A Thinker's Guide to the Philosophy of Religion

Allen Stairs
University of Maryland, Department of Philosophy

Christopher Bernard
University of Maryland, Department of Philosophy

PEARSON
Longman

New York • San Francisco • Boston
London • Toronto • Sydney • Tokyo • Singapore • Madrid
Mexico City • Munich • Paris • Cape Town • Hong Kong • Montreal

Publisher: Priscilla McGeehon
Editor-in-Chief: Eric Stano
Executive Marketing Manager: Ann Stypuloski
Project Coordination, Text Design, and Electronic
    Page Makeup: Integra Software Services Private Limited
Senior Cover Design Manager: Nancy Danahy
Cover Illustration/Photo/Photo Disc: Getty Images Inc.
Senior Manufacturing Buyer: Alfred C. Dorsey
Printer and Binder: R. R. Donnelly and Sons
Cover Printer: Hamilton Printing Company

Library of Congress Cataloging-in-Publication Data
Stairs, Allen.
    A thinker's guide to the philosophy of religion / Allen Stairs,
Christopher Bernard.
    p.   cm.
    Includes bibliographical references (p.   ).
    ISBN 0-321-24375-7
    1. Religion—Philosophy.   I. Bernard, Christopher, 1972–
II. Title.
BL51.S62585 2006
210—dc22
                                                              2006015700

Please visit us at www.ablongman.com

ISBN 0-321-24375-7

1 2 3 4 5 6 7 8 9 10—DOC—09 08 07 06

Contents

Introduction

Once upon a time, we were told that there were three topics that shouldn't be talked about in polite company: sex, politics, and religion. Lately, American political discourse has included much in the way of sex and religion and stirred this up with politics into a rather unholy stew, so we promise we won't try to influence your politics. We certainly don't plan to give you advice on your sex life. But we hope that we can help you think more clearly about religion.

What aspect of religion will be our focus? We'll start by telling you what we are not going to talk about. We're not Bible scholars, so we won't have much to say about scripture. We're not priests or pastors, and our job isn't to provide you with spiritual guidance. We're not experts in comparative religion, and we won't be able to satisfy your curiosity about Islam, Buddhism, or any other specific religion.

Instead, we will discuss the evidence for and against the existence of God and related topics. Perhaps the two most popular worries about belief in God have to do with evidence and evil. If God exists, are there good reasons to think so, or must we just take this claim on faith? If an all-powerful and all-good God does exist, why does he allow innocent children to suffer? These questions will occupy a good deal of our time.

Before we consider whether there is sufficient reason to think God exists, we need to have a rough idea of what we mean by *God*. Is God in space and time? Does God change? Does saying that God is all-powerful actually make sense? We discuss these of issues in the first chapter.

We then have a section on the evidence for the existence of God. Here we discuss the arguments for God, miracles, and religious experience. Next, we turn to the question of belief without evidence. What if there is no evidence for God or if the evidence is poor? Can belief in God still be rational? We then discuss the evidence against God, specifically whether suffering is a disproof of God's existence.

We then consider some broader questions. If God doesn't exist, can there be objective morality? There is a rich diversity of religions in the world but they seem to contradict each other. Is one religion the true religion? If so, is everyone else going to a flaming hereafter? What are the special problems that religious language presents? How should we think about life after death?

We talk about these questions as philosophers. Philosophy is mainly concerned with ideas and reasons. Ideas can sometimes be confused and muddled. The philosopher's job is to straighten out and bring clarity to our concepts. We are not as concerned with what people believe as why they believe it. That said, the philosopher is not a psychologist. We are interested in the logical reasons people have for holding their beliefs, not the psychological ones.

Questions of religious belief tend to call forth particularly strong reactions, and so we'd like to say something about an assumption that has guided our thinking in writing this book. In our view, believing that God exists, believing that God does not exist, and being unsure about God's existence can all be intellectually respectable positions. There's room for reasonable disagreement on this issue.

Please don't get the impression that we're saying anything goes, or that one opinion is as good as another, or that reasons and arguments don't matter. We aren't saying anything remotely like that. Some opinions are beyond the pale. For example, although some people still think that slavery is acceptable, that opinion simply can't be defended by any good arguments. This doesn't mean you shouldn't try to reason with people who are in favor of slavery, but you can reason with the confidence that the position you're arguing against is bankrupt.

We don't think the situation with religion is like that. We don't think that atheism is a bankrupt position. There are serious reasons, worthy of your serious consideration, why someone might be an atheist; a person can be an atheist in good intellectual conscience. We think the same goes for belief in God. There are serious reasons, worthy of your serious consideration, that might lead someone to believe in God; a person can be a theist in good intellectual conscience.

We stress this because religion, like politics, is one of those areas where people tend to think that anyone who disagrees with them is a fool or worse. Atheists are often contemptuous of believers; believers often dismiss atheists. We think the subject is too complicated for that.

On the other hand, there are mindless believers and mindless non-believers. Some people hold their views about religion as matters that are simply beyond any sort of discussion. These people are often supremely convinced that they're right, but if they ever found themselves in a corner with someone who thought otherwise and had thought about it seriously, they would run out of things to say very soon.

We don't want you to be like that. We want you to understand that thinking, arguing, and reasoning are important if we're serious about the truth. They help keep us from making mistakes and, if the arguments and evidence are good, they help lead us in the right direction. But we also want you to take seriously the idea that however strongly you may hold your views on religion, you can find someone just as smart and thoughtful as you who sees things differently. That doesn't mean you're both right—it means that you both need to be open to the possibility that you might be wrong.

We have now come full circle and are back at the starting point of good philosophy—reasons and arguments. Our goal is not to help you to justify the position you already hold. Our job is to challenge you to think critically and not to reinforce your religious beliefs, or lack thereof.

Because philosophy deals with reasons and arguments, it is the kind of thing that needs to be read more than once. After you've read a chapter for the first time, you may find it helpful to look over the "At a Glance" section at the chapter's end. (These summaries will make more sense if you've already read the chapter.) This section should make it easier for the ideas to gel when you re-read the chapter. You can look up bold-faced words in the Glossary, where you'll sometimes get additional information.

Occasionally, you'll see sections marked with an asterisk. This will let you know that what follows is a bit more demanding than the rest of the chapter. If this book is the text in a course you are taking, your instructor may or may not assign those sections. That said, we've tried hard to make them clear and have included them because the arguments they discuss are often among the most fascinating in the field and take you deeper into contemporary debates.

We don't want to be coy about the fact that we have our own opinions and positions on these subjects. One of the reasons this book has two authors is to minimize bias in our presentation. We also don't want to push our views on you and so, in the interest of full disclosure, we think it's important for us to say something about our religious perspectives.

Allen Stairs doesn't subscribe to a religious creed and wouldn't count as orthodox by the standards of any major religion. He's equally appalled by the dismissive attitude that many academics take toward religion and by the intellectual brittleness of many believers.

Christopher Bernard's views are closer to traditional Christianity. However, he has taught philosophy of religion at a secular university and has a master's degree from a theologically liberal seminary. He believes we all must be willing to openly and honestly consider arguments that run counter to our own views.

This is a dual use book: it was purposely written for the general reader and the college student. It is meant to be a notch above a pure introduction, a little bit more sophisticated than something written for intellectual beginners. On the other hand, it doesn't assume that you already know anything about the philosophy of religion, nor that you're already experienced at philosophical argument. It pays attention to major figures in the history of philosophy of religion but also introduces you to ideas that have only entered the debates in the last few years. We start each chapter by letting you know where we plan to go, and at the end of each chapter, there's a summary to help you see where you've been. All textbooks try to be clear; some end up being dry. We've tried hard not to let that happen.

Thanks to our former student Kevin Ford for creating the stereogram found in Chapter 11. Allen Stairs would like to acknowledge the Arts and Humanities Council of Montgomery County for its support during the writing of this book. He also benefited from conversations with Sam Kerstein, Ray Martin, and Chris Morris. Panera Bread in Silver Spring, Maryland, provided a congenial environment for writing chunks of this book. He is grateful to his father for helping him learn how to argue and to his children Alex and Jenelle for putting up with a philosopher father. Finally, he thanks Cathrine Nelson for her love and support.

Christopher Bernard would like to thank Mary Bernard for her enormous patience, support, and love. He would also like to thank Christopher, Abigail, Jonah, and Jacob for putting up with their dad's unwillingness to wrestle during particularly intense periods of writing.

A Note to Instructors

This book is a sophomore-level introduction to the philosophy of religion in the analytic mold. By using the term "analytic," we mean that it reflects the vicissitudes of our training. For instance, neither of us knows enough about Continental or Thomistic approaches to the philosophy of religion to discuss them knowledgeably. By calling the text sophomore-level, we don't mean that a freshman couldn't use the text and do well. We also don't mean that the reader must have had previous courses in philosophy. We mean that the material is aimed at readers who are a bit more intellectually sophisticated than brand-new college students often are. On the other hand, the book isn't aimed at someone who is looking for the kind of in-depth and detailed treatment that someone who's already familiar with the basics of the philosophy of religion might want. Sophomore-level or not, we still want this book to serve an introduction to the field.

Some introductory books devote relatively little time to the contemporary literature of the topics they cover. Given the way that the philosophy of religion has blossomed in the last three decades or so, we thought it was important to include more recent discussions, such as newer approaches to divine command theories, Plantinga's externalist version of Reformed epistemology and his modal version of the ontological argument, and the controversy over intelligent design as propounded by Dembski and Behe.

We've tried to include all the perennial topics—arguments for God's existence, the argument from evil, and so on—and also topics that have received more sustained attention only in recent years—for example, Reformed epistemology and religious diversity. Still, some instructors might want to fill existing gaps in other ways. We think that a discussion of various approaches to scripture can be a useful thing for students finding their first exposure to the philosophy of religion, but because analytic philosophers of religion have had relatively little to say on this topic, we've omitted it. We also haven't discussed atheism and naturalism as separate topics, though relevant ideas, arguments, and concepts emerge at various points in the text.

In addition to being analytic in approach, this book focuses almost entirely on the theistic tradition, in particular, on classical theism. If someone were to complain that religion is much broader than classical theism, we would agree emphatically. However, the field of analytic philosophy of religion is what it is, and it is the field we're trying to introduce. That said, we haven't entirely ignored other ways of thinking about religion. Both in the chapter "Concepts of God" and in the chapter on religious diversity, there are discussions of religious traditions and points of view that fall outside classical theism.

Each chapter begins with a paragraph that sets the stage for what's to come—not a summary of the chapter but a posing of the problem. We hope that this addition will help students enter more easily into the arguments and issues. At the end of each chapter is a summary that recaps the major points from the chapter. These summaries don't include every issue or topic raised in the text itself. Some instructors will be more inclined than others to pursue the nuances, but we felt that we serve more students well by making our summaries more skeletal. We've also included some web resources and suggestions for further reading.

A few sections are marked with asterisks. These are either a little more demanding or a little less central. We recommend that you have a look at these before you assign them. They are:

- Chapter 1 (Concepts of God): Section 4.2.2, on omniscience and freedom
- Chapter 3 (The Cosmological Argument): Sections 2.1 and 2.2, on the Kalam argument
- Chapter 4 (The Ontological Argument): Section 6, on Plantinga's ontological argument
- Chapter 6 (Religious Experience): Section 5, discussion of Alston
- Chapter 10 (God and Morality): Section 6, God, obligation, and the "Queerness Problem"

In each case, it's entirely possible to teach the chapter respectably to beginners without asking students to read those sections, though leaving them out would sometimes require omitting some of the more fascinating parts of the contemporary literature. We leave it to the instructor's judgment to decide what will work best.

The book includes an extensive glossary. Glossary terms are written in bold when they first appear in a chapter, and we typically provide a brief explanation of each term when it first occurs. Most glossary entries are brief and can be helpful for students to use when reviewing. A few entries, such as probability and modal logic, are longer and provide interested readers with more detail than the text strictly requires.

The chapters are independent. Though they occasionally refer to one another, each is meant to be free-standing. (The Glossary helps make this work.) The order of the chapters has a rationale: from the general idea of God, arguments for God's existence, further sources of support for belief, arguments against belief, and finally, miscellaneous topics. However, instructors should have no difficulty omitting chapters or ordering the topics differently.

Though we've tried to provide broad coverage, we don't make any pretense of being comprehensive or unerring in our choices. In any given chapter, we're likely to have left something out that an instructor might want to cover, or to have covered something the instructor might want to leave out. However, what we hope is that each chapter provides a coherent approach to the issue that will equip students to think about it more effectively and get more out of other (possibly more advanced) readings on the same topic.

Finally, we're sure that every instructor will disagree with at least some claim we make or find at least some argument defective. We could say that this is all deliberate—that like Persian rug makers, we included flaws in each chapter so as not to presume to be God-like. For better or worse, we can't make any such claim. However, what we do know from our own experience as teachers is that in learning to be philosophers, students get at least as much out of hearing their professor disagree with an author as in hearing them agree. Either way, we hope we've produced a book that will help your students think clearly and well about the fascinating topics that make up the philosophy of religion.

CHAPTER 1

Concepts of God

*God and gods are often claimed to have various attributes,
such as being supernatural, or being present everywhere, or
being perfect. In this chapter, we explore several ways of
thinking about God and a few apparent paradoxes, with
special emphasis on the God of classical theism: a being who is
all-powerful, all-knowing and perfectly good.*

Decades from now, scholars may wonder why people in the early years
of the twenty-first century were writing Ph.D. dissertations and academic essays on *Buffy the Vampire Slayer*. Whatever the answer to that
question, the show did raise the occasional philosophical conundrum. In
the fifth season, Buffy spends most of her time battling Glory, a high-
heeled *fashionista* with great hair, uncanny strength, a band of remarkably unattractive minions, and a serious mean streak. Oh, and one other
thing: Glory is a god, trapped in our dimension and trying to get herself
back home.

All this is just a story, but does it even make sense? This isn't just a
way of asking whether anything remotely like this ever happened. Does
calling a being like Glory a god mean anything? What would count as a
god, anyway? And what's the difference between a god and God?

In this chapter, we'll explore the concepts of gods and, most importantly, of God. Although we'll pay most attention to the idea of God in
classical theism, we will look at a number of variations on the theme of
divinity. We'll also consider some puzzles about the idea of God.

1 GOD, GOD, AND GODS

Start with a point of grammar. The word *god* with a lower-case "g" isn't a name; it's a descriptive term. Although saying exactly what would count as a god is difficult, one thing that's clear is that there could be more than one of them. The ancient Greeks for example, worshipped a whole pantheon with enough gods to populate a good-sized mountaintop. On the other hand, *God* is a name, or better yet, a title, and it's a title that's generally understood to refer to a single being if it refers to anything at all. If there are two or more equally viable candidates for the title "God" then *God* does not exist, though some gods do. God, if God there be, is unique.

Monotheism is the belief in a single god. **Polytheism** is the belief that there's more than one god. Judaism, Islam, and Christianity are perhaps the most well-known monotheistic religions, though not the only ones (Sikhs, for example, are monotheists, as are Zoroastrians and Baha'is). There are many polytheistic religions, including Taoism, Shinto, and Hinduism. (Hinduism recognizes a large number of gods, although many Hindus see all these gods as manifestations of a single divine reality.)

Interestingly enough, some of the best-known arguments from the monotheistic tradition don't do much to support monotheism. In Chapter 3, we'll consider the **Cosmological Argument**, which tries to explain why the physical universe exists at all. In one of its forms, this argument points out that there are chains of causes in the world and argues that any such chain has to have a first member. However, leaving aside whether the first member would have to be a god at all, this wouldn't show that there needs to be a unique first cause. For example, there might be four separate deities, one for each of the four fundamental forces of nature.

One classic argument implies that only one being is worthy of the name God. It's called the **Ontological Argument**, and we'll discuss it in Chapter 4. It tries to prove the existence of a being so great that no greater being can be conceived. There couldn't be two such beings. If there were, neither of them could have unlimited power, because neither would have power over the other. We'll have more to say later about the sort of being that the ontological argument concerns itself with.

2 NATURE AND SUPERNATURE

A being that deserves to be called God would have to have some very special qualities. Zeus for example, wouldn't do. However, if God exists, then God is at least a god, so it might be worth asking what a being would have to be like to count as a god at all. Most people would say that at the very minimum, a god would have to be supernatural. However, that raises a question: what does "supernatural" mean?

The answer isn't obvious. Suppose there's such a thing as magic—suppose that charms and spells really work. It's not entirely clear what would be gained by calling this strange power supernatural. Why wouldn't finding out that magic is real amount to discovering that the world has some surprising natural laws?

Whatever the answer, suppose a being exists who isn't made of the stuff that anything in the physical world is made of, and perhaps isn't made of any "stuff" at all. Suppose that this being somehow made the physical universe and has unlimited power over it. In that case, there would be a clear break in the order of things. It would make sense to use the words "supernatural" and "natural" to label what's on either side of the break. We can imagine variations on this theme. In one version, God creates the physical world out of nothing. This is what Christians, Jews, and Muslims usually believe about God. Another version (which some people find in the first verses of the Bible) says that God didn't create the world from nothing but imposed order on a pre-existing chaos. ("Chaos" in this sense refers to raw matter in such a confused state that it doesn't have any real form at all.) On this view, God didn't create matter where there was none before, but God did make incoherent, formless matter into a coherent world. That's still pretty impressive. Counting a being who could do this as supernatural seems reasonable.

The Church of Jesus Christ of Latter-Day Saints (the Mormons) offers an interesting variation on the familiar concept of God. According to the Latter-Day Saints, God has a body not unlike our bodies. This means that God is a physical being who occupies the same space and time that we do. God has a son, Jesus Christ, who also has a physical body and who also is divine. Under the direction of God the Father, Latter-Day Saints believe that Jesus Christ created what we think of as the physical world by imposing order on chaos. Because the physical world was created by a physical being with a body, there had to be organized matter before the Universe was assembled: the bodies of the Father and the Son. Presumably, some laws would have governed both those bodies and the process of bringing order out of chaos. This blurs the line between natural and supernatural. In fact, Mormon philosopher and theologian Sterling McMurrin argues that God as understood in Mormon theology shouldn't be described as supernatural.

If we look at world religions both now and in the past, things get even blurrier. For example, the Greek gods were immortal beings with extensive but far from complete control over what we think of as the natural world. Supernature, it seems, comes in degrees. Still, the god of classical theism is supernatural by any measure.

3 PERFECTION

We now have a little more clarity on what a god is, but not every being who would count as a god would also count as the God of classical theism. Classical theism sees God in a way that leaves no doubt about whether we're talking about a mere god. It says that God is a perfect being.

3.1 Three Central Perfections

What would it mean to say that God is a perfect being? Here are three things that most theologians would insist on:

- God is **omnipotent**; that is, God is all-powerful.
- God is **omniscient**; that is, God is all-knowing.
- God is **omnibenevolent**; that is, God is entirely good.

We'll refer to these attributes as the *central perfections*. As we'll see in Chapter 9, these characteristics give rise to the argument from evil, which is the most important argument for the nonexistence of God.

In Section 4, we'll explore some paradoxes and puzzles that arise when we consider the central perfections more carefully. In the remainder of this section, we'll look briefly at some more controversial attributes that a perfect being might possess.

3.2 Necessary Existence

It's often claimed that a perfect being would have to have **necessary existence**—that by its very nature, a perfect being couldn't fail to exist. We'll run into the idea of a **necessary** being again in later chapters, but this characteristic is more controversial than the three central perfections. Not everyone agrees that the concept of a necessarily existing being makes sense. If it doesn't, then necessary existence could hardly be a perfection.

3.3 Eternal or Everlasting?

Theologians agree that a perfect being would have no beginning and no end, but there's more than one way to understand this. Many theologians say that God has no beginning and no end because God isn't in time at all: God is *eternal.* Other thinkers say that God isn't eternal but *everlasting*: God is in time but didn't begin to exist and will never cease to be. We'll revisit this distinction when we discuss omniscience in Section 5.

3.4 Changing or Unchanging?

The question of whether God is in time is closely related to the question of whether God changes. If God does change, then God is everlasting and not eternal because change implies time.

Some theologians argue that a perfect being wouldn't change. After all, they ask, what reason could there be for change in a being who is already perfect? Another reason that some people give for saying that God is changeless is that various scriptural passages appear to say so. For example, Malachi 3.6: "For I the Lord do not change . . ." However, other interpreters read these passages not as saying that God is absolutely unchanging but only that his love and trustworthiness don't change.

3.5 Omnipresence

Many people believe that a perfect being would have to be *omnipresent*, or present everywhere. Just what omnipresence would amount to isn't easy to say. Here are some possibilities.

If a pantheist conception of God is correct, then the world and God are identical. In that case, God is everywhere at least in the sense that some part of God is at every place. Pantheism has a drawback for perfect-being theology: the world is clearly not a perfect place. If God is identical with the world, it would follow that God isn't perfect.

Another view is that even though God isn't identical with the world, God pervades the world in the way that a soul might be thought of as pervading a body. Yet another view, advocated by the great physicist Isaac Newton (1642–1727), is that space is God's "sensorium," the seat of God's thoughts and ideas. Each of these views goes some way to making sense of what it would mean to say that God is omnipresent but none is widely accepted.

All three of the views we've just described seem to give God a spatial aspect. Some ways of thinking about omnipresence avoid that consequence. For example, God keeps the world in existence. Because this applies to every part of the world, it provides a way of saying that God is present everywhere even if God isn't spatial: God is present as sustaining cause.

There are other, even more abstract ways of understanding omnipresence, but believers might complain that all this high-flying **metaphysics** misses the point. Many believers feel that they experience the presence of God directly even though they might be hard-pressed to explain exactly what this amounts to. Explainable or not, the believer might insist that this presence of God that he sometimes senses is real, always and everywhere, even when we aren't aware of it.

3.6 Does God Have Feelings?

We have feelings. Does God? If we suffer and if God has feelings, we might expect God to feel sorrow, especially if God really loves us. However, many theologians think that if we believe God has feelings like ours, we're ignoring the profound difference between us and God.

Some theologians, St. Thomas Aquinas (c.1225–1274) among them, believe that sorrow is negative and therefore not something that could apply to a perfect being. If we grant that this argument is correct (and it's not clear that we should), it would still leave room for God to have other feelings that don't imply imperfection–perhaps feelings such as joy and love.

Process theology insists that God does have feelings and that these feelings allow God to suffer with us. As process theologians argue, a God whose love merely consisted in doing good things for us without being able to feel genuine sympathy and compassion for us would be a cold and less than fully admirable being (see Cobb and Griffin 1976, pp. 44 ff.). However, once again we'll raise a thorny issue without trying to resolve it.

4 PUZZLES AND PARADOXES

It's time to return to the central perfections: omnipotence, omniscience, and omnibenevolence. Classical theists agree that God has these three characteristics. In the case of omnipotence and omniscience, there's a long history of worries about whether these concepts lead to paradoxes and we'll look at these debates in some detail. As for omnibenevolence, anyone who thinks that there's no objective difference between good and evil or between right and wrong will think that the idea of omnibenevolence makes no sense. In fact, as we will point out again in Chapter 10, the whole question of just what sorts of properties "goodness" and "badness" or "rightness" and "wrongness" might be is a vexing one. For now, we'll set this issue aside and assume that there is a real difference between good and evil. This raises questions about whether God's omnibenevolence is compatible with God's omnipotence and omniscience—the famous **Problem of Evil**. However, because we devote a whole chapter (Chapter 9) to that problem, we'll wait until then before we discuss omnibenevolence any further. For now, we'll look at the puzzles raised by the concepts of omnipotence and omniscience.

4.1 Paradoxes of Omnipotence

At first, it sounds straightforward: God is omnipotent, which means that God is all-powerful. However, this is just an English translation of a Latin word. We need more than this to be sure we're dealing with a consistent concept. One way to think about omnipotence is by way of the idea of limits on power. Your power and ours is limited. There are things we can't do. If God is omnipotent, then we might want to say that God's power is unlimited.

The inference from "God's power is unlimited" to "There's nothing God can't do" is tempting but not as obvious as it seems. There certainly seem to be some things that God can't do, no matter how much power God has. Two traditional examples: God can't make a square circle, and God can't create a stone so heavy that God can't lift it. Let's begin with the first of these.

4.1.1 Square Circles

We can put the problem of the square circle this way:

1. If God is omnipotent, then God has unlimited power (definition of omnipotent).
2. If God has unlimited power, then God can perform any action (premise).
3. Therefore, if God is omnipotent, then God can perform any action (from 2 and 3).
4. Making a square circle would be performing an action (premise).
5. Therefore, if God is omnipotent, then God can make a square circle (from 3 and 4).
6. No one can make a square circle (premise).
7. Therefore, God can't make a square circle (from 6).
8. Therefore, God is not omnipotent (from 5 and 7).

Notice that if our argument is correct, what it really shows is that no being could be omnipotent—that the very idea of omnipotence is incoherent. But how good is the argument? If we accept the definition, then the argument depends on three premises, and although each of them can be called into question, we'll start with statements 2 and 6.

Statement 2 is doubtful. For example, as Joshua Hoffman and Gary Rosenkrantz point out, if we consider a necessary fact (e.g., the fact that $2 + 2 = 4$), then no one makes it so (Hoffman & Rosenkrantz 2002). But the fact that God can't make $2 + 2$ equal 4 hardly seems like a limitation on God's power.

As for statement 6—no one can make a square circle—some philosophers, such as René Descartes (1596–1650), have claimed that it's within God's power to make square circles, and more generally, to make impossibilities true. Other philosophers, such as St. Thomas Aquinas, disagree. They say that if something is impossible, then the fact that God can't make it so doesn't limit God's power. We agree and will try to explain why.

We say it's impossible that $2 + 2$ should be anything other than 4 at least, it is if "2", "+", "=", and "4" have their usual meanings. This means that God can't make $2 + 2$ equal 5, but not because God is somehow weak. It's because nothing would count as doing the job.

The case of the square circle makes the problem even clearer. Think about a computer screen. Ignoring multiple colors, things get "drawn" on the computer screen by turning some pixels on and leaving others off. The monitor for the computer that this chapter was written on has a resolution of 1024×768 pixels. Obviously, drawing a perfect circle on a computer screen is not possible because there are only finitely many pixels on the screen. However, this won't change the point we want to make. Since the monitor has 786,432 pixels in total, and since each one can be off or on, arithmetic gives us a whopping $2^{786,432}$ different ways for pixels to be on and off. This is a vast number (10 followed by over 230,000 zeros). A large but much smaller number would count as drawing a circle on the screen. Likewise, a large but much smaller number would count as drawing a square on the screen. However, not a single one of the $2^{786,432}$ different arrangements would count as drawing a square circle. Improving the resolution of the screen wouldn't help. Even if we made each pixel into a mathematical point, no combination of pixels being off and on would count as a square circle, even though infinitely many would count as a square and infinitely many would count as a circle.

To keep the story simple, we'll stick with the usual, more limited computer screen. Notice that each of the $2^{786,432}$ combinations of pixels on the computer screen is possible. But no matter which one we pick, it simply doesn't count as being a square circle. Suppose, then, that we ask God to make a square circle on the screen. God has the power to turn pixels on and off in any combination whatsoever. Still, God can't make a square circle from the pixels on the screen.

Is this a limitation on God's power? It's hard to see how. The point we've been making is that no matter what God did, it wouldn't count as drawing a square circle because *nothing* would count as drawing a square circle. The problem has nothing to do with God's power. The problem is that we haven't asked God to do anything definite. Saying the words "draw a square circle" may appear to be asking something definite of God but, as the old saying goes, appearances can be deceiving. Nothing would count because the words "square circle" don't pick out any arrangement of pixels at all.

In order for a "task" to be a genuine task, something should count as success at doing it. That's the problem with the square circle. Making a square circle isn't a genuine task. It's what's sometimes called a **pseudo-task**—a task that nothing would count as actually carrying out. It's not obviously a limitation on anyone's power—God included—that they can't perform a pseudo task.

How do we tell when something is a pseudo-task? General answers are hard to come by, but one sure sign is if the task involves a self-contradiction. "Square circle" is arguably a self-contradiction. To be a circle, all points in the figure must be equidistant from the center. But in a square, the points are at varying distances from the center. That means one and the same thing (being equidistant from the center) would have to be true and false of some points for a square circle to exist. The trouble is that nothing counts as making a contradiction true.

4.1.2 All Stones Great and Small

If we agree that God could be omnipotent without being able to make impossible things true, then we can dispense with at least some of the puzzles about omnipotence. However, it's not clear that all the problems can be solved this way. How about the idea of a stone so heavy that God can't lift it? This creates a dilemma: if God can't make such a stone, then there's something God can't do, in which case—so it seem—God isn't omnipotent. But if God can make a stone that he can't lift, then there's still something God can't do: lift that stone. Either way, it seems, God can't be omnipotent.

This argument, like the previous one, is really trying to show that no being could be omnipotent—that the very idea of omnipotence makes no sense. Perhaps we might try to deal with this case in the way that we dealt with the problem of the square circle. Making a square circle is a pseudo-task. Square circles are impossible, and if we agree that omnipotence doesn't call for being able to perform pseudo tasks, there's no problem with the idea that an omnipotent being can't make a square circle. If we could show that asking God to make a stone so heavy that he can't lift it amounts to asking God to perform a pseudo-task, the problem would be solved.

This approach might not seem very promising at first. As George Mavrodes points out (Mavrodes 1963 pp. 221–223), even though "Jones can draw a square circle" seems to be a contradiction, "Jones can make a thing too heavy for him to lift" isn't a contradiction at all, and asking Jones to do this isn't asking him to perform a pseudo task.

Of course, Jones isn't God. Mavrodes thinks the phrase, "a stone too heavy for God to lift," amounts to the phrase, "a stone which cannot be lifted by the being whose power is sufficient to lift anything." This second phrase seems to be self-contradictory. If that's correct, asking God to make a stone too heavy for even God to lift is asking God to perform a pseudo task.

A cheap trick might seem to undermine Mavrodes' argument. Suppose we ask God to do two things: first, give up omnipotence and become weaker; second, in that weakened state, make an *exceptionally* heavy stone by putting together things that are at the limit of God's now-reduced lifting powers. That might sound like a recipe for God to do what any of you can do—make something that exceeds your lifting powers.

We could wonder if asking God to give up omnipotence makes sense, but leave that worry aside. The trouble with the cheap trick is that it avoids the real question: can an omnipotent being, *while remaining omnipotent*, make a stone so heavy that this same omnipotent being can't lift it? That's the question that Mavrodes thinks leads to a contradiction if we answer "yes."

You might still feel a little suspicious. For Mavrodes' solution to work, the phrase, "being whose power is sufficient to lift anything," has to make sense. You might suspect that anyone who was really skeptical about the idea of omnipotence would also be skeptical of this idea. As it turns out, it may not matter. Perhaps Mavrodes' analysis is correct, but suppose not. Mavrodes points out that even then, the problem may amount to much less than meets the eye. Suppose you decide that, strictly speaking, omnipotence is an incoherent notion and you decide to make do in your theology with the idea that God has as much power as possible, short of full (but perhaps contradictory) omnipotence. Where would that leave us? Consider the stone again and think about it not via some indirect reference to God's powers but as it is in itself. Could God make a 10,000-ton stone and be able to lift it? Surely, the answer is yes. The same holds for a ten-million-ton stone, or a ten-billion-ton stone or a ten **googol** ton stone. (A googol is 1 followed by 100 zeros.) In fact, what's clear is that there's no upper limit here. No matter how heavy the stone you think of, there's no problem with the idea that there could be a being who could both make it and lift it. We only run into confusion when we describe the stone indirectly, by reference to God's powers. If the only tasks God can't perform are quirky, self-referential ones like this—defined by way of God's own powers—this may be power enough for all religiously interesting purposes.

The puzzles of omnipotence seem to be puzzles for the theologian and the philosopher but not for the ordinary believer. However, when we come to omniscience, at least some of the issues feel a little more urgent.

4.2 Problems of Omniscience

Classical theism says that God is omniscient—all-knowing. This raises two kinds of problems. One has to do with feelings. If God doesn't have feelings, then we seem to have a type of knowledge that God doesn't have: knowledge of what feelings are like. The other problem is the threat of a conflict between God's omniscience and human freedom. Briefly, if God is omniscient, then God presumably knows what you are going to choose to do before you do it. But in that case, how could your choice be free? In an essay in the *Routledge Encyclopedia of Philosophy*, Thomas Flint sets the issues forth very clearly, and our discussion is indebted to his.

4.2.1 Feelings Again

The God of classical theism is all-knowing, but what does this mean? It seems to mean that God's knowledge has no limits, but how do we describe this limitless knowledge? Here's one possible answer: for every **proposition**, God knows whether it's true or false. Is this an adequate definition of omniscience?

Imagine a man blind from birth who knows everything science has to tell us about color vision. This man knows a vast array of true propositions about human vision. However, with all of this propositional knowledge (as we'll call it), most of us know something that he doesn't know—what it's like to see colors. (Our example is based on one due to Frank Jackson, an example that has played an important role in recent discussions in the philosophy of mind. See Jackson 1982.)

Knowing how things feel or what having certain experiences is like seems to be a genuine type of knowledge. If God's knowledge is entirely a matter of knowing propositions, then God doesn't know what human joy feels like, or human pain. The idea that God doesn't know what our suffering is like seems to be a serious gap in the divine stock of knowledge.

If God has the right range of feelings, this particular problem doesn't come up. If there's a problem with the idea that God has feelings, then anyone who wants to say that God is omniscient will have to make the case that being omniscient doesn't call for the sort of "knowledge" we obtain by having feelings.

But we will leave this problem unresolved and turn to a rather worrisome issue: if God is omniscient, this seems to imply that God knows what we are going to do before we do it. But if that's so, it may seem that we couldn't possibly be free. This wouldn't be a contradiction in the very idea of omniscience, but it would create a conflict between an important theological idea and a belief about human nature that many people would be very reluctant to abandon.

Some theologians and philosophers would argue that it's a mistake to think of God's knowledge as in any way compelling us to do what we do. Intriguingly, others argue that God could be omniscient without knowing what we will do in the future because the facts about our future decisions don't yet exist for God to know! The next, somewhat advanced section considers this problem in more detail.

*4.2.2 Freedom

Many people believe that humans are free in a very strong sense; they make at least some decisions that aren't determined or strictly caused by any prior conditions. Suppose this picture is correct, and suppose that tomorrow Jones will make a free decision about whether to take a job as a carnival barker. We'll suppose the laws of nature and the facts up to now don't settle what Jones is going to do. However, if God really is omniscient, doesn't God already know what Jones will do? Doesn't God either know that Jones will take the job or know that he won't? In fact, didn't God already know yesterday, or 10,000 years ago what Jones will do tomorrow?

Now we add a bit of metaphysics. The past can't be changed. If it's true that Mary went to Cleveland yesterday, then no one can do anything about that fact now. In a certain sense, from our present point of view, this fact about Mary is a necessary truth. It's necessary in the sense that absolutely nothing can be done about it. But this raises a puzzle. To see why, we need a widely accepted principle of **modal logic**—the logic of **possibility** and **necessity**.

First, we'll illustrate: suppose you believe that something couldn't be otherwise—for example, suppose you believe that nothing could be water unless it's H_2O, and so you believe that "Water is H_2O" is a necessary truth. And suppose you believe—reasonably enough—that from this it follows that water contains hydrogen, that "Water is H_2O" strictly implies "Water contains hydrogen." Then you should also believe that "Water contains hydrogen" is a necessary truth. Here's the general principle:

> **Transfer of Necessity:** If P is necessary, and if P strictly implies Q, then Q is necessary as well.

Put slightly differently, from

> Necessarily P, and
> Necessarily, if P then Q

it follows that

> Necessarily Q.

Suppose that, as a matter of fact, God knew yesterday that Jones is going to take the job tomorrow. Then being a fact about the past, this fact about God's knowledge would be necessary in the way that any fact about the past is, or so it seems. But the following is a necessary truth no matter what statement X stands for:

> If God knows that X is true, then X is true.

It's not that God's knowledge makes things true. The principle just cited holds even for mortals like us. It simply reflects the fact that you can't know false things, though of course, you can mistakenly *believe* false things. This gives us the following argument:

1. Necessarily, God knew yesterday that Jones will take the job tomorrow (premise based on God's omniscience and the unchangeable nature of the past).
2. Necessarily, if God knew yesterday that Jones will take the job tomorrow, then Jones will take the job tomorrow (because it's impossible to know something that's false).
3. Therefore, necessarily Jones will take the job tomorrow (from 1, 2, Transfer of Necessity).

Now we see the problem: if it's necessary that Jones will take the job tomorrow, it's not clear how this could be a free choice. Apparently, Jones isn't free after all.

When we discussed the problems of omnipotence, the worry was that the concept itself was incoherent. The worry here is different: saying that God is omniscient undermines the belief that humans can make free choices.

All of the replies we'll discuss have one thing in common—they question the first premise that God knows or knew necessarily that Jones will take the job. Here are several ways of calling the premise into question.

*4.2.2.1 Soft Facts Suppose a truth is strictly about the past and doesn't include any reference to later times. For example, consider this truth:

Vincent van Gogh was born in 1853.

This is a fact that's entirely about the past. It's also clear that nothing anyone could do will change it, or at least so we'll assume. Let's use the term *hard fact* to refer to facts that are strictly about the past, and let's grant that hard facts are necessary in the sense that nothing can be done to change them, not even in principle. Nonetheless, some facts that appear to be about the past aren't really just about the past. For example, suppose Jones truly believed yesterday that you would be reading a philosophy book today. That Jones believed this is a fact strictly about the past. After all, he could believe whatever he believed quite apart from how things would actually turn out. However, the fact that he this belief that Jones held yesterday was true isn't just a fact about yesterday. The truth of the belief brings today into the picture. This sort of fact about the past—a fact that depends partly on facts about the future—is often called a *soft fact*. As Thomas Flint points out, "Unlike hard facts about the past, soft facts need not be seen as necessary" (Flint 1998, p. 110). If this is correct, we can challenge the first premise of the argument above. It deals with a soft fact, and soft facts don't have to be necessary.

Let's spell this out further. Suppose that right now you are reading this page of your own free will. The fact that Jones believed yesterday that you would be reading this page today is a hard fact about the past. However, why not say this? The fact that Jones truly believed this—that his belief was correct—is only a fact because of a free choice you made today. If you had decided not to read this page, then Jones's belief wouldn't have been true. Likewise, the argument would go, the fact that God knew yesterday that Jones will take the job tomorrow isn't simply a fact about the past. It's true because Jones actually accepts the job tomorrow. In that case, then perhaps it's not necessary at all. But if that's right, the first premise of the argument above, which requires that necessarily God knew this, would be false.

This seems promising but Flint reminds us that there's a reply. If God *believed* yesterday that Jones will take the job tomorrow, then that is a hard fact—a fact entirely about the past, just as it's a fact entirely about the past that Jones believed yesterday that you would read this book today. But Jones and God are different. The fact that Jones believes something may have little connection with whether it's true. Not so for God. Some would insist that *necessarily*, God's beliefs are true. In that case, we get a new argument:

1. Necessarily, God believed yesterday that Jones will take the job tomorrow (hard fact about the past).
2. Necessarily, if God believed yesterday that Jones will take the job tomorrow, then Jones will take the job tomorrow (theological principle).
3. Therefore, necessarily, Jones will take the job tomorrow (Transfer of Necessity).

It's not clear that we can solve the problem by distinguishing between hard and soft facts.

*4.2.2.2 God as Outside Time Some theologians and philosophers reject the very idea that we can talk about what God knew yesterday. As we saw earlier, some theologians say that that God is not just everlasting but is eternal—is outside time. If that's true, then the argument we've just reviewed depends on a faulty assumption. God didn't believe *yesterday* that Jones will take the job tomorrow. God's beliefs, the argument would go, can't be described in the language of time at all.

This might not seem to help. Suppose God is outside time. (For a related discussion, the reader might want to look at "Eternity" Stump and Kretzmann, 1981.) If God really is omniscient, and Jones takes the job, doesn't God know this necessarily? If so, we can still construct an argument like the one we constructed above:

1. Necessarily, God knows (timelessly) that Jones will take the job (supposed consequence of God's omniscience).
2. Necessarily, if God knows that Jones will take the job, then Jones will take the job (because no one can know false things).
3. Therefore, necessarily, Jones will take the job.

Once again, we seem to end up with the conclusion that Jones isn't free, but once again we can call that troublesome first premise into question. We need to reflect on what saying that necessarily God knows that Jones will take the job would mean. Suppose that Jones really is going to take the job and that God, surveying the scheme of things from eternity, sees this. If God is omniscient, then no matter what X is, we have:

O: Necessarily, if X is true, then God knows that X is true.

This seems to be a perfectly good way of saying what it means for God to be omniscient. Now assume that X is, in fact, true. It simply doesn't follow from this assumption that *necessarily*, God knows that X. The following is not a correct principle of reasoning:

1. Necessarily, if X, then Y.
2. X.
3. Therefore, necessarily Y.

For example, necessarily, if George Washington was over 6' tall, then he was over 5' 10". This is just arithmetic. Furthermore, George Washington was over 6' tall. But the statement that necessarily, he was over 5' 10" is false. If he had had rickets, for example, he might well never have grown to be taller than 5' 10". If the view we're considering is correct, then what God actually knows depends on what's actually true. If we start with the very plausible assumption that there's nothing necessary about the fact that Jones will take the job, then the fact that God *knows* that he will take the job is a contingent fact—contingent on what Jones actually decides to do. In that case, the first premise is false and the argument fails. God's omniscience amounts to the principle that we labeled "O" above: necessarily, if something is true, then God knows it. That doesn't make the truths that God knows necessary.

4.2.2.3 Open Theism The third solution goes in a very different direction. It assumes that God is everlasting, but exists within time. However, it also takes a particular view of what time is like. According to the open theist, at least some things about the future aren't fixed. Suppose once again that Jones will freely decide tomorrow whether to take the job. The open theist says that if the decision really will be a free one, then there simply is no fact of the matter today about what Jones will do. The proposition that he will take the job isn't true, nor is the proposition that he won't. Neither will be true or false until he actually makes the decision. But in that case, even God doesn't know what Jones will do because there's nothing for God to know. There simply is no fact one way or the other. Once again, the premise that necessarily, God knows that Jones will take the job turns out to be false.

This view is called **open theism**, and it rests on two premises. One is that when we say that God is omniscient, all we can reasonably expect is that God knows every fact or truth that is actually there to be known. The second premise is that some aspects of the future—particularly things that will result from free choices—aren't yet fixed and so aren't yet real. Therefore, the fact that God doesn't know them isn't a blot on God's omniscience.

Open theism has been defended in recent years by a number of theologians and philosophers (see Clark Pinnock, et al., *The Openness of God*) but it's controversial. Some thinkers believe it doesn't do justice to God's omniscience. Others question the idea that statements about future free choices are neither true nor false. Nonetheless, open theism injects a lively alternative into the debate. Its views on the nature of God's knowledge are not unlike those of process theology, which also holds that what God knows depends in part on what creatures decide to do in response to God.

5 A BEING OR NOT A BEING

So far, we've assumed throughout our discussion that God is a being and wondered what attributes God might have. Interestingly enough, not everyone agrees that God is a being in the first place.

It's not easy to spell out just what we mean when we call something a being, but some things seem clear. For example, the Dalai Lama is a being and so are you. It also seems correct to say that an animal is a being, and for purposes of this discussion, even correct to call an inert physical object such as a rock a being. Water isn't a being, although a particular body of water such as Lake Michigan might be. And even though the Dalai Lama is a being, his height or shape isn't.

What about such things as concepts or numbers? Are they beings? The best answer is probably that they aren't. Numbers and concepts are examples of what philosophers call *abstract objects*, which is more or less a way of saying that they aren't objects in the ordinary sense at all.

If God is a person, as Jews, Christians, Muslims, Sikhs, and many others would say, then it seems perfectly clear that God is a being. However, some thinkers have denied that God is a being at all. This tradition goes back a long way but in recent times, it was advocated by the Protestant theologian Paul Tillich. Anything that is not absolutely ultimate couldn't be God, according to Tillich. As he saw it, if we identify God with any being whatsoever, we've identified God with something less than ultimate and, in fact, Tillich says, are guilty of a sort of **idolatry**, of worshiping something that isn't really God. (Tillich's *Dynamics of Faith* is often recommended as an introduction to his thought.)

Needless to say, not everyone finds this line of thought convincing, and it's tempting to argue that it makes no sense. After all, if we say that God isn't a being, how is this different from saying that God doesn't exist at all?

Saying that something isn't a being doesn't necessarily make it unreal. Even though the shape of your desk isn't a being, your desk still has a shape. Still, this isn't what Tillich has in mind. The reason many philosophers wouldn't count the shape of your desk as a being is that the shape of your desk is a quality or property or, in the language of Aristotelian philosophy, an "accident" of the being or thing that is your desk. That gives the desk's shape a sort of second-class or dependent status. Tillich doesn't want to say any such thing about God. Instead, Tillich would say that when we talk about God, we are talking about something deeper than beings and their qualities. We are talking about the very ground of being—of what lies behind the possibility of beings at all.

This isn't an easy notion to grasp, though it has roots in ideas that long predate Tillich. The theology of St. Thomas Aquinas contains closely related ideas. Some people have interpreted mystical thinkers such as Meister Eckhardt as saying similar things, and Tillich's view has antecedents in "negative theology," which claims that we can't make positive claims about God but can only say what God is not. In any case, what we see by including Tillich in our survey is that concepts of God range from the idea of a fully physical being, as Latter-Day Saints would claim, to denying that God is a being at all.

6 GOD AND LANGUAGE ABOUT GOD

So far, everything we've had to say is very "philosophical." We've discussed God in terms of hifalutin concepts from metaphysics and theology. Some thinkers object that this is very far from the way that believers really think about and experience God. Some thinkers would also insist that however fascinating terms like "omnipotence" or "omnipresence" might be, the real vocabulary that lights up religious life is much more concrete. The Bible portrays God as walking in the garden in the cool of the evening, as fashioning the first human from the clay, and as bargaining with Abraham. This sort of talk may have a strong element of metaphor or symbol, but it's vital to people's religious imaginations.

We also have a certain vocabulary that we use to talk about God, and at least in Christianity and Judaism, this vocabulary carries connotations that some theologians see as harmful. God is referred to as Father and as Lord. Even though the God of the theologians is neither male nor female, the dominant imagery for talking about God in Christianity and Judaism is male. Even though most believers agree that God is neither male nor female, we get a sense of how strongly entrenched the male image of God is by noticing how strange it still sounds to most people to hear God referred to as "She." Indeed, in some Christian denominations, using feminine language to refer to God is controversial, even though almost all sides agree that God is not literally male. Feminists complain that these ways of thinking about God reinforce unfortunate stereotypes, institutions, and ways of behaving. They say the history of theology has contributed to this tendency by picturing a hierarchical universe ruled over by a God whose **transcendence**—God's utter difference from the world we inhabit—has been emphasized over God's **immanence**, that is, over God's deep and thorough presence in the world.

One solution might be to direct our sights away from metaphor and poetry and back to the abstract vocabulary of philosophy and theology. We could stop using terms like "Father" or "Lord" and restrict ourselves entirely to non-metaphorical terms. Feminist theologians such as Sallie McFague believe that avoiding metaphor would be a mistake and many believers would agree. Religious belief is not the same as philosophical speculation. It's an affair of the heart as well as the mind. Because most believers will continue to think of God in the more concrete and poetic terms of real-life devotion, McFague thinks that rather than abandon metaphor, it's important that we develop other metaphors for thinking about God. In her book, *Models of God*, she explores the images of God as mother, lover, and friend, and suggests that there is much to be gained by thinking of the world as God's body.

Whatever we make of McFague's metaphors, the fact is that theology and philosophy are only a part of how people actually think about God. This chapter has mostly stressed the abstract, but if there is such a thing as religious wisdom, it isn't the same thing as mastering the intricacies of abstract metaphysics and theology. The typical believer may well decide to leave those sorts of questions to the professionals. But then again, the typical computer user can leave questions about how computers work to professionals. That doesn't mean these more abstract questions don't matter. It would be a mistake to think that philosophical and theological debates don't make a difference for how religious groups and religious leaders behave and, ultimately, for how ordinary believers conceive of the divine.

7 EPILOGUE: GOD AND RELIGION

Before we leave this chapter, it's worth asking just what God and religion have to do with one another. The answer is, quite a bit but not as much as some people think. That's for two reasons. First, it's perfectly possible to believe that God exists without being religious. Second, being religious without believing that God exists is also possible.

To illustrate the first point, consider the ancient Greek philosopher Aristotle (384–322 BCE). Aristotle believed that there was an intelligent "first cause" that was ultimately responsible for all change and motion, but this was what we might call a purely philosophical belief. As Aristotle conceived it, the first cause had no interest in us, was certainly not responsive to prayers, wasn't something or someone we could enter into a relationship with, and wasn't anything that Aristotle ever thought of worshipping. It would be strange to think of the mere philosophical belief that Aristotle's first cause exists as a way of being religious.

On the second point, one good place to begin is with a brief discussion of a major religious tradition: Buddhism. It would be wrong to say that Buddhism simply rejects the supernatural. Many Buddhists believe that gods do exist. However, these gods aren't thought of as creators of the universe or rulers of various parts of nature. In one important respect, gods are like us. They are on the path to final Nirvana.

It's possible to exaggerate the differences. Many Buddhists believe that it makes perfect sense to pray to the Buddha, whom they believe still to exist in some other realm and to be capable of helping us in our journey toward enlightenment. But at least some people who call themselves Buddhists—especially in the Western world—play down the supernatural aspects of Buddhism (see Batchelor 1998; Keown 1996).

Apart from variants on Buddhism, some Unitarians consider themselves to be religious but don't believe in God. There is even an Anglican priest, Don Cupitt, who remains a priest but rejects belief in a supernatural deity (see Cupitt, *Sea of Faith*). Ursula Goodenough is a cell biologist who clearly has a reverential, religious attitude toward nature but is also a thoroughgoing naturalist (Goodenough 2000).

This might puzzle some readers. They might ask, what is the point of religion without God? However, there's no tidy definition of the term "religion It's what philosophers call a "family resemblance concept." When we look at religions, we find various overlapping practices, traditions and beliefs that resemble one another in various ways but don't share a common essence. What many of these non-theistic ways of being religious share with more familiar religions is a certain attitude—a sense of awe about the universe, of sacredness in nature, and a certain humbleness in the face of mystery. If someone who feels this way calls herself religious, then who are we to quarrel?

AT A GLANCE: CONCEPTS OF GOD

1. God and gods
   - Monotheism is the belief in a single god.
   - Polytheism is the belief in many gods.
   - The word "God" (upper-case "G") is meant as a title for a unique being.
2. What is supernatural?
   - To count as God, a being would have to be supernatural.
   - The word "supernatural" doesn't have a clear meaning.
   - A nonphysical being that created the physical world would count as supernatural by any definition.

Characteristic	Definition
Supernatural	Has significant control over large parts of nature
Omnipotent	All-powerful
Omniscient	All-knowing
Omnibenevolent	Perfectly good
Omnipresent	Present everywhere
Necessary Existence	Impossible to not exist
Eternal/Everlasting	Eternal is existing outside of time whereas everlasting is existing throughout time
Immutability	Unchanging

3. Perfect being
    3.1. Three central perfections. According to most theologians:
        • God is omnipotent: all-powerful.
        • God is omniscient: all-knowing.
        • God is omnibenevolent: entirely good.
    3.2. Necessary existence
        • If God exists necessarily, God can't fail to exist.
    3.3. Eternal or everlasting
        • If God is eternal, God is outside time.
        • If God is everlasting, then God is in time but didn't begin to exist and won't stop existing.
    3.4. There is a debate about whether God is completely unchanging.
    3.5. Omnipresence could mean various things. Alternatively:
        • Pantheism: God is identical with nature.
        • God is not identical with nature but pervades the world the way a soul is thought to pervade a body.
        • God is omnipresent by causing the world to stay in being at every moment.
    3.6. There is a debate about whether God has feelings.
4. Puzzles and paradoxes
    4.1. Omnipotence
        • If God is omnipotent, this seems to imply that there's nothing God can't do. But there seem to be things that even God couldn't do.
        4.1.1. The square circle
            • God can't create a square circle, and so is not omnipotent.
            • The argument:
                1. If God is omnipotent, then God has unlimited power (definition).
                2. If God has unlimited power, then God can perform any action (premise).

3. Therefore, if God is omnipotent, then God can perform any action (from 1 and 2).
4. Making a square circle would be performing an action (premise).
5. Therefore, if God is omnipotent, then God can make a square circle (from 3 and 4).
6. No one can make a square circle (premise).
7. Therefore, God can't make a square circle (from 6).
8. Therefore, God is not omnipotent (from 5 and 7).

- Creating a square circle is a pseudo task; nothing would count.
- Being unable to perform a pseudo task isn't a limit on a being's power.

4.1.2. The stone paradox

- God arguably could not create a stone so heavy that he couldn't lift it.
- Mavrodes argues: in God's case (but not in ours), creating such a stone amounts to a pseudo task.
- Also: there is no limit to the size of the stone God could create.
- We only get puzzles when we define the task by reference to God's power.

4.2. Omniscience
4.2.1. Feelings

- Problem: if God has no feelings, there seem to be things we know that God doesn't.
- Solution: perhaps omniscience only calls for knowing which propositions are true.

4.2.2. Free will

- The argument:
  1. Necessarily, by omniscience, God knows what we will do.
  2. Necessarily, if something is known, it is true.
  3. Therefore, by the Transfer of Necessity, what we will do is necessary, hence not free.
- This puzzle arises whether or not God is in time.
- One solution:
  1. Saying God is omniscient means necessarily, if some proposition X is true, then God knows this.
  2. This doesn't imply that X itself is necessary; X many depend on a free choice.
- Another solution:
  1. Open theism: not all statements about the future are already true or false.
  2. If something is not already true or false, nothing now exists for God to know.

5. There is a debate about whether it's correct to think of God as a being.
6. Metaphors for God
   - Sally McFague suggests thinking of God as mother, or as lover, or as friend.
7. God and religion
   - Agreeing that there is a god or God doesn't entail being religious.
   - Being religious doesn't entail believing in God or gods.

WEB RESOURCES

For a discussion of omnipotence, see the entry by Joshua Hoffman and Gary Rosenkrantz in the Stanford Encyclopedia of Philosophy at http://plato. stanford.edu/entries/omnipotence.

The section of Boethius's Consolation of Philosophy, in which he sets forth his account of how divine omniscience is compatible with human freedom, is in Chapter V, beginning on p. 163. This is also online at http://etext.lib.virginia.edu/latin/boethius/boephil.html.

CHAPTER 2

The Design Argument

Nature appears to display purpose and complexity. Some theists see this as evidence for the existence of God. Critics argue that purpose in nature can be explained without postulating the existence of God. In this chapter, we explore the argument for God's existence based on apparent design in nature. We explain the main criticism of the argument— the evolution objection—and various theistic replies to it, including an important reformulation of the design argument. We then explore traditional philosophical objections to the argument.

INTRODUCTION

Labels give us information about products. They tell us what a product is and who made it. Some designer labels indicate quality. Others merely reflect the latest fad. Many theists argue that the universe has a designer label attached to it. They point to incredible features of nature as evidence of design. They contend this apparent design amounts to a designer label telling us that God designed the world.

1 THE WATCH AND THE WATCHMAKER

1.1 The Stone and the Watch: Goal-Directed Complexity

The best known proponent of the design argument is the eighteenth-century English theologian, William Paley. Paley asks us to imagine two scenarios. Suppose that while walking through a field, you came across a stone and wondered how it came to be. One answer might be that, for all we know, the stone has always existed. Now suppose you were walking through a field and came across a watch. Could you explain the existence of the watch by saying that, for all we know, it has always existed? Paley doesn't think so. He argues that from the existence of the watch, we legitimately infer the existence of an intelligent being who designed and created it—a watchmaker (Paley 1802, p.4).

What is the difference between the stone and the watch that makes us think one was designed by an intelligent being and the other was not? Paley argues that the difference is a matter of **teleology**. A teleological system is a system with **goal-directed complexity**. The watch is complex in the sense that it has several parts, like wheels, gears, and springs. It is goal-directed because its parts work together towards a particular goal—keeping time. Paley argues that teleological systems are best explained by a designer. The watch displays teleology. It's a goal-directed system; the stone isn't. This is why we think the watch was designed and the stone wasn't.

1.2 "Living Watches:" Goal-Directed Complexity in Nature

Paley argues that animals, plants, and insects are like "living watches" because they display at least as much teleology as human-made watches. As Paley sees it, the goal-directed complexity we observe in nature is evidence that nature is the product of intelligent design. He thinks that just as the best explanation of the watch is a watchmaker, so the best explanation of "living watches" is a supernatural watchmaker—God. To appreciate Paley's argument, it might be helpful to look at an example of what he has in mind.

1.2.1 The Eye: An Example of Teleology in Nature

Animals need information about their environment to survive and thrive. One way animals gather information is by using their eyes. Paley argues that a careful examination of the eye reveals that it is a sort of "natural watch," displaying goal-directed complexity. He thinks this is best seen by comparing the eye to a human-made optic device like a telescope, but an even better comparison might be a camera.

Cameras and eyes work in very similar ways. The following chart records some familiar resemblances between the eye and a camera:

Camera Structure	Eye Structure	Function
Lens	Cornea/Lens	Focuses Image
Aperture	Pupil	Regulates amount of light reaching sensor
Film	Retina	Light-sensitive medium that registers light pattern

There are other similarities between cameras and eyes. For example, they both have an inner surface that minimizes the scattering of stray light. There are also obvious and important differences. But Paley argues that even these differences demonstrate the superiority of the eye over the telescope and, by extension, a camera:

> every indication of contrivance, every manifestation of design which existed in the watch, exists in the works of nature, with the difference on the side of nature, of being greater and more, and that in a degree which exceeds all computation . . . the contrivances of nature surpass the contrivances of art, in the complexity, subtlety, and curiosity of the mechanism; and still more, if possible, do they go beyond them in number and variety . . . (Paley 1802, p.13).

In the case of the camera, it seems even clearer that the eye is superior. For example, the retina is far more sensitive to light than film. It takes only one or two photons to stimulate the retina. The retina is so sensitive that the eye is equipped with neural filters that only allow a visual signal to travel to the brain if at least ten photons arrive in less than 100 milliseconds.

The eye also functions over a much wider spectrum of light availability than a typical camera. It automatically and quickly adapts to light changes. It has a superior automatic focus system and is able to improve contrast automatically. The eye is extremely sensitive to touch. This sensitivity help protect it from damage. There are more nerve endings in the cornea than anywhere else in the body. Just before surgery, anesthesiologists sometimes test the corneal reflex by touching the eyelashes in order to determine how unconscious a patient is.

If we were walking in a meadow and came across a watch, a telescope, or a camera, we would rightly infer it was designed by an intelligent being. Paley thinks we should draw the same conclusion about "biological watches" like the eye. We should take the goal-directed complexity we see in nature as evidence that the world was designed and created by God.

1.3 What Kind of Argument Is This?

The design argument is an *a posteriori* argument, that is, it is an **argument** based on experience and observation rather than abstract reasoning alone. There are two common ways of understanding the form of the design argument: as an **argument from analogy** or as an **abductive argument**.

1.3.1 Argument from Analogy

The basic idea of an argument from analogy is that when two things are similar in many important and relevant ways, they are probably similar to each other in the way at issue. For example, rats and humans are very similar when it comes to getting cancer from certain chemicals. For this reason, we use rats to determine whether some particular chemical causes cancer in humans. We infer that if that particular chemical causes cancer in rats, it's likely to also cause cancer in humans.

Arguments from analogy take the following form:

1. Two things, x and y, share the properties $P_a, P_b, \ldots, P_y$.
2. x has the property P_z.
3. Therefore, y probably has the property P_z.

Unlike deductive arguments, the conclusions of even the best arguments from analogy are only probably true. Knowing that some chemical doesn't cause cancer in rats doesn't guarantee that it won't cause cancer in humans. It just means it is probably safe for humans.

Arguments from analogy are not uncommon in philosophy. Bertrand Russell, for example, uses an argument from analogy to argue that other people have minds even though we can't perceive their thoughts directly. Other people are similar enough to us in physical structure and behavior that it seems reasonable to infer that they have minds. For example, if a person acts the way we act when we're in pain, it is reasonable to conclude that they have the same inner sensations of pain that we do.

Hume thinks the design argument is an argument from analogy because it rests on the principle that "similar causes prove similar effects, and similar effects similar causes" (Hume, p. 31). According to the design argument, organisms and human-made machines are alike in that they both display a considerable amount of teleology. The conclusion is that they are both most likely the result of similar causes—intelligent designers. We can summarize the argument this way:

1. Organisms and machines are both complex goal-directed objects.
2. Machines were created by an intelligent being.
3. Therefore, organisms were probably also created by an intelligent being.

1.3.2 Abductive Argument

A second way to view the design argument is as an **abductive** argument, that is, an inference to the best explanation. We reason abductively when we conclude that something is true because it makes the most sense of the available facts. Many philosophers think that the design argument is best formulated as an abductive argument. On this understanding, the argument claims that a designer is the best explanation of the goal-directed complexity in nature. Consider the following two hypotheses:

- The design hypothesis: nature is the product of a designer.
- The natural hypothesis: nature is not the product of a designer.

According to the abductive version of the design argument, the teleology we observe in nature is less surprising if the design **hypothesis** is true than if the natural hypothesis is true.

2 THE BLIND WATCHMAKER: DARWIN'S SCIENTIFIC OBJECTION

2.1 The Objection from Evolution

Two kinds of objections arise against the design argument—scientific and philosophical. The most important objection to the design argument is the scientific objection from **evolution**. According to this objection, we don't need to posit God to explain apparent design in nature; it can be explained by natural processes alone. According to evolution, organisms are adapted to survive and reproduce in their environments by a natural process involving two components: random genetic mutation and natural selection.

Here's the basic idea: life in nature is a competition to survive. During the course of this struggle, random genetic mutations occur that result in organisms acquiring new traits or characteristics. If a new trait gives an organism an advantage at the four Fs (feeding, fleeing, fighting, and reproducing), then it's more likely to spread throughout the population.

As Charles Darwin explains, the new trait is "selected" by nature to be passed to future generations because organisms with the new trait are better equipped to survive and have offspring. Eventually, over many generations, the new trait will spread throughout the entire population and the population as a whole will have acquired a new trait. If this process is repeated many times with various traits, a population will accumulate enough new traits that it will no longer be the same species as the original population. A new species will have emerged.

Darwin maintains that we can see the power of evolution to explain the amazing characteristics of organisms by looking at artificial selection. Artificial selection is the intentional modification of a species through human intervention in animal or plant reproduction to foster desirable traits. For example, the domestic chicken is the result of artificial selection. A random genetic mutation would cause a particular chicken to be a bit larger than the rest. When farmers noticed a larger chicken in a population, they would select it to breed with other large chickens. Over time, the entire population of domestic chickens acquired the trait of being large. This process resulted in domestic chickens that are about four times larger than their wild ancestors and that, according to Colonel Sanders, make for much better eating.

Making a chicken larger is one thing but radically changing a population is something else. Darwin points out, though, that artificial selection has led to pretty radical changes in animal populations. Consider the enormous variety of dogs. Wild dogs originally looked something like a wolf. From wild dogs, humans have created a wide variety of dogs. The differences between a St. Bernard and a Teacup Poodle are not minor. Evolution works on the same principles, except that characteristics are not selected by people but by nature. If random genetic mutations and artificial selection can accomplish such radical change in a population of dogs, surely genetic mutations and natural selection can do so in other species.

With the process of evolution in mind, let's reconsider Paley's example of the eye. Can the existence of the eye be explained by a gradual accumulation of traits? The majority of scientists think so. Oxford biologist Richard Dawkins explains how the eye could have arisen by natural processes alone. He assumes that our distant ancestors probably started out with some "rudimentary patch of light-sensitive pigment."

Human skin is light sensitive. When you take your watch off in the summer, your skin is lighter where the watch was. Your skin is light sensitive and "records" when it has been exposed to light. If the radiation from the sun is strong enough, your skin records light exposure within hours. Dawkins argues that early "eyes" might have started out as something a bit more sensitive than the light sensitivity of normal skin: "Perhaps it could just tell the difference between day and night" (Dawkins 1996, p. 140). An organism with a mutation that allowed it to sense light— even if just barely—had an advantage over competing organisms. This advantage would contribute to its survival and reproduction and be passed on to its offspring.

Any mutations that improved the sensitivity of this patch of light-sensitive cells, no matter how small, would also be selected and passed to future generations. Over time, this process would lead to better and more sophisticated light-sensing organs and eventually to eyes. Dawkins provides a detailed account of how this might have happened and points out that we find organisms with eyes that actually display the various intermediate stages (Dawkins 1996, pp. 138–197). The objection to the design argument from evolution is a powerful objection. If apparent design can be explained by natural processes alone, no need exists to posit God and hence the rug is pulled out from underneath the design argument.

Defenders of the design argument appreciate the seriousness of this objection. They counter the objection from evolution in two basic ways. The first is to argue that, despite appearances, evolution can't account for apparent design in nature. This response to evolution involves arguing over the facts of biology. This is the route taken by **scientific creationists** and **intelligent design theorists**. The second is to concede that evolution explains apparent design in biology but shift the debate to apparent design in physics. Let's consider each strategy in turn.

2.2 Creationism

It's important to be clear about the meaning of certain key terms at the outset of this discussion on **creationism**. For our purposes, creationism is the general view that God created the universe. Creationism in this very broad sense is compatible with evolution. It is not uncommon for people to think that God created the universe and that he used the mechanisms of evolution as part of the process. People who hold this view are sometimes referred to as "**theistic evolutionists**."

2.2.1 Scientific Creationism

Scientific creationists are creationists who argue that science supports the existence of God and a more literal reading of Genesis. They accept microevolution—change within a species—but reject macroevolution, or change from one species into another. Scientific creationists contend that humans were created directly by a special act of God and are not directly related to other animals. They believe that the universe is relatively young, about 6,000 to 10,000 years old, and that Noah's flood played an important role in the formation of the Earth's geology. Outspoken scientific creationists like Henry Morris and Duane Gish make various arguments. Consider two.

First, they argue that an examination of the fossil record undermines evolution because it does not record transitional forms. Scientific creationists claim that if evolution occurred, we would expect the fossil record to contain fossils of intermediate species that "link" two species together. Morris and Gish claim that we have yet to find such fossils. They argue the lack of "missing links" in the fossil record is powerful evidence against evolution.

Second, scientific creationists insist that a major problem with evolution is its reliance on random genetic mutations to acquire traits that contribute to an organism's survival and reproduction. Their argument is that the vast majority of mutations are harmful to a species, not helpful. Only in comic books are mutations beneficial. Creationist James Perloff puts the argument this way:

> Mutations are almost universally harmful. In human beings they are classed as "birth defects." They often result in death or sterility. People today suffer from more than 4,000 disorders caused by gene mutations. Down's syndrome, cystic fibrosis and sickle cell anemia are familiar examples. But what benefits can we list from mutation? Who hopes their child will be born with one? (Perloff 1999, p. 25)

There are many scientific problems with scientific creationism but we will focus on three. First, consider the gaps in the fossil record. Contrary to scientific creationist claims, fossils of transitional forms or so-called "missing links" do exist. In 1861, just two years after *The Origin of Species* was published, scientists discovered fossils of *Archaeopteryx*, a prehistoric bird with important features of a reptile. It has wings and feathers, like a bird, but it also has many skeletal features of reptiles that birds don't have. The vertebrae in the trunk region are free, not fused like other birds. The neck attaches to the skull in the rear, not from below. The sacrum consists of 6 vertebrae like reptiles, not 11 to 23 vertebrae like birds.

Other well-documented transitional fossils exist between whales and land mammals and in the evolution of the horse. True, scientists don't have transitional fossils for connecting every species, but this is to be expected. Fossilization is a very rare process. Only a select few organisms are fossilized for posterity. Further, evolution is a slow and gradual process. Together these two facts suggest that very little of the evolutionary process would be recorded in fossils. In other words, large gaps in the fossil record are not unexpected.

Second, it's not at all clear that most mutations are harmful. Evidence suggests that most mutations are neutral. According to one study, there are about 3 deleterious mutations out of 175 per generation in humans (Nachman & Crowell 2000). Further, beneficial mutations are not as rare as creationists claim. They are common enough that we observe them in everyday life. Consider antibiotic resistance in disease-causing germs. Consider also pesticide resistance in agricultural pests. These mutations give these organisms a survival advantage.

There is an important asymmetry between harmful and beneficial mutations that's very important for this debate. Beneficial mutations are far more likely to be preserved precisely because they are helpful. Harmful mutations are less likely to be preserved. Even if more mutations were harmful than beneficial, the beneficial ones would be preserved at a much higher rate. Therefore, most surviving mutations are beneficial.

Third, one of the most important objections to creation science isn't a scientific objection but a philosophical one: creation science is not a science at all. In the early and mid-1980s, American courts ruled that teaching creation science in public schools ran afoul of the First Amendment's prohibition against the government's establishment of a state religion. Critics of creation science hold that to be a genuinely scientific explanation, a theory must appeal to natural processes alone. Genuine science does not, indeed cannot, explain nature by appealing to supernatural beings. Critics contend that at best, creation science is a pseudoscience like astrology.

2.2.2 Intelligent Design Theory

Intelligent design theory (ID) is an updated critique of evolution that was formulated, in part, to avoid this criticism by distancing itself from religion. Intelligent design theory is made up of two component claims:

1. Scientific theories may legitimately posit intelligent agents as an explanation of apparent design in nature.
2. Some parts of nature are best explained as the product of intelligent design.

Let's consider each component in turn.

2.2.2.1 Intelligent Design and the Nature of Science The first component of ID is not a scientific claim but a philosophical one. It's a claim about the nature and limits of science. There's an important difference between scientific questions and philosophical questions *about* science. "How does a human kidney work?" is a scientific question. It's answered using the tools of science, especially observation and experimentation. "What is science?" is a philosophical question about science. It's answered using philosophical methods, such as the analysis concepts. Scientists, because of their experience, have a special perspective for considering the question, "What is science?" But being good at doing science doesn't necessarily make someone good at philosophizing about it. In any case, when scientists propose an answer to the question, "what is science?" they are practicing philosophy, not science.

ID claims then that there is a proper place in science for inferring intelligent design. Unlike scientific creationists, however, proponents of ID go out of their way to point out that "intelligent designer" does not necessarily mean "God." Intelligent design theory doesn't claim that the intelligent designer is God. In fact, it has nothing to say about God whatsoever. It makes a much more modest claim than scientific creationism, namely, that nature bears signs of intelligent design. It is "officially" agnostic about who the designer or designers are. William Dembski, a leader in the ID movement, explains it this way:

> A biological theory of intelligent design holds that a designing intelligence is required to account for the complex, information-rich structures of living systems. At the same time, it refuses to speculate about the nature of the designing intelligence (Dembski 2001, p. 8).

Most ID advocates do believe that God is the designer of nature. They argue that this is their personal view and not the conclusion of intelligent design theory itself. Michael Behe, a leader in the ID movement, puts it this way:

> I myself do believe in a benevolent God ... But a scientific argument for design in biology does not reach that far. Thus while I argue for design, the question of the identity of the designer is left open. Possible candidates for the role of designer include: the God of Christianity; an angel—fallen or not; Plato's demi-urge; some mystical new age force; space aliens from Alpha Centauri; time travelers; or some utterly unknown intelligent being. Of course, some of these possibilities may

seem more plausible than others based on information from fields other than science. Nonetheless, as regards the identity of the designer, modern ID theory happily echoes Isaac Newton's phrase, *hypothesis non fingo* [I will not speculate] (Behe 2001, p. 165).

But what other candidates for an intelligent designer exist? As the above quote suggests, ID advocates claim that it's at least conceptually possible that life on earth was designed by space aliens, time travelers, and so on. These possibilities seem far-fetched and implausible but remember that we are talking about a *philosophical* claim about science, not a *scientific* claim.

Philosophy has a different set of tools than science does and plays by a different set of rules. So far, we are just trying to understand the concept, or definition, of science. Philosophers often use implausible examples to find the boundaries of a concept or idea. In fact, extreme **thought experiments** are sometimes very helpful at clarifying concepts. Let's consider the possibility of space aliens as intelligent designers and see how this idea is supposed to clarify the concepts of science and intelligent design.

Suppose some technologically sophisticated alien species exists on another planet. This society is far more advanced scientifically than we are. Its experts are particularly adept at genetic engineering and creating the building blocks of life: amino acids, proteins, nucleic acids, and so on. They regularly design all sorts of exotic organisms, from the ground up. Suppose someday humans discover a planet populated exclusively by plants and animals designed by these aliens. Unknown to us, this planet is the aliens' version of a wildlife preserve, so no signs of alien civilization are found on the planet. Could human scientists, in principle, discover that these organisms were designed?

According to ID, scientists can legitimately infer such design depending on what the organisms were like. Nothing about the nature of science forces us to conclude that life on this alien planet was completely the result of non-intelligent processes. Now suppose that the human scientists could tell that the life on this planet was designed but had no clue who designed it. Intelligent design theorists argue there is nothing unscientific about noticing design and at the same time having no opinion about who the designer is. Just as importantly, these scientists didn't cross the boundary from science into religion.

They claim this admittedly unrealistic example tells us something about the nature of science that applies to the debate about evolution.

Merely inferring that an intelligent designer exists doesn't disqualify a theory as unscientific. Neither does it mean that the intelligent designer is God.

Dembski and other ID theorists attempt to bolster their view of science by pointing out a particular scientific project, the Search of Extraterrestrial Intelligence (SETI). SETI looks for signs of intelligent life elsewhere in the universe by examining radio waves from space and was funded by NASA until 1993. Dembski argues that if inferring intelligence from complex patterns of radiation is legitimate science, then inferring the existence of an intelligent designer from complex patterns in biology is also legitimate science.

So is ID genuine science? Most scientists and many philosophers of science don't think so. Critics argue that advocates of ID have subtly misconstrued the debate over the scientific status of ID. Proponents of ID act like the chief complaint against it has to do with the legitimacy of invoking intelligent agents as scientific explanations. It isn't. The main complaint, though others exist, focuses on the legitimacy of including the supernatural in scientific explanations. Confusing these two issues creates the impression that if it's okay for scientists to infer intelligent design in organisms, then ID is legitimate science.

Critics insist ID is not science, regardless of the role intelligent causes play in science because it ultimately allows for supernatural explanations. Perhaps ID doesn't claim that a supernatural cause directly and immediately explains irreducible complexity. The problem is that it allows for the possibility of supernatural explanations in science at all. Its failure to rule out supernatural causes undermines its claim to scientific legitimacy.

Whether or not that's a good reason for thinking that ID isn't science, we can ask a significant, though often neglected question about this debate: why does it matter whether ID is legitimate science? The answer is that it doesn't matter as much as the parties to the debate might think. Whether ID is science is important to scientific practice. It's important to questions of education policy, research funding, and the law. It doesn't matter, though, in the broad debate between theists and atheists over the existence of God.

The design argument concerns whether apparent design in nature constitutes evidence for God. The quality of that evidence is what is important, not whether the evidence is classified as scientific, philosophical, or otherwise. An empirical debate about whether certain observations count as evidence for God cannot be won merely by defining words a certain way. If there's evidence for God, there's evidence for God. It doesn't matter whether that evidence is scientific but whether it's good enough to justify belief in God. The important question, for our purposes, is about the quality of the evidence for design, not its category.

2.2.2.2 Intelligent Design's Scientific Arguments

Let's now turn to the second claim of ID, that parts of nature are best explained as the product of intelligent design. ID empirical arguments tend to center on two concepts: **specified complexity** and **irreducible complexity**. For brevity's sake, we will focus our attention on irreducible complexity.

Biochemist Michael Behe claims that irreducible complexity throws a monkey wrench into the theory of evolution. Just what is irreducible complexity? A system is irreducibly complex if it's composed of several well-matched, interacting parts such that the removal of any one part causes the whole system to cease functioning. Behe cites a mouse trap as an example of irreducible complexity:

> The mousetrap depends critically on the presence of all five it its components; if there were no spring, the mouse would not be pinned to the base; if there were no platform, the other pieces would fall apart; and so on. The function of the mousetrap requires all the pieces: you cannot catch a few mice with just a platform, add a spring and catch a few more mice, add a holding bar and catch a few more. All of the components have to be in place before any mice are caught. Thus the mousetrap is irreducibly complex (Behe 1998, p. 178).

A mouse trap missing even one piece will not kill mice. On the other hand, a typical wrist-watch is not, strictly speaking, irreducibly complex. If one removed the glass face from the watch, it would still function.

Behe argues that irreducibly complex biological systems can't be explained by evolution. Remember that evolution happens in small steps and that each step must have survival value to be "selected" by nature. However, in the case of irreducibly complex systems each small step doesn't have survival value because each part of the system is useless by itself. It's only when every piece of the system is present that the system function and has survival value. Consider the mouse trap again:

> You can't start with a platform, catch a few mice, add a spring, catch a few more mice, add a hammer, catch a few more mice and so on: The whole system has to be put together at once or the mice get away (Behe 1996, p. 111).

Thus, irreducibly complex systems could not have evolved in the piece-meal way evolution works:

> An irreducibly complex system cannot be produced directly by numer-ous, successive, slight modifications of a precursor system, because any precursor to an irreducibly complex system that is missing a part is by definition nonfunctional. Since natural selection can only choose systems that are already working, then if a biological system cannot be produced gradually it would have to arise as an integrated unit, in one fell swoop, for natural selection to have anything to act on (Behe 1996).

Behe gives several examples of irreducible complexity in nature but the "poster child" is the bacterial flagellum. The bacterial flagellum is a bacterial propulsion system that resembles a boat motor. It consists of a motor, a rotor, and a propeller. Like all motors, the bacterial motor has a stator (stationary element) and a rotor (rotating element). The energy to move the motor is generated by acid flow through a bacterial membrane. This rotates a rod (driveshaft) with a hook-shaped protein (universal joint) attached to the end. A whip-like filament (propeller) is attached to the hook and acts as a contact surface to move the bacteria (Behe 1996, pp. 69–73).

For the system to work, it must have at least three functional parts: motor, rotor, and propeller. Behe argues that like the mouse trap, if any one of those parts is missing, the system will not function. According to Behe, this means that the bacterial flagellum could not have come into existence by means of small, incremental steps as evolution requires. Behe argues the bacterial flagellum is just one of many "molecular machines" that display irreducible complexity and amount to "a loud, clear, piercing cry of '*design!*'" (Behe 1996, p. 232).

What are we to make of the scientific claims of ID? Most scientists find them unconvincing. Let's first consider the claim that irreducibly complex systems can't develop in small successive steps. One problem with Behe's argument is that it doesn't take seriously the possibility of individual parts of a system arising independently of each other with functions that change later.

Consider again the mousetrap. Biochemist Kenneth Miller points out that the individual pieces of a mousetrap can have other useful functions. Take away the catch and the metal bar and you have something that could be used as a paper clip. The paper clip function of the structure is a useful function, so it would be "selected." If later mutations resulted in a change from the paper clip function to, say, a mouse-killing function, the structure would continue to be "selected." At no point did the structure lack a useful function, even if the function changed.

In this way, small successive changes can result in an irreducibly complex system. If the other parts of the mousetrap arise in similar ways—with an independent function that later changes—one sees how irreducibly complex systems can arise naturally. With the structures already present, it isn't hard to see how their individual functions could change in such a way that they together form a new system with a new function. Biologist Robert Dorit puts it this way: "The correct metaphor for the Darwinian process is not that of a First World engineer, but that of the Third World auto mechanic who will get your car running again but only if parts already lying around can be used for the repair" (Dorit 1997). For example, Dorit points out that the set of genes that originally

> involved specifying the pattern of segmentation in insects has now been found to assist in the proper development of the vertebrate hindbrain (a structure that has no counterpart in segmented insects). This . . . is an exquisite piece of molecular machinery, precisely of the sort that the author finds so imponderable in a Darwinian world (Dorit 1997).

Let's return to the bacterial flagellum. Scientists have long been interested in how germs make us sick. Bacteria produce toxins that destroy the cells of the host organism they infect. These toxins are delivered by a tiny syringe that pierces the cell wall and secretes the poison into the host's cell. Miller informs us that research into this secretion system revealed that ten of the parts that make up the secretion system are the same parts that make up the bacterial flagellum. Miller explains:

> This means that a portion of the whip-like bacterial flagellum functions as the 'syringe' that makes up the . . . secretory apparatus. In other words, a subset of the proteins of the flagellum is fully-functional in a completely different context—not motility, but the deadly delivery of toxins to a host cell. This observation falsifies the central claim of the biochemical argument from design—namely, that a subset of the parts of an irreducibly complex structure must be, 'by definition non-functional.' Here are 10 proteins from the flagellum which are missing not just one part but more than 40, and yet they are fully-functional in the . . . [secretory] apparatus (Miller 2003, p. 300).

It's interesting to note a possible intermediate step in the transformation of this secretion system into a movement system. One common way for bacteria to move is by secreting a trail of material that they then glide along "in a manner reminiscent of slugs" (Musgrave 2005, pp. 74–75). The secretion system functioning as a secretion system is used for movement. A possible connection then begins to emerge between bacterial secretion systems and movement systems. This potential connection is bolstered by the fact that "in many gliding eubacteria, the secretory systems rotate and are driven by proton-motive force, as are the eubacterial flagella" (Musgrave 2005, p. 75).

3 THE FINE-TUNING DESIGN ARGUMENT

A second way of responding to the evolution objection to the design argument is to shift the debate from biology to physics, from anatomy to astronomy. This strategy takes biological evolution completely off the table because, even if evolution is true, random genetic mutation and natural selection are *biological* mechanisms and cannot explain design in *physics*.

3.1 The Argument

Philosopher Robin Collins offers the following analogy. Suppose that when humans finally arrive on Mars, we find a clear domed structure containing plant and animal life. Suppose further that the environment in the biosphere is perfect for life. The temperature is 80°F. The relative humidity is 50%. The biosphere has an oxygen-recycling system and a system for the production of food and water. If we came across such a biosphere, we would most likely conclude that it was made by an intelligent designer. The alternative explanation, that the biosphere came about as a result of natural processes alone, is so unlikely and improbable that we would scarcely consider it.

Proponents of the design argument point out that life is very fragile and can only exist in certain narrowly defined conditions. Life is as picky as Goldilocks. For it to exist, the universe cannot be too hot or too cold—it must be just right. Fortunately for us, the universe is "just right." It is, in effect, a biosphere with an environment fine-tuned to render life possible. They further argue that the **probability** of the universe being fine-tuned for life just by chance is so low that the best explanation is that the universe was not suited for life by coincidence but by design.

Proponents of the fine-tuning design argument, like William Lane Craig, point to statements by scientists like Princeton physicist Freeman Dyson, who notes that "there are many . . . lucky accidents in physics.

Without such accidents, water could not exist as liquid, chains of carbon atoms could not form complex organic molecules, and hydrogen atoms could not form breakable bridges between molecules." In short, life as we know it would be impossible. Theoretical physicist Paul Davies claims that with regard to the basic structure of the universe, "the impression of design is overwhelming."

The apparent fine-tuning of the universe involves the laws of physics and **physical constants**. Physical laws regulate the universe whereas physical constants describe the value of those regulations. An analogy can be made here with civil laws. Every state has a speed-limit law but the value of the speed limit is different from state to state.

Consider the law of gravity. Gravity is the mutual force of attraction between all particles or bodies that have mass. Without gravity, life couldn't exist. Masses would not clump together to form stars or planets, and hence the existence of complex, intelligent life would be impossible. But the universe's simply having gravity is not enough. The strength, or value, of gravity must be just right. If it were a little stronger, land-based animals anywhere near the size of humans would be crushed (Collins 2003, p. 189–191). If it were even greater, all stars would have been red dwarfs, which are too cold to support life-bearing planets (Craig 2003, p. 156).

Alternatively, if the gravitational constant were a little weaker, all stars would have been blue giants, which burn too briefly for life to develop. If it were even weaker, no stars or other solid bodies could form. According to physicist Paul Davies, a change in the strength of gravity by only one part in 10^{100} would have prevented a life-permitting universe (Craig 2003, p. 156).

Consider the strong nuclear force. The strong nuclear force is a short-range force that operates within an atomic nucleus. It holds nuclei together against electrical repulsion. Without it, life would be impossible because protons and neutrons could not bind together and, hence, no atoms with an atomic number greater than hydrogen would exist. As with gravity, the mere existence of this force isn't enough for life. It must have a narrowly defined strength, otherwise life would be impossible.

A 1% increase of the strong nuclear force would result in almost all carbon being burned into oxygen. A 2% increase would preclude protons formation from quarks, preventing the existence of atoms. A 5% decrease of the strong nuclear force would unbind deuteron, which is essential to nucleo-synthesis, leading to a universe composed only of hydrogen. The strong force must be within 0.8 to 1.2 of its actual strength or all elements with an atomic weight over 4 would not have formed (Craig 2003, p. 156).

If the value of the weak nuclear force had been greater, the Big Bang's nuclear burning would have proceeded past helium to iron, making fusion-powered stars impossible. If it had been weaker, stars would consist mainly of helium. Helium stars have a maximum life of 300 million years and are less stable than hydrogen stars (Collins 2003, p. 189; Craig 2003, p. 156).

Defenders of the fine-tuning design argument contend that life appears to be balanced on a razor's edge. The laws and constants of physics are "just right" for life to exist. The odds of any one of these constants being just right are extremely low. The odds that all of them are just right for life are incredible. As William Lane Craig puts it, "the existence of life depends on a conspiracy of initial conditions that must be fine-tuned to a degree that it is literally incomprehensible and incalculable" (Craig and Sinnot-Armstrong 2004, p. 9).

Proponents of the fine-tuning design argument contend that it is vastly more probable that a universe that is life-prohibiting rather than life-permitting should exist. Despite incredible odds, every condition necessary for the universe to be life-permitting has been met. They argue that the best explanation of the fine-tuning of the universe for life is that it was designed by an intelligent designer.

3.2 Objections to the Fine-Tuning Design Argument

Let's first consider objections specifically directed at the fine-tuning version of the design argument before we turn to philosophical objections to the design argument in general.

3.2.1 The Other Forms of Life Objections

One objection to the fine-tuning argument is based on the possibility of other forms of life. Life as we know it could not exist if the laws and constants of physics were much different than they are, runs the objection, but that doesn't mean that life *per se* couldn't exist. For all we know, other forms of life radically different from ours, like non-carbon forms of life, could exist even if the constants of physics were different.

Theists reply that this objection doesn't take into account that many of the parameters appealed to by the fine-tuning argument are necessary not just for the existence of life but for the existence of more fundamental and basic physical structures such as molecules and atoms. For example, according to Craig, a 2% increase in the strength of the strong nuclear force would preclude protons forming from quarks, preventing the existence of atoms altogether (Craig 2003, p. 156). It is difficult to see how any kind of organism could exist if there were no atoms whatsoever.

3.2.2 The More Fundamental Law Objection

Another objection to the fine-tuning argument is that as far as we know, there could be a fundamental law underneath the laws of physics. This more basic fundamental law might cause the constants of physics to have the values they do. According to this objection, universes with different laws or constants are not real physical possibilities, and so, it is not improbable that the constants of physics fall within the life-permitting range.

Proponents of the fine-tuning argument have several countermoves available to them. First, they contend that this suggestion is completely speculative. We simply have no reason to think it is true. Second, at most this objection simply pushes the improbability of the fine-tuning back a step to the fundamental physical law that supposedly necessitates a universe suited for life. If true, this might actually be stronger evidence of design. After all, how likely is it that, just by chance, the universe happens to *require* all physical laws and constants be fine-tuned for life? The notion that the universe had to be life-permitting is often called the **Strong Anthropic Principle** and, if true, is typically considered evidence of design.

Third, physicist Paul Davies points out that even if the laws of physics were necessary, the initial conditions aren't. Even if the rules are fixed, the starting point isn't. For example, the initial entropy of the early universe was low. There is no reason to think it had to be low. It could have been otherwise (Davies 1992, p. 169; Craig 2003, p. 166).

Fourth, philosopher John Leslie points out that various physical models show how different sorts of universes might have been created. If these four responses are correct, there was nothing inevitable about the fine-tuned universe we find ourselves in (Craig 2003, p. 156).

3.2.3 The "Any Universe is Equally Improbable" Objection

According to this objection, it might be improbable that the universe has the physical laws and constants that it has but the fact that it does have this particular set of laws is as probable as its having any other set, so we shouldn't be surprised that it has the particular set that it does. Consider a lottery: the odds that Mary wins the lottery are extremely low, but the odds that any particular person wins the lottery are equally low. Mary's winning does not surprise us. It doesn't require any special explanation. Every particular outcome of the lottery is equally unlikely, so no particular outcome should surprise us.

The same holds for the universe. The universe had to have *some* set of physical laws and constants and each possible set of laws is equally improbable. The fact that our universe has a set that makes it life-permitting should be no more or less surprising than if it had a set that was life-prohibiting. It should surprise us no more than Mary winning the lottery.

One problem with this objection is that it focuses on bare probability. Advocates of the design argument are not merely pointing to the extremely low probability of a fine-tuned universe existing by chance. They argue that this possibility is both improbable *and* surprising. The idea here is that some events are merely improbable, whereas others are improbable and surprising. Events that are improbable and surprising seem to demand an explanation.

The philosopher Roger White offers several helpful examples (White 2003). We wouldn't be surprised, for instance, if Mary won a lottery with 1 billion participants. But we would be surprised if John won three lotteries in a row, each of which had 1000 participants. But both events have the same odds: 1 in a billion. The second case is more surprising than the first and would probably make us suspect cheating. The odds that a monkey punching the keys on a typewriter would produce the text, "ʃ dsjf`s`hsjsjs@," is identical to the odds that the monkey would type, "I want a banana!" However, the former is not surprising whereas the latter is. The odds that a person gets any three specific "normal" bridge hands in a row is the same as getting three perfect bridge hands, yet the first requires no explanation whereas the second event does. Indeed, in such a case we would surely suspect cheating.

Equally Improbable Events

Improbable Event	Improbable and Surprising Event
Mary won a lottery with 1 billion participants	John won three lotteries in a row, each of which had 1000 participants
A monkey at a typewriter typed "ʃ dsjf`s`hsjsjs@"	A monkey at a typewriter typed "I want a banana!"
Any three particular bridge hands in a row	Three perfect bridge hands in a row

The difference between the events in the two columns is not entirely clear. White suggests that the critical element of surprising events is that they undermine our assumptions about the circumstances in which they occur (White 2003, p. 239). Improbable and surprising events demand an explanation because there is a plausible, non-*ad hoc* **explanation** (i.e., not merely contrived for the purpose) that, if true, makes the events less surprising.

Advocates of the design argument maintain that a universe fine-tuned for life belongs in the right column of the table above and, hence, demands an explanation. The existence of a fine-tuned universe is not only improbable but it's improbable *and* surprising. It's made less surprising if there's a God that designed it that way.

Second, Craig invites us to consider a different analogy than the lottery. Suppose you have a large container with 1 billion balls in it. All of the balls are black except for one, which is white. On the one hand, the odds that any particular ball is picked from the container are 1 in a billion. On the other hand, it's far more likely that a black ball is chosen than a white one.

Any two particular universes might be equally improbable but the number of universes that are life-prohibiting far outnumber the number of universes that are life permitting. That means the odds that our universe would be life-permitting are much lower than the odds that it would life-prohibiting (Craig 2003, p. 167).

3.2.4 The Anthropic Principle Objection

One of the most important objections to the fine-tuning argument is the objection from the anthropic principle. There are two versions of the anthropic principle:

- *The Weak Anthropic Principle (WAP)*: The physical laws and constants scientists can expect to observe are restricted by the conditions necessary for their presence as observers.
- *The Strong Anthropic Principle (SAP)*: The physical laws and constants of the universe are restricted to those ranges that allow the emergence of life.

Our discussion will focus on the weak anthropic principle. According to WAP, "what we can expect to observe must be restricted by the conditions necessary for our presence as observers" (Carter 1974, p. 291). Notice that this is a principle about what we can expect to observe. It describes an **observational selection effect**. An observational selection effect occurs when the method scientists use to collect information skews their data. The particular way scientists observe the world can result in a selection of data that does not accurately reflect reality.

For example, if you were studying the length of the population of fish in a particular lake, you might use a net to collect random samples of fish and measure their size. Now suppose the net you used had 7-inch holes in it. This net would skew your sample by only netting fish that are 7 inches or longer. The method you used to make your observations and collect your data resulted in a sample of fish that does not accurately reflect the fish population of the lake (Sober 2003, pp. 43–44).

WAP is considered an observational selection effect because it asserts that our existence as observers limits the selection of data we should expect to observe. In the fish example, the net caused the selection effect. According to WAP, our very existence results in a selection effect.

The objection to the fine-tuning argument from the anthropic principle is this: given the fact that we exist, it is not surprising that we observe that the constants are right for a life-permitting universe. If the laws of nature were not fine-tuned, we would not be here to notice that fact. Our existence as observers gives rise to a selection effect, making it unsurprising that we observe a universe fine-tuned for life.

John Leslie argues that the anthropic principle objection is flawed. He invites us to consider the following analogy: suppose a prisoner is dragged before a firing squad of 200 expert marksmen. They aim their rifles precisely at his heart. The order to fire is given and the marksmen shoot. When the smoke clears, the prisoner observes that he is still alive. All of the expert marksmen missed. Should the prisoner be surprised by his observation that he is alive? If the anthropic principle objection is correct, he shouldn't. After all, if the marksmen had not missed, the prisoner would not be around to make the observation that they missed.

Leslie argues that the problem with the objection can be readily seen in this analogy. It's true that:

> *The prisoner should not be surprised that he does not observe that he is dead.*

After all, if he were dead, he would not be able to make any observations. But this is different than saying that:

> *The prisoner should not be surprised that he observes that he is alive.*

The prisoner should be surprised by his observation that 200 expert marksmen missed him. His continued existence is very improbable under the hypothesis that they missed him by chance. It is not improbable under the hypothesis that there was some reason why they missed him.

When thinking about the universe, a similar mistake is made. The statement is true that:

> *Observers should not be surprised that they do not observe that the laws and constants of physics are not fine-tuned for life.*

But this is not the same as saying that:

> *Observers should not be surprised that they observe that the laws and constants of the universe are fine-tuned for their existence.*

The existence of a life-permitting universe is improbable under the hypothesis that it exists merely by chance. It is not improbable under the hypothesis that it was intentionally designed to be life-permitting.

3.2.5 The Many Universes Objection

Perhaps the most important objection to the fine-tuning argument is the many universes objection. According to this objection, there are many universes, maybe even an infinite number of them. The laws and constants of physics vary from universe to universe. In most universes, the laws and constants of physics are not life-permitting. However, some small number of universes have life-permitting qualities. So, the fact that at least one life-permitting universe exists is not improbable.

The idea here is that the more chances there are for an event to occur, the more likely it is to occur. To be dealt a perfect bridge hand with one deal is improbable, but if you were dealt an enormous number of bridge hands (say 10^{20}) it might be very likely that at least one of them would be a perfect bridge hand. Similarly, if there are vastly many universes, it's likely that at least one of them would be life-permitting.

Defenders of the design argument charge that there's no evidence for multiple universes. For example, Craig contends that the only reason some advocate multiple universes is to avoid the conclusion of the fine-tuning argument (Craig 2003, p. 171). It's not entirely clear, though, that there is no independent evidence for multiple universes. According to some physicists, **superstring theory** (an important idea in contemporary physics that is beyond the scope of this chapter) might provide independent reasons to think that multiple universes exist, but this is unclear. String theory is on the very frontiers of science and is less developed than other areas of science. The upshot is that just how good this objection is depends on an empirical debate that is just beginning.

4 HUME'S PHILOSOPHICAL OBJECTIONS TO THE DESIGN ARGUMENT

So far, we have examined Paley's design argument and noted the important impact of Darwin's theory of evolution on it. We then set out a form of the design argument that is immune from the evolution objection, and the objections to it. Now we consider philosophical objections to the design argument in general, objections that apply to both the biological and the fine-tuning design arguments. The classic critique of the design argument was made by David Hume, an eighteenth-century Scottish philosopher. Hume wrote before Paley, so his criticisms were not aimed directly at Paley's argument but at arguments very similar to Paley's.

4.1 The Bad Analogy Objection

If the design argument is an argument from analogy, then the most straightforward way to criticize it is to undermine the analogy. This is precisely what Hume did. He argued that human artifacts and natural objects are so different that the comparison between them breaks down.

This objection has merit but only applies to versions of the design argument that are formulated as argument from analogy. Many philosophers point out that the design argument can be formulated differently. For example, Elliot Sober argues that the design argument is best formulated as an abductive argument, or an inference to the best explanation (Sober 2003, p. 28). Formulated this way, the design argument is immune from this criticism. The thrust of the abductive argument is not that watches and universes are similar so they probably have similar causes but rather that an intelligent designer explains apparent design in nature better than competing hypotheses. The point of the analogy between the watch and the universe is that the underlying reasoning for thinking they were designed is similar.

4.2 The "Who Designed the Designer?" Objection

Hume objected that if the design argument works, it proves more than the theist wants. It proves that God was designed by some sort of super-designer. The crux of the design argument is that teleology is best explained by intelligent design. Hume pointed out that God is a teleological being. If goal-directed complexity demands a designer, then God must have a designer. George Smith puts the argument this way:

> If the universe is wonderfully designed, surely God is even more wonderfully designed. He must, therefore, have had a designer even more wonderful than He is. If God did not require a designer, then there is no reason why such a relatively less wonderful thing as the universe needed one (Smith 1980, p. 56).

This objection can be pushed even further, for surely the designer of God is goal-directed and complex, so the designer of God must also have a designer:

> There must be a super-designer who designed god. But a super-designer would require a super-super-designer, and so on, ad infinitum. Thus, by the premises of the teleological argument, we are led to an infinite series of transcendental designers—a "solution" that leaves much to be desired (Smith 1989, p. 259).

At this point, the theist might be tempted to argue that not all goal-directed complexity requires a designer. The chain of designers has a stopping point and that point is God. But this reply to the "Who designed God?" objection seems arbitrary. If not all teleological objects require a designer, then does the universe really require one? In other words, if there is a stopping point to the regress of designers, why not make it the universe rather than God?

What can theists say in reply to this objection? First, they can offer reasons to think that God is a better stopping point for any potential regress of designers. The design argument basically claims that teleology cannot ultimately be explained by mindless matter alone. One reply is that mindless matter does in fact contain sufficient resources to ultimately explain all teleology by itself. In that case, the question of where to stop the chain of designers comes down to this question: which is a *better* candidate for the ultimate repository of teleology—mind or mindless matter? Theists might think that our general experience of the world provides grounds for making a special connection between mind and design that doesn't exist in the case of mindless matter. Design, so the claim goes, just provides a more natural fit with mind than mindless matter.

A second reply involves pointing out that the design argument can be formulated in a way that avoids the "Who designed the designer?" objection. What gets this objection off the ground is the premise that all goal-directed complexity demands a designer. If the argument is formulated without this premise but as an abductive argument, then it should avoid this objection altogether, for then the argument is not claiming that all teleology demands a designer. It just claims that the best explanation of the goal-directed complexity in nature is a designer.

Now the atheist might ask what the best explanation is for the teleology in God, but the theist is not required to say that it is some super-designer just because they think that the best explanation of design in nature is a supernatural designer. In fact, given God's nature as an eternal, non-space-time being, a super-designer of God looks to be a poor explanation.

The atheist might question the legitimacy of the theist's appeal to God's "eternal nature." But the theist might point out that we are comparing the probability of two theories against a certain bit of evidence. The theist's theory includes their concept of God. They aren't adding that God is eternal in some cheap *ad hoc* way to get around an objection. The idea that God is an eternal, non-spatio-temporal being is a deep part of many theological views and is motivated independently of the argument from design. On this view, the theist's response amounts to pointing out that given the nature of this theory, certain objections just don't arise. If God didn't have a beginning because he is supposed to be eternal, then asking "Who designed God?" makes no sense.

Continuing in that same vein, remember that the design argument makes a claim about the best explanation of goal-directed complexity. According to theism, God isn't complex: he isn't a thing with parts that fit together in a certain way, so the types of design questions we ask about complex physical systems just don't arise.

The debate could continue. The atheist might object that, complex object or not, something is deeply puzzling about this supposed being. At the very least, though, the usual version of the "Who designed the designer?" objection seems too simple.

4.3 The "It Doesn't Prove Theism" Objection

If Hume's last objection was that the design argument proves too much, this next objection is that it proves too little. He argues that even if one grants all of the premises of the design argument, this doesn't prove that the God of traditional theism exists. The God of traditional theism is all-powerful, all-knowing, and completely good. What kind of God must exist in order to design and create a universe like ours? He would have to know a lot, but would he have to know everything? He would have to be powerful, but would he have to be all-powerful? Hume didn't think so. He thinks that a less powerful being, one with, say, 90% of God's knowledge and power could design and create our universe. Such a being would be very knowledgeable and very powerful but not all-knowing and all-powerful. Consequently, it would not be the God of traditional theism.

In addition, Hume points out that the design argument doesn't prove that just one God designed the world. The mere fact that the universe is the product of design does not mean it was designed by one being. Most human artifacts were designed by multiple designers. He thinks it is at least as likely that the universe is the product of a design team. If the conclusion of the design argument makes monotheism and polytheism equally likely, then it doesn't prove monotheism. If it doesn't prove monotheism, then it doesn't prove traditional theism.

Hume further points out that there are what appear to be design flaws in the universe. Scientists like Stephen Jay Gould argue that the thumb of a panda bear is not well designed. The human eye seems to be wired backwards, resulting in a blind spot in the human visual field. The human birth canal seems poorly designed, resulting in unnecessary complications in child bearing. Even worse, the world contains so much unnecessary pain and suffering. Surely an all-knowing, all-powerful, perfectly good God would not have designed things this way. So the designer of the world, if one exists, is most likely not all-knowing, or not all-powerful, or not completely good. Thus, he is not the God of traditional theism.

Even if Hume grants the premises of the design argument, he claims, it wouldn't prove theism but maybe some form of polytheism involving powerful gods who are less than perfectly moral. Even worse, it might just prove some sort of intelligence or intelligences that are not gods at all. At best, it is an argument for beings like the gods of ancient Greece— numerous and flawed.

Theists admit this objection highlights a limitation of the argument but it does not make the conclusion of the argument insignificant or unimportant. After all, if the design argument proves that Zeus and Aphrodite exist, then atheism is false. While it might not prove **classical theism**, it would disprove atheism. Demonstrating the existence of at least one intelligent designer of the world would not be insignificant. Once the existence of a designer was established, the theist could offer different arguments to extend the conclusion of the design argument to the effect that only one designer exists that is all-knowing, all-powerful, and perfectly good. Sober writes:

> Paley, perhaps responding to this Humean point, makes it clear that his design argument aims to establish the existence of the designer, and that the question of the designer's characteristics must be addressed separately. Does this limitation of the design argument make the argument trivial? Not at all—it is not trivial to claim that the adaptive contrivances of organisms are due to intelligent design. This supposed "triviality" would be big news to evolutionary biologists (Sober 2003, p. 36).

5 CONCLUSION

The argument from design continues to capture people's imaginations—and spawn bitter arguments. The purely philosophical objections of the sort Hume offers can most fairly be said to produce a stand-off. The "Who designed the designer?" objection is not trivial but neither is it conclusive. There are reasonable countermoves the theist can make. Evolution delivers a serious blow to the argument from biological design but it can be circumvented by deploying the fine-tuning version. However, the design argument is subject to other objections, some more serious than others. The safest thing to say is that this debate will likely continue for a long time with eager partisans on either side.

AT A GLANCE: THE DESIGN ARGUMENT

1. Paley's Biological Design Argument
    1.1. Formulated as an Argument from Analogy
        - Premise #1: Organisms and machines are both complex goal-directed objects.
        - Premise #2: Machines were created by an intelligent being.
        - Conclusion: Organisms were probably also created by an intelligent being.
    1.2. Formulated as an Abductive Argument
        - Premise #1: Organisms and machines are both complex goal-directed objects.
        - Premise #2: Intelligent design is the best explanation of complex goal-directed objects.
        - Conclusion: Organisms were probably also created by an intelligent being.
2. Darwin's Evolution Objection
    2.1. The Evolution Objection
        - We do not need to posit God to explain apparent design in nature; it can be explained by natural processes alone. According to evolution,

organisms are adapted to survive and reproduce in their environments by a natural process involving two components: random genetic mutation and natural selection.

2.2. Creationism

- Creationism is the view that God created the universe. Stated generally, it is compatible with the view that God indirectly created the universe via physical laws and evolution.

2.2.1. Scientific Creationism

- Scientific creationism is a form of creationism that uses science to support the existence of God and a more literal reading of the book of Genesis. Adherents tend to believe that the universe if very young, only 6,000 to 10,000 years old; that Noah's flood is an important fact explaining earth's geology; and that God created humans directly in such a way that humans are not biologically related to other animal life.
- Scientific creationism has many problems including evidence contradicting its claims about transitional fossils and harmful mutations, and that it doesn't count as science.

2.2.2. Intelligent Design Theory (ID)

- Intelligent design theory is a view consisting of two basic theses:
  1. Scientific theories can legitimately posit intelligent agents as an explanation of apparent design in nature.
  2. Some parts of nature are best explained as the product of intelligent design.

2.2.2.1. ID and the Nature of Science

- Most scientists do not think that ID is science. However, the scientific status of ID is not as important as it is often thought to be. Whether it is science is central to public policy and legal question but not very important to whether apparent design in nature is evidence that God exists. A mere definition cannot settle that debate.

2.2.2.2. ID's Scientific Claims

- One central scientific argument of ID is that evolution cannot account for irreducible complexity. Michael Behe claims that instances of irreducible complexity abound in nature, including the bacterial flagellum. Critics point out that irreducible complexity can be accounted for in evolutionary terms by an indirect process involving parts arising independently of one another with useful functions. The functions of these parts later change to different functions as parts of a new system that has survival value. The bacterial flagellum seems to have developed this way from a prior secretion system.

3. The Fine-Tuning Design Argument
   - The fine-tuning design argument is a reformulation of the design argument that attempts to make it immune from the evolution objection. It does so by focusing on design in physics and cosmology where the elements of biological evolution—random genetic mutation and natural selection—do not apply.
4. Hume's Philosophical Objections
   4.1. The Weak Analogy Objection
      - The design argument is based on a weak analogy at best: "the dissimilitude is so striking, that the utmost you can here pretend to is a guess." Hume's point has several aspects (i.e., the universe is unique, nothing else is like it; the universe is more like an organism than a machine; we only have a small sample to make the inference).
      - Possible Replies
        1. All analogies presuppose dissimilarity. The important question is whether they are similar in the relevant respect. Paley's argument is that they are similar in that they both show goal-oriented order.
        2. Contrary to popular opinion, Paley is not making an argument from analogy but is giving an abductive argument, i.e., an inference to the best explanation.
        3. The universe might be unique but not all of its properties and features are unique.
        4. The sample size we have for most inductions is small relative to the size of the universe (we only know about our small corner of the universe). Why should this analogy be any different?
   4.2. The "Who Designed the Designer?" Objection
      - If goal-oriented complexity demands a designer as an explanation, then doesn't God need a designer to explain himself because he is goal-oriented?
      - Possible Replies
        1. The theist might argue that thinking mind is a better candidate than mindless matter for the ultimate repository of design is entirely reasonable. Our experience seems to connect minds and designs in a special way. This connection between designs and mindless matter is importantly different and weaker.
        2. The design argument need not be formulated in a way that says that all goal-oriented complexity requires a designer. It can be formulated as an abductive argument, i.e., an inference to the best explanation.
   4.3. The "It Does Not Prove the Existence of the Traditional Theism" Objection
      - Even if the design argument is sound, it does not prove the existence of the traditional theistic God. A committee of gods rather than one god

could have designed the universe. Nothing about the design of the universe indicates that the designer is perfect, incorporeal, omniscient, or omnipotent. In fact, plenty of "bad design" is found in the universe to indicate that God is not perfect.

- Possible Replies

    1. If the design argument is granted, even if it does not prove the God of classical theism, it certain makes a significant conclusion and shows that atheism and **naturalism** are false.

    2. Once we establish some sort of God, we would naturally ask more questions about the nature of this God. Other arguments would be able to add to our understanding of the nature of God and leads us in the direction of the God of classical theism.

FURTHER READINGS AND WEB RESOURCES

The Classic Design Argument

Hume, D. (1989). *Dialogues Concerning Natural Religion.* Amherst, MA: Prometheus Books. Available online at http://www.philosophyofreligion. info/humedcnr.html.

Paley, W. (1963). *Natural Theology.* New York: The Bobbs-Merrill Co. The complete text is online at http://www.hti.umich.edu/cgi/p/ pd-modeng/pd-modeng-idx?type=header&id=PaleyNatur.

Evolution

Dawkins, R. (1996). *The Blind Watchmaker: Why the Evidence of Evolution Reveals a Universe without Design.* New York: W. W. Norton & Co.

Dennett, D. C. (1995). *Darwin's Dangerous Idea.* New York: Simon & Schuster.

Creation Science

Morris, H. M. (1974). *Scientific Creationism.* San Diego, CA: Creation-Life Publishers.

Intelligent Design

Behe, M. (1996). *Darwin's Black Box: The Biochemical Challenge to Evolution.* New York: The Free Press.

Dembski, W. A. (1999). *Intelligent Design: The Bridge between Science and Theology.* Downers Grove, IL: InterVarsity Press.

Shanks, N. (2004). *God, the Devil and Darwin: A Critique of Intelligent Design Theory.* New York: Oxford University Press.

The General Debate

Manson, N. A. (Ed.) (2003). *God and Design.* New York: Routledge.

CHAPTER 3

The Cosmological Argument

Did the material world have a cause? If so, was the cause divine? Can chains of causes stretch back forever? Why do physical things exist at all? These are the sorts of questions addressed by the various cosmological arguments for the existence of God—arguments that we scrutinize in this chapter.

They're the sorts of thoughts that come to you late at night, when you're trying to sleep and your mind isn't quite under your control. The universe is vast. Maybe it has a purpose and maybe it doesn't, but the fact that it exists at all is somehow a wonder. Does it have a beginning? If it does, how could it have started? And if it doesn't, how could it always have just been here? Why is there anything at all? The cosmological arguments (there are several) are attempts to provide answers to such ultimate "Why?" questions. They will be our subject in this chapter.

Cosmological arguments come in two broad kinds. One looks at chains of causes: this is caused by that, which was in turn is caused by that, and so on, and tries to show that these chains can't go on to infinity. The other kind begins with the thought that some things didn't have to be and asks how the existence of such things could be explained. We'll start with the first kind of argument.

1 ST. THOMAS AQUINAS'S SECOND WAY

In his *Summa Theologica*, St. Thomas Aquinas (c.1225–1275) presents his "Five Ways" for proving God's existence. All of these arguments are *a posteriori* arguments, based on facts we discover through experience.

Ways One through Three are the ones that usually get the most attention in discussions of cosmological arguments. The First and Second Ways are similar, so we'll concentrate on the Second in this section. Later on, we'll turn to the Third Way.

The Second Way deals with what Aquinas calls **efficient cause**. In particular, Aquinas is interested in the causes of the very existence of things. Many commentators understand Aquinas to be talking about sustaining causes—causes that keep things in being. We'll read the argument this way. It's not entirely clear just what count as efficient or sustaining causes, but perhaps the air that keeps us alive or the Sun that provides much of Earth's energy might be examples.

We can set the argument forth as follows:

1. Some things have efficient causes.
2. Nothing can be its own efficient cause (because it would have to be prior to itself).
3. Therefore, chains of efficient causes exist.
4. A chain of efficient causes can't go on to infinity. (More on this point in a moment.)
5. Therefore, there must be a first efficient cause (which everyone calls God).

The argument begins with an observable fact: there are things that depend on other things to keep them in existence. Let's call these **dependent beings** or dependent things. Statement 4 is the heart of the argument and we'll look at it carefully in a moment. Meanwhile, we'll mention two criticisms but not pursue them.

First, if the premises are true, they show that every chain of efficient causes has a first member, but they don't show that every such chain has the *same* first member. This means the argument doesn't show that just one God exists. Second, even if there is a single first cause, the argument by itself doesn't show that whatever it is deserves to be called God. For all it says, the first cause might be some sort of nameless abstraction that's of no religious interest at all. Let's set these objections aside for now. Aquinas is aware of them and has relevant things to say elsewhere in his work, whether or not those things are good enough to do their job. We will focus on the argument for the existence of the first cause.

Why can't a chain of efficient causes be infinite? Here's what Aquinas says:

> Now to take away the cause is to take away the effect. Therefore, if there be no first cause among efficient causes, there will be no ultimate nor any intermediate causes; all of which is plainly false. Therefore, it is necessary to admit a first efficient cause, to which everyone gives the name God. (Pegis translation 1945, pp. 22–23)

The word "ultimate" might be confusing here. You exist at the end of a chain of efficient causes. The "ultimate" cause of you is the cause that's directly responsible for sustaining you, perhaps the air or the Sun. Assuming that there is a first member to the chain of causes that sustain you, the ones between the first and the ultimate are "intermediate." The argument itself is a *reductio ad absurdum*. It says that if we suppose no first cause exists, we get the absurd result that there are no intermediate causes, no ultimate causes and therefore no dependent beings at all. This would mean that *you* don't exist, which is plainly absurd. However, when we try to spell out the details, things get foggy. Suppose Z is something that exists in the here and now— Zelda, for example. Suppose there's an efficient cause Y that keeps Zelda in existence, making Zelda a dependent being. Perhaps Y has an efficient cause X, which might in turn have an efficient cause of its own. Aquinas says that this series of efficient causes can't be infinite, but why not?

It's hard to tell, because what Aquinas actually says is very compressed. Here are three possibilities. First, Aquinas says that taking away a cause also takes away its effect. He's right about that, but perhaps he thinks that "taking away" the first cause is the same thing as eliminating a cause. If this is what Aquinas had in mind, then the confusion might be rooted in pushing the language of "taking away the cause" too far. If someone says no first cause exists, she isn't saying that some particular cause has been eliminated. She's saying that anything we might identify as the first cause turns out to have a cause of its own.

A second possible reason for thinking a first cause must exist might be the idea that any series must have a first member. This is true for a series like the line in the grocery store or the counting numbers. The trouble is that there are other series that don't have first members—for example, the series of all integers, positive and negative.

A third reason: even if some kinds of infinite series are possible, this fact doesn't mean that infinite causal series are possible. Perhaps there has to be some "original impetus" to get the causal series going or some unmovable place to "anchor" the chain. Perhaps Aquinas's claim is that without an uncaused first cause, no causal series would exist at all. The problem is that the believer in the possibility of infinite series will simply disagree. In fact, Aquinas could be accused of **begging the question**. The assumption that a causal series must have a first member amounts to another way of saying that it can't be infinite, but that's exactly what Aquinas needs to prove.

In spite of the difficulties here, most of us don't think infinite chains of sustaining causes exist. Perhaps the air sustains you. The air wouldn't be air unless the molecules that make it up were stable, so perhaps the air needs a sustaining cause as well. The likely candidate would be a combination of various physical forces. It could be that there are sustaining causes for these forces, which in turn have sustaining causes, and so on, but our guess is that most readers think the buck stops long before infinity. As far as we know, most physicists agree. They might disagree about where the stopping point is, but they agree that there is one. It seems that most of us accept something like Aquinas's conclusion, whether or not we agree with his reasoning.

Why we agree is more difficult to say. It would be nice to have a good argument for our conviction. So far, we don't have one, and even if we agree that infinite chains of sustaining causes or explanatory principles don't exist, this doesn't yet tell us that there is one first cause that deserves to be called God. Still, the fact that we share at least part of Aquinas's intuition is interesting.

2 THE KALAM COSMOLOGICAL ARGUMENT

Aquinas tried to convince us that a certain sort of infinite collection is impossible: a chain of simultaneous causes. When most people think of an infinite series of causes, what they have in mind is a series stretching back in time. If that sort of series is impossible, then the world had a beginning.

The Kalam cosmological argument tries to show that the world has a beginning, caused by God. The roots of the argument are in medieval Islamic philosophy, but in recent years it has been developed by the American philosopher of religion William Lane Craig. Craig (Craig 1992) considers a tree of possibilities and prunes off the branches that don't lead to God. Either the universe had a beginning or it didn't. Craig argues that it did. Either that beginning was caused or it wasn't.

Craig argues that it was. Either that cause was personal or it wasn't. Craig argues that it was personal:

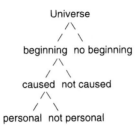

At each node, Craig maintains that we can cut off the branch on the right.

The part of the argument that Craig spends the most time on is the first step, which tries to show that the universe had a beginning, and that's the part we'll concentrate on. Here's the idea: use the word "events" for things that happen—thunderclaps, changes in temperature, births, deaths, atomic collisions, and so on. If the universe had no beginning, then there has been an infinity of events, stretching back into time with no end. However, Craig argues that infinite collections of actual things or events would lead to absurdity and that such collections are therefore impossible. If this argument is **sound**, the world must have had a beginning.

What sorts of absurdities does Craig have in mind? Here's an example: If infinite collections of things really could exist, then there could be a bookshelf with infinitely many books on it. But the mathematical theory of infinity seems to imply the absurd consequence that if every other book were removed from the shelf, then not only would the same number of books remain as there were to begin with but it would be possible to rearrange the remaining books to fill up all the infinitely many gaps in the shelf. Because Craig takes this to be patently absurd, he concludes that infinite collections of real physical things or events are impossible. However, the problem is that many philosophers and mathematicians would insist that there is no absurdity here at all. What we see is merely that infinite collections have some surprising properties. If that's the correct reaction, then the Kalam argument is no improvement on Aquinas's as a way of ruling out a certain sort of infinite series. The reader who is interest in the details should proceed to the next two sections; others can skip ahead to Section 2.3.

*2.1 Finite and Infinite

Why say that the universe had a beginning? Craig offers some scientific reasons. One is that cosmologists say the world began with the **Big Bang**.

Another is that a physical principle called the Second Law of Thermo-dynamics says the universe is winding down and so could not have been around forever. These reasons are interesting but science is in flux. Some scientists think a series of universes might have existed, each with its own Big Bang. The Second Law of Thermodynamics doesn't rule this out because thermodynamic principles break down in the extraordinary con-ditions of the Big Bang. But Craig has another argument and if it's correct, it amounts to a proof that the universe had a beginning. It goes like this:

1. An actual infinite cannot exist.
2. A beginningless series of events in time is an actual infinite.
3. Therefore, a beginningless series of events in time cannot exist.

The argument is **valid**, and the second premise seems obviously true. This means that if the first premise is true, so is the conclusion. Why should we accept the first premise?

First, what's an "actual infinite?" It's an infinite collection of space-time *objects*, such as stones or elephants, or *events*, such as lightning strikes and finger-snaps. Abstract entities like numbers or truths don't form an actual infinite and interestingly, on Craig's view neither do points nor regions of space-time. This point is important. If Craig agreed that an actual infinite could be made up of space-time points or regions, then denying that actual infinites exist would be difficult. Just think about two points one meter apart and the infinity of points between them.

You might wonder why Craig wouldn't count an infinite collection of space-time points as an actual infinity. This attitude might seem arbitrary, and worse, it might seem to be a dodge designed to keep his argument out of trouble. However, some philosophers argue that space and time aren't real things to begin with; they are abstractions—ways of talking about how concrete objects and events are related. If that's correct, Craig's move doesn't seem so arbitrary and so we'll let it pass. At least for the sake of argument, we'll accept Craig's restrictions on what would count as an actual infinite and see how well he does at proving that actual infinites are impossible.

To understand Craig's defense of the first premise, we need to say a bit about the mathematical theory of infinity. Suppose you didn't know any number words but you wanted to show that these two **sets** are the same size:

{a, b, c, d, e} {v, w, x, y, z}

You could do this by showing that there's a way to pair things up so that every letter in the first collection is paired with exactly one letter in the second collection with nothing left over:

```
a   b   c   d   e
|   |   |   |   |
v   w   x   y   z
```

In modern mathematics, this is what saying that the number of things in the first set is the same as the number of things in the second collection means. On the other hand, if we tried the same trick with the following two sets, we'd see that something would always be left over in the second set:

```
{a, b, c, d}   {v, w, x, y, z}

a   b   c   d
|   |   |   |
v   w   x   y   z
```

We can extend this concept of "same number" to infinities. Two infinite sets contain the same number of objects if there is a one-one pairing of the members of the two sets. Take the infinite set of all counting numbers: 1, 2, 3, 4, 5, . . . Now consider the even numbers. This is still an infinite set, and it's a **proper subset** of the counting numbers: Every even number is a counting number but not vice versa. All the same, by this definition these two sets have the same number of members. It's easy to describe a way of pairing all the even numbers with the counting numbers so that nothing is left over:

```
1   2   3   4   5    6    7    8    9
|   |   |   |   |    |    |    |    |
2   4   6   8   10   12   14   16   18
```

Saying that these two sets have the same number of members might sound odd but remember: all that "same number" means on this definition—for finite or for infinite sets—is that the two sets can be paired up one-to-one. The definition agrees with common sense in the finite cases and extends the notion of "same number" to deal with infinities. There's no

contradiction here, as Craig himself agrees. Keep in mind that Craig is not criticizing the mathematical theory of infinity. When he says that there can't be an actual infinity, he means an infinite set of concrete events or objects in space and time.

*2.2 Are Actual Infinite Collections Absurd?

According to Craig, if we assume that actual infinite collections exist, we get absurd consequences. Here's one of his examples: Suppose we have an infinitely long library shelf with infinitely many books sitting on it, all in a row. Imagine that the spines are colored alternately red, black, red, black, and so on. Suppose we lent out all the black books. That would mean we had lent out an infinite collection of books. But how many would be left? According to the theory of infinities, the answer is that we'd have exactly the same number as when we started.

Craig seems to think this idea is absurd, and for a finite bookshelf, it would be. If we take every other book off a shelf with ten books on it, we are left with a smaller number of books than when we started. However, we aren't imagining a finite bookshelf and the example of the even numbers and the counting numbers shows that we can expect surprises when we deal with infinities— mathematical or concrete.

This might not seem very satisfying. Isn't there some sense in which there are fewer books on the shelf after the black ones are gone? The answer is yes, if we're careful about what we mean. The set of red books is a proper subset of the set of all the books; that is, every member of the set of red books is also a member of the total set of books but not vice versa. In this sense, there are "fewer" *red* books than *books*. This is like the case of the even numbers and the counting numbers. In one sense, (proper subset) there are fewer even numbers than counting numbers, but in another sense (pairing of elements), there are not fewer. This second sense is what mathematicians have in mind when they use the phrase, "same number."

Craig sees other difficulties. Once we lend out the books, there are infinitely many gaps in the shelf. But without adding a single book, we can fill up all the holes. Just move the second remaining book down a space, then move the third remaining book down two spaces, the fourth down three spaces, and so on. Since we never run out of books to move, this will leave us with a shelf that has no gaps. Isn't this absurd?

That depends on what counts as an absurdity. A contradiction internal to a statement itself certainly counts. If we assume that the square root of two can be written as one integer divided by another, such as 33,333 ÷ 23,570, then there is a mathematical proof that we can derive a contradiction from this very statement: Some one number is both even and odd. (We'll spare you the details.) Another sort of absurdity is a conclusion that contradicts a known, uncontroversial fact. This is the idea behind Aquinas's Second Way. He tried to show that if we assume no first cause exists, we end up contradicting the known fact that there are dependent beings.

Which sort of absurdity does Craig think we have here? By Craig's own admission, there's no internal contradiction in assuming all the gaps can be filled by rearranging the books. The mathematical theory of infinities, which Craig accepts, says that there is a "mapping" that behaves this way. In other words, there's a consistent description of a rearrangement of the books that has just this result. Presumably, Craig means that assuming the existence of this infinite bookshelf leads to a contradiction with known facts. What facts?

Lets' agree that *we* couldn't rearrange the shelf to fill up all the gaps. It would be an infinite task requiring infinite amounts of energy and, since the speed of light is a cosmic speed limit on moving the books, it would take an infinite amount of time. We can't do that—we're finite. However, assuming that the infinite bookshelf exists doesn't imply that we can do any such thing. No contradiction yet.

This might seem like cheating. Suppose we had infinite energy available to us, and suppose that there was no cosmic speed limit so that the books could be moved faster and faster. Now don't we have a contradiction with a known fact?

What known fact? The only candidate seems to be the very claim at issue—that there's no way to rearrange all the remaining books so that the shelf has no gaps. The idea that this is possible is strange and surprising, but that's very different from saying that it's absurd. Even accepted science contains some strange and surprising things. The special theory of relativity tells us that whether two things happen at the same time depends on who's asking the question (or more accurately, on their state of motion). It also tells us that the amount of time that passes between two events (say, two collisions in outer space) depends on the path in space-time between those events. Before Einstein, this idea seemed completely absurd. Even after Einstein, many people have trouble accepting it. But these apparent "absurdities" are now part of basic physics.

The concept of infinity is subtle, and if actual infinities exist, some surprising things are true of them. However, there is plenty of room to doubt that the surprises are outright absurdities. To the extent that this is so, Craig hasn't made his case.

2.3 The Rest of the Kalam Argument

Whether Craig's argument is any good or not, it's plausible that the physical universe had a beginning. After all, as Craig points out, cosmologists tell us that the physical universe as we know it began sometime around 15 billion years ago with the Big Bang. Suppose we grant this. What then?

Craig's next task is to show that the beginning had a cause. In his view, we don't need much in the way of argument to get this conclusion. He says,

> [P]robably no one in his right mind sincerely believes that the universe could pop into existence uncaused out of nothing. [p. 70]

It's probably true that very few people think the universe as we know it—with all its structure and complexity—just "popped into existence" But here's another possibility: The physical universe is nothing more than the whole complicated collection of events that physics studies, and this collection just happens to have a first member. There's no time nor space nor anything else before the universe, and so the universe didn't "pop into existence"; it simply *is* without being caused. Perhaps this idea is wrong. But if so, this isn't just obvious.

However, suppose that the physical universe has a cause. Thinking that this cause couldn't have come into existence itself just before the first event might be reasonable because then *it* would be the first event and we'd have to face the question of what caused it. As Craig sees it, this suggests that the cause of the universe must be eternal. But if that's so, he asks, why isn't the universe itself eternal?

Craig thinks we get the best answer if we assume that the cause is personal. Then we can say that the eternal cause of the universe intended from eternity to create a universe in time.

What should we make of this? If the universe had a beginning and if the beginning was caused, then the idea that the cause was the eternal intention of a personal being might well be as good an answer as any other. Whether this is the only possible answer is much harder to say. The main thing that's clear about this sort of question is that not much is clear.

3 CONTINGENCY

Proving that every series of causes must have a first member is a difficult thing to do. However, there's another approach to our worry about why there's something rather than nothing. In an article written several years ago, Richard Taylor asks us to imagine that while wandering in the woods, we come upon a large translucent ball, about as tall as an average adult (Taylor 1983, pp. 90 ff.). This would be very odd, and the existence of this thing would cry out for some sort of explanation. You wouldn't believe that it had just always existed and you'd be sure that something else is responsible for its existing at all. However, Taylor makes another claim: The existence of this great sphere is not really any more puzzling than the existence of a rock or a tree. The only difference is that we're used to rocks and trees, and so we take them for granted. If we think about it, Taylor insists, the fact that there are any physical objects at all is puzzling.

The objects around us, simple and complex, are **contingent**. It's perfectly possible that they might not have existed at all. This is what makes us ask why they do exist. Perhaps some things don't need their existence explained. Perhaps abstract things like numbers are real and exist "of their own nature," or have **necessary** existence, as often said. However, ordinary space-time objects seem clearly not to exist necessarily. It's all too easy to imagine them not existing at all. Perhaps meditating on this thought will lead us to God.

3.1 Aquinas on Contingency

We'll start our exploration with Aquinas's Third Way. Aquinas considers a special case of contingent things: things that come into being and later on cease to be, things that by their nature are "generated and corrupted," in his phrase. Aquinas offers another *reductio ad absurdum*, meant to infer God's existence from the fact that this special class of contingent things exists. For shorthand, we'll call such things *evanescent* because by nature they each have a beginning and an end in time. Here's the argument:

1. Suppose that everything that exists is an evanescent thing.
2. By its nature, each evanescent thing is nonexistent at some time.
3. Therefore, if every thing were evanescent, there would have been a time when nothing existed.
4. However, something can't come from nothing.

5. Therefore, if everything were evanescent, nothing would be in existence now (because it would have had to come from nothing).
6. This contradicts the fact that there are things in existence now.
7. Therefore, our original supposition is false: Not everything that exists is an evanescent thing.

We used "evanescent" as a technical term to mean things that are generated and corrupted. If not everything is by nature generated and corrupted, then according to Aquinas, something must exist that has a different sort of nature. According to Aquinas, it's something whose existence is *necessary*. Whatever we make of this idea, there's a serious problem in the argument we laid out. Step 3 is supposed to follow from steps 1 and 2, but it doesn't. Even if each individual thing is evanescent, it doesn't follow that at some past time, nothing existed. Compare these two claims:

a. If each thing fails to exist at some time or other, then at some one time, everything failed to exist.
b. If each person has a mother, then one person exists who is the mother of everyone.

It's clear that (b) is false. But (a) seems to embody the same sort of reasoning as (b). In any case, if we reject Craig's proof that infinite series are impossible, describing what it would be like for (a) to be false is easy. Just imagine an overlapping collection of objects, stretching back in time as far back as time stretches:

In this picture, every object is generated and corrupted—is evanescent—but there is no time when all of them are nonexistent at once. Aquinas's Third Way won't work.

3.2 Sufficient Reason

Whether or not every contingent thing is evanescent, it's clear that there are contingent things that might not have existed at all. Many people balk at the idea that there might be no explanation for these contingent things. Furthermore, even if we allow infinite chains of explanation, this might not be good enough to explain what's really bothering us. In an infinite chain of explanations of contingent things, each individual thing gets an explanation but we still seem able to ask, "Why do any contingent things exist at all?"

There's an idea that some people have thought will help make sense of this—the **Principle of Sufficient Reason**. A little more accurately, there is a collection of principles with this name. The first one was introduced by the German philosopher Leibniz in the early eighteenth century, and his version says:

> No fact can be real or existent, no statement true, unless there be a sufficient reason why it is so and not otherwise (Leibniz 1714, para. 32).

If this were correct, it would guarantee that there's a sufficient reason for the existence of contingent things. Unfortunately, Leibniz's version of the principle is too strong. It's quite possibly a fact that no people are exactly 5' 9.8759" tall, and because only finitely many people exist, *some* such statements will be true. Referring to this particular, specific height, does this fact have a sufficient reason? It's not obvious that it does.

Here's another version of the Principle, this one formulated (though ultimately rejected) by the contemporary American philosopher, William Rowe:

> [T]here must be an explanation (a) of the existence of any being, and (b) of any positive fact whatever (Rowe 2001, p. 20).

Why not just make do with part (a)? Because we can imagine that limited "local" explanations can be found for each being (you exist because of your parents, who exist in turn because of their parents, and so on) but no explanation for the larger fact that any contingent beings exist at all. Part (b) is meant to take care of this difficulty. The reference to "positive facts" also gets around the problem of explaining why no one is exactly 5' 9.8759" tall because the fact that nothing has a certain property isn't a "positive fact" in Rowe's sense.

Just what exactly should count as a positive fact is not easy to spell out; sometimes one and the same fact can be stated in positive or negative form (for example, "All dogs are mammals" and "No dogs are non-mammals"). However, there seem to be some clear examples ("Jenny is 5' 5" tall" would clearly be a positive fact, whereas "Jenny is not 5' 5" tall" would be a negative fact) and so let's assume that the distinction can be made clear.

Rowe uses the word "explanation" but that term needs some clarifying. In the context of discussions of the Principle of Sufficient Reason, a sufficient reason must entail what it explains; the fact explained must follow from the fact that does the explaining. (For a discussion of "entails," "follows from," and related notions, see the Glossary entry on **validity**.) For example,

(A) Sample X of water freezes

follows from

(B) All water freezes when cooled below 0° Celsius,
and sample X of water is cooled below 0° Celsius.

There's no way for (B) to be true unless (A) is true too.

In addition to implying what they explain, sufficient reasons must also be true because false "facts" don't explain anything. This still isn't enough to get at the idea that sufficient reasons provide explanations. The contingent truth that horses and cows exist implies that horses exist but obviously doesn't explain it. That said, there are such things as explanations and we'll assume that there's a way of filling in the details of what counts.

Some positive facts are necessary and we might agree that they are "self-explaining." For example, that 2 + 3 = 5 is a positive fact but it's also a necessary fact, and as such it doesn't require a sufficient reason beyond itself. However, contingent positive facts don't seem to be self-explaining. If the principle that Rowe formulates is true, then each such fact—including the fact that any contingent things exist at all—will be explained by something else.

3.3 Is the Principle of Sufficient Reason True?

The hope is that we can use the Principle of Sufficient Reason to argue that God is the sufficient reason for the existence of contingent things. Unfortunately, the way the world actually works, it's very likely that the Principle of Sufficient Reason is false. Suppose some uranium atom decays at exactly 3:00 PM Greenwich Mean Time tomorrow and emits a particle. The emission of the particle at 3:00 PM is a positive contingent fact, but according to many physicists, the most that can be said is that there was a certain probability that the decay would happen. In that case, there is no sufficient reason for the decay. Science leaves the Principle of Sufficient Reason doubtful.

Perhaps physics could be revised to give a sufficient reason for atomic decays but there's a deeper question. *Could* every positive contingent fact have a sufficient reason? Several philosophers—including Rowe—have made a strong case that the answer is no. The problem is that the sum total of all contingent facts is itself a contingent fact. If we think it needs an explanation, nothing would be left to do the explaining. Here's a sketch of an argument for this conclusion based on an essay by John O'Leary-Hawthorne and Andrew Cortens (1993):

Suppose we take the "sum" or **conjunction** of all positive contingent facts, as in

> *There are trees* and *There are dogs* and *The Empire State Building is in New York* . . . .

and so on. What we end up with is still a positive contingent fact. Call this overstuffed fact *F*. Now suppose there's a sufficient reason for *F*, which we'll call *R*. There are two possibilities:

1. The sufficient reason R is a necessary truth.

   This can't be right, because the only things implied by necessary truths are other necessary truths. This is a standard principle of **modal logic**, the branch of logic that deals with possibility and necessity. A necessary truth is one that would hold in every possible situation. But if X implies Y, then Y must hold whenever X holds. This means that whatever a necessary truth implies must hold in every possible situation, which amounts to saying that the thing implied is another necessary truth. We can sum this up in a principle that we met in Chapter 1:

   > **Transfer of Necessity:** If X is a necessary truth and X implies Y, then Y is also a necessary truth.

   Now we see the problem. Our totality of contingent facts *F* is a contingent fact itself. No necessary truth can imply a contingent truth, so no necessary truth can imply *F*. But that means no necessary truth can be sufficient for *F*.

The other possibility is:

2. The sufficient reason *R* is a contingent truth.

   The trouble here is that it's hard to see what sort of contingent fact could do the job. The idea of a self-explaining contingent fact is very puzzling. Saying that the explanation for the existence of lions is the fact that lions exist just seems wrong. No one we know of has offered any more plausible examples. So it seems that *F* can't explain itself. But no "part" of *F* could do the explaining either because a "part" of *F* wouldn't imply *F*. (As an illustration, consider the truth, "Boston is in Massachusetts and Toronto is in Ontario." This fact isn't implied by the "part" that says "Boston is in Massachusetts.")

The only remaining possibility is that *R* is a negative fact, but though we won't argue the point in detail, it's hard to see how a negative contingent fact could explain a positive contingent fact. Since we've exhausted the possibilities, the consequence is that at least some positive contingent truths don't have sufficient reasons. The Principle of Sufficient Reason, it seems, can't possibly be true—at least, not in the form that Rowe considers.

3.4 Does the Fact that the Principle of Sufficient Reason is False Matter?

The argument we've just examined shows that the totality of contingent facts can't have a sufficient reason. Perhaps that's not surprising. But suppose we could start with something necessary, add the right dash of contingency, and end up with a satisfactory answer to the question of why contingent things exist, even though what we got didn't explain literally every contingent truth. This would be a considerable accomplishment.

Here's a suggestion from Quentin Smith: First, suppose that God exists necessarily and that God has complete free will, so nothing determines or necessitates God's decisions. Now suppose that God wills the existence of contingent things. This fact—the fact about God's will—won't have a sufficient reason; it's an exercise of God's free choice, and God could have chosen otherwise. (Remember that "sufficient reason" is a technical term; sufficient reasons must imply what they explain.) But if we add some plausible premises about God (e.g., that God is omnipotent), then it would follow from those premises and God's willing the existence of contingent things that they actually would exist. That would be the sufficient reason for the existence of contingent things.

Notice that this act of will on God's part wouldn't have to explain the existence of every single contingent thing. Suppose that one of the things God's act of will creates is a contingent thing—let's call it X—that randomly creates other contingent things. (Quantum theory allows for this sort of possibility. When particles decay, they create other particles.) Now suppose that Y is some other contingent thing (a subatomic particle, perhaps) to which X randomly gave rise to. There wouldn't be a sufficient reason for the existence of Y even though there would be a sufficient reason why at least some contingent things exist. The explanation would be God's free act of will in creating X.

Smith doesn't think God's will is the only possible sufficient reason for the existence of contingent things. We can agree that there is nothing necessary about the existence of ordinary physical objects like Taylor's sphere. However, what about space-time itself? Perhaps it's impossible for space-time not to exist. In that case, space-time would be a "necessary being" in the way that some say God is. Suppose that as a matter of contingent fact, this necessarily existing space-time fits some of the more exotic principles of quantum physics and includes something called a quantum mechanical vacuum. The nature of a quantum vacuum, so the physicists say, is that it randomly creates various kinds of particles. This would explain why concrete, contingent things exist: space-time, a necessary thing, contingently gives rise to them.

Let's stand back from this example a bit and state the underlying ideas. First, there can be contingent facts about things that exist necessarily. What God wills is contingent, even if God's existence is necessary. Exactly what space-time is like is a contingent matter, even if the existence of space-time is necessary. (Whether God or space-time really exists necessarily is another matter.)

Second, some contingent *fact* about a necessary thing might explain why contingent *things* exist. What God contingently wills, if a necessarily existing God exists, could do the trick; so could the fact (if it is one) that a necessarily existing space-time contingently happens to fit certain quantum-mechanical principles. Smith argues on this basis that at least this version of the principle of sufficient reason is true:

> *Smith's Principle of Sufficient Reason*: There is a sufficient reason for the fact that contingent things exist.

3.4.1 Reasons and Explanations

Smith's idea is interesting but his two cases aren't clearly on par. Smith is saying that if a necessarily existing space-time contingently fits certain quantum principles, we have a sufficient reason for the existence of contingent things. In the technical sense of "sufficient reason," this is true. But you might wonder why should space-time fit these particular quantum principles? Haven't we just left ourselves with another puzzle?

What this suggests is that a principle of sufficient reason might not be what we want after all. If Smith is right, there could be a sufficient reason for the existence of contingent things that wouldn't be a *satisfying* reason. Interestingly enough, there could also be satisfying reasons that aren't sufficient reasons. To see this, return to the idea that God might will concrete, contingent things to exist.

Suppose that a necessarily existing God freely created the world around us for good reasons. On the one hand, the fact that God made this choice would be a sufficient reason for the existence of the world, but this choice itself wouldn't have a sufficient reason in the technical sense. The fact that there is a good reason for doing something doesn't imply that God will do it. After all, there might be other things, also with good reasons, that God could do instead. Because God could have done otherwise, the facts about God don't entail that God would create the world. However, if God created the world for good reasons, those reasons would make what God did intelligible—they would make sense of God's decision and provide a satisfying reason for it, even if not a sufficient reason.

Suppose Betsy is deciding whether to go to graduate school, either in philosophy or in psychology. She finally decides that though she's attracted to the intellectual freedom of philosophy, she appreciates the fact that as an experimental psychologist, she'll be working with data and she's always had a passion for finding patterns in data. She decides to become a psychologist.

We normally suppose that she could have decided otherwise in some deep sense of "could." We normally suppose that Betsy's reasons make sense of her decision without compelling it. This would mean that her decision to become a psychologist didn't have a sufficient reason, but it would be silly to say that it didn't have an explanation in a broader sense than we've considered so far and, indeed, an explanation that brings the buck to a stop in an appealing way. Her decision is based in the reasons that guided it, and if these reasons are good ones, they can provide explanations that don't cry out for further explanation themselves.

Suppose someone asks you why you took an aspirin. You say, "I wanted my headache to stop and aspirin cures headaches." If the person went on to ask why you wanted your headache to stop, you would quite rightly see that as a silly question. The point is that even if your choice was free, and therefore had no sufficient reason in the technical sense (people can and sometimes do decide not to do things that there are good reasons for), the fact that headaches are painful is a perfectly adequate explanation for wanting them to stop. Explanations don't need to be sufficient in the technical sense to be adequate or satisfying.

3.5 The Principle of Satisfying Reasons

Let's put all this together. Various principles have been called "the principle of sufficient reason." Some seem false or even impossible. A weaker principle that might be true is that there is a sufficient reason for the existence of contingent things. Smith has argued that this could be true but one of his suggestions—a necessarily existing space-time that happened to fit the rules of quantum theory—wouldn't obviously give us a satisfying reason for the existence of contingent things. It would seem perfectly reasonable to wonder why space-time happens to have these peculiar properties. An explanation in terms of the choices a necessarily existing God made seems different. Even if it's a contingent truth that God chose to create the world of contingent things, if God had good reasons for doing this, those reasons could provide a satisfying explanation for the choice—and hence for the existence of contingent things—even if they don't provide sufficient reasons.

If all this is right, we might have stumbled on a principle that could let our insomniac get to sleep.

> **The Principle of Satisfying Reasons:** The fact that there are contingent things has a satisfying reason.

We haven't given a full theory of what makes for a satisfying reason. The reasons that lie behind decisions are plausible examples of satisfying reasons for contingent facts. However, they might not be the only examples. Recall Smith's space-time case. We don't pretend to understand the physics but there's a possibility here that shouldn't be overlooked. Suppose that for people who understand the details, it's appealing and natural to assume that space-time fits the relevant quantum principles. Suppose that this assumption is simple (for physicists, at least), elegant, contains all sorts of pleasing symmetries, and seems as "natural" as any other choice. This might add up to a satisfying reason. If so, and if thinking that space-time exists necessarily really makes sense, this could amount to a satisfying nontheistic answer to the question, "Why do any contingent things exist?"

We can go a step further. Suppose that a pleasing, "natural" physical theory of a necessarily existing space-time doesn't require that contingent physical things will come into existence but merely makes this outcome very likely. This might still be good enough for a satisfying explanation. Suppose you flipped a fair coin 1000 times and got 530 heads. The fact that the coin was fair wouldn't give a satisfying explanation for the exact number of heads, and perhaps nothing else would either. But the fact that the coin was fair would give a satisfying explanation for the fact that the number of heads was close to 50%. The Principle of Satisfying Reasons doesn't require that there be *sufficient* reasons for the existence of contingent things. Still, we need to ask, "Why think that the Principle of Satisfying Reason is true?"

We doubt very much that there's a convincing argument to show that we must accept this principle. Nonetheless, there are principles that people, including hard-nosed philosophers, accept that seem within the bounds of the reasonable even though they can't be proved. For example, some philosophers think that laws of nature are mere superficial patterns—nothing more than special kinds of correlations that just happen to hold. However, other philosophers (and many scientists) think there's something deeper to laws than that, even if saying just what is very difficult. We think that people who hold the stronger view aren't being unreasonable.

As we noted earlier, most people also think that the principles governing nature bottom-out at some point; they don't form an unending chain. We noted that this is something most of us have in common with Aquinas, even if none of us—Aquinas included—have good arguments to show that it's true.

Perhaps then the Principle of Satisfying Reason is in the category of principles that could be rejected, and are rejected by some reasonable people, but that don't have to be rejected for someone to qualify as reasonable. In the realm of questions that we've been considering in this chapter, perhaps that's the most we can hope for.

So where does that leave us? It leaves us with a principle that might or might not be true, and if true, might or might not require the existence of God. This is a situation that some people will find frustratingly ambiguous. But we're trying to solve the deepest mysteries of the universe. We may have to settle for whatever we can get.

AT A GLANCE: THE COSMOLOGICAL ARGUMENT

Broadly speaking, the cosmological arguments try to explain why a physical world exists at all.

1. Aquinas's Second Way

   - Aquinas argues that chains of efficient or sustaining causes can't go on to infinity. There must be a first efficient cause, which he identifies as God. His argument against infinite chains of efficient causes is obscure. He might be confusing the denial of a first cause with removing a cause from a series; he might be illicitly applying truths about finite chains to infinite chains; or he might think there is something special about chains of causes, although he doesn't say clearly what that would be except that he thinks they must have beginnings. The argument looks like this:

Premise #1: Some things have efficient causes.
Premise #2: Nothing can be its own efficient cause (because it would have to be prior to itself).
Premise #3: Therefore, chains of efficient causes exist.
Premise #4: A chain of efficient causes can't go on to infinity.
Conclusion: Therefore, a first efficient cause must exist (which everyone calls God).

2. The Kalam Cosmological Argument
   - This argument tries to show that actual infinite series are impossible. If so, the world had a beginning.
   - The reasons are that this beginning would have to have been caused rather than uncaused and that the cause would have been personal rather than impersonal.

   2.1. Finite and Infinite
      - Craig argues that no actual infinite series (made up of physical objects or events) is possible.
      - In the mathematical theory of infinities, two sets have the same number of things if the members can be paired one-to-one.
      - This implies that the number of even numbers is the same number as the number of counting numbers.

   2.2. Are Actual Infinities Absurd?
      - Craig accepts the mathematical theory of infinity when applied to mathematical objects.
      - Craig thinks the theory yields absurdities if applied to collections of actual objects or events.
         1. For example: It would imply that if we remove every other book from an infinite bookshelf, the same number of books remains.
      - Problem: Craig doesn't clearly demonstrate that such consequences are absurd.

   2.3. The Rest of the Kalam Argument
      - This calls for showing that the beginning of the world was caused and that the cause was personal.
      - Craig insists that no "sane person" thinks otherwise.
      - Problem: This is not an argument.
      - Craig argues that positing a personal cause is the only way to get a satisfactory explanation. Whether this is right is difficult to say.

3. Contingency
   - Some things are contingent—they didn't have to exist.

3.1. Aquinas's Third Way

1. Suppose that everything that exists is evanescent (comes into being and goes out of being).
2. Each evanescent thing is nonexistent at some time.
3. Therefore, if every thing were evanescent, there would have been a time when nothing existed.
4. Something can't come from nothing.
5. Therefore, if everything were evanescent, nothing would be in existence now.
6. Things are in existence now.
7. Therefore, not everything that exists is an evanescent thing.

• Aquinas's proof depends on a fallacy. He doesn't show that one time would exist when everything fails to exist at some time.

3.2. The Principle of Sufficient Reason

• Rowe's version: Every thing has an explanation, and every positive fact has an explanation—an explanation that implies what it explains.
• If the principle is correct, then the fact that contingent things exist has an explanation.

3.3. Is the Principle of Sufficient Reason True?

• Things like atomic decay suggest that the principle is actually false.
• It can be argued that the principle must be false.

1. Let F be the conjunction of all contingent facts.
2. F is contingent.
3. Therefore, no necessary fact can explain F (or else F would not be contingent).
4. F can't explain itself.
5. No part of F could explain F.
6. No negative fact could explain F.
7. Therefore, F has no explanation and the Principle of Sufficient Reason is false.

3.4. Does the Fact that the Principle of Sufficient Reason is False Matter?

• Quentin Smith argues that a related principle might be true:

1. There is a sufficient reason for the existence of contingent things.

• This could work in two possible ways:

1. God exists necessarily, and God contingently wills that contingent things exist.
2. Space-time is a necessary thing and contingently fits certain quantum principles.

3.4.1. Reasons and Explanations

• Sufficient reasons might not be satisfying reasons. (Smith's suggestion about space-time might be an example.)

- Satisfying reasons (such as the good reasons for making a certain choice) might not imply what they explain, and so might not be sufficient reasons.
- Satisfying reasons might be good enough to provide understanding.

3.5. The Principle of Satisfying Reasons

- This principle would say that there is a "satisfying" explanation for the existence of contingent things.
- This principle might not be provable.
- This principle might be reasonable to accept.
- Even if the principle is true, something other than God might provide the reason for the existence of the physical universe.

WEB RESOURCES

You can find the Five Ways online at http://www.newadvent.org/summa/100203.htm.

Leibniz enunciates the Principle of Sufficient Reason in his *Monadology*, which you can find online at http://philosophy.eserver.org/leibniz-monadology.txt.

There is A detailed discussion of the cosmological argument in the Stanford Encyclopedia of Philosophy, available at http://plato.stanford.edu/entries/cosmological-argument.

Quentin Smith's discussion of the Principle of Sufficient Reason is online at http://www.qsmithwmu.com/a_defense_of_a_principle_of_sufficient_reason.htm.

CHAPTER 4

The Ontological Argument

One especially intriguing family of arguments holds that we can prove God's existence by reason alone, simply by reflecting on the concept of God as a perfect being. We consider three such arguments in this chapter.

An excerpt from a real conversation, overheard by one of this book's authors: the young priest, dressed in blue jeans, was seated across from a student in a booth in the university cafeteria. "I don't know, Father," the student said. "I'm just not sure whether I really think there's a God."

"But don't you see?" the priest said. "In order even to doubt that God exists, you have to talk about God."

"Oh!" said the student. "I never thought about it that way!"

This priest might have been a good pastor but as a philosopher, he had a ways to go. If we could prove that you have to believe in God by an argument like this, we could also prove that you have to believe in the Loch Ness Monster and Santa Claus. Still, there's an intriguing idea here. What the priest was trying to say is that there's something incoherent about doubting God's existence, and a famous family of philosophical arguments tries to show more or less that. These various arguments are versions of the *Ontological Argument*, our subject in this chapter.

1 ANSELM'S ONTOLOGICAL ARGUMENT

Many people have formulated ontological arguments, including seventeenth-century philosophers René Descartes and Gottfried Leibniz and twentieth-century logician and mathematician Kurt Gödel. In this chapter, we'll concentrate on three versions: one by St. Anselm of Canterbury, an eleventh-century bishop and theologian; a variant on Anselm's argument that Normal Malcolm drew attention to a few decades ago; and an intriguing form of the argument due to the contemporary philosopher Alvin Plantinga. We begin with Anselm. (For the text of his argument, see Charlesworth, 1965.)

The argument begins with a definition: God is "a being than which none greater can be conceived." In other words, for something to count as God, it must be so great that there is simply no possibility for anyone, no matter how knowledgeable or clever, to so much as conceive of a greater being. It's important to understand that this definition doesn't just concern itself with the limits of what any particular human being might be able to imagine. What it's really saying is that to count as God, a being must be absolutely perfect—no room for improvement. There may be other possible definitions of God, but no matter. Proving that such a being exists would be quite an accomplishment. It's also hard to see how it could fail to have religious significance.

Anselm's argument takes the form of a *reductio ad absurdum*. He imagines an **atheist**—a "fool," as he puts it—who has said to himself that there is no God. Anselm then tries to show that this position leads to an absurdity and therefore must be false. We can reconstruct his argument as follows:

1. By definition, God is a being than which none greater can be conceived.
2. A being that exists in reality is greater than a being that exists only in the understanding.
3. The fool understands the concept of God as the being than which none greater can be conceived.
4. Therefore, God exists in the fool's understanding.
5. Suppose God exists only in the understanding and not also in reality.
6. Then by (2), we can conceive of a greater being, namely one that also exists in reality.
7. Therefore by our supposition (5), we can conceive of a greater being than God.
8. Because (7) contradicts (1), the supposition (5) has led to a contradiction.
9. Therefore, (5) is false; God exists in reality and not just in the understanding.

2 EXISTING IN THE UNDERSTANDING

Anselm's argument seems to depend on comparing two things: a being that exists only in the understanding and a being that also exists in reality. However, a being that exists only in the understanding is not a being at all. What are we comparing?

We can answer this question in at least two ways. The first is to frame the argument in terms of possible beings (we'll explain what this means later in the chapter). The second is to frame the argument in terms of ideas or concepts—in terms of ways of conceiving of God. Here are two concepts, made up arbitrarily for purposes of illustrating our point.

> Deity A: a being that is perfectly good and perfectly powerful.
>
> Deity B: a being that is perfectly good, perfectly powerful and that has unlimited knowledge.

Think of these as two ways of conceiving of God. Which amounts to conceiving of God as greater? Deity B, of course. Perfect goodness and perfect power are perfections, but the concept of Deity B includes an extra perfection: unlimited knowledge. We'll assume in what follows that we can make sense of Anselm's argument roughly this way. The atheist conceives of God as omnipotent and all-knowing and perfectly good, but as lacking existence. Anselm would say that we can conceive of an even greater being, one that has the perfection of existence. Because the atheist takes himself to be conceiving of the being than which none greater can be conceived, his view results in a contradiction, or so Anselm would say.

3 THE PERFECT ISLAND?

The first known critic of Anselm's argument was a monk named Gaunilo. (See Charlesworth, 1965) Gaunilo believed that God exists, but he didn't think that Anselm's proof was **valid**—he didn't think the conclusion followed from the premises. His most interesting objection was that if we reason as Anselm does, we can prove things that are clearly not true. In particular, suppose we hear someone talk of the Lost Island, an island greater than any other island. Gaunilo objects that if we say that the Lost Island doesn't exist, Anselm's reasoning will lead us to a contradiction. If the Lost Island exists only in the understanding, then we can conceive of an even greater island, namely one that also exists in reality. But this hardly proves the existence of The Lost Island.

If The Lost Island were merely greater than any actual island, the objection wouldn't work. However, most people understand Gaunilo's objection to run along these lines. Define The Lost Island as the island than which none greater can be conceived. Now go through the steps of the argument above, but substitute "The Lost Island" for "God" and replace "being" with "island." We have an argument with the same form but with an absurd conclusion: an island really exists than which none greater can be conceived. In that case, the objection would go, something must be wrong with Anselm's argument.

Many readers of the Ontological Argument seem to think that this amounts to a knock-out punch. However, as William Rowe has pointed out (Rowe 2001, p. 35), there's a promising reply. For the Ontological Argument to work, the definition must make sense. Anselm thinks that the idea of a being than which none greater can be conceived is a coherent idea and, for the moment, we'll assume he's right. However, just because the idea of a being than which none greater can be conceived makes sense, it doesn't follow that the idea of an island than which none greater can be conceived also makes sense. What would this island be like? How big would it be? Would it ever rain on the island? What would the average temperature be? What kind of vegetation would it have?

There are no good answers to these questions. In fact, it may be that no matter what worldly kind of thing we pick—hockey player (Rowe's example), French chef, business suit, tattoo needle—it won't make sense to talk about one than which none greater can be conceived. The problem is that when we talk about any of these things, we're talking about something that's inherently limited and, perhaps, inherently imperfect. However, Anselm's argument deals with beings as such, quite apart from any more limited categories. When it comes to beings, we can say some definite things about what one would have to be like if none greater could be conceived. Such a being would have to be all-powerful. It would have to be morally perfect. It would have to know everything. In short, it would have to be the God of **classical theism**. It would have to be a perfect being. But while "perfect being" arguably makes sense, "perfect island" doesn't.

Or is this right? What about the idea of a leaper than which none greater can be conceived? (We thank an anonymous referee for this suggestion.) Isn't this something we can make sense of? This would be someone whose ability to leap was unlimited. The word "island" isn't understood in terms of functions or goals; words like "leaper" or "mathematician" are. But wouldn't a leaper who exists in reality be greater than one who exists only in the imagination? If so, we're back to Gaunilo's objection.

Perhaps. But could a leaper conceivably leap from Earth to Proxima Centuri (a distance of about 2 light years)? After all, a leap is accomplished by using your leg muscles and not by a nuclear-powered rocket engine. Is a mathematician than which none greater can be conceived one who can produce a proof for any provable theorem, no matter how long the proof? How quickly must they be able to do it? Or does the mathematician just "see" the truth of the theorem, in which case she isn't really doing mathematics. (In fact, if God exists, then God is presumably such a "mathematician.") Perhaps both examples are coherent, but this is not entirely clear. And perhaps Gaunilo's objection still stands but his island example won't do, and providing the right example may not be easy.

4 IS EXISTENCE A PERFECTION?

If Anselm's argument works, then adding existence to a concept is adding a perfection. However, for this to be true existence would have to make some difference to what a thing is like. It would have to add some enhancing feature to the thing. For that to be so, existence would have to be a property or quality or a characteristic. This is open to doubt. The great eighteenth-century philosopher Immanuel Kant argued that existence is not a property or quality at all. In his vocabulary, existence is not a **predicate**.

Kant may be right. A genuine predicate should tell us something about what a thing is like. Suppose someone tells you that her brother is six feet tall, has red hair, weighs 170 pounds, is near-sighted, and has freckles on his nose. Each of these descriptions tells you more about what her brother is like. But suppose she adds that her brother exists. This would be an odd thing to say but, more to the point, it wouldn't help you pick her brother out of a line-up. It tells you that she really has a brother and that someone actually fits the description she has given you, but it doesn't contribute anything to your idea of what her brother is like. This would make sense if Kant is correct: existence is not a quality or property or predicate. However, in that case it's also not a perfection. But if it's not a perfection, then it doesn't add to God's greatness.

Here's the point in tidier form:

1. If Anselm's argument succeeds, then existence must be a perfection.
2. For existence to be a perfection, it must be a predicate.

3. Therefore, if Anselm's argument succeeds, existence must be a predicate.
4. Existence is not a predicate.
5. Therefore, Anselm's argument does not succeed.

The debate over Statement 4 is not entirely settled among philosophers. However, even if existence is not a predicate, a related concept offers a way to avoid Kant's objection.

5 NECESSARY EXISTENCE: THE ANSELM-MALCOLM ARGUMENT

If Kant is correct, Anselm's argument—as we've spelled it out so far—fails. However, Norman Malcolm pointed out several decades ago that if we read a little further, we find a subtly but importantly different version of Anselm's argument (Malcolm 1960). Anselm said that among beings that exist, we can distinguish between the ones whose nonexistence is conceivable and the ones whose nonexistence is not conceivable. The second sort of being is greater.

Malcolm says that the concept of the being than which none greater can be conceived includes the concept of **necessary existence**. Anselm doesn't use that phrase. Instead, he talks in terms of conceivability: of a being such that it's inconceivable that it should not exist. However, he means *absolutely* inconceivable—inconceivable by anyone, no matter how smart or sophisticated or insightful. This comes close enough to the **metaphysical** notion of necessary existence that the difference may not be worth worrying about. In any case, here is the passage from Anselm that spells out the argument that Malcolm wants us to consider:

> [I]t is possible to conceive of a being which cannot be conceived not to exist; and this is greater than one which can be conceived not to exist. Hence, if that, than which nothing greater can be conceived, can be conceived not to exist, it is not that than which nothing greater can be conceived. But this is a contradiction. (Malcolm 1960, p. 45)

Anselm claimed that we have a concept of God as a being so great that a greater being can't be conceived. If we examine this concept he adds, we see that part of what it includes is the inconceivability of this being's nonexistence; expressed in Malcolm's terms, it includes the being's necessary existence. Therefore, if we say that God can be conceived not to exist, we've contradicted ourselves. But if God's nonexistence is inconceivable, then we have to agree that God does exist. More formally:

1. The concept of God is the concept of a being so great than none greater can be conceived.
2. A being whose nonexistence is conceivable is not as great as a being whose nonexistence is inconceivable.
3. Therefore, the concept of God is the concept of a being whose nonexistence is inconceivable.
4. If a being's nonexistence is inconceivable, then the being exists.
5. Therefore, God exists.

On the face of it, this is a powerful argument—we'll call it the Anselm-Malcolm argument. However, we're in tricky conceptual territory. We need to look more carefully. We'll start by asking if the Anselm-Malcolm argument gets around Kant's objection.

5.1 Is Necessary Existence a Predicate?

Perhaps Kant is correct in claiming that existence is not a predicate. However, this doesn't seem to hold for necessary existence. Saying that something exists necessarily adds some significant information about what the thing is like. One way of understanding information is that it rules out possibilities. If you learn that the murderer fired the weapon with his left hand, you can rule out the possibility that Jones, whose left hand was amputated, was the killer. If you learn that the new chair of the philosophy department is a woman, you can rule out the possibility that either author of this book is the new chair. What if you are told that a being has necessary existence—that its nonexistence is inconceivable? Then you can rule out a great many things. For example: you can rule out that this being is a building or a stone or an ordinary person. Things of each of these sorts can easily be conceived not to exist. In fact, if God's nonexistence is inconceivable, then nothing that's limited in time and space could possibly be God. It's easy to conceive of such things not existing. Just think of how things are in a time or place where they don't exist. When we're told that God's nonexistence is inconceivable, we are given information about what God is like, even though it's negative information. Kant's reasons for denying that existence is a predicate don't apply to necessary existence. So far, the Anselm-Malcolm argument seems to be on track.

5.2 Does Anything Exist Necessarily?

Some philosophers are suspicious of necessary existence. They believe that existence is inherently a **contingent** matter and that the very idea of necessary existence is absurd. If this is correct, then the Anselm-Malcolm argument is in trouble.

It's certainly true that most things don't exist necessarily, This is especially true of ordinary physical objects and kinds of stuff. Ships, shoes, stars, sealing wax, salamanders, sodium—all of these can easily be conceived not to exist. However, Malcolm points out that there are theorems that say such things as, "Infinitely many prime numbers exist." This seems to tell us that these numbers really do *exist* and since their existence is guaranteed by the laws of mathematics, they would seem to exist necessarily.

Of course, if the only things that exist necessarily are things like numbers—purely abstract objects—this wouldn't help the Anselm-Malcolm argument. However, the question was whether anything at all exists necessarily, and if numbers do, we have an answer to that general question, even if showing that *God* exists necessarily requires more work.

Not everyone would accept Malcolm's interpretation of theorems like the proof that infinitely many primes exist. Philosophers disagree about whether such theorems really commit us to the existence of numbers. One group of philosophers—often called Platonists—insist that numbers are real entities even though they aren't physical things. Their opponents, often called Nominalists, say that statements like, "there exists a prime number between 17 and 23," can be translated into more complicated statements that don't require the existence of numbers at all. The details of this debate are beyond our scope, and we won't try to spell them out. However, if the Nominalists are correct, Malcolm hasn't given us a clean example of something that exists necessarily. That wouldn't show that nothing exists necessarily, though it would leave us wanting a clear, uncontroversial example of necessary existence.

This discussion raises a third issue: is necessary existence a perfection? Suppose numbers exist necessarily. Does this somehow make them better? It's not obvious that it does. Wouldn't a necessarily existing evil being be worse than one that existed only in the understanding?

Perhaps numbers are somehow better for existing necessarily, and perhaps a necessarily existing evil being is actually better than an evil being that exists only in the understanding. Later we'll see a version of the Ontological Argument that avoids these questions. Meanwhile, we'll shelve the doubts and continue to assume that necessary existence is a perfection.

5.3 Definitions and Concepts

If Anselm and Malcolm are correct, then it's part of the very concept of God that God exists necessarily. On the one hand, this might make it difficult to see how anyone could say that God doesn't exist. On the other hand, there's something puzzling in the idea that we should be able to prove the existence of something as impressive as God just by analyzing a concept.

Kant believed that even if the idea of God includes necessary existence, this still doesn't guarantee that God exists. We can grant that the following is true if we understand it appropriately:

God is omnipotent.

This is true as a matter of what's contained in the concept of God, just as "unicorns have golden horns" is true as a matter of what's contained in the concept of a unicorn. However, if we simply deny that God exists at all—if we "reject the subject"—then we don't have to agree that an omnipotent being exists. Likewise, if we say,

God exists necessarily.

we can agree that necessary existence is part of the concept or "definition" of God but deny that any being actually fits the definition.

Or so Kant thought. Malcolm thinks this is confused. In his view, Kant is treating "God exists necessarily" as a hypothetical statement:

If God exists, then God exists necessarily.

He also thinks that because Kant holds out the possibility of "rejecting the subject," he is really saying this:

If God exists (and it's possible that he doesn't) then he exists necessarily.

In Malcolm's view, there's a contradiction lurking here. Once we see that it's part of the very idea of a being than which none greater can be conceived that it exists necessarily, then there's no room left for the parenthetical remark. It's as though we're saying:

> *God exists necessarily, but it's possible that God doesn't exist.*

which has every appearance of being a contradiction.

In fact, things aren't so simple. We can find interesting reasons for adopting the hypothetical approach quite apart from questions about God. These reasons suggest a way of understanding the word "possible" in that parenthetical remark so as to remove the appearance of contradiction. An example will help.

In the previous section, we contemplated the idea that numbers exist necessarily but we pointed out that there's a dispute among philosophers over whether numbers really exist at all. However, both sides would agree to this: if numbers exist, then they exist necessarily. Now put yourself in the place of someone who isn't sure whether the Nominalists or the Platonists are correct. (The authors of this book fall into that category.) You might very well say:

> *If numbers exist (and it's possible that they don't),*
> *then they exist necessarily.*

What you mean here by "possible that" is "for all I know." The word "possible" is being used in its *epistemic* sense—the sense having to do with our knowledge. There is an unresolved dispute about numbers and you might well think you don't know which side is correct. If numbers really exist, they exist necessarily—but maybe it's a confusion to think they exist at all.

Perhaps the same is true of God. The skeptic (or the philosopher analyzing neutrally) might agree: necessary existence is part of the concept of God, just as it's part of the concept of numbers. However, whether anything actually fits the concept is a further question, both in the case of numbers and in the case of God. Our neutral philosopher is saying: "If God exists, he exists necessarily, but I don't know whether he does exist." This at least seems to be a coherent position.

There are other ways of trying to get a sound argument out of the idea that God exists necessarily. They rest on the idea that if something is necessarily true in the metaphysical sense of "necessarily", then it would be true no matter what the world was like—it would be true in every possible world, as it's sometimes put. This leads to a striking consequence: if it's *possible* that a necessary being exists, then such a being *must* exist. (Otherwise, there would be a "necessary truth" that wasn't true in every possible situation.) The most sophisticated such argument is due to Alvin Plantinga and it's discussed in the next section. However, all such arguments are highly controversial. It's difficult to get skeptics to agree that the being whose existence is at issue really is possible to begin with. Section 6, which is a bit more advanced, makes its way through these issues.

*6 POSSIBLE WORLDS AND THE POSSIBILITY OF A NECESSARY BEING

The Ontological Argument depends crucially on the **modal** notions of possibility, impossibility, and necessity. Modern **modal logic** has developed powerful tools for thinking about these concepts, and those tools have led to intriguing new versions of the Ontological Argument. Very briefly (details to follow), some philosophers argue that if we admit that God's existence is even possible, we have no choice but to agree that God exists. To explore this thought, we need to look at modal logic more carefully. Sections 6.1 and 6.2 owe a debt to William Rowe's essay, "The Ontological Argument" (commissioned for *Reason & Responsibility*) though we develop the point differently than Rowe does.

*6.1 Possibility in the Metaphysical Sense

As we've already seen, the word "possible" has more than one sense. In the epistemic sense, "it's possible that" amounts to "for all I know." The ontological argument isn't an epistemic argument. It deals with possibility and necessity in the strong or metaphysical sense—a sense that has to do with the way things are, quite apart from what we know. When we say in the metaphysical sense "It's possible that X," we don't mean that X might be true for all we know. We mean that X represents a way things could be or might have been whether or not we know if X is actually true.

It's important to be clear about this. Consider this odd-sounding claim:

> *It's possible that New York City has only 100,000 inhabitants.*

In the epistemic sense, this isn't possible at all for most of us. Most of us know that millions of people live in New York City. But in the metaphysical sense, this sentence is true. It's true because things could have turned out so that New York only had 100,000 inhabitants. This metaphysical sense is the one you should keep in mind for what follows.

*6.2 Possible Worlds

Modern modal logic makes extensive use of the idea of a possible world. There are many ways of understanding possible worlds, but the approach we'll adopt holds that a possible world is a way that the totality of things could be. A few philosophers think of possible worlds as full-blown concrete entities but most think of them as abstract—complex structures of propositions or properties. In any case, the actual world is a way things could be, and so we count it as a possible world.

There are also possible worlds (infinitely many of them) in which no people exist. There are possible worlds in which George Washington was not the first president of the United States. There are possible worlds in which no stars or planets exist, and on and on. On the other hand, there are no possible worlds in which $2 + 2 = 5$, no possible worlds in which bachelors are married, and no possible worlds in which all people are over six feet tall and some people are under six feet tall.

Metaphysical possibility is sometimes called logical possibility, but that's a bit misleading. It suggests that to figure out whether something is possible, all we need to do is figure out if the sentence that describes it is consistent. However, many philosophers would disagree. It's not a contradiction to say that water is not H_2O. The word "water" doesn't mean H_2O; English speakers knew how to use the word "water" long before chemistry came on the scene. However, many philosophers would say that science made a discovery: it's the very nature of water to be made of H_2O, and so there are no possible worlds where water is not H_2O. We discovered this through science, these philosophers would say, but it's still a metaphysical necessity. Logic alone doesn't settle all questions about metaphysical possibility.

Something is possible in the metaphysical sense so long as there's at least one possible world where it's true—whether we know it or not. Something is necessary in the metaphysical sense if it's true in every single possible world. This leads to an interesting result: if it's *possible* that something is necessarily true, then it *is* necessarily true. A diagram will help.

Pretend that there are only finitely many possible worlds. They are the labeled points in the box:

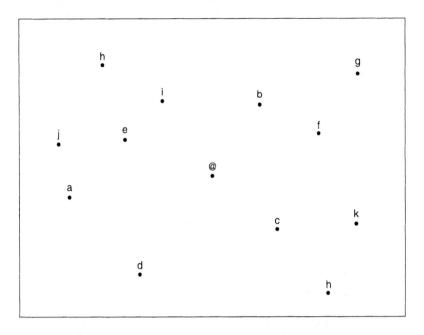

The actual world is labeled "@." Now suppose that angels don't exist necessarily, but they're possible beings. Then some world or worlds exists—perhaps *e* and *i* for example—where the statement

Angels exist.

is true. However, it doesn't follow that they exist at the actual world @. On the other hand, consider the statement,

$$2 + 2 = 4$$

This statement is necessary, and so it is true at every possible world.

Now consider the statement,

Numbers exist necessarily.

Suppose that it's possible that this statement is true. Then there is some possible world—let's say *g*—where the statement is true. That means that in *g*, numbers exist necessarily. But if it's true at world *g* that numbers exist necessarily, then it's true at world *g* that "numbers exist" is true in every world. This is what it means for a statement to be necessarily true. However, if it's true at *g* that numbers exist in every world, this amounts to saying that numbers exist in every possible world, period. Therefore, if it's so much as possible that numbers exist necessarily, then numbers really do exist necessarily. Of course, that in turn means that it's true in @, the actual world, that numbers exist.

The same goes for any statement of the form, "It's possible that X is necessary." Such a statement is true if some possible world exists where "X is necessary" is true. But in that case, "X" itself is true in every world. And that in turn means that it's necessary that X. But now notice the theological consequence: suppose we agree that "God exists necessarily" is possibly true. In that case, we've agreed that it's true, period. Suppose then that we ask the atheist to agree that God as understood by Anselm is a possible being. The atheist should reply that we've asked him to give away the store! An atheist who understands the implications of Anselm's concept of God will not agree that God is a possible being.

This response may seem strange. How could anyone deny that it's at least possible that God exists? Here's one way to answer: let's use the word "Deity" to mean a being that is omnipotent, omniscient, and perfectly good. Notice that necessary existence is not part of our definition of the word "Deity." The atheist can say, "I admit that a *Deity* is a possible being. Admitting this only guarantees that a Deity exists in some possible world. However, I don't admit that God as Anselm understands him is a possible being. If I did, I would be admitting that a Deity exists in every possible world, including the actual world." In other words, the atheist can agree that a being *almost* like Anselm's God is possible. He simply draws the line at agreeing that a *necessarily existing* Deity is possible.

This may make sense of how the atheist can deny that Anselm's God is a possible being. However, it may seem that by refusing to go all the way and admit that Anselm's God is possible, the atheist's only motive is to avoid Anselm's conclusion. Alvin Plantinga offers a version of the ontological argument that calls for a more thoughtful response and we discuss it in the next two more advanced sections.

*6.3 Plantinga's Argument

Suppose Superman exists in some world *b* as a being with the sorts of super powers that he has in the comic books. Whether or not Superman is the most impressive thing in that world, he's still quite extraordinary. To use Plantinga's vocabulary, Superman has a high degree of excellence in that world; Plantinga uses the word "excellence" to talk about how good something is strictly from the point of view of a given world. That might seem to be an odd qualification but its point will be clear soon.

We've assumed that Superman exists in some world or other. However, we think that he doesn't exist in every world and, in particular, he doesn't exist in this world. Though it sounds a bit peculiar, we can say that Superman's degree of excellence in this world is very low. In fact, it's probably safe to say it's zero because Superman doesn't live here at all. There may be yet other worlds where Superman exists but without all the powers he has in world *b*. For example, perhaps there's a world *e* where Superman—the same being that exists in world *b*—has all the powers we think of him as having except for super speed. In world *e*, Superman has a high degree of excellence but less than he has in *b*.

Excellence, as Plantinga is using the term, is a measure of a thing's virtue, goodness, and so on, in a given world. Now introduce the idea of *greatness*. As Plantinga uses the word "greatness," it's a measure of a thing's excellence across different worlds. If we ask about a thing's degree of excellence, we're always asking strictly from the point of view of a given world. If we ask about a thing's greatness, the question isn't just about any particular world—it's about the overall pattern of excellence that the thing has across worlds.

Once again, pretending that there are only finitely many worlds will help. Suppose the worlds are *a* through *k* plus the actual world @. Here's a table that sets forth Superman's excellence in each world:

a	*b*	*c*	*d*	*e*	*f*	*g*	*h*	*i*	*j*	*k*	@	Greatness
2	10	0	0	9	3	0	1	1	6	0	0	32

The last entry is Superman's greatness, which is determined by his excellence in all worlds. We've represented greatness in this table as though we simply add across worlds. Since there are infinitely many possible worlds, a coherent scheme would have to be more complicated. However, this is a matter of detail, and we'll assume that there is a way of sorting it out. What's important is that greatness calls for cross-world comparison.

Now suppose that in some world—say, *c*—a being exists that fits the description of a Deity. In that world, the being has maximal excellence. Can we imagine a greater being? That depends on the deity's excellence in other worlds. Suppose that in world *c*, the Deity has maximal excellence but in world *d*, this Deity is not a deity at all and is no greater than Elvis. Reasonable people might disagree on just how great that is, but it's certainly not up to the standards of godliness. To repeat, the crucial idea is this: to determine a being's excellence at a world, we need only look at what the being is like in that world. To determine a being's greatness at a world, we need also to look at its degree of excellence in other possible worlds.

We're almost ready to state Plantinga's argument but first we need to define *maximal greatness*. A being has maximal greatness at a world *x* if it has maximal excellence in every world. Plantinga adds that a being has maximal excellence only if it is omniscient, omnipotent, and perfectly good, and so fits the concept of God that we find in classical theism. With this in mind, here is Plantinga's argument. We'll combine his words with some steps marked by a "†" that fill in the reasoning.

1. It is possible that there be a being that has maximal greatness.
2. So there is a possible being exists that in some possible world *w* has maximal greatness.
3. A being has maximal greatness in a world only if it has maximal excellence in every world.
4. So there is a possible being that has maximal excellence in every world.†
5. A being has maximal excellence in a given world only if it has omniscience, omnipotence, and moral perfection in that world.
6. So there is a possible being that has omniscience, omnipotence, and moral perfection in every world.†
7. Therefore, there is a possible being that has omniscience, omnipotence, and moral perfection in the actual world. In other words, God exists in the actual world and in all other worlds† (Plantinga 1977, p. 108).

Because premises (2) and (3) are matters of definition and premise (5) is a reasonable inference from the meaning of "maximal excellence," everything depends on premise (1). You will accept this argument only if you agree that it's possible for there to be a being with maximal greatness. Plantinga is well aware of this. In fact, he doesn't think his argument proves God's existence, since the first premise is too controversial. But in that case, what's the point of the argument?

Plantinga's reply is that accepting premise (1) isn't irrational. Therefore, he thinks the argument shows that it's at least rationally acceptable to be a theist.

*6.4 Assessing Plantinga's Argument

Suppose someone doubts that theism is rational. Why should they agree with Plantinga that it's rational to accept his first premise? As it turns out, Plantinga never provides a positive argument for saying this but perhaps he thinks this is more or less obvious. Whether or not that's his view, the reasonableness of his first premise is actually very far from obvious. William Rowe asks us to consider the property of being in *less than perfect company*. A person in a possible world has this property if every person in that world, human and non-human, has some flaw, even if only a small one. Rowe writes:

> It may be that we enjoy (or are burdened with) this property in the actual world. But even if we are not, surely, one would think, it is *possible* that this property be instantiated. Surely there is some possible world in which every person has some imperfection, however, slight (Rowe 1996a, p. 199).

Why is this important? Because if there is even a single world where every person has some imperfection, then there's no world that contains a being with maximal greatness. Why not? Because if there's a world where some being has maximal greatness, then that being has maximal excellence in every world. However, a being with maximal excellence doesn't have any imperfections. If the "possibility" that Rowe proposes really is possible, then the first premise of Plantinga's argument is false.

Now "being in less than perfect company" certainly sounds like a possible property. To begin with, it's logically consistent to assume that we're in less than perfect company, though that's not enough to settle the issue. However, we can say more. As many people see it, the evils we find in this world makes it at least reasonable to suspect that this world is one in which we are in less than perfect company. That's why the **Argument from Evil** (see Chapter 9) is a challenging problem. And even if the evil in our world can be explained, it's not difficult to imagine worlds quite a bit worse than ours, where the amount of evil would be devilishly hard to reconcile with God's existence. It's hard to see why we should doubt that the range of possible worlds has this sort of variety. Put another way, if we don't know that "being in less than perfect company" is possible, then do we know enough about possibility to know that a nonphysical, omnipotent, omniscient, perfectly good being is possible? What could make believing this more reasonable than believing that it's possible to be in less than perfect company?

Plantinga could reply that what's possible and impossible isn't just obvious. However, that would cut both ways, which is why we wouldn't expect Plantinga to say it. It's at least as puzzling that maximal greatness is possible as that being in less than perfect company is *not* possible. At the very least, this would seem to impose a burden of proof on Plantinga: tell us why these seeming possibilities really aren't possible after all, and do it in a way that doesn't amount to simply asserting that maximal greatness is possible. Otherwise, it's not clearly rational to accept Plantinga's first premise.

7 EPILOGUE

The Ontological Argument, in all of its forms, is deeply fascinating even if it's flawed. Plantinga's version is generally agreed to be the most sophisticated but, as we have seen, even it has its problems. The problems with Plantinga's argument help explain why someone who rejects

It is possible that God exists necessarily.

need not simply be trying to avoid Anselm's conclusion. The point doesn't just apply to atheists like the one discussed in Section 6.2. Even someone who believes that an omnipotent, omniscient, perfectly good being exists in the actual world might balk at the idea that every possible world must contain such a being. Such people would presumably say that they do believe in God, but that God couldn't be quite what Anselm or Malcolm or Plantinga take him to be. In fact, such people might even say that this amounts to a proof that necessary existence is not a perfection. After all, if they're right, it's something that God couldn't possibly possess and it would be a peculiar perfection that couldn't apply to God.

AT A GLANCE: THE ONTOLOGICAL ARGUMENT

1. Anselm's Ontological Argument
   - The argument is a reductio.

     Premise #1: God is a being than which nothing greater can be conceived.
     Premise #2: We understand the words, "A being than which nothing greater can be conceived."
     Premise #3: Whatever is understood is in the understanding (mind).
     Premise #4: Therefore, a being than which nothing greater can be conceived exists in the understanding (from 2 and 3).

Premise #5: Either a being than which nothing greater can be conceived exists in the understanding but not in reality, or a being than which nothing greater can be conceived exists both in the understanding and in reality.

Premise #6: Assume (to show false by *reductio*) that a being than which none greater can be conceived exists in the understanding but not in reality.

    (a) A being than which nothing greater can be conceived can be thought to exist in reality.

    (b) Existing in reality and in the understanding is greater than existing in the understanding alone.

    (c) A being than which nothing greater can be conceived (if it exists in the understanding alone) is not a being than which nothing greater can be conceived, for another being greater than it can be conceived—namely, the same being that exists in reality. A contradiction results from the original assumption, allowing us to conclude that it is false.

Conclusion: Therefore, a being than which nothing greater can be conceived (God) exists in the understanding and in reality (from 4, 5, and 6c).

2. Existing in the Understanding
   - We can replace talk of "existing in the understanding" with talk of concepts.
   - The question becomes, is the concept of a being that lacks existence as great as the concept of a being that also actually exists?

3. The Perfect Island
   - Gaunilo: Anselm's argument if correct, would prove the existence of an island than which none greater can be conceived.
   - Possible reply: "the island than which none greater can be conceived" is not a coherent concept.

4. Is Existence a Perfection?
   - Kant: existence is not a predicate (quality or property).
   - If so, then existence is not a perfection, and so it does not make God greater.

5. The Anselm/Malcolm Argument
   - Defines God as (in one sense) a necessary being.
   - A being than which none greater can be conceived would have be so great that its nonexistence is inconceivable.

   5.1. Necessary Existence a Predicate
      - Necessary existence seems to be a predicate.
      - If we are told that something exists necessarily, we know something about it (for example, not an ordinary space-time object).

5.2. Some philosophers doubt that anything exists necessarily. It's difficult to find clear examples. Numbers might qualify but some philosophers (Nominalists) argue that mathematics doesn't require the literal existence of numbers.

5.3. Definitions and Concepts

- Kant: even if "God exists necessarily" is a matter of definition, we can still say that God doesn't exist by "rejecting the subject."
- Malcolm: this is like saying, "If God exists (and it's possible that he doesn't), then he exists necessarily," a seeming implicit contradiction.
- Reply: if the word "possible" in parentheses is understood in the epistemic sense and the word "necessary" is understood in the metaphysical sense, the appearance of contradiction goes away.

6. To assess the ontological argument fully, we need to explore concepts from modal logic—possibility and necessity.

6.1. Possibility in the Metaphysical Sense

- Something is metaphysically possible if it could be or could have been true.

6.2. Possible Worlds

- Something is possible if it's true in at least one possible world.
- Something is necessary if it's true in all possible worlds.
- This entails that if God is by definition a necessary being, then if it's possible that God exists, God does exist.
- Possible reply: God as Anselm and Malcolm understand God is not a possible being; an omnipotent, omniscient, and omnibenevolent being is a possible being, but not a necessary being.

6.3. Plantinga's Argument

- Define "maximally excellent being" relative to a given world: a being that possesses all perfections in that world.
- Define "maximally great being" as one that possesses maximal excellence in every world.

Premise #1: It's possible that a maximally great being exists.
Premise #2: If it's possible that a maximally great being exists, then such a being actually exists.
Conclusion: Therefore, a maximally great being actually exists.

- Explanation of Premise 2: a maximally great being has maximal excellence and hence exists in every world (is necessary). See Heading 6.2 above.

6.4. Rowe's Objection

- Plantinga doesn't say he can prove that a maximally great being is possible.
- However, he thinks it's reasonable to believe this.
- Rowe objects that it's not obviously reasonable. It would rule out a possible world where every being is flawed to at least some degree.

WEB RESOURCES

You can read Anselm's Ontological Argument online at http://www. fordham.edu/halsall/source/anselm.html.

Kant's argument is available at http://www.fordham.edu/halsall/basis/ anselm-critics.html#KANT.

A survey of the Ontological Argument can be found in the Stanford Encyclopedia of Philosophy: http://plato.stanford.edu/entries/ ontological-arguments/.

There is also a survey in the Internet Encyclopedia of Philosophy at http://www.iep.utm.edu/o/ont-arg.htm#H4.

CHAPTER 5

Miracles

Miracle stories are found in almost all religions, but the eighteenth-century philosopher David Hume argued that the evidence for believing in a miracle could never be good enough. This chapter examines the problems and prospects for establishing the existence of miracles.

On January 28, 2003, at about four o'clock in the afternoon, Luis Nivelo, a Christian from Ecuador, was cutting fish in a market in a Hasidic Jewish community north of Manhattan. He picked up a 20-lb carp but before he could club it, it started to speak. Mr. Nivelo couldn't understand what the fish was saying, but needless to say he was shocked to hear it talk at all. He called for the shop's owner, Zalmen Rosen. The fish was speaking Hebrew, Mr. Rosen reported. It prophesied the end of the world. It told Mr. Rosen to go and pray. It identified itself as the soul of a local man who had died a year ago. Mr. Rosen frantically tried to kill the carp but ended up whacking his own thumb with the knife and was taken away in an ambulance. After all that, Mr. Nivelo butchered the *wundercarp* before it could enlarge upon its astonishing utterances.

In the spirit of full disclosure, *The New York Times* reporter who wrote the story didn't witness any of it himself and doesn't exactly endorse the idea that the fish really spoke (*The New York Times*, March 15, 2003, Late Edition–Final, Section A, p. 1). However, there's every reason to believe that two witnesses would claim otherwise, though Mr. Nivelo can't vouch personally for what the fish was saying.

Miracle stories raise lots of questions but we can boil them down to two: are miracles possible? And supposing they are, could we ever be in a good position to believe one had happened? Let's start with the first question.

1 ARE MIRACLES POSSIBLE?

The fish story is, well, fishy. Other miracle stories have commanded more respect, but if some philosophers are right, miracles are simply impossible. The problem is supposed to be that miracles are exceptions to natural laws, and natural laws by definition can't have exceptions.

David Hume, the eighteenth-century Scottish philosopher, offered the definition that lies behind most modern discussions of miracles. Hume writes that a miracle is

> a transgression of a law of nature by a particular volition of the Deity (Hume 1975, henceforth, *Enquiry*, p. 115).

In other words, a miracle is something that would happen only if God intervened and overrode a natural law. What's a natural law? According to one influential view, at the very least it's a regularity with no exceptions. For example, it's a law that copper conducts electricity. On the regularity view, this means that every single piece of copper conducts electricity when a current is applied to it. But now put these definitions together. A miracle is a transgression or violation of a natural law; that would make it an exception to the law. But by the definition on offer, laws of nature can't have exceptions. If all this is correct, the very idea of a miracle is a contradiction.

Think about it. For all this argument says, God might have raised Jesus from the dead. It's just that if he did, we wouldn't be able to call it a miracle because it wouldn't actually be a law that people never rise from the dead. This is silly. If the Resurrection really happened, it should count as a miracle on any reasonable definition. The best solution is the obvious one. The laws of nature we should say, are laws of *nature*—regularities that hold when there's no intervention from outside nature. If there's a God who created nature, then a miracle would be something that happens when God overrides the laws of created nature. Whether we call divine interventions "exceptions" to the laws or not, the laws of nature won't rule them out because the laws don't tell us what happens if God intervenes. (Mackie 1982, pp. 18–22 discusses this very clearly. For a more general discussion, see Hoffman and Rosenkrantz 1994, pp. 167–168.)

2 HUME'S "EVERLASTING CHECK"

It appears that we can't rule miracles out on purely "philosophical" grounds. Suppose someone reports a miracle. Could we ever have good reason to believe her? Hume thinks the answer is no. He writes:

> I flatter myself, that I have discovered an argument . . . which, if just, will, with the wise and learned, be an everlasting check to all kinds of superstitious delusion (*Enquiry*, p. 110).

What Hume seem to mean—or what he's often taken to mean—is that his argument will forever rule out the possibility of any reasonable person accepting a report of a miracle. If that's right, it's an impressive accomplishment. How does Hume make his case?

2.1 Hume's Argument

Imagine you hear a supposed eyewitness report of something so strange that it appears to contradict the laws of nature. What should you think? Here's Hume's answer:

> . . . as a firm and unalterable experience has established these laws, the proof against a miracle, from the very nature of the fact, is as entire as any argument from experience can possibly be imagined (Enquiry, p. 114).

Notice that Hume isn't just saying, "miracles are very unlikely, and so you should be careful about believing miracle stories." That might be true (though there's more room to argue than Hume admits) but it would hardly be a reason for Hume to boast that he's found "an everlasting check." In Hume's view, if someone says she's seen a miracle, then at the very least she's saying that she's seen something that violates a law of nature; otherwise, it wouldn't deserve to be called a miracle. When are we justified in counting something as a law of nature? According to Hume, only when no exceptions have ever been found anywhere, at any time, in any circumstances. Miracles aren't just unlikely; in Hume's view, they are extraordinarily improbable.

Hume uses the word "proof" for this sort of evidence and his point is that we can't seriously call something a miracle unless we also agree that the prior evidence against it amounts to a proof in this sense. This appears to put the believer in a dilemma, as J. L. Mackie points out (Mackie 1982, p. 25). He wants to convince us that a miracle really has occurred. However, by the logic of his own position, he must insist that any supposed miracle violates a law of nature. As Hume sees it, this means he has to agree that, apart from the testimony, what he wants us to believe is remarkably, exceedingly improbable.

Where does this leave us? In a famous passage, Hume gives gave us an illustration:

> When anyone tells me, that he saw a dead man restored to life, I immediately consider with myself, whether it be more probable, that this person should either deceive or be deceived, or that the fact, which he relates, should really have happened . . . If the falsehood of his testimony would be more miraculous, than the event which he relates; then, and not till then, can he pretend to command my belief or opinion (*Enquiry*, p. 116).

Once again, a miracle is a violation of a law of nature and the raising of the dead would surely count. We aren't justified in counting something as a law of nature unless we have a "proof" that it's true—extensive and completely uniform evidence. In Hume's view, this means that apart from the testimony, the probability that the miracle occurred is extremely low. Now add the testimony to the evidence. If the witness is careful enough and reliable enough, you might think it's very unlikely that he's wrong. The question is, how unlikely? Hume agrees that if witnesses like this one had been found to be completely reliable in all circumstances, we would have a "proof" that such a witness is never wrong. In that case, it would be "proof against proof" and the stronger proof would win.

Strictly speaking, Hume allows that we could find ourselves in a position to agree that a miracle had occurred. However, the rest of his chapter on miracles reads much more like an extended argument that this will never happen. According to Hume, the history of miracle stories is a history of gullibility, deceit, and wide-eyed wonder. Miracle stories typically come from uneducated and uncritical witnesses but even people of good sense have a love of the fantastic that leads them to believe amazing tales. Add to that the phenomenon of religious enthusiasm and outright fraud and the result is a long history of religious fantasy posing as fact. Given a choice between believing that a law of nature was violated and that someone is exaggerating, lying, or confused, Hume thinks it will be no contest for the careful thinker. It will all but certainly never be more likely that the miracle happened than that the witness is wrong.

2.2 Probability and Hume's Argument

For what is to come, we need to say a little more about **probability**. Suppose someone robbed the bank last night. One hypothesis is that Bill did it. The evidence is that his fingerprints are on the door of the safe. This might sound significant until we learn that Bill works in the bank. His fingerprints would likely be on the safe whether or not he's the thief. In the language of probability, the **conditional probability** that Bill's fingerprints are on the door given that he is the thief is essentially the same as the conditional probability of finding his prints there even if he's not the thief.

The evidence doesn't count very strongly against Bill. We'll say it has little or no **relevance** to the hypothesis that Bill is the thief. Intuitively, it wouldn't be surprising to find Bill's fingerprints on the safe even if he's not the thief. On the other hand, suppose that a set of fingerprints that match Sam's turn up there as well. Sam has no connection with the bank and no obvious good reason to be anywhere near the safe unless he is the thief. The probability of finding his prints on the safe given that he's *not* the thief is much lower than the probability of finding his prints given that he *is* the thief. In this case, finding Sam's prints there is surprising if he's not the thief. The evidence has high relevance and counts against Sam much more dramatically.

"Counts against" is one thing; "settles the matter" is another. We're trying to get a grip on the **posterior probability** that Sam is the thief— the probability, in light of the evidence, that he committed the crime. But to think about this, we need to think about the **prior probability** of our hypothesis. That is, we need to ask: suppose we didn't have this piece of evidence. How likely would we think the hypothesis was? Put another way, given our general background knowledge minus the evidence in question, how probable is the hypothesis?

Suppose the prior probability that Sam committed the robbery is very low. For example, imagine that he has no obvious motive (he's extremely rich) and has an excellent alibi for the time the robbery was committed (several witnesses say he was at a business meeting in another city). Then it would still be puzzling that those prints were on the safe but, all things considered, the evidence might not be good enough to make a case against him. The posterior probability might still be too low.

Using the concepts from this example, we can put Hume's argument in probabilistic terms. First, given that miracles are violations of laws of nature, the prior probability of any miracle story will be extremely low. Second, given a host of human tendencies—gullibility, love of wonder, dishonesty, and various others—people can be expected to tell miracle stories whether miracles are real or not. That means the relevance of testimony for miracles will be low. Combining the low relevance of the testimony and the low prior probability of the miracle hypothesis, Hume's argument is that the posterior probability will be low as well—testimony for a miracle will almost certainly never be good enough to convince a reasonable person. In brief,

1. The prior probability of any miracle is always low.
2. The relevance of testimony for the miracle is always low.
3. Therefore, the posterior probability of the miracle in light of the testimony is low.

This raises two important questions. First, is the relevance of testimony as low as Hume suggests? In other words, are witnesses as unreliable as Hume seems to believe? Second, do miracles always have low prior probability? We'll start with the first question.

3 WITNESSES

Let's agree that witnesses to miracles are often unreliable. If Hume's point were simply that we should proceed very carefully when we hear reports of miracles, we could all agree. However, Hume isn't just giving practical cautions. He claims that he found an "everlasting check," and he seems to think that it should convince any reasonable person never to believe a report of a miracle. The problem is that his points about witnesses are too general. For example, some people have made a career out of debunking the supernatural—The Amazing Randi, a former stage magician who has written books "supernatural" fraud, is a good example. People like this don't get caught up in religious enthusiasm; if anything, they might be accused of being hostile to any hint of the supernatural. If someone like this reported a miracle, Hume's cautions wouldn't apply nearly so straightforwardly.

Hume's broad-brush generalization about the unreliability of witnesses is an overstatement. We can all imagine witnesses who are sober, skilled, cautious, and fair-minded enough that if they reported a miracle, we'd take their testimony very seriously. However, the obvious reply is that miracles are so intrinsically improbable that even the best witnesses we could reasonably imagine wouldn't be good enough. And so we need to turn to the question of the improbability of miracles.

4 ARE MIRACLES IMPROBABLE?

Even if reliable witnesses to miracles are likely to be few and far between, it's hard to argue that there simply couldn't be. On the other hand, when we are asking about the prior probability of miracles, Hume might appear to be on more solid ground. Hume says that to be justified in counting something as a natural law, we must have wide-ranging and completely consistent experience in its favor. This seems to make it inevitable that miracles have very low prior probability. In fact, things aren't quite so simple.

4.1 Evidence for Laws and the Probability of Miracles

Imagine a world like the one pictured in parts of the Bible: God steps in often in ways that leave no room for misunderstanding. In a world like that, natural laws would still exist—including the ones that the miracles overrode. But in a world like that, there would be nothing improbable about miracles.

There's no paradox here. As we pointed out earlier, laws of nature are laws of *nature*. They tell us what happens when there's no supernatural intervention. Richard Otte puts it this way:

> Evidence for a law of nature will be evidence about how the world behaves when God does not intervene (Otte 1996, p. 153).

And as Otte reminds us, this tells us nothing about what would happen if God did intervene.

We can make a further point: the evidence for a law of nature tells us nothing about the probability of miracles. This is important. Hume sees evidence for laws of nature as automatically amounting to evidence against miracles. We think that's a mistake. In other words, we are saying that there is a flaw at the heart of Hume's argument. Evidence for laws of nature is evidence for what happens when God doesn't intervene, and that tells us nothing about how likely it is that God will intervene.

This point applies even if you think this world is very far from the sort of world that the Bible depicts. There could be strong reasons, perhaps combining theological argument and certain kinds of experience for thinking that certain kinds of miracles are very likely. Our point isn't that in fact anyone has such reasons; perhaps no one does. Our point is that Hume's reasoning is flawed. Knowing how nature behaves when God doesn't intervene doesn't imply anything at all about the likelihood of divine intervention.

4.2 Anything Goes?

Even if there's nothing in the concepts of natural laws and miracles that requires miracles to be improbable, Hume might still insist that the facts provide ample evidence for his conclusion. For example, he writes:

> It is no miracle that a man, seemingly in good health, should die on a sudden: because such a kind of death, though more unusual than any other, has yet been frequently observed to happen. But it is a miracle, that a dead man should come to life; because that has never been observed in any age or country (*Enquiry*, p. 115).

Hume might say the same thing about other miracles. He might say: we don't simply have "uniform experience" that things work a certain way when God doesn't intervene. We have uniform experience that God *doesn't* intervene—that laws of nature don't get overridden by supernatural powers, period.

Unfortunately, this won't do. As C. S. Lewis points out, Hume's resurrection example is a case of **begging the question**—of arguing from a premise that the opposition couldn't be expected to accept (Lewis 1947, ch. XIII). Many people believe that a dead man has come to life and Hume's mere insistence to the contrary isn't likely to change their minds.

4.3 Probabilities and Theoretical Arguments

There's a more general point. Suppose a scientist reports a new experimental result that contradicts a well-known principle of science. If we looked at things Hume's way, we'd have to say that in light of the "uniform experience" against the new result, what the scientist reports is remarkably unlikely. However, this is much too simple. Science takes some hypotheses more seriously than others—for example, if the hypothesis would provide good explanations for things that are very puzzling otherwise, or if the hypothesis is simpler and more elegant than the alternatives. In general, what we'll call theoretical arguments sometimes raise the prior probability of a hypothesis.

The point goes beyond science. If there are good reasons to think God might exist, that raises the probability of miracles. The reasons don't need to amount to proof. Suppose someone thinks that if God exists, the probability is, say, 95% that there would be at least some miracles. As it happens, she thinks it's more likely than not that God doesn't exist, but she still think the arguments and evidence for God can't simply be dismissed. For example, suppose she puts the probability of God's existence at 10%. Suppose she also believes that *assuming* God's existence, the probability of a miracle occurring is 95%. Then the rules of probability require her to say that the probability of God existing and a miracle occurring is almost 10% (10% of 95% is 9.5%). Since a miracle is an act of God (no God, no miracle), this gives the probability that at least some miracles will occur. For those who like formulas, the rules of probability say

$$\text{prob (God exists)} \times \text{prob (miracles occur/God exists)}$$
$$= \text{prob (miracles occur \& God exists)}$$

Using the numbers from our example, we get

$$10\% \times 95\% = 9.5\%$$

Different people might assess the probabilities in different ways, but the point remains that even a religious skeptic could think that miracles aren't wildly improbable. It will depend on how unlikely she thinks God's existence is, and on how likely she thinks miracles would be *if* God exists.

5 WHAT IF MIRACLES ARE IMPROBABLE?

All we've argued so far is that Hume's arguments for the improbability of miracles don't do their job. Someone might still think that there are better arguments elsewhere. In any case, even if someone were persuaded that miracles overall aren't desperately improbable, the probability of any particular miracle story might be very low. Take the fish story we started with, for example. What if we take that point of view and assume that Hume was correct—that miracles have a very low prior probability? We'll explore that question in this section, and we should acknowledge from the start that our discussion owes a very large debt to John Earman's book, *Hume's Abject Failure*, and to Jordan Howard Sobel's essay, "On the Evidence of Testimony for

Miracles: A Bayesian Interpretation of David Hume's Analysis," found in *The Philosophical Quarterly* 37 (1987).

5.1 Lotteries and Low Probabilities

Even when a hypothesis has low prior probability, it might be very easy for testimony to establish the hypothesis. As commentators on Hume pointed out in the nineteenth century, lotteries are a good example. Suppose a lottery has a million tickets. You read in the newspaper that the winning ticket was #387,542. The prior probability of that ticket winning is only 1 in 1 million, but you believe the newspaper without skipping a beat. Shouldn't Humean-style reasoning lead us to be more skeptical?

The answer is no. Suppose you are the one who holds ticket #387,542. You read the paper and you're trying to decide whether you should believe the paper. If #387,542 really is the winner, it's very likely that the paper would report it; getting a six-digit number right isn't very difficult. But what if #387,542 isn't the correct number? Newspapers make mistakes of course, but we would expect those mistakes to be more-or-less random and not to be biased in favor of certain numbers. The probability that the newspaper would report #387,542 if it isn't the correct number is very low; after all, there are 999,999 different ways to go wrong. This low probability offsets the low prior probability that your ticket was the winner. The math works out. Suppose that on average, the paper transcribes a lottery number incorrectly one time in a 1000. There's nothing special about your number, and so given what you read in the paper, the chances are 999 out of 1000 that you really are the winner. (Readers can consult Sobel for mathematical details.)

5.2 Why Prior Probability Matters for Miracles: A Probability Fable

The lottery example shows that even if prior probabilities are low, testimony could easily produce a high posterior probability. But lotteries are a bad model for miracles. Imagine two countries, Wonderland and Glumdom. In both countries, there are plenty of miracle stories. However, Wonderland is blessed by the gods; real miracles are common there. The gods are less kind to Glumdom; real miracles are far scarcer there. The two countries cooperate on theological affairs and they share a certain official, the Miracle Checker. Her job is to investigate miracle claims. In Wonderland, let's imagine that fully half of the cases that look like miracles really are. (We're imagining this from the point of view of the gods, who actually know, as opposed to the point of view of the Wonderlanders, who can be mistaken.) In Glumdom, however, only one such case in 1,000 is a real miracle.

To make things easy to follow, we'll assume that the Miracle Checker is never wrong about a real miracle: the conditional probability is 100% that X is a miracle given that the Miracle Checker says it is. Nonetheless, she makes occasional mistakes in dealing with cases that only look miraculous—frauds, psychosomatic cures, hidden forces of nature, and so on. Specifically, given a fake miracle, she mistakes it for the real thing one time out of 100. Now suppose that the Miracle Checker investigates 1,000 miracle claims in Wonderland. What would we expect from a "god's-eye" perspective? First, we'd expect that there would be about 500 real miracles in the lot and that she'd correctly identify all of them. Of the other 500 cases, we'd expect her to misidentify 5 of them as real miracles. (One out of 100 equals 5 out of 500.) That means that she would report 505 miracles, of which 500 would be genuine. In Wonderland, when the Miracle Checker declares something to be a miracle, the chance that she's right is 500/505, or about 99%.

Suppose she also investigates 1,000 miracle claims in Glumdom. We would expect that one of these would be real and that she would spot it. Of the remaining 999, we would expect her to guess incorrectly that 10 of them are real miracles. (10% of 999 is 9.99—close enough to 10.) In other words, she would report 11 miracles, of which only one would be real. In Glumdom, when the same Miracle Checker declares something to be a miracle, the chance that she's right is only 1 out of 11, or about 9%.

What's the difference? Not the Miracle Checker—she's the same person using the same skills. The difference is the prior probability of a miracle. The lower that probability, the harder it is for her testimony to make the miracle believable. Why isn't this case like the lottery case? Suppose that #387,542 isn't the winner. What's the chance that the paper would say that it is? Because there are so many ways to go wrong, the answer is: very low. But when the Miracle Checker is investigating a report of something that—as the gods know—isn't really a miracle, there is essentially only one way for her to go wrong: by saying that it really is a miracle. Whether she says this depends only on her skills at diagnosing miracles. Even if those skills are good, enough fake miracles will make for a high rate of "false positives"—of cases where she says that something is a miracle when it isn't. So Hume is right about this much: prior probability does matter when it comes to miracles.

5.3 Clouds of Witnesses: The Power of Independent Testimony

In some ways, our fiction is too fictitious. Expecting one miracle report out of 1,000 to be true is wildly optimistic, especially for spectacular miracles like resurrections. Suppose we agree and, for the sake of a number, suppose we think the prior probability of a resurrection story being true is only 1 in 1 quadrillion. (That's 1 in 1,000,000,000,000,000.) Suppose our Miracle Checker investigates an apparent resurrection. Once again, to keep things simple, imagine that if the resurrection is real, she would certainly say so, and as before, if it's not, the chance that she would make a mistake and say that it is comes to 1 in 100. Given her testimony, what's the probability that a resurrection really occurred?

The answer is about 1 in 10 trillion. That's still low, though it's quite a bit better than 1 in 1 quadrillion. But suppose that we get an independent report of the same miracle from an equally skilled miracle checker. Now what's the probability? Because we've already got some positive evidence, we have a new probability of 1 in 10 trillion to replace the old prior probability of 1 in 1 quadrillion, and that's where the new calculation begins. The new answer is about 1 in 100 billion. Once again, this is low but you may be able to see the trend. In fact, if we had a total of eight such independent reports, the probability would rise from a measly 1 in 1 quadrillion to over 90%.

Here's a simple way to think about it. The chance that one miracle checker would make a mistake when confronted with a bogus miracle is 1 in 100. That's not high, but given how common bogus miracles are, it means that one bit of testimony will never be good enough. The chance that eight different miracle checkers would make this same mistake is vastly lower. It's $.01^8$, which is 1 in 10 quadrillion. In Hume's language, it would be a greater "miracle" if all these witnesses were wrong than if the miracle itself actually happened. Whether this counts against Hume or simply illustrates his overall point about needing to decide which would be the greater "miracle," it's intriguing how quickly independent reports could raise the posterior probability.

Of course, it's unrealistic to imagine that a reasonable witness would correctly identify all miracles. Perhaps it's also unrealistic to assume that a real miracle checker would only mistake one non-miracle out of 100 for the real thing. Suppose our miracle checker reports real miracles as miracles only 90% of the time and mistakes a bogus miracle for a real one 5% of the time. If 13 independent witnesses with these credentials testified to the resurrection miracle described above, that would raise the probability to 95%. The basic point is the same: it's highly unlikely that a large number of skilled people would independently make the same mistake.

Of course, skilled independent witnesses might be difficult to find, but that's not the point. Hume's argument is supposed to be an "everlasting check," and so we're asking a question on principle: *could* testimony establish a miracle? In principle, with enough witnesses, the answer is yes.

Hume wouldn't disagree that this is true in principle. Still, it may be surprising that even with very low prior probabilities, a relatively small number of independent witnesses could provide good reason for thinking a miracle had occurred.

6 MIRACLE AGAINST MIRACLE

Even if miracles are very improbable and even if the skills of witnesses are limited, it's at least possible that enough testimony could make it likely that a miracle had occurred. However, Hume makes a further argument. Different religions use different miracle stories to support their doctrines. If two religions disagree fundamentally, they can't both be correct. As Hume sees it, this means that miracle stories from conflicting religions cancel one another out. According to Hume, it's as though a judge hears testimony from two witnesses who say that Murphy committed a crime and two other witnesses who claim that Murphy was a hundred miles away when it happened.

Witnesses might disagree but that doesn't mean all the witnesses are equally believable. The miracle stories of religion X could be much more credible than the ones on behalf of religion Y. More importantly, Hume's courtroom analogy contains a flaw. If Biff says that Benny stole the diamonds and Bud says he didn't, the two stories contradict one another. If a Hindu miracle tale says that Jasbir was miraculously cured of his illness and a Christian story says the same thing about Jedediah, the two stories don't conflict. Both could be true.

Whether a genuine miracle happened is one thing, but whether a particular religion gives the best explanation for it is another. The connection between miracles and religious doctrines is not as tight as Hume's argument requires. Suppose someone was convinced that Jesus rose from the dead. From there to the core doctrines of Christianity is a long way. You could believe in the Resurrection without believing in the doctrines of the Incarnation (Jesus was literally God made flesh) or the

Trinity (God is three persons in one being). Miracles and their detailed interpretations aren't the same. A real miracle in a Hindu setting doesn't exclude an equally real miracle in a community of Jews. All that's ruled out is that the correct interpretation of one miracle should be inconsistent with the correct interpretation of the other.

Hume might insist on a different point: using a miracle story as evidence for a particular religion is a problem if competing religions offer equally credible miracle stories. We can agree with this, but it doesn't undermine the point that real miracles could occur and even be known to occur in different religious contexts. It could be clear that something *is* a miracle even when it's not clear what the best detailed theology might be.

7 MIRACLES AND "MIRACLES": ANOTHER FABLE

A related point bears further discussion. A miracle isn't just an event that goes against what we expect of nature. On the definition we've been using, it's an act of God. On our definition, if you agree that something is a miracle, you've agreed that a supernatural being exists. However, for any strange happening, it's always at least possible that instead of being a miracle, it's a result of natural processes that we don't understand. That means there are two hurdles to establishing a miracle: making the case that the unusual event happened at all, and making the case that if it did, it was an act of God.

Some philosophers have suggested that we should always prefer a natural explanation to a supernatural one, but this isn't obviously so. The question is what makes the most sense of things overall, and the answer could be that a theological explanation is the best one. Suppose the ruler of a certain country is a brutal dictator who requires his subjects to worship him as a god. Most people are afraid of the dictator and at least outwardly they do as he says. However, a small sect of peaceful religious resisters refuses to go along with the dictator's demands.

As time passes, the resisters gain sympathy. More and more people refuse to worship the dictator. Finally, he has the three leaders arrested and has their trial broadcast on television. He allows reporters and camera crews from respected news organizations around the world to film the events. The leaders are charged with treason and sedition. They are told that unless they renounce their faith and worship the dictator, they will be burned alive in a blast furnace. When they refuse, the dictator's minions shackle and bind them. As millions of horrified people watch on their televisions, the three leaders are tossed into a furnace so hot that even their captors are severely burned. But as the cameras reveal and witnesses later testify, the leaders don't die. Instead, viewers see images of the resisters praying among the flames. In their midst is a fourth figure, an angelic being, praying with them and comforting them. The dictator is stunned. He orders the furnace shut down. The three leaders emerge calm and unharmed as the dictator falls on the floor, weeping and begging forgiveness.

Some readers will recognize the story as a modernized version of the tale of Shadrach, Meshach, and Abednego from the biblical book of Daniel. That story might well be a legend, and ours is an admitted fiction; however, two points stand out. First, as we've told the story, faking the events would be extremely difficult. Second, if you became convinced that the events really took place, there would be nothing perverse about interpreting them as miraculous. In fact, someone might well say that our story would so obviously be a miracle that looking for a naturalistic explanation would be perverse. We'll settle for the more modest claim: seeing the events as a miracle would be perfectly reasonable—a case of supernatural intervention in the natural world.

8 SMALL WONDERS

Perhaps the story of Shadrach, Meshach, and Abednego has a real-world counterpart, but a reasonable person might well have doubts. In fact, a reasonable person might think that no scriptural miracles are beyond reasonable doubt. As for modern miracle stories, what we tend to get are doubtful healings, weeping statues, talking fish. In fact, we're willing to concede: so far, there have been no miracle stories that can't be reasonably doubted. That's different from saying that none can reasonably be believed, but it might make the theoretical victory over Hume's arguments seem hollow.

In light of this, we can ask how miracles fit into the scheme of things for believers. Occasionally, philosophers talk as though someone hears of something remarkable, decides it's real, and reasons that it could only make sense if God exists. Perhaps some people come to religion this way but many don't. For example, we doubt that many people read the story of the Resurrection, consider the evidence objectively, decide that the story is true, convert to Christianity, and proselytize by inductive argument.

Some believers are leery of miracles and tend not to take the classical miracle stories of their own religions literally. Interestingly, even these believers tend to believe in a God who acts in the world. This might or might not be puzzling, but two questions are worth asking here: what does believing in a God who acts in the world mean, and does this entail believing in miracles?

Our answer to the first question won't be very precise. People who believe in a God who's active in the world often tend to see at least parts of their lives in terms of gentle nudges, holy coincidences, moments of grace. The things that happen to them—at least some of the time—seem to be more than chance. It might be a compelling insight, a danger averted, or meeting the right person at just the right time. Whatever it is, it will seem to have meaning.

This sort of thing seems different from the clearly miraculous in at least two ways. First, cases like this are well within the power of unaided nature. This introduces a complication into the notion of a miracle. What if something is of a sort that could have happened naturally but wouldn't have happened on this occasion if God hadn't intervened? That could still amount to a divine intervention in the natural order, but it's not what people usually have in mind when they think of a miracle.

The second difference is that believers usually think of a miracle as a clear sign from God. The sorts of small events we're talking about aren't like that. Any particular example could be chance. Even the believer might agree that, taken one event at a time, it would be impossible to be sure what simply happened and what revealed the hand of God. Overall, however, the believer sees something more than mere randomness. Think of an abstract expressionist painting. Many of the details—a splash of paint exactly here or just this shape there—might be matters of chance. Some things could differ without significantly changing the whole. But overall, the pattern of shapes and colors is no fluke. This is the way some believers see the world. It's also a way that some people come to be believers. Gradually, they come to feel that something lies behind the episodes of ordinary life. Belief in God gives them a way of making sense of how things seem.

This has implications for the discussion of miracles. Miracles if there are any, are part of a broader range of religiously significant events. Some might be striking cases natural laws being overridden. Some might be seemingly natural events that actually are divine interventions. And some might really be natural events, but natural events whose seeds and meaning were built into the universe from the beginning. Full-blown miracles may not be as religiously important as is sometimes thought. The believer's sense may be that God doesn't perform stunts. A believer might expect grand miracles to be rare. Nonetheless, someone who sees the world in terms of hints and whispers will approach the more central religious miracle stories differently than the skeptic does. If you gradually come to believe that your life makes a certain kind of sense, this might shift your prior probabilities; it might make you more open to the possibility that some full-blown miracles aren't so unlikely after all. Two people who start from different places might see the same evidence very differently.

9 CONCLUDING UNSATISFYING POSTSCRIPT

The sense that things make sense has plenty of problems. We tend to project patterns on events that really are random, as various psychological experiments have shown. However, at least in the natural realm, not all pattern detection is projection. Sometimes events do have patterns and sometimes we do detect them. The believer believes something similar. It would be nice to have a clean way to sort all this out, but there's no easy way to confirm or dismiss the believer's way of resolving the religious ambiguity of experience. Unfortunately, the problem of miracles is set against this background.

What then can we say? First, Hume's case against miracles is flawed. His common-sense cautions are reasonable but his more ambitious argument fails. His argument that miracles are by nature improbable is open to serious criticism. He doesn't pay enough attention to possible differences in credibility among witnesses and he doesn't seem to appreciate the way in which a relatively small number of good witnesses could provide strong reason for believing even something with very low prior probability. His argument that "competing" miracles from different religions cancel one another is fallacious. Whether John Earman is correct in describing Hume's efforts as an "abject failure," Hume's boast that he has found an "everlasting check" is an exaggeration.

Second, however, even if Hume's argument fails, this doesn't show that miracles are real. There is no substitute for proceeding case-by-case, even if most cases can be easily dismissed. Third, the evidence in particular cases will look different to different people and there is no simple way to sort out which starting points are better or worse. Doing that calls for combing though a lot of theological and philosophical argument and for paying careful attention to people's background experiences—including the sorts of religious experiences discussed in Chapter 6.

Finally, the conceptual territory around the very idea of a miracle is complicated and the complications matter. For those on both sides who would like things to be tidy, this will be a disappointment. What it shouldn't be is a surprise.

AT A GLANCE: MIRACLES

1. Defining Miracles
   - Problem: if laws of nature are exceptionless regularities and if miracles are exceptions to laws of nature, then miracles are impossible.
   - Solution: define laws of nature as regularities that hold when no intervention from outside nature occurs.
2. Hume's Position
   - Hume believed he had discovered "an everlasting check" against accepting reports of miracles.
   2.1. Hume's Argument
      1. A miracle is a violation of a law of nature.
      2. To count something as a law of nature, we need very strong evidence.
      3. A miracle is a violation of a law of nature.
      4. Therefore, for something to count as a possible miracle, the evidence against it must be very strong.
      5. The probability that a witness might be lying, exaggerating, or confused is always much higher than the probability that the law of nature was violated.
      6. Therefore, a witness's testimony can never make it likely that a miracle occurred.
   2.2. Hume's Argument in Probability Terms
      1. The prior probability of any miracle is always low.
      2. The relevance of testimony for the miracle is always low.
      3. Therefore, the posterior probability of the miracle in light of the testimony is always low.
3. Witnesses
   - Objection: Hume overstates the unreliability of witnesses.
   - Some potential witnesses are extremely careful and extremely unlikely to lie or exaggerate.
   - Reply: miracles are so improbable that even the best witnesses couldn't establish them.

4. Probability of Miracles
   - The claim that miracles are intrinsically improbable isn't as strong as it appears.
   4.1. Strong evidence for laws of nature doesn't automatically make miracles improbable:
      - A miracle is a supernatural intervention.
      - Laws of nature are regularities that occur apart from supernatural intervention.
      - Evidence for a law of nature is evidence based on how nature behaves when God doesn't intervene.
      - Therefore, evidence for laws of nature tells us nothing about how common miracles are.
   4.2. Hume Begs the Question
      - When he says that no one has ever seen a dead man come back to life, Christians will not agree.
   4.3. Theoretical Arguments
      - If there are good reasons to believe in God aside from miracles, then those reasons would raise the general probability of miracles.
5. What If Miracles Are Improbable?
   5.1. Lotteries
      - Witnesses can easily establish winning numbers in a lottery, even though the prior probability is low.
      - This is because the probability of mistakenly reporting any particular number is very low; for a given number, the chance of a "false positive" is low.
   5.2. Miracles
      - Low prior probabilities do matter in the case of miracles.
      - The reason is that if miracles are very rare, then even a skilled witness has a high probability of "false positives."
   5.3. Independent Witnesses
      - The combined testimony of independent witnesses can be powerful.
      - This is because the probability of all the witnesses being wrong is extremely low.
6. "Competing" Miracle Stories
   - Hume thinks that miracle stories from different religions cancel one another out.
   - This ignores the difference between the fact of a miracle occurring and the best religious explanation of the miracle.
   - Hume could still be right on a more limited point: using miracle stories from one religion as evidence for that religion is problematic if there are equally credible miracle stories from other religious traditions.

7. Establishing a Miracle
   - Establishing a miracle calls for two things:
     1. Establishing that the event in question actually occurred.
     2. Establishing that it was an act of God.
   - It's possible to describe cases that would do both.
8. A Broader Understanding of Miracles
   - In actual religious practice, large-scale miracles might not be terribly important.
   - A believer might think God can intervene in many ways:
     1. Obvious violations of natural laws.
     2. Events that might seem natural but are actually divine interventions.
     3. Natural events with religious significance "built into" nature.
9. Summary
   - Hume's case is flawed.
   - This doesn't show that miracles are real; we must proceed case-by-case.
   - How people assess the evidence will depend on their background assumptions.
   - The concept of the miraculous is more complicated than it might seem.

WEB RESOURCES

Hume's discussion of miracles is in Section X of his *Enquiry Concerning Human Understanding*, which can be found at http://www.etext.leeds.ac.uk/hume/ehu/ehupbsb.htm.

The Stanford Encyclopedia of Philosophy has a good summary discussion of miracles. Go to http://plato.stanford.edu/entries/miracles.

CHAPTER **6**

Religious Experience

Many people see religious experience as an important source of support for belief in God. Recently, a number of philosophers have argued that believers are entitled to take religious experience at face value, with the same attitude that we take toward seeing, hearing, and so on. Other philosophers think that the best way to explain the phenomenon of widespread religious experience is by positing the existence of God. We look at both approaches.

One of the most remarkable tales of determination, perseverance, and sheer courage is the story of Sir Ernest Shackleton's ill-fated attempt in the early years of the twentieth century to cross Antarctica. Before the trek overland could even begin, Shackleton and his men found their ship trapped in the polar ice of the Weddell Sea. Over a year later, Shackleton and a small crew set off in a 20-foot boat to sail the 800 miles from Elephant Island, where the rest of the crew waited to be rescued, to South Georgia Island. After a harrowing journey across the open sea, Shackleton and two of his crew walked over the mountains and the ice to the island's whaling station. In his memoir, Shackleton writes:

> When I look back at those day I have no doubt that Providence guided us, not only across those snow-fields, but across the storm-white sea that separated Elephant Island from our landing place on South Georgia. I know that during the long and racking march of thirty-six hours over the unnamed mountains and glaciers of South Georgia it seemed to me often that we were four, not three. I said nothing to my companions on

123

the point, but afterwards Worsley said to me, "Boss, I had a curious feeling on the march that there was another person with us." Crean confessed to the same idea. One feels "the dearth of human words, the roughness of mortal speech" in trying to describe things intangible, but a record of our journeys would be incomplete without a reference to a subject very near to our hearts (Shackleton 1998, p. 211).

Although Shackleton offers little interpretation beyond the word "Providence," most readers will identify what he reports as a religious experience. That will be our subject in this chapter. We'll ask what counts as religious experiences, how they might be explained, and what support they might provide for religious belief.

1 WHAT IS RELIGIOUS EXPERIENCE?

When we talk about religious experiences, we'll be talking about experiences that seem to the people who have them to reveal something about the nature of things. For example, it may seem to a person that an angel is speaking to her. Following Roderick Chisholm and Richard Swinburne, when we use the word "seems" here, what we mean is that the person is inclined to take the experience at face value—to say that an angel really is speaking to her. More generally, when it seems to someone in this sense that they are experiencing something, this means they are inclined to take the experience as **veridical**—as really revealing what it seems to reveal. Swinburne calls this the **epistemic** sense of the word "seems," the sense in which we take how things seem to be to tell us how they actually are. Whether any religious experiences actually are veridical is one of the issues we'll need to address.

1.1 Swinburne's Classification Scheme

Sometimes it seems to people that they are having an experience of the divine, to use Richard Swinburne's preferred term. Because we're especially interested in questions about the existence of God, we'll pay a lot of attention to these cases. Swinburne has provided a classification scheme for such experiences and many other philosophers have made use of Swinburne's way of sorting things out. Here are his five categories.

1. Experiencing the divine in ordinary, publicly observable objects. For example, someone might have the sense that she's seeing God's creative handiwork while looking at the sky or the sea. It's not a matter of taking the sky to be God but a sense of encountering God through the publicly observable object.

2. Experiencing the divine in some unusual, publicly observable object. Examples might include appearance of the Virgin Mary or an angel.

3. Experiencing the divine through private experiences that can be described in the ordinary language of the senses. Here dreams might provide examples. The dream can be described in the language of shape, color, sound, and so on. But sometimes, both while in the midst of the dream and after waking up, the dreamer has the strong sense of having encountered the divine.

4. Experiencing the divine through private sensations that can't be described in ordinary vocabulary. By their very nature, such experiences would be hard to convey. As Swinburne characterizes them, it's as though the person having the experience had a "sixth sense." Imagine a member of a society of deaf people who suddenly develops a sense of hearing. She would be aware of a new kind of sensation that she would have no vocabulary for describing. Perhaps this is as close as we can come to capturing what Swinburne has in mind.

Some authors take Swinburne to be talking about experiences of the presence of God. Peterson et al. quotes St. Teresa of Avila:

> I saw Christ at my side—or, to put it better, I was conscious of him, for neither with the eyes of my body nor with those of the soul did I see anything (Petersen et al. 2003, p. 18).

Teresa insists that nonetheless Christ was beside her, watching all that she did. The experience that Shackleton and his crew had might also fit in this category.

Swinburne's fifth category is the most rarified of all:

5. Experiencing the divine without any sensations at all. Swinburne writes:

> It seems to the subject, perhaps very strongly, that he is aware of God or of a timeless reality or some such thing, and yet not because he is having certain sensations; it just so seems to him, but not through his having sensations (Swinburne 1979, p. 251).

Just how this differs from the fourth category is not easy to say. If the awareness is "like" something—that is, if it has a distinctive "feel"—then what it is "like" might well count as the sensation, even if we find it impossible to describe. If the awareness isn't "like" anything, then the difference between this category and simply having a strong belief isn't clear.

2 AN ARGUMENT FROM RELIGIOUS EXPERIENCE?

Many philosophers have talked about arguments from religious experience. The idea is that religious experience provides premises for an explicit argument that God exists. However, a number of philosophers have rejected this way of understanding religious experience. If you open your eyes and seem to see a tree, you simply believe that there's a tree in front of you. You don't reason to this conclusion and you don't think any sort of reasoning is necessary. For many people, that's how beliefs based on religious experience are. It's not a question of reasoning from experience; it's a question of seeming to experience the divine and simply forming a belief—that God is present, or is comforting you, or is perhaps unhappy with something you've done. As many philosophers see it, this is a perfectly appropriate way to respond to a religious experience.

Michael Martin objects. He thinks this confuses two things: how a belief is arrived at and what justifies it. He writes:

> For example, in order to be able to justify my spontaneous perceptual belief that there is a brown table in front of me, it would seem necessary in principle to be able to argue thus: Spontaneous beliefs of a certain sort occurring under certain conditions are usually true, and my belief that there is a brown table in front of me is of this sort and occurs under these conditions. Consequently, my belief is probably true (Martin 1990, p. 156).

Let's unpack this a bit. Suppose you are in normal light, not having ingested any strange substances, and not having any known tendencies to hallucination, and you have the sense that you are seeing a brown table. As a result, you find yourself *believing* that there is a brown table in front of you. That would be an example of a "spontaneous perceptual belief." But now suppose that for whatever reason, you feel the need to justify your spontaneous perceptual belief—to make the case that it's reasonable to believe that there really is a table in front of you. Martin is saying that to do this, you would have to maintain that this sort of spontaneous perceptual belief—roughly, one that you form by looking around in "normal" conditions—is usually true. Because this particular belief is of that general sort, you would argue that it is probably true. According to Martin, the justification of beliefs based on religious experience would have to have a similar structure:

1. Religious beliefs formed in certain circumstances are usually true.
2. This particular religious belief was formed in those circumstances.
3. Therefore, this religious belief is probably true.

Whatever we make of the case of religious experience, what Martin has to say about ordinary perception seems more than a little odd. If for some reason you needed to justify your belief that you're seeing a table in front of you, perhaps you'd do it the way Martin suggests, but the real question is: when would you ever need to justify a belief like that? When would it be unreasonable for you to simply believe what you seem to see without bothering about the justification? Whatever the answer, the circumstances would clearly have to be very unusual. In the language of Chapter 7, beliefs that come on us spontaneously as a result of ordinary sensory experience seem to be clear cases of **properly basic beliefs**— beliefs that it's perfectly reasonable to hold without any argument at all. If this is right, then Martin's objection gets off on the wrong foot. We almost never need to justify our ordinary perceptual beliefs, and that is a very good thing. Most of us, including most philosophers, would have very little idea how to spell out the circumstances that usually hold when we have true perceptual beliefs. Very few philosophers would agree that this leaves such beliefs unjustified. Of course, whether the same can be said of beliefs based on religious experience is another matter.

3 NATURALISTIC EXPLANATIONS OF RELIGIOUS EXPERIENCE

In the next section, we'll begin to look closely at the idea that we can simply take religious experience at face value. Before that, we'll consider one common skeptical reaction to religious experience. It's not unusual to hear it said that religious experience can be explained in a completely natural, "scientific" way. In particular, there's considerable interest in explanations that tell us what occurs in the brain when people have religious experiences.

Suppose we could figure out the neural correlates of religious experience. Would this show that religious experience can't tell us anything about the divine? Would we have "reduced" religious experiences to mere brain events? The quick reply is that every experience is grounded in the brain, including ordinary perceptual experiences. That hardly shows that seeing, hearing, and so on can't tell us anything about the world outside our heads. Why should research that reveals the brain processes that underlie religious experience count against a religious understanding of those experiences?

The answer is that by itself, it doesn't. However, depending on the details, it could.

3.1 The God Helmet

Dr. Michael Persinger of Laurentian University has invented a gadget
that he claims can make many people have religious experiences. It's
essentially a football helmet decked out with strategically placed electro-
magnets that stimulate the brain's temporal lobes, and it's come to be
known as the "God Helmet." Persinger claims that a significant fraction
of the people he's experimented on have a **sense of presence** during the
experiment. Like Shackleton and his men, they feel as though some
unseen person is present. Many of his subjects find the experience deeply
significant. What's going on?

Here's a journalist's version of the underlying theory:

> Simplified considerably, the idea goes like so: When the right hemi-
> sphere of the brain, the seat of emotion, is stimulated in the cerebral
> region presumed to control notions of self, and then the left hemisphere,
> the seat of language, is called upon to make sense of this nonexistent
> entity, the mind generates a "sensed presence" (Hitt 1999).

We're in no position to assess the plausibility of this explanation. Instead,
we want to use the God Helmet as part of a **thought experiment**—an
imaginative attempt to explore a concept. Suppose that something like the
theory just sketched is correct. What, if anything, would that suggest?

First, notice that the theory tells us something about why people
who use the God Helmet should have the kind of experience they have.
The explanation is in terms of the functions of the affected areas of the
brain and their relationship to one another. It goes beyond merely setting up correlations and offers at least a sketch of an account of why the
experience feels the way it does.

Now suppose Persinger's technique is perfected to the point where
he can induce a sense of presence in 90% of people who put on the
God Helmet. Are people who have experiences of presence while using
the God Helmet having genuine experiences of the presence of God?
The answer could be yes; the fact that the experience was induced in
a lab doesn't prove otherwise. However, we're guessing that you won't
be drawn to that possibility. The experiences seem to be perfectly well
accounted for without supposing that they are veridical. Given what's
being done to the brain, we would expect people to have a sense of
presence even if no being is presenting itself at all.

By itself, this hardly threatens the claims of religious experience.
Even if the God Helmet were simply a reliable way of creating an

illusion, that wouldn't show that experiences of God's presence outside the lab are nonveridical. After all, suppose scientists find a reliable way to conjure up the sensation that you're seeing the Taj Mahal. It would hardly follow that people who go to Agra and seem to see the Taj Mahal are mistaken. In their case, the best explanation of the experience is that the Taj Mahal is a crucial cause of the brain state that underlies the experience. Likewise, the best explanation for spontaneous religious experiences could be that they're caused by God.

All the same, let's carry our fiction a little further. Suppose scientists come up with hypotheses about the kinds of natural conditions that can cause the sorts of brain changes that the God Helmet induces. Suppose that over time, evidence builds up that when people spontaneously have a sense of God's presence, one or more of these conditions is typically present. In that case, we'd have strong evidence for a purely natural account of religious experience—or at least of one kind of religious experience. What are the crucial features of the account we're imagining? Roughly, they are these five:

1. The account would tell us what goes on in the brain during the religious experience.
2. The account would explain why these neurological events should produce experiences of this particular sort.
3. The account would provide evidence that certain sorts of natural conditions can put the brain into the relevant states.
4. The account would set forth the mechanisms that explain how the natural conditions affect the brain.
5. The account would provide strong evidence that these natural conditions are typically present when people have religious experiences.

If we had all of this for a particular kind of religious experience, we'd have good reason to think that it could be explained without any talk of the supernatural. We'd have reason to believe that people would have these experiences whether or not a God exists.

3.2 Implications

What does our exercise in science fiction imply about religious experience as things stand now? The answer is: more or less nothing. In the case of experiences of God's presence, we don't have a good story that fits our five conditions. We have some tantalizing evidence relevant to (1) and (2) but very little that makes (3), (4), and (5) plausible (though the reader might want to look at Rick Strassman's *DMT: The Spirit Molecule*). However, our point wasn't to show that experiences of God's presence can actually be explained naturally. Our point was to say something about what such an explanation would be like if one were possible. At the same time, satisfying all of our five conditions clearly won't be easy, and we're not holding our breath waiting for it to happen.

4 TAKING RELIGIOUS EXPERIENCE AT FACE VALUE, PART I: RICHARD SWINBURNE

In what follows, we'll assume that there's no good naturalistic explanation of religious experience sitting on the horizon, and we'll turn to a major issue in the recent literature. Over the past two decades or so, philosophers have given a good deal of thought to the question of whether religious experience can be taken at face value in the way that, for example, seeming to see a tree typically can. In this section and the next, we'll look at what two philosophers, Richard Swinburne and William Alston, have to say on this question.

4.1 Swinburne's "Principle of Credulity"

Swinburne offers the following thought:

> [I]t is a principle of rationality that (in the absence of special consider-ations) if it seems (epistemically) to a subject that *x* is present, then probably *x* is present; what one seems to perceive is probably so (Swinburne *op cit*, p. 254).

He calls this the **Principle of Credulity** because it's a principle telling us when we should be "credulous," that is, when we should simply believe. We operate by something like this principle in most ordinary circumstances. For example, we believe that when someone seems to see a table in front of them, it's most likely because a table is really there. That means that when this happens to you, it's perfectly reasonable for you to believe that you really are seeing a real table.

What about apparent experiences of the divine? Here's what Swinburne says:

> [I]n the absence of special considerations, all religious experiences ought to be taken by their subjects as genuine, and hence as substantial grounds for belief in the existence of their apparent object—God, or Mary, or Ultimate Reality, or Poseidon (Swinburne *op cit*, p. 270).

For many, this will be a big jump. It's one thing to say that if we seem to see a table, it's reasonable to believe that a table really is there. It would be quite another thing to say that if we seem to be having a conversation with Poseidon, he's probably present.

Swinburne tries to deal with this sort of problem by offering four restrictions on the Principle of Credulity. According to Swinburne, the principle doesn't apply in any of the following situations:

1. Either the person reporting the experience isn't reliable (e.g., they are on drugs) or else the circumstances make the experience unreliable (e.g., the lighting produces illusions).
2. The person has often been wrong about the sort of thing they claim to experience (e.g., the person says they saw an oriole in a tree several hundred feet away, but they've typically been wrong about this sort of thing in the past).
3. What the person says they perceived very probably wasn't present or didn't happen (e.g., John claims to have seen David walking across the street, even though David has been paralyzed since birth).
4. Even if what the person claims to have seen was present, it probably didn't cause the perception (e.g., even though the president is actually in the hotel, the hotel is also the site of a convention of professional presidential impersonators and so, most likely, you saw one of them).

Swinburne argues that the atheist isn't in a good position to object to religious experience on any of these grounds. The discussion is quite detailed but we can capture its essence as follows:

- On Restriction 1: People who have religious experiences are not typically drug addicts or mentally disturbed.
- On Restriction 2: Short of actually proving that God doesn't exist, showing that people who have religious experiences usually aren't reliable about them would be difficult.
- On Restriction 3: Once again, this would call for showing that God very probably doesn't exist. The burden here is on the atheist.
- On Restriction 4: If God exists, then God is everywhere and underlies all cause and effect. That means (so says Swinburne) that if God exists, any apparent perception of God was caused by God.

4.2 The Principle of Credulity Assessed

The Principle of Credulity is an interesting starting point for thinking about knowledge and experience, but we need to be careful not to be credulous about the Principle itself. There's something right about the Principle, but it gets its credibility from ordinary experiences of publicly observable objects—the kinds of cases where it's possible to compare our own impressions with other people's and where doing so usually leads to substantial agreement. We'll call these "public experiences." Perhaps the Principle should be extended beyond public experiences but that's surely open to doubt, and Swinburne doesn't offer any arguments for thinking it should.

A more systematic look at Swinburne's five categories makes the problem clearer. Start with cases like sensing God's handiwork in the majesty of the heavens. If you are having an experience like that, your friend looking at the same sky might be having an experience of the meaningless of the material world. Is this the sort of case where we think that what a person seems to sense is probably real? If so, this isn't just obvious.

How about experiences of very unusual objects? Swinburne's own third restriction says we can't apply the Principle if what's reported is very unlikely to exist in reality. If the vision was of Queen Elizabeth I—who died in 1603—we wouldn't think the Principle of Credulity applied. Why should it apply if what the person seems to see is the Virgin Mary or a bush that burns without being consumed? Swinburne doesn't tell us.

As for Swinburne's remaining three categories, all of them have to do with private experiences—experiences that can't be straightforwardly checked by what other people experience. That isn't a problem by itself. If you feel that you have a headache, it's perfectly reasonable for you to believe that you do even though other people can't feel your headache. What makes Swinburne's final three categories different is that they are private experiences that are supposed to give information about reality outside your head. They are very different from the ordinary kinds of experiences that make the Principle of Credulity seem reasonable at first blush. The cynic might say that we wouldn't believe someone who said he sensed the presence of little green men on the far side of the Moon. Why should we believe him if he says he senses God?

Our point isn't that the cynic is correct. Our point is that there are some very obvious questions about just how far the Principle of

Credulity can be extended. Swinburne doesn't address these perfectly reasonable worries. William Alston offers an approach that avoids some of the difficulties that Swinburne faces. Section 5, which is somewhat more advanced, looks at what Alston has to say.

*5 TAKING RELIGIOUS EXPERIENCE AT FACE VALUE, PART II: WILLIAM ALSTON

William Alston explores what he calls non-sensory experiences of the presence of God, and so we're somewhere in the territory of Swinburne's fourth and fifth categories. The experiences of Shackleton and his men seem to fit this description, as do those described in the quote from St. Teresa of Avila. Alston thinks that such experiences aren't rare even if they're not altogether common, and he understands them as apparent direct awareness of God. Our discussion is based mainly on his book, *Perceiving God*.

*5.1 Doxastic Practices

One important difference between Swinburne and Alston is that Alston's view depends on the idea of a **doxastic practice**. The word "doxastic" comes from a Greek word meaning "opinion" or "belief," and the easiest way to explain the idea of a doxastic practice is by way of examples. Deductive reasoning is a doxastic practice; we use it to come up with new beliefs by reasoning from previously known facts. The practice consists in certain ways of making inferences, certain ways of checking inferences, and certain ways of criticizing them. Furthermore, deductive reasoning is a "socially established practice." It's been used for a very long time by many people who understand themselves to be doing the same sort of thing, subject at least broadly to the same rules.

There are many other doxastic practices. Two important examples are the use of memory as a source of information and the practice of gaining knowledge by sense perception. The use of sense perception is important enough that Alston gives it its own label: SP.

*5.2 Doxastic Practices and Rationality

Swinburne's Principle of Credulity would allow a lot of strange experiences to be taken at face value. For Alston, we don't even get what's called *prima facie* justification unless the experience fits into a socially established practice. In other words, without a connection to a socially established practice, we aren't entitled to treat the experience as reliable even in a preliminary way. Spontaneously feeling that you've being contacted by aliens from beyond the solar system isn't enough.

Alston uses the term "mystical practice" for the practice of forming beliefs about God on the basis of non-sensory experiences like St. Teresa's. His more specific interest is Christian mystical practice, or CMP for short. CMP is mystical practice within the framework of Christian ideas and beliefs, but a good deal of what Alston says can be generalized to other traditions.

The existence of an established tradition of criticizing and evaluating the outcomes of CMP is important for Alston's position. For example, Alston thinks broad agreement would be found among Christians that an apparent experience of God isn't genuine if it deals with trivial matters, or tends to make a person's character worse, or appears to involve God commanding something that's clearly immoral. Alton's two main claims are:

1. It's *prima facie* rational to engage in CMP because it's a socially established doxastic practice.
2. It's unqualifiedly rational to engage in CMP because we don't have good reasons to see it as unreliable or in some other way defective enough to count as irrational.

Let's look at each of these in turn.

5.2.1 Socially Established Practices and Prima Facie *Rationality*

Alston claims that participating in any socially established doxastic practice is *prima facie* rational. In one way, this isn't saying a lot. A *prima facie* rational practice might turn out to be completely irrational when we look at it more closely. However, if the practice is "socially established," then Alston thinks we can say this:

> It is reasonable to suppose that a practice would not have persisted over large segments of the population unless it was putting people into effective touch with some aspect(s) of reality and proving itself as such by its fruits (Alston 1991, p. 170).

Whether this is really reasonable is open to doubt. Astrology has been around for a long time and accepted by many people. Is assuming that it puts people in touch with reality reasonable? The answer is hardly an obvious yes. The problem is that a practice can stick around for many reasons and not all of them have anything to do with whether it "puts people into effective touch with reality." The practice might persist because it gives people an illusion of control, or it might persist because it serves the purposes of those in power. Still, Alston doesn't take the fact that something is *prima facie* rational to mean that it is genuinely rational when all relevant considerations are taken into account, and so perhaps we should grant Alston this point—at least to see where the argument leads.

*5.2.2 The Unqualified Rationality of Engaging in CMP

Our question is whether CMP is rational without any need for qualifications. Alston takes an "innocent until proven guilty" approach: so long as we don't have some good positive reasons to think that CMP is unreliable, it will be rational all things considered to engage in it. He proceeds by examining various reasons for thinking that CMP isn't rational and, in each case, he argues that these reasons aren't good enough. Here are some of the highlights.

Someone might argue that CMP leads to serious inconsistency. Different Christian believers sometimes come to conflicting conclusions, and CMP sometimes conflicts with the output of other doxastic practices. (For example, if someone believes God is telling him that creation stories in Genesis are literally true, then that belief conflicts with science.) Alston points out that other practices, including SP (using sense perception to form beliefs about the world) and science, also lead to these sorts of inconsistencies. If we reject CMP because it sometimes leads to inconsistency, we'll have to reject those practices too. As for conflict with science, when it comes to the big questions (e.g., Does God exist? Can we sometimes sense this God?), science doesn't tell us that CMP is wrong. Science is simply not in the business of settling questions about God's existence and nature.

Alston also admits that if we try to justify CMP, we'll be caught in a kind of circularity because we'll inevitably make use of information derived from CMP itself. However, he points out that any doxastic practice will face the same difficulty. Consider SP. Suppose someone believes that a deer was eating the lettuce in the garden because they saw it happen. If we want to check on this claim, we'll no doubt go to the garden and have a look at the lettuce patch. To do that, we'll need to use SP, but this sort of circularity hardly makes it irrational to form beliefs using sense perception. Even if CMP can only be checked by using CMP itself, this doesn't show that it's an irrational practice. If we say otherwise, we're unfairly applying a different standard to CMP than to SP.

With SP, we can make predictions about what we should expect to see in the future based on what we've seen in the past. If you seem to see a deer nibbling the lettuce and then running away, you fully expect that if you go to the garden, you'll see bite marks on the lettuce. And when we refine SP with science, the predictions can be extremely detailed; CMP isn't like that. We can't make many predictions about who will perceive God's presence and under what circumstances, and we can't predict much about the details of the experiences. This is a major difference between CMP and some of our most important doxastic practices. Does it show that CMP doesn't really count as rational?

Alston doesn't think so. Suppose God really exists and that we really can perceive him in the way that Alston has in mind. We wouldn't expect God to appear at our beck and call. That means we wouldn't expect to be able to say much about when and where we would have experiences of God's presence. But in that case, criticizing CMP for not giving us much in the way of predictions isn't fair. God isn't like the lettuce in the garden. Holding CMP to the standards we use for SP is applying the wrong standard.

Read narrowly, this reply seems reasonable. If God isn't the sort of being we could make these sorts of predictions about, it would be unreasonable of CMP to pretend otherwise. That said, there's still something a little troubling about this reply. Suppose a group of people become convinced that they are in occasional hazy contact with ghosts. They can't say much about them; it's just that they sometimes seem to sense their presence. Suppose we aren't convinced and we point out that in addition to not offering much detail, no one seems to be able to predict what conditions will lead to one of these experiences. Would we be satisfied if they replied by saying that there's no reason to think a ghost should appear whenever and wherever we want it to? The problem we might think, is that if ghosts are supposed to be this elusive, then even if people do sometimes experience them we might never be in a good position to know this.

In spite of this, Alston believes that CMP benefits from a certain kind of self-support. People who engage in CMP see it as a way to come to know God better and to become what God wants them to be. This process of coming closer to God and God's will is what Alston and the tradition refer to as "sanctification," and Alston believes that from within the practice of CMP, there's good evidence that CMP leads to sanctification.

Of course, some people become religious fanatics, but let's grant Alston that what he calls sanctification is much more typical. His point is that this provides some positive reason for taking CMP seriously, and we can allow that. The question is just how far that gets us.

*5.3 Religious Experience and Religious Diversity

When we discussed consistency earlier, we ignored an obvious point. Many mystical practices are more-or-less equally well established socially. Furthermore, it's not obvious that there are neutral arguments that put one of these practices in the lead. Given this situation, how could sticking with one particular practice be rational—CMP, in Alston's case?

William Hasker offers an analogy. Suppose you're playing hide-and-seek. You know that Johnny is hiding in one of the four rooms upstairs, but you only have time to look in one room. Suppose you pick the sewing room. Perhaps you just have a hunch, but what you don't have is any evidence that gives a reason for picking this room. Hasker writes:

> [I]t is more likely than not that the room you have chosen is the wrong one, and that your "method" is unreliable (Hasker 1986, pp. 139–140).

Hasker continues:

> If there are several schemes for interpreting religious experience which are alternative to, and incompatible with, Christianity, and if there is no decisive reason for thinking those schemes to be incorrect, then there is a good reason to think the Christian practice unreliable (p. 141).

Alston isn't persuaded. He offers his own analogy but it will take a bit of setting up.

You might see the drawing here (we'll meet it again in Chapter 11) as a rabbit or as a duck. More generally, how we think about things can make a difference to how things seem to us. Think about how your whole

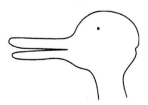

view of a person can shift depending on what you believe about him. One person might see the way he behaves as cold and arrogant. Another person might see the very same behavior as shyness and social awkwardness. The person literally looks different to us depending on which of these points of view we adopt.

Alston's analogy is more complex. Most of us see things in the physical world as separate objects or, at least, as collections of separate objects. For example, a stone is a solid thing. This way of thinking was described by Aristotle over 2000 years ago and we'll call it the Aristotelian view—but it's not the only possibility. The philosopher Alfred North Whitehead (1861–1947) thought that *processes* were fundamental. Think perhaps of swirls of energy. On this view, "objects" aren't really solid permanent things at all. Even a rock is not so much a thing as a collection of processes that happen to form a stable pattern.

Most of us tend to see things the Aristotelian way. But Alston asks us to imagine that the second way—the process view—is the basic way of seeing the world for certain cultures. There would be two very different versions of SP: the one we operate with, that sees what's in our visual field in terms of objects, and this other, process-oriented view, that interprets what's given in sense perception as a complicated collection of processes without solid, underlying objects. What we need to imagine to grasp the point of the analogy is that these different approaches are paired with highly developed doxastic practices—practices that lead to very different ways of seeing the world.

Alston takes this to be an analogy for the variety of mystical practices we actually find—Christian, Muslim, Buddhist, and so on. He asks: suppose we came upon other cultures whose sensory practices were like the process practice. Should that convince us that we're irrational to stick with our Aristotelian practice? Alston says no:

> In the absence of any external reason for supposing that one of these competing practices is more accurate than my own, the only rational course for me is to sit tight with the practice of which I am a master and which serves me so well in guiding my activity in the world (Alston 1991, p. 274).

This is just a way of saying that CMP hasn't been shown to be irrational. But if that were all we could say, Alston thinks this would not be very impressive. Unless there is more, the facts of religious diversity would "reduce the epistemic status [of CMP] to an alarming degree" (p. 276).

Fortunately, Alston thinks, there's more to be said. It's not just that a practice like CMP hasn't been shown to be unreliable. As we've already noted, it gets a good deal of self-support from the fact that it helps people grow in "sanctity, in serenity, peace, joy, fortitude, love and other 'fruits of the spirit'" (p. 276). Because CMP produces these benefits, Alston thinks it is reasonable for the believer to see the practice as providing access to ultimate reality.

*5.4 Evaluating Alston on Diversity

Has Alston met the challenge of diversity? There's room to quarrel.

*5.4.1 Religious Instrumentalism

Begin with Alston's hypothetical case of the variation on SP. In one way, what Alston says is reasonable: you should stick with the practice you've mastered. However, one way to stick with the practice is to believe that its output is not just useful but true. Philosophers would call this a *realist* response. Another way commits us to less. This way would agree that following the practice you know is useful, but it would remain agnostic on the deeper question of whether the world is made up of objects or processes. Philosophers would call this an instrumentalist approach. In the philosophy of science, there is a debate about when we should take a theory to give us a true picture of reality. Some philosophers and scientists say that we often don't need to settle that question. We can take scientific theories to be intellectual tools or "instruments" that are useful for predicting experimental results and for controlling parts of the world, but theories can serve as instruments whether or not they give us true pictures of reality. The old Earth-centered picture of the heavens is still a useful instrument for navigating the oceans but that doesn't mean it's true.

In the case Alston imagines—that of differing ways of "seeing" objects—the instrumentalist approach has much to recommend it. The real evidence for deciding among rival views about the basic nature of matter will come from physics, and we already know that whatever the true story is, it's likely to be very different from what common sense tells us.

For many purposes, the moment-to-moment outlook of an instrumentalist can be a lot like belief. Compare our attitude toward the Earth and the Sun. None of us believes at the "theoretical" level that the Earth sits still while the Sun revolves around it. However, we don't keep that "theoretical" knowledge in mind from moment to moment. In daily life, we think of things as though the Earth is still and the Sun is in motion.

It's possible to take a similar attitude toward religious practice. A person could lead her devotional life as a Christian or a Hindu or a Jew and use the practices of her tradition as ways of deepening her spiritual life, to use the vague but popular phrase. At the daily level of religious practice, she thinks and sees things in light of her background tradition. At the same time, she could take the attitude that though things seem a certain way when seen through the lens of her mystical practice, they might be quite different in reality. After all, she might say, the divine is a deep mystery that may well be beyond what we can fathom. And to some extent, many believers already do operate this way. We suspect that in their devotional lives, most believers anthropomorphize God (that is, think of God in human terms) well past the point that they would allow to be true as a matter of good theology.

The attitude at issue here is what we might call *religious instrumentalism*. It would say: follow your practice because it "works" on a day-to-day "spiritual" level, but don't get caught up in questions about whether your practice captures the deep truth about the universe. This approach is similar to the kind of religious pluralism set forth by John Hick that we'll discuss in Chapter 11. Alston maintains that it's reasonable not just to think that one's usual religious practice is useful; he goes the extra step and claims that it's reasonable to think it gets at the truth. However, it can be argued that if the question is what's true and whether we know it, religious instrumentalism is more reasonable. Religious instrumentalism can admit that changing practices or giving up the one you've mastered is difficult. And it can also admit that following CMP (or any of various other mystical practices) is "spiritually useful," to put it crudely. But in contrast to Alston, religious instrumentalism sees no reason to go further.

*5.4.2 Self-Support

The point about instrumentalism is relevant to Alston's comments about self-support. As we noted, Alston sees the "fruits of the spirit" alluded to above as providing a type of self-support for CMP. Let's grant that CMP leads to tangible spiritual benefits and that this gives the Christian a reason to continue the practice. However, Jews, Muslims, Buddhists, Hindus, and many others can say the same thing—following their own practice brings spiritual benefits. The problem with this type of self-support as a defense of CMP is that it seems to provide at least as much reason for being an instrumentalist as for being a realist. It shows that CMP, like many mystical practices, is "spiritually useful" but gives no reason for thinking that the deliverances of CMP are more likely to be true than those of Hindu mystical practice or Zoroastrian mystical practice, for example.

Still, we can say a bit more here. Alston sees these spiritual benefits as a reason for thinking that CMP brings people into contact with Ultimate Reality. He admits that people who follow other mystical practices could say the same thing about their own practices. Could there be room for more than one camp to be at least partly right? Alston doesn't address this, or at least not in any clear way, but another approach does.

6 AN INFERENTIAL APPROACH: GARY GUTTING

Like Swinburne and Alston, Gary Gutting is interested in experiences that seem to be direct, non-sensory perceptions of God. Unlike Swinburne and Alston, he probes the question of what we can reasonably infer from the fact that these experiences are so widespread. Gutting is not saying that we are simply entitled to take these experiences at face value. Rather, he is offering an argument: over a long span of time and across a variety of cultures, many people have had what seem to them to be experiences of a good and powerful being who cares about us. Gutting claims that the cumulative weight of all these experiences provides good evidence that such a being exists.

Notice that this being may or may not be the God of traditional theism. The being is experienced as good but Gutting doesn't claim that it must be perfectly good. Likewise, this being is experienced as powerful but, once again, not necessarily as all-powerful. But if Gutting is correct, we have reason to believe that a good and powerful supernatural being exists who cares about us. The belief that such a being exists provides the best explanation for the fact that such experiences are so common and for various important facts about the experiences.

6.1 Gutting Pro and Con

Alston discusses Gutting's approach explicitly and rejects it. His reason is that if we cut mystical practice loose from any particular tradition, we leave ourselves with no background practice of criticism and assessment for sorting the more plausible from the less plausible. In Alston's view, this means we can't even have *prima facie* or "initial" justification for experiential beliefs unless the beliefs are set within the context of a doxastic practice—a practice of criticizing and evaluating the beliefs the experiences tend to call forth.

This isn't a strong objection. Alston and Gutting are doing different things. Alston is asking, "When is simply taking religious experience at face value rational?" and part of his answer is that a socially established doxastic practice must exist that forms the background for evaluating the experiences—just as in the case of vision or memory. Gutting is doing something different. He's looking for the best *explanation* for the fact that many people, across many cultures, seem to experience the presence of a powerful, loving being. If his explanation is a good one, then even people who have never had a religious experience might accept it. Further, even though Gutting doesn't draw on the evaluative practices of any particular religious tradition, he's still operating within a broad doxastic practice of sifting evidence and providing explanations, and he offers some explicit criteria. First, if religious experiences of a good and powerful being are veridical, Gutting thinks we should expect that people who have had such experiences will be likely to have them again. Second, we should find that other people will have the same sorts of experiences, and third, that people who have them will tend to become better people. We would expect all this because of the goodness and power of the being the experiences appear to reveal. As Gutting reads the evidence, we find all three of these things.

Gutting's approach has advantages over both Alston's and Swinburne's. First, it doesn't rest on anything like the Principle of Credulity, and so it doesn't have to give credit to all of the odd experiences that seem to fall within the scope of that Principle. Second, Gutting's claims are modest enough that the problem of religious diversity is much less of an issue for him than it is for Alston. For example, Christians and Sikhs could both be correct in thinking they experience a divine being, even though they can't both be correct about just what this being is like. At the same time, the experiences Gutting describes could serve as part of a case for more specific claims. For example, the experiences don't reveal that this being is infinitely powerful or perfectly good. As some commentators have pointed out, it's not clear that a religious experience by itself could reveal such things. (How would we know from any finite experience that the being is infinitely powerful or perfectly good?) That still leaves room for the experience to be part of a larger case for the God of classical theism or even for the more specific claims of a particular religion.

Of course, the world is full of striking experiences. The ones Gutting describes are not uncommon, but so are many other types of experiences that we may or may not take as seriously. Many people—sane, healthy people—claim to have seen ghosts. Some people claim that they are in touch with the spirits of the dead. The list could go on. Someone might worry about just how much Gutting's argument would end up showing. Furthermore, because Gutting's argument is an **abductive** argument—an argument that his explanation is the best explanation for the phenomena it considers—a thorough evaluation of it would have to ask whether there are other explanations—for example, from psychology or neuroscience—that are at least as good.

7 FINAL THOUGHTS

As we might have expected, it's not easy to come to a definitive judgment on the status of religious experience. In this brief final section, we'd like to widen our view a bit and make a connection between this topic and another.

Our first point is that though we've focused on religious experiences that have the quality of perception, there is a very wide range of phenomena that a serious study of religious experience would have to take account of, and some of these experiences aren't really very exotic at all. Go back for a moment to Swinburne's first category of experiences of the divine: experiencing the divine in ordinary, publicly observable objects. This is very much like the sort of thing that Plantinga discusses in connection with the *sensus divinitatis*, as discussed in Chapter 7. It's also like the sorts of things that John Hick describes when he says that the data of religion include a great deal of what he describes as "ordinary human experience," but experience that, as it seems to the believer, "mediate[s] the presence and activity of God" (Hick 1964, p. 243). It's difficult to say how many believers have had experiences that they would describe as perceptions of God, but our guess is that most have had more diffuse experiences in which it seemed to them that something was somehow due to God's presence or activity. Our guess is that experiences like this are at least as important for the average believer as the more exotic or colorful religious experiences that have often occupied the attention of philosophers.

Our second point is that when deciding how strongly to count the more exotic cases of religious experience as evidence of God, the answer will depend in part on how probable or improbable the person doing the evaluating takes God to be in the first place. Someone who thinks the existence of God is extremely unlikely might well see such experiences as not raising the probability of God's existence much at all. Someone who is more open to the possibility that God exists might find that the same sort of experience is enough to raise the probability over some crucial threshold. As we saw in the chapter on miracles, the *prior probability* of a hypothesis—in this case, the hypothesis that God exists—makes a difference when we're assessing the evidence for the hypothesis. This doesn't mean that all judgments of prior probability are equally reasonable, but it does complicate the process of sorting things out.

Our third point is that the resemblances between miracles and religious experiences actually run a little deeper. We noted when we discussed miracles that for many believers, cases that fall short of clear miracles—hints and whispers, as we put it—are very important. But many of these same experiences would also count as seeing the divine in ordinary things and hence, by Swinburne's criteria, as religious experience. The overlap is also clear at the other end of the scale: a vision of the Virgin Mary would count as a religious experience but it also would fall quite straightforwardly into the category of candidate for a miracle. None of this should be surprising. If a miracle is what happens when God breaks into the natural order, then veridical religious experience, if such there be, is a miracle all by itself.

AT A GLANCE: RELIGIOUS EXPERIENCE

1. What is Religious Experience?
   • An experience that the person having it is inclined to take as a veridical experience of God or some aspect of the divine.

   1.1. Swinburnes' Classification of Religious Experience

Types of Religious Experience	Example
Experiencing the divine in ordinary, publicly observable objects.	Seeing the blue sky, majestic mountains, or starry heavens as the handiwork of God.
Experiencing the divine in some unusual, publicly observable object.	Appearances of angels, the Virgin Mary, or Jesus that other people who are present can see.
Experiencing the divine through private experiences that can be described in the ordinary language of the senses.	Joseph's religious dreams or Paul's vision of Jesus on the road to Damascus. Others present do not share the experience.
Experiencing the divine through private sensations that can't be described in ordinary vocabulary.	St. Teresa of Avila's "sixth sense" awareness of the presence of Christ. A general awareness of God's love.
Experiencing the divine without any sensations at all.	A bare and vague awareness of divine reality.

2. How Is Religious Experience Supposed to Justify Belief in God?

- Some philosophers say, *indirectly through an argument*: religious experience is data that is best explained by the hypothesis that God exists.
- Other philosophers say, *directly by experience*: religious experience directly justifies belief in God without an argument, just as sense perception of a tree directly justifies the existence of a tree without an argument.

3. Naturalistic Explanations of Religious Experience

- Religious experiences likely correlate with certain brain states.
- This is true of experience in general, and so doesn't show that religious experience isn't veridical.

3.1. What the "God Helmet" Suggests

- There are ways that science could undermine the evidential value of religious experience.
- This would happen if scientists discovered the neural correlates of religious experience, discovered how they produce the experiences, and showed that natural conditions typically trigger the neural conditions.

3.2. Implications

- Though science might someday undermine the evidential value of religious experience, at this time, no strong case can be made for a naturalistic explanation.

4. Taking Religious Experience at Face Value

- Many philosophers of religion argue that we are entitled to take religious experience at face value—as veridical experience.

4.1. Swinburne Offers a *Principle of Credulity*

- In the absence of special considerations, if it seems to a subject that X is present, then probably X is present.
- Special circumstances would include:
  1. Unreliable person or circumstances.
  2. Person has often been wrong about this sort of thing.
  3. What the person "perceived" probably wasn't there.
  4. Even if the thing reported was there, it probably didn't cause the perception.
- Swinburne argues that none of these exceptions typically apply to religious experience.
- Swinburne's argument:

  Premise #1: If it seems to a person that X is present, then it is likely that X is present, unless there is other evidence that undermines the existence of X (Principle of Credulity).

  Premise #2: Religious experience makes it seem to some persons that God is present, so it is likely that God exists, unless there is other evidence that undermines the existence of God.

Premise #3: There is no other evidence that undermines the existence of God.

Conclusion: Therefore, it is likely that God exists.

4.2. Critique of Swinburne

- The Principle of Credulity gets its plausibility from ordinary, public experience.
- It doesn't clearly extend to cases where, for example, one person "sees" God's handiwork in the sky and his friend "sees" the meaninglessness of the universe.
- In some public cases (e.g., a burning bush that isn't consumed), we can apply Swinburne's Exception (3) above.
- It also doesn't clearly extend to Swinburne's "private" cases—where private experience is supposed to reveal a non-private reality.

5. William Alston

- Alston also defends the view that religious experience can be taken at face value.

5.1. Doxastic Practices

- Doxastic practices are central to Alston's approach.
- A doxastic practice is a socially established practice of evaluating and criticizing particular ways of forming beliefs.

5.2. The Rationality of Christian Mystical Practice (CMP)
Alston claims

- It's *prima facie* rational to engage in CMP because it's part of a socially established doxastic practice.
- CMP is rational all things considered, because we don't have a good reason to think that it is defective.
- Alston's argument in schematic form:

Premise #1: If some belief-forming process is a doxastic practice, then it is *prima facie* reasonable to think that beliefs formed on this basis are justified.

Premise #2: Christian mystical practice constitutes a doxastic practice.

Premise #3: Therefore, it is prima facie reasonable to think that beliefs formed on this basis of Christian doxastic practice are justified.

Premise #4: There are no inconsistencies within CMP or between it and other doxastic practices sufficient to override the *prima facie* rationality of CMP.

Premise #5: If there are no inconsistencies within CMP or between it and other doxastic practices sufficient to override the *prima facie* rationality of CMP, then it is reasonable to form beliefs based upon Christian mystical practice CMP is reasonable.

Conclusion: Therefore, it is reasonable to form beliefs based upon CMP is reasonable.

5.2.1. On *Prima Facie* Rationality

- Alston argues that the long-standing existence of a practice is reason to think something is reasonable about it.
- This is open to challenge by examples like astrology.

5.2.2. Rationality, All Things Considered

- Alston considers various potential sources of difficulty:
  1. Inconsistency
  2. Circularity
  3. Lack of predictions
- On (1) and (2), he says that CMP is no worse off than science, for example.
- On (3), he argues that the subject matter makes this an inappropriate standard.
- He also adds that CMP gets self-support from the facts of sanctification.

5.3. Religious Diversity

- CMP conflicts with many religious traditions that also have long-established doxastic practices.
- Alston offers an analogy: If several competing sensory practices existed, all equally well-established, we would be rational to stick with the one that we have mastered.
- Also, we must remember that CMP gets self-support from the facts of sanctification.

5.4. Critique of Alston on Religious Diversity

- Alston's analogy with other possible sensory practices could only justify religious instrumentalism.
- Other mystical practices have the same sort of self-support that CMP has.

6. Gutting

- Gutting thinks that the widespread occurrence of similar religious experiences is best explained if a powerful, good being exists who cares about us.
- Gutting's argument:

  Premise #1: Over a long span of time and across a variety of cultures, many people have had what seem to them to be experiences of a good and powerful being who is concerned about us.

  Premise #2: The best explanation of Premise 1 is that some sort of God exists.

  Conclusion: Therefore, some sort of God probably exists.

6.1. Evaluating Gutting

- Gutting's approach is third-person, unlike the first-person approaches of Swinburne and Alston.
- He can appeal to general standards for evaluating explanations.

- In his favor:
    1. He doesn't need anything like the Principle of Credulity.
    2. He can more easily meet the problems of religious diversity.
  - Potential problem: His approach might justify too much.
7. Final Thoughts
   - For most believers, religious experiences will be diffuse rather than exotic or highly specific.
   - People will evaluate the genuineness of experiences using their background beliefs. These will affect prior probabilities.
   - Evaluating religious experiences resembles evaluating apparent miracles because a genuine religious experience would be a type of miracle.

FURTHER READING AND WEB RESOURCES

John Hick discusses some of the issues presented here in a very clear way that anticipated later discussion. See his essay, "Skeptics and Believers," in Hick 1964.

William James's *The Varieties of Religious Experience* is a classic study of our topic. Go to http://www.des.emory.edu/mfp/james.html#varieties for links to the full text and to discussions of James's ideas.

Rudolph Otto's *The Idea of the Holy* is another classic text on religious experience. You can find a summary of his ideas at http://academic.brooklyn.cuny.edu/english/melani/gothic/numinous.html.

CHAPTER 7

Reformed Epistemology

Some theists spend a lot of time making arguments for the existence of God. They seem to think that the rationality of belief in God depends on whether there are good arguments for it. But is this right? In this chapter, we explain a view according to which belief in God can be rationally justified, even if there are no good arguments for the existence of God. Along the way, we explore some important ideas in the theory of knowledge.

Bertrand Russell, one of the greatest philosophers of the twentieth century, was once asked what he would say if he died, found himself standing before God, and were asked why he had not believed. He replied, "I'd say, 'Not enough evidence, God! Not enough evidence!'" Russell's view that belief in God is not justified because it lacks evidence is widespread. Former Christian minister turned pop atheist Dan Barker explains that, "I am an atheist because there is no evidence for the existence of God. That should be all that needs to be said about it: no evidence, no belief" (Barker 1992, p. 87).

The criticism expressed by atheists like Russell and Barker is often called the **evidentialist objection**. According to the evidentialist objection, belief in God is **unjustified** or **unwarranted** because there is insufficient evidence that God exists. The argument has two premises:

The Evidentialist Objection

Premise #1: If there is insufficient evidence that God exists, then belief in God is unjustified.

Premise #2: There is insufficient evidence that God exists.

Conclusion: Therefore, belief in God is unjustified.

Naturally enough, most theists disagree with the likes of Russell and Barker. But there's an important difference among theists here. Some agree with the first premise of the evidentialist objection but disagree with the second. They think the atheist is correct when he claims that belief in God is not justified if there's no evidence for God but disagree that there's insufficient evidence for God. These theists think that **natural theology**, the project of trying to prove or demonstrate the existence of God from nature, provides good **arguments** for the existence of God.

Other theists disagree with the first premise. They think that belief in God can be justified even if there's no evidence for the existence of God. This second view is known as **Reformed epistemology** because it's advocated by philosophers who see their defense of theism stemming from the **Protestant Reformers**, particularly John Calvin. In earlier chapters, we examined the arguments for the existence of God. In this chapter, we will focus on Reformed epistemology, particularly the work of Alvin Plantinga.

1 THE EVIDENTIALIST OBJECTION

To understand the evidentialist objection, we must understand how the terms "justified" and "evidence" are used.

1.1 Justification

Roughly speaking, knowledge is thought of as having three components: belief, truth, and justification. This view of knowledge is a bit simple and has been criticized, but it will suffice for our purposes. (We'll say more about problems with it later.) All three of these elements are required for knowledge. First, to know something you first must believe it. Someone doesn't know that the earth is 93 million miles from the Sun if they don't believe it. Second, you can't know something if it's false. Someone can't know that the Sun is 10 miles from Earth because it isn't. Third, true beliefs must be justified to count as knowledge. Suppose Rachel strongly believes that she will win the lottery tomorrow and she believed it for no reason or for a bad reason. Perhaps she believes it because she read it in the tea leaves, or simply because it amuses her. Suppose that she does win the lottery.

Her belief that she would win the lottery was true but it wasn't knowledge. It was a lucky guess, and lucky guesses are just that—it wasn't at all likely that what she believed would turn out to be true. For true belief to be knowledge, it must be grounded in a way that somehow makes it more likely to be true.

The exact nature of justification is controversial. For now, let's just say that a belief is justified if it's held for good reason. Rachel didn't know she would win because she had no good reason to think so.

1.2 Evidence

In a criminal trial, evidence might include fingerprints, a drop of blood, a strand of hair, or testimony. In philosophy, "evidence" has both a broad and a narrow sense. In the broad sense, evidence is anything a person has access to that's relevant to the truth of some **proposition**. This includes sense experience, memory, testimony, arguments, and inferences. In the narrow sense, evidence is propositional—a matter of statements and arguments.

The evidentialist objection is typically understood as using "evidence" in the narrow sense. It amounts to saying that belief in God is unjustified because it's not based on any good arguments. For example, J. L. Mackie writes that

> any rational consideration . . . [of theism] will involve arguments . . . [theism] must be examined by either deductive reasoning or, if that yields no decision, by arguments to the best explanation; for in such a context nothing else can have any coherent bearing on the issue (Mackie 1982, pp. 4, 6).

1.3 What Kind of Objection Is the Evidentialist Objection?

The evidentialist objection is a *de jure* objection. Objections to theistic belief typically fall into two categories: *de facto* and *de jure*. *De facto* objections try to show that no God exists, whereas *de jure* objections try to show that we aren't justified in believing that God exists, whether or not God actually exists. *De facto* objections are **metaphysical**, having to do with the way reality is, whereas *de jure* objections might be **epistemic**, having to do with the requirements for beliefs to be rational, or they might be psychological. The evidentialist objection is not that God doesn't exist but that belief in God is unjustified. It is a *de jure* objection about what we are entitled to believe, not a *de facto* objection about what is actually true.

De Facto Objections	*De Jure* Objections
The Argument from Evil: God doesn't exist because evil does.	*The Evidentialist Objection*: Belief in God is unjustified because it lacks evidence.
Contradictory Attributes: God doesn't exist because some divine attributes, like mercy and justice, are inconsistent with each other.	*Freud's Complaint*: Belief in God is irrational because it is an illusion that results from wish-fulfillment.
Divine Attributes Incoherent: God doesn't exist because some divine attributes, like omnipotence, are incoherent and unintelligible.	*Marx's Complaint*: Belief in God is irrational because it results from a perverted and unhealthy social order.
	Nietzsche's Complaint: Belief in God is irrational because originates in slave morality and the resentment of the oppressed.

1.4 What Kind of Reply Should We Expect?

As we've said, the evidentialist objection is a *de jure* objection. It claims that we aren't justified in believing in God. Perhaps somewhat surprisingly, Reformed epistemologists do not reply by arguing that God actually exists. Rather, they argue that belief in God is not necessarily unjustified just because it's not based on **arguments**.

To many, this is unsatisfying. They want to know whether God actually exists. They are more concerned with *de facto* questions than *de jure* ones. This concern deserves a response. First, Reformed epistemologists genuinely think that the problem with the evidentialist objection is the first premise. They think it involves a subtle **epistemological** mistake—one that should not be allowed to go unchallenged.

Second, there is an advantage to replying to the first premise of the evidentialist objection rather than the second. It makes for a more modest reply. To try to demonstrate the existence of God is more ambitious than to argue that belief in God can be justified without arguments. Making a more ambitious argument, when nothing more extensive is needed, is riskier. It amounts to biting off more than you need to chew.

Third, some natural theologians tend to view the arguments for God as so strong that they can be rejected only on pain of irrationality.

Reformed epistemologists take a less optimistic view. They acknowledge that theistic proofs can provide some rational support for theism but they also think room exists for honest disagreement about just how strong the arguments are. So there are reasons for replying to the evidentialist objection in a way that doesn't attempt to prove God's existence, despite the fact that some people find this less satisfying.

1.5 A Tale of Two Projects

There are two ways to undermine the premise of an argument. You can argue that there is no good reason to think the premise is true, or that the premise is simply false. Reformed epistemologists take both approaches to undermining the first premise of the evidentialist objection. Let's call the first approach the negative project and the second approach the positive project.

The goal of the negative project is to show that no good reason exists to think that we need arguments to be justified in believing in God. This doesn't mean that the evidentialist's premise is false. It just means that no one has yet offered any good reasons to think it is true. Alternatively, the goal of the positive project is to show that belief in God can be justified independently of arguments. The negative project is defensive because it blocks moves made by critics of theism. The positive project is offensive because it endeavors to show that belief in God can be justified without evidence.

2 THE NEGATIVE PROJECT

Evidentialism—the idea that good arguments are required for belief in God to be justified—has appealed to many people. There are several reasons why. We will examine two.

2.1 Reason #1: Every Belief Must Be Justified by an Argument

Why might someone think that belief in God must be justified with arguments if it is to be justified at all? One might think that no belief is justified unless there is a good argument for it. W. K. Clifford, whom we discuss at greater length in Chapter 8, seemed to have this in mind when he wrote that "it is wrong, always, everywhere, and for anyone to believe anything upon insufficient evidence" (Clifford 2003 (1901), p. 367). This would obviously include belief in God.

The problem with this suggestion is that it's an overgeneralization. First, not everything we justifiably believe could be based on good arguments. If every justified belief requires an argument, then the premises of that argument would also need to be established by a second argument. But then the premises of this second argument would have to be established by a third argument, and so on. This process would either have to be circular or else continue *ad infinitum*. **Circular arguments** have obvious problems. The problem with an **infinite regress** of arguments is that we don't have an infinite amount of time to construct one. Clearly, at least some of the things we're justified in believing don't require arguments.

Second, there are clear examples of things we're justified in believing without arguments. For example, when we have a toothache we experience the pain and on that basis, we form the justified belief that we have a toothache. We do *not* quickly run through this sort of implicit argument in our mind:

> *Premise #1*: If I am experiencing pain in my tooth, then I am having a toothache.
>
> *Premise #2*: I am experience pain in my tooth.
>
> *Conclusion*: Therefore, I am having a toothache.

Or consider what **logicians** call "the law of non-contradiction:" that no claim is both true and false at the same time. We believe this, but we don't believe it on the basis of arguments. It's notoriously difficult—if not impossible—to establish, in a noncircular way, that the laws of logic are **truth-preserving**—that they never lead from truth to falsity. Clearly, not everything we're entitled to believe must be justified by an argument.

Perhaps the epistemological principle should not be that every belief must be justified by an argument but that it must be *able* to be justified by an argument. One problem with this suggestion is that we are justified in believing plenty of things that no one has been able to demonstrate with a good argument. If the history of philosophy has taught us anything, it has taught us defeating radical **skepticism** is extremely difficult, if not impossible. The work of philosophers like Rene Descartes, David Hume, and Bertrand Russell has shown us how difficult providing strong arguments for our common sense beliefs about the world is—that physical sticks and stones exist, that the Sun will rise tomorrow, or that other persons with minds exist. Yet most of us, including most philosophers, think we're justified in believing these things. If we're right, not everything we believe requires an argument.

2.2 Reason #2: Classical Foundationalism

From the preceding discussion, we learned that some beliefs are justified even if they aren't based on arguments. That gives us two categories of justified beliefs: those that are justified independently of arguments, and those that aren't. The question is: In which category is belief in God? According to the evidentialist objector, it's in the latter category. But why think that? What criteria should we use to organize beliefs into one category or the other?

Alvin Plantinga thinks that belief in God is typically categorized as a belief that requires arguments because of the influence of a historically important epistemological theory—classical **foundationalism**. As Plantinga puts it, "the evidentialist objection to theistic belief is rooted in classical foundationalism" (Plantinga 1983, p. 90). Classical foundationalism allows that some beliefs can be justified without arguments, but belief in God isn't one of them. Let's see why.

2.2.1 The Architecture of Belief: The Building and the Web

Classical foundationalism is a species of foundationalism. To understand classical foundationalism, we need to familiarize ourselves with foundationalism in general. Foundationalists take as their starting point the fact that some beliefs are based upon others. Suppose that when you wake up, you look outside and notice your driveway is wet. You might form the belief that it rained last night. Your belief that it rained is based upon other beliefs, namely, that when it rains your driveway gets wet and that your driveway is wet. In turn, those beliefs are based on other beliefs. Our beliefs form chains of inference and seem to take on a certain structure:

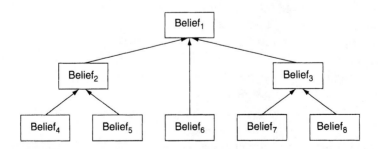

What is the shape of this structure? Here are three possibilities. The chain of inference might be infinite, circular, or terminate at some base or foundation. Foundationalists favor the third option.

A chain of inference might be infinitely long. One belief might be based on another belief and so on, *ad infinitum*. One problem with this possibility is that it assumes finite human minds are capable of believing an infinite number of things. This is pretty clearly false.

The chain of inference could be circular. One belief is based on another belief, but the chain isn't infinite because it eventually loops back on itself. For most of our beliefs, this seems psychologically false. Try an experiment: you believe you are reading a book. Ask yourself why you believe that. Trace the chain of inference as far back as you can. Does it loop back on itself forming a circle? Very few of our beliefs appear to do that. More importantly, arguing in a circle is usually considered to be a fallacy—a mistake in reasoning. A circular chain involves beliefs eventually justifying themselves and thus "pulling themselves up with their own bootstraps"—something that won't just obviously work.

Foundationalists think the best option is the third one: chains of inference terminate at some base. These foundational beliefs are something like epistemic axioms. They're starting points from which all other beliefs are eventually inferred. Foundationalism then is a view about the structure of one's beliefs. According to foundationalism, the structure of one's beliefs resembles a building with a foundation and a superstructure. The beliefs in the foundation of the structure are non-inferred, or **basic beliefs**. The beliefs that comprise the superstructure are inferred or **non-basic beliefs**.

There are two types of basic and non-basic beliefs: justified and unjustified. A non-basic belief is justified if it is inferred from other justified beliefs using the appropriate methods of reasoning. A non-basic belief is unjustified if it is inferred from unjustified beliefs or is improperly inferred from justified ones. Properly basic beliefs are beliefs that are both basic and justified. Any basic belief that is not justified is not properly basic. Foundationalists disagree among themselves about what makes a basic belief justified.

We noted earlier that there are two categories of justified beliefs: those that are justified independently of arguments and those that aren't. This fits nicely with foundationalism. Beliefs that are justified independently of arguments are properly basic beliefs and are in the foundation of our belief structure. Beliefs that must be justified by arguments or inferences are properly non-basic beliefs and are in the superstructure of belief structure.

The alternative to foundationalism is **coherentism**. Coherentism is a view about the belief structure, according to which the structure of one's beliefs resembles a web. Coherentists disagree with foundationalists that justification is linear. They view justification as holistic in nature. A belief is justified if it coheres with the total system of one's beliefs—if it fits well into the total web of belief.

2.2.2 Foundationalism: Modern and Classical

There are several varieties of foundationalism. The main difference between them is over which beliefs are properly basic and why. An historically important version of foundationalism is modern foundationalism. In many ways, modern foundationalism is a response to epistemic skepticism. As such, one of the main motivations of foundationalism is the quest for certainty. The French philosopher René Descartes, using the foundationalist's metaphor of a building, explains his project as a search for a certain foundation for knowledge:

> Some years ago now I observed the multitude of errors that I had accepted as true in my earliest years, and the dubiousness of the whole superstructure I had since then reared on them; and the consequent need of making a clean sweep once in my life, and beginning again from the very foundations ... reason convinces me that I must withhold assent no less carefully from what is not plainly certain and indubitable than from what is obviously false (Descartes 1971, p. 61).

He proposes rejecting any opinion that can be doubted, pushing doubt as far as it can go to see if anything survives this process. If something does, he proposes to use that as the certain and indubitable foundation of knowledge. After all, if the foundation is certain and the rules of inference never take us from a true belief to a false one, the superstructure should also be certain. Descartes eventually concludes that he can doubt everything except that he thinks and that he exists. After all, he must exist to doubt that he exists. This is where his famous argument, *Cogito ergo sum*, or "I think, therefore I am," originates. For Descartes, his belief that he exists is properly basic.

The problem with Descartes' foundation is that he can't build much from it. How do you infer that sticks and stones exist from the bare fact that you exist? Other philosophers have proposed different beliefs as properly basic.

Modern foundationalism is the type of foundationalism that counts only two types of belief as properly basic: **self-evident beliefs** and **incorrigible beliefs**. Self-evident beliefs are beliefs that are obviously true considered in themselves. If you understand them, you simply see that they are true: *2 + 2 = 4* and *all bachelors are unmarried males* are self-evident. You see that they are true just by understanding them.

Incorrigible beliefs are beliefs you can't be mistaken about. Sally's belief that her tooth hurts is incorrigible. The mere fact that she feels the pain *makes* it true. Her belief that she is having the experience of reading a book is incorrigible. She might be mistaken that she is reading a book but she can't be mistaken that it *seems* to her that she is reading a book.

Like Descartes' version, this version of modern foundationalism is motivated by the quest for certainty. Modern foundationalists think that self-evident and incorrigible beliefs are infallible—that they cannot be false. So any beliefs validly inferred from this foundation will also be certain.

Classical foundationalism is almost identical with modern foundationalism. The only difference is that classical foundationalists count three types of beliefs as properly basic: self-evident beliefs, incorrigible beliefs, and beliefs that are evident to the senses. Beliefs that are evident to the senses are sometimes called **perceptual beliefs**. They include beliefs like *a tree is in front of me*, *the tree has yellow leaves*, and *I am wearing shoes* (Plantinga 1983, pp. 57–58). The addition of perceptual beliefs to the list of properly basic beliefs gives the foundationalist more material to work with in building the structure but it comes at the expense of certainty. Perceptual beliefs are not infallible.

2.2.3 Getting to the Root of the Objection

We're now in a position to see why Plantinga thinks the evidentialist objection is rooted in classical foundationalism. According to classical foundationalism, only beliefs that are self-evident, incorrigible, or evident to the senses are properly basic. Every other belief must be justified by inference or argument. Belief in God is not self-evident, incorrigible, or evident to the senses. Therefore, according to classical foundationalism, it's not properly basic and must be justified by argument. This is why Plantinga thinks that those who object to the idea that belief in God can be properly basic might be assuming classical foundationalism or something like to it.

2.2.4 The Problem with Classical Foundationalism

Plantinga attacks the evidentialist objection by attacking the classical foundationalism in which he believes it is grounded. If classical foundationalism is wrong, then we still haven't been provide a reason to think that belief in God requires an argument to be justified.

Plantinga offers three main criticisms of classical foundationalism. First, it suffers from the same malady as Descartes' foundationalism. There just aren't enough properly basic beliefs to ground our everyday knowledge claims. Classical foundationalism can't justify our belief in other minds, the past, a self that persists through time, or inferences about the future based on what has happened in the past. The foundation is just too meager (Plantinga 1983, pp. 59–60). As Kelly Clark puts it, classical foundationalists are "trying to make epistemological gold out of base metals" (Clark 2000, p. 276). Its failure to justify these sorts of beliefs seems to lead to skepticism and partially explains the focus on skepticism among modern philosophers.

Second, Plantinga points out that classical foundationalism sets a standard of justification that it doesn't meet itself. It claims that all justified beliefs are either properly basic or inferred from properly basic beliefs. But classical foundationalism isn't properly basic because it is not self-evident, incorrigible, or evident to the senses. Nor is it clear how it could be inferred from properly basic beliefs "as far as I know, no classical foundationalist has produced any such argument" (Plantinga 2000, p. 95).

Third, it artificially exalts the role inference, or reason, plays in knowledge. According to classical foundationalism, except for the very few properly basic beliefs, all justified beliefs are based on deductive, inductive, or abductive inferences. It assumes the faculty of reason produces more reliable beliefs than **faculties** like memory and perception. If I have a memory of eating cereal for breakfast but I cannot justify this by inferential reasoning, I am justified in my belief, despite what classical foundationalists might say. Why should the demands of reason trump experience? The eighteenth-century Scottish philosopher Thomas Reid makes this point beautifully:

> Reason, says the skeptic, is the only judge of truth, and you ought to throw off every opinion and every belief that is not grounded on reason. Why, sir, should I believe the faculty of reason more than that of perception?—they came both out of the same shop, and were made by the same artist; and if he puts one piece of false ware into my hands, what should hinder him from putting another? (Reid 1997, p. 169)

Classical foundationalism has serious problems. If it's supposed to provide the main reason for thinking evidentialism is true, then evidentialism is in trouble. As Plantinga puts it, "insofar as the evidentialist objection is rooted in classical foundationalism, it is poorly rooted indeed" (Plantinga 1992, p. 135).

We've examined two prominent reasons to think that the first premise of the evidentialist objection is true. Both appear to suffer from serious failings. According to Plantinga, this means that we have no reason, so far, to think that belief in God can only be justified by a good argument. However, this doesn't mean that belief in God is justified without evidence. It just means that no one has yet offered a good reason to think it is required.

3 THE POSITIVE PROJECT

The aim of the positive project is to defend the view that belief in God can be properly basic. If it can be, then the evidentialist objection is mistaken because it claims that belief in God can only be justified by arguments.

3.1 Plantinga's Proposal: Reidian Foundationalism and Belief in God as Properly Basic

Although Plantinga contends that classical foundationalism is flawed, he doesn't have a problem with foundationalism *per se*. In fact, he thinks that something like the foundationalism of Thomas Reid is correct. Reid notices the same type of problems with modern and classical foundationalism discussed above. He argues for an expansion of the foundation of knowledge to include beliefs like memory and perception.

According to Reid, our minds have several belief-producing mechanisms. Inference, or reason, is just one of them; memory, sight, smell, and taste are others. Beliefs formed from these other mental processes might not be able to be justified by inferences, but they don't need to be. Consider our sense of smell:

> There is a smell, is the immediate testimony of the sense; There was a smell is the immediate testimony of the memory. If you ask me, why I believe that the smell exists? I can give no other reason, nor shall ever be able to give any other, than that I smell it . . . the evidence of sense, the evidence of memory [and the evidence of reason] . . . are all distinct and original kinds of evidence, equally grounded on our

constitution: none depends upon, or can be resolved into another. To reason against any of these kinds of evidence is absurd; nay, to reason for them is absurd (Reid 1997, p. 29).

So beliefs based on perception and memory should generally be considered properly basic and be included in the foundations of our knowledge. They aren't justified by argument, inference, or reason, but they are ways of knowing that are equal with reason. They are the epistemic siblings of reason, not its peasant subjects.

Plantinga picks up on Reid's line of reasoning and proposes a further expansion of the foundations of knowledge to include belief in other minds, the past, a self that persists through time, enumerative induction, and most controversially, belief in God. If belief in God can be properly basic, then belief in God can be justified without arguments. This is an important claim because it completely undermines evidentialism. Let's see if he can defend it.

3.2 Argument that Belief in God is Properly Basic

For a belief to be properly basic, it must meet two conditions: it must be basic, i.e. not inferred from other beliefs, and it must be justified. Plantinga argues that belief in God meets these conditions. Let's consider the two conditions one at a time.

3.3 Is Belief in God Basic?

It's important to note, right off the bat, that Plantinga argues that belief in God is basic for many theists but not necessarily for all theists. His contention is that belief in God *can* be and often is properly basic, not that it always is. Some people might very well believe in God on the basis of theistic arguments. He just doesn't think that this is typical.

He makes his case by pointing out that most people don't believe in God because of arguments. Think about all the billions of people who believe in God world-wide and throughout history. How many of them believe in God because they have read and been convinced by the **cosmological, teleological,** and **ontological arguments**? During many periods in human history, a large segment of people were illiterate. Most people today don't even know what philosophy is, let alone have a familiarity with the traditional philosophical proofs for God.

Reformed epistemologists are fond of using their grandmothers as examples here. Grandma believes in God, but not because she has read St. Thomas Aquinas, William Paley, or St. Anselm of Canterbury. Most theists are like Grandma. They believe God exists and may even live lives of great faith without ever being exposed to theistic arguments, let alone convinced by them. So Reformed epistemologists conclude that most theists hold belief in God in the basic way.

One might object that although most theists have not been formally exposed to the theistic proofs, they have considered them in less formal ways. It doesn't take an educated person to look at the world and wonder how it came to be. You don't have to have read Paley's design argument to wonder at apparent design in nature.

The question though is not whether most theists have had these sorts of thoughts but *how* they had these thoughts. Do they think these thoughts and infer the existence of God, or do these thoughts inspire a belief in God? Reformed epistemologists contend that looking at a beautiful mountain range or the starry heavens triggers the belief in God without going through an inferential process. (We'll have more to say about this later).

3.4 Is Belief in God Justified?

There is a reasonable case that many, if not most, theists do not believe in God on the basis of arguments, and so it appears that belief in God can be basic. The next phase of the argument is to establish that such beliefs can be justified. This is the heart of Plantinga's positive project.

Is belief in God justified independent of arguments? The answer is that it depends. It depends on the meaning of "justification." The difficulty here is not merely verbal. Real disagreement exists among philosophers as to what justification amounts to. At the beginning of this chapter, we said that a belief is justified if it is based on a good reason. At this point, we need to leave that provisional definition and be more precise.

At the beginning of this chapter, we said that knowledge is (roughly) justified true belief. This view of knowledge was famously criticized in a three-page, 1963 article by the philosopher Edmund Gettier. Discussion and debate about Gettier's article led to many of the developments in the theory of knowledge that surround Plantinga's defense of religious belief. Having a basic understanding of Gettier's criticism might be helpful.

Gettier offers a counterexample rather like the following for thinking of knowledge as justified, true belief. Suppose that you are walking down a hallway in a building at your local college. As you pass by a room, you see what you take to be a person sitting there by herself. You then form the belief that at least one person in the room. You later learn that what you saw was not a person but an extremely well-made manikin. However, completely unknown to you, there is a person in the room, out of your line of vision. Your belief that a person is in the room is justified and true but it doesn't amount to knowledge.

Gettier-style counterexamples show us that the criteria for knowledge outlined in the justified true belief account aren't sufficient for knowledge. There are various ways of responding to the difficulty that Gettier raises, but the strategy that Plantinga adopts is to see Gettier problems as showing a defect in our previous understanding of justification. Plantinga offers an analysis that takes Gettier counterexamples into account, and he uses the term "warrant" for the concept that plays the role of justification in his analysis of knowledge. Let's take a closer look at two very rough pictures of justification and warrant.

3.5 Two Types of Justification: Justification and Warrant

Classically, justification is what must be added to true belief to yield knowledge. For our purposes, there are basically two types of theories of epistemic justification. We will distinguish between them by calling one type "justification" and the other "warrant." Plantinga uses more-or-less the same terminology (Plantinga 2000, p. 178). In Plantinga's earlier writing, he focused mainly on justification; in his later writing, he focuses on warrant. He argues that belief in God can be properly basic on either view.

3.5.1 Justification: Epistemic Obligation and Internalism

The classical picture of justification has two main components: "epistemic obligation," as it's called, and introspective awareness. The basic idea of epistemic obligation is that we have an obligation to try our best to make sure everything we believe is true. We have a duty to try to ensure that our epistemic house is in order.

This general obligation gives birth to other epistemic obligations. For example, if you have a duty to try to believe only true things, then you might be obligated to not form beliefs about a person who is a long distance away in the dark. You might have a duty not to believe that you had chocolate cake on your fifth birthday if the memory is very vague. You must do your best to believe only true things, so you should try to at least temper beliefs formed from seeing things from a distance in the dark or based on very vague and distant recollections.

This "epistemic obligation" view of justification implies **internalism**. Internalism and **externalism** are rather complex concepts. Rather than go too deeply into that labyrinth, we will provide a simplified account of those two ideas. Internalism is the view that the ability to reflect on the reasons for believing something is essential to justification. If you have obligations about how to form beliefs, then you must be able to examine the reasons for your beliefs introspectively to make sure they do not flout any duties. The obligation to do your best to ensure your epistemic house is in order implies that you have the ability to inspect your epistemic house.

According to this view of justification, a belief, then, is justified if two conditions are met: it was formed without disregarding our epistemic duty to try our best to ensure that what we believe is true, and we can reflect inwardly on the factors that confer justification.

3.5.2 Warrant: Proper Function of Cognitive Faculties

We have various cognitive faculties: the ability to reason, to call on memory, to form beliefs based on perception, and so on. **Warrant** is whatever must be added to true belief to make it knowledge, and according to Plantinga, a belief has **warrant** if the belief is produced by cognitive faculties that are properly functioning and are functioning in circumstances in which those faculties are designed to operate. We will henceforth use the word "warrant" in this sense. For example, Sally's belief that her car is in the driveway is warranted if it's formed by her properly functioning visual system (e.g., not by optical illusions, hallucinations, or other malfunctions) in conditions in which they were designed to operate (e.g., proper lighting and distance).

On Plantinga's view, warrant doesn't depend on the fulfilling of epistemic duties but on the reliability of the cognitive process that produced the belief. At the heart of Plantinga's view of warrant are properly functioning cognitive faculties rather than obligations and duties.

Furthermore, warrant is **externalistic** not internalistic. A belief can have warrant even if the individual doesn't know what gives the belief warrant. Sally doesn't have to know that her eyes are functioning properly or that they are operating in the circumstances for which they were designed for her belief to have warrant. What's important is that they are functioning correctly.

Notice also that with justification, we have a larger say in whether our beliefs are justified. We have more control because justification depends on us fulfilling our epistemic duties and making sure our epistemic house is in order. Warrant doesn't directly depend on us. All that matters for warrant is whether our belief is produced by properly functioning cognitive faculties, and this is something we have far less direct control of.

	Justification	*Warrant:*
Does a belief have justification/warrant?	It was formed without disregarding one's epistemic duty to try to ensure that what is believed is true.	It was produced by cognitive faculties functioning properly in circumstances in which they were design to operate.
Does the individual have to be able to know what justifies/ warrants belief?	Yes: Internalism	No: Externalism
How much direct control over justification/warrant does the individual have?	More direct control	Less direct control

3.6 Two Arguments that Belief in God Can Be Properly Basic: Justification and Warrant

Plantinga argues belief in God is both justified and warranted. Because the concepts are different, he offers two arguments: one for justification and one for warrant. Let's look at both.

3.6.1 Justification of Belief in God

Plantinga argues that it is pretty clear that belief in God is justified in the "epistemic obligation" sense described above. He thinks this because justification in this sense requires a low threshold. To be justified, one need only fulfill her epistemic duty to try to ensure that what she believes is true.

Suppose a believer does her level best to make sure her belief about God's existence is true. She open-mindedly reads the standard atheist arguments against the existence of God. She reflects on the problem of evil and alleged inconsistencies in the nature of God. She also reads Nietzsche's, Freud's, and Marx's critiques of religious beliefs.

Alternatively, she reads the arguments for the existence of God but does not believe in God *because* of them. She has had religious experiences in which she took God to be comforting, loving, and encouraging her. During worship services, prayer, or Bible reading sessions, she has a strong sense of the majesty and awe of God. She may sometimes even feel as if she is in God's very presence. She might feel what she takes to be the Holy Spirit enlightening her as previously bewildering passages of scripture suddenly become crystal clear. She mulls over her experiences:

> After long, hard, conscientious reflection, this all seems to her more convincing than the complaints of the critics. Is she then going contrary to duty in believing as she does? Is she being irresponsible? Clearly not. There could be something defective about her, some malfunction not apparent on the surface. She could be mistaken, a victim of illusion or wishful thinking, despite her best efforts. She could be wrong, desperately wrong, pitiably wrong ... nevertheless, she isn't flouting any discernable duty. She is fulfilling her epistemic responsibilities; she is doing her level best; she is justified (Plantinga 2000, p. 101).

She has fulfilled her obligations according to the theory of justification sketched above. She has done her level best to make sure what she believes is true. She has considered the arguments and experiences pro and con. She has introspective access to that which she takes to confer justification, her rich inner spiritual life:

> [H]ow can she possibly be blameworthy or irresponsible, if she thinks about the matter as hard as she can, in the most responsible way she can, and she still comes to these conclusions? (Plantinga 2000, p. 101)

Plantinga maintains not only that someone can hold her belief in this way but that many people do. If he's correct, then their belief in God is not only basic but is justified.

3.6.2 Warrant and the Aquinas/Calvin Model

For Christian belief to be warranted, it must be produced by properly functioning cognitive faculties and in circumstances in which those faculties are designed to operate. To show this, Plantinga would have to demonstrate that God exists and that he has endowed us with a cognitive faculty that produces belief in God.

He doesn't pretend to be able to establish this. Plantinga is content to argue that if Christianity is true, then belief in God is warranted. He is not even arguing that belief in God is warranted. Plantinga argues that it is warranted on the condition that Christianity is true.

One might object here that this thesis is both too obvious and too modest. It's too obvious because, clearly, if Christianity is true, then God exists. It's too modest because even if successful, it doesn't show that belief in God is warranted, let alone that God exists.

The criticism that Plantinga's thesis is too obvious is based on a subtle misunderstanding. He doesn't claim that if Christianity is true, then God exists. Rather, he contends that if Christianity is true, then belief in God is warranted. There's an important difference between these two claims. The first claim is trivial because the truth of Christianity logically entails the existence of God. The second claim is not as modest as it might seem. Critics of theistic belief have long charged that whether God exists or not, there's no good reason to believe that God exists. In other words, they point out that God could very well exist, but belief in God could still be unwarranted. Plantinga's argument would undermine this type of *de jure* objection. If he is correct, the truth of Christianity carries with it the mechanism for warranted theistic belief. This means that if Christianity is true, then belief in God is probably warranted. The *de jure* objections would then collapse into *de facto* objections: To show that belief in God isn't warranted, the critic would have to argue that, in fact, God doesn't exist. Contrary to popular opinion, this shows that whether belief in God is warranted depends on whether the belief is true.

Plantinga defends his claim by way of a model of how knowledge of God might work. If this model is true, then belief in God is warranted. Plantinga doesn't argue that the model is true. Rather, he argues that it's true "for all we know." If he can successfully show that (1) if his epistemic model of theistic belief is true, the theistic belief is warranted; and (2) if the epistemic model is true "for all we know," then he has succeeded in showing that as for all we know, belief in God is warranted.

The model he proposed is based on the philosophical and theological views of St. Thomas Aquinas and John Calvin. In their honor, he names this model the "A/C Model." The basic idea of the A/C Model is that God has designed humans with a cognitive mechanism that triggers belief in God in certain circumstances. According to the A/C Model, when a person finds herself themselves believing in God when she is staring at majestic mountains or the starry heavens above, this is due to part of the mind that triggers belief in God.

Our beliefs arise in part through cognitive processes. Some of the processes rest on inferences and can include awareness of the reasoning process that's part of the belief-forming mechanisms. Other belief-forming cognitive processes don't involve inferential processes of which we are or can be aware. They are the result of unconscious mechanisms that spit out a particular belief output when given the appropriate input. When I have the input of seeing a tree, I automatically form the belief that a tree is in front of me. We don't infer or reason that a tree exists; we see a tree and our perceptual belief mechanism kicks out the appropriate belief.

According to the A/C Model, God designed humans with a *sensus divinitatis*—a divine sense. The *sensus divinitatis* is a cognitive mechanism that outputs a belief in God given the correct sort of input. If this is correct, the input of seeing majestic mountains and starry heavens produces the output of a belief in God. Religious experience, worship, or Bible study may stimulate the *sensus divinitatis* to kick out a belief in God.

Suppose that the A/C Model is true. Does the truth of the model mean that belief can be warranted without evidence? It does, given the account of warrant sketched above. Recall that a belief is warranted if the belief is produced by properly functioning cognitive faculties in circumstances in which those faculties are designed to operate. If God designed our minds to cause belief in God when they are triggered by the appropriate stimulus, then belief so caused is warranted.

Notice further that belief caused in this way doesn't necessarily involve arguments or even religious perception. All it requires is that the belief is triggered by the stimulus God designed it to be triggered by. Triggers can include arguments and religious experience but they don't have to.

Is the model true? Plantinga thinks it is but doesn't think he can prove it. He is content to argue that it could be true. We have no reason to think it is false, according to Plantinga. When Plantinga argues that the A/C Model is possibly true, he doesn't mean "could be" in the weak sense. He doesn't merely mean that it is logically possible. He's making a stronger possibility claim. He claims that it is epistemically possible. The model is true "for all we know." Thus for all we know, belief in God is warranted without evidence, arguments, or inference.

4 OBJECTIONS

There are several objections to Plantinga's Reformed epistemology. We will limit our comments to the two main objections.

4.1 The Great Pumpkin Objection

The first objection is this: if belief in God is properly basic, then any belief can be properly basic.

> It is tempting to raise the following sort of question. If belief in God is properly basic, why cannot just any belief be properly basic? Could we not say the same for any bizarre aberration we can think of? What about voodoo or astrology? What about the belief that the Great Pumpkin returns every Halloween? . . . If we say that belief in God is properly basic, will we not be committed to holding that just anything, or nearly anything, can properly be taken as basic, thus throwing wide the gates to irrationalism and superstition? (Plantinga 1983, p. 74)

Plantinga calls this objection the "Great Pumpkin Objection." His thinking on these issues has developed over time and we will organize our discussion around that development.

4.1.1 Early Plantinga and the Great Pumpkin Objection

In his early writings, Plantinga argued that the Great Pumpkin Objection amounts to this: if we reject the classical foundationalist criteria for proper basicality and do not replace it with other criteria, then we're left without any rules for deciding when a belief is properly basic. Without such rules, anything and everything can legitimately count as properly basic.

Plantinga made two replies to this objection. First, the mere fact that we lack criteria for distinguishing between two things doesn't mean we can't differentiate them. Supreme Court Justice Potter Stewart made this point when he famously said that even though he can't define pornography, he knows it when he sees it.

To understand Plantinga's response, it's helpful to consider the abortion debate. On one construal of that debate, opponents of abortion claim that fetuses are persons and hence have a right not to be killed. Advocates of permitting abortion argue that fetuses are not persons and thus a woman has a right to terminate her pregnancy under certain circumstances. Viewed this way, the moral status of abortion depends on whether a fetus is a person. But what is a person? What distinguishes persons from non-persons? What are the criteria of personhood?

Suppose proponents of abortion rights argue that something is a person if and only if it can reason at the level of a newborn baby. Abortion opponents reject that criterion. By rejecting that criterion, they aren't obligated to count just anything as a person, even if they don't offer their own criteria. We know, even without widely agreed-upon criteria, that rocks aren't persons but normal adult humans are. (Needless to say, this example isn't intended to settle the abortion debate.) Likewise, Plantinga argues that just because he rejects the classical foundationalist's criteria for proper basicality and does not offer his own, does not mean he must accept just anything as properly basic. He can still know, without criteria, that $2 + 2 = 4$ is properly basic and belief in the Great Pumpkin is not.

Although in his earlier writings Plantinga didn't suggest criteria for proper basicality to replace the classical foundationalist's criteria, he did suggest a method for arriving at such criteria. He argued that we shouldn't begin with criteria for proper basicality and then judge whether a belief is properly basic using those criteria. Rather, we should first examine our beliefs to see which ones are properly basic. Once we have a set of properly basic beliefs, we can examine their similarities to each other and differences from beliefs that aren't properly basic, and from these characterizations form criteria for counting beliefs as properly basic.

Returning to the analogy of the abortion debate, we shouldn't begin with a general definition of a person and then use that to decide which particular things are persons. Rather, we should collect a relevant set of examples of persons and non-persons and develop general criteria for personhood by characterizing the similarities and differences among and between these particular examples. Similarly, Plantinga thinks we should develop criteria for proper basicality from a relevant set of particular examples of properly basic beliefs.

Opponents and proponents of abortion rights might disagree about which particular things are persons, and so they might come to different definitions of a person. Theists and atheists might disagree with which beliefs count as properly basic and thus develop different criteria for proper basicality. Plantinga admits that this inductive method will not help settle any argument between atheists and theists and so is not polemically useful, but he doesn't think it must be:

> Criteria for proper basicality must be reached from below rather than above; they should not be presented as ex cathedra, but argued to and tested by a relevant set of examples. But there is no reason to assume, in advance, that everyone will agree on the examples. The Christian will of course suppose that belief in God is entirely proper and rational ... followers of Bertrand Russell and Madelyn Murray O'Hare may disagree, but how is that relevant? (Plantinga 1992, p. 140)

4.1.2 Later Plantinga and the Great Pumpkin Objection

In his early works, Plantinga was committed to there being a difference between properly and non-properly basic beliefs, but he didn't say what the difference was supposed to be. He just suggested a method for developing the criteria for proper basicality.

In his later writings, Plantinga specified the difference in terms of warrant. The difference between belief in the Great Pumpkin and belief in God is that belief in the Great Pumpkin isn't produced by properly functioning cognitive faculties in circumstances in which those faculties are designed to operate, whereas a belief in God is.

In other words, when later Plantinga applies the method for arriving at criteria for proper basicality suggested by earlier Plantinga (along with other general theorizing about knowledge), the result is criteria for proper basicality based on his view of warrant. A belief is properly basic if it is held in the basic way and produced by properly functioning cognitive faculties in circumstances in which those faculties are designed to operate. Plantinga thinks that belief in God meets these criteria, whereas belief in the Great Pumpkin doesn't.

4.2 Son of the Great Pumpkin Objection

Atheist philosopher Michael Martin raises a similar objection:

> Although Reformed epistemologists would not have to accept voodoo beliefs as rational, voodoo followers would be able to claim that insofar as they are basic in the voodoo community they are rational and, moreover, that Reformed thought was irrational in this community. Indeed, Plantinga's proposal would generate many different communities that could legitimately claim that their basic beliefs are rational ... Among the communities generated might be devil worshipers, flat earthers, and believers in fairies, just so long as belief in the devil, the flatness of the earth, and fairies was basic in the respective communities.

Plantinga understands the "son" of the Great Pumpkin Objection to be the following sort of argument:

> *Premise #1*: If Reformed epistemologists are warranted in claiming that belief in God is properly basic, then voodoo epistemologists are warranted in claiming that belief in voodoo is properly basic.
>
> *Premise #2*: Voodoo epistemologists are not warranted in claiming that belief in voodoo is properly basic.
>
> *Conclusion*: Therefore, Reformed epistemologists are not warranted in claiming that belief in God is properly basic.

Plantinga criticizes the Son of the Great Pumpkin Objection by pointing out that it is possible that Reformed epistemologists are warranted in believing that belief in God is properly basic and at the same time voodoo epistemologists are not warranted in believing that voodoo belief is properly basic. If he's correct, then the first premise is false and the objection fails. The thrust of his criticism is appealing. After all, why think a connection exists between whether Reformed epistemologists are warranted in believing Reformed epistemology and voodoo epistemologists being warranted in believing voodoo epistemology? On the surface, for one to be warranted while the other isn't seems possible.

Still, this reply seems to miss the point. After responding to the Son of the Great Pumpkin Objection, Plantinga raises the following objection "in the spirit of the Son of the Great Pumpkin Objection": the heart of Plantinga's case is that a model exists—the A/C Model—that, if true, makes belief in God warranted independent of arguments. He then argued that the A/C Model is true as far as we know. Could not voodoo epistemologists or Great Pumpkin epistemologists make a similar argument with equal cogency?

It seems *prima facie* possible for a voodoo epistemologist to describe a model—call it the "voodoo model"—that, if true, makes belief in voodoo warranted independent of arguments. It doesn't seem too far-fetched to think the voodoo epistemologist could also argue that the voodoo model is true "for all we know." If such a case can be made, the Reformed epistemologist and the voodoo epistemologist are, for all we know, in the same epistemic boat. This seems closer to the objection Michael Martin had in mind.

Plantinga responds here by conceding that something like this might be true for other theistic religions like Judaism, Islam, and some forms of Buddhism and Hinduism. But it doesn't seem to be true for a host of other beliefs like voodoo, philosophical naturalism, the belief that the Earth is flat, or Humean skepticism. Consider Humean skepticism: Hume tells us that we ought to be skeptical of our belief forming processes. Hume thinks that many of our belief-forming processes lead us to believe things that are unlikely, arbitrary, or dubious. This skepticism about our belief-forming processes raises doubt about the very cognitive processes that cause us to be skeptical. Plantinga argues that this raises serious doubt about whether we can find a model such that if Humean skepticism is true, then we are most likely warranted in believing that it is true. The upshot is that the truth of Humean skepticism decreases the likelihood that our beliefs are reliably formed. This includes our beliefs about the truth of Humean skepticism. The truth of Humean skepticism then makes it less likely that our beliefs about Humean skepticism are true. Alternatively, the truth of the A/C Model makes the belief that God exists more likely. Thus, Plantinga argues, it's far from obvious that just any belief system can make an analogous argument to the Reformed epistemologists' system with equal cogency.

Plantinga's reply to this objection amounts to saying that the objection is correct in some cases (Judaism, Islam, etc.) but not in others (Humean skepticism, voodoo, etc.). That is to say, there may be other religious points of view that can argue that if their claims are true, their adherents could *know* this without evidence, but there are limits to the range of beliefs for which this can reasonably be claimed. At best, Plantinga has reduced the scope of the objection. Rather than "throwing wide the gates to irrationalism and superstition," he seems to be conceding that Reformed epistemology at least "partially opens the gates" to other world religions and perhaps more exotic beliefs.

What's more, his claim—that the truth of Humean skepticism does not make it likely that our cognitive faculties are reliable, —is plausible because Humean skepticism takes a skeptical and critical view of our belief-forming processes. Because it's an epistemic theory, it is self-referential. However, it is not obvious how the truth of belief systems like voodoo or the Great Pumpkin—which are not primarily views about knowledge, let alone systems of skeptical views of knowledge—make our belief in them less likely. In other words, Plantinga's reply seems to rule out only a very few types of systems and does not apply to bizarre beliefs like that of the Great Pumpkin.

5 CONCLUSION

Reformed epistemologists, like Alvin Plantinga, have enriched the philosophy of religion with well thought-out and sophisticated epistemic views. They have undermined crass forms of evidentialism that were once commonplace in the philosophy of religion and exposed an unwarranted favoring of inferential ways of knowing. In short, Plantinga's negative project seems more-or-less successful.

Alternatively, the positive project seems to have problems somewhere in the vicinity of the father and son Great Pumpkin Objections, though to spell out the problem in precise terms is difficult. Early in Plantinga's career, he was fond of saying that belief in God is in the same epistemic boat as other common beliefs like the belief in other minds.

The problem with the positive project is that it's hard to see how Reformed epistemology and Great Pumpkin epistemology are not in the same epistemic boat. Plantinga's reply to the Son of the Great Pumpkin Objection partially concedes this point but tries to limit the scope of the objection. At best, he seems to have limited the scope to a minor extent. The door to bizarre beliefs might not be wide open but it is open enough to raise doubts about the positive project.

AT A GLANCE: REFORMED EPISTEMOLOGY

1. The Evidentialist Objection

   Premise #1: If there is insufficient evidence that God exists, then belief in God is unjustified.
   Premise #2: There is insufficient evidence that God exists.
   Conclusion: Therefore, belief in God is unjustified.

2. Knowledge
   * Knowledge is justified, true belief.

   2.1. Roughly Two Views of Justification
      * *Justification*: A belief is justified if and only if it was formed without disregarding one's epistemic duty to try to ensure that what is believed is true and the individual knower has introspective access to that which confers justification on a belief.
      * *Warrant*: A belief has warrant if and only if it was produced by cognitive faculties functioning properly in circumstances in which they were designed to operate. The individual knower need not have introspective access to that which confers warrant on a belief.

	Justification	*Warrant*
Does a belief have justification/warrant?	It was formed without disregarding one's epistemic duty to try to ensure that what is believed is true.	It was produced by cognitive faculties functioning properly in circumstances in which they were design to operate.
Does the individual have to be able to know what justifies/warrants belief?	Yes: Internalism	No: Externalism
How much direct control over justification/warrant does the individual have?	More direct control	Less direct control

3. The Argument that Belief in God is Properly Basic
   3.1. The basic point: The belief that God exists can be justified and warranted without arguments for the existence of God.
   3.2. The Argument

   Premise #1: If a belief is basic and justified/warranted, then it is properly basic (definition).
   Premise #2: Belief in God is basic and justified/warranted (premise).
   Conclusion: Therefore, belief in God is properly basic.

4. Argument for Premise #2
   4.1. Argument that the belief that God exists is justified

   - Justification is a low threshold to meet. A person must merely meet their epistemic obligations. It seem clear to Plantinga That someone can meet one's epistemic obligations and still believe in God.

   4.2. Argument that the belief that God exists is warranted

   - The Aquinas/Calvin (A/C) Model: God designed humans with a divine sense, a cognitive mechanism that outputs a belief in God's existence given the correct sort of input. It can be triggered by seeing majestic mountains, religious experience, worship, or Bible study.
   - If the A/C Model is true, the belief that God exists is warranted. Further, the A/C Model is true as far all we know.

5. The Great Pumpkin Objection
   5.1. The Objection: If belief in the existence of God is properly basic, why can't the belief in the existence of the Great Pumpkin also be properly basic?
   5.2. Replies

   - Early Plantinga Reply #1: the Reformed epistemologist has simply rejected a particular set of criteria about proper basicality and not

replaced it with a set of his own. Rejecting a criterion or definition does not commit one to the view that there is no definition (e.g., we may reject a particular definition of porn and do not have a replacement definition, but this doesn't mean we don't know porn when we see it).
- Early Plantinga Reply #2: although Reformed epistemologists don't have criteria for proper basicality, they do suggest an inductive method for arriving at some.
- Later Plantinga Reply: we have new criteria that might apply to a belief in God's existence but not to a belief in the Great Pumpkin's existence.

FURTHER READINGS

Kenny, A. (1983). *Faith and Reason.* New York: Columbia University Press.

Martin, M. (1990). *Atheism: A Philosophical Justification.* Philadelphia: Temple University Press.

Parsons, K. M. (1989). *God and the Burden of Proof.* Buffalo, NY: Prometheus Books.

Plantinga, A. (1983). "Reason and Belief in God." In A. Plantinga and N. Wolterstorff. *Faith and Rationality: Reason and Belief in God.* Notre Dame, IN: Notre Dame University Press.

Plantinga, A. (2000). *Warranted Christian Belief.* New York: Oxford University Press.

CHAPTER 8

Faith and Pragmatic Reasons for Belief

Some people say that religious belief is a matter of faith, but this term needs defining. Others say that we can sometimes have good reasons for believing something even if those reasons don't make it more likely that the belief is true. These are called pragmatic reasons. William James and Blaise Pascal both offered pragmatic arguments for believing in the existence of God. This chapter examines faith and pragmatic reasons, and looks at the role our emotions and passions might legitimately play in religious belief.

Some believers take themselves to know that God exists, and perhaps they do. Other believers don't take themselves to know. They might have doubts about the usual arguments. They might have had tantalizing experiences that hint of divinity, but they may find those experiences too difficult to read—not enough to add up to knowledge.

Some believers see lack of evidence as a good thing. Soren Kierkegaard, the nineteenth-century Danish thinker, believed that true faith calls for an infinite commitment. As he saw it, if we knew that God exists, we couldn't demonstrate that sort of commitment. Others say that belief must be freely chosen to have any religious value. If we knew that God existed, then there wouldn't be room for the free and willing decision to believe.

Then some don't believe at all. Some wish they could. Others think that religious belief is an intellectual vice. Like the believers who say they do not know, these non-believers don't think the evidence for God is good enough. Even if we understand the word "evidence" broadly—as meaning anything that can count toward the truth of beliefs, or make them more probable—these people think that when considered strictly on the evidence, religious belief fails the test. The question for this chapter is whether it's acceptable to believe if we think the **epistemic** justification comes up short. However, "epistemic justification" is a lumbering sort of phrase. In this chapter, we'll use the term "evidence," understood broadly, or sometimes "grounds" or "basis."

1 FAITH

Some people would say that our topic is faith. Many people will say that faith is exactly what we substitute when we don't have solid support for a belief. No doubt this is one of the ways the word "faith" is used. In this way of looking at things, faith and knowledge are like oil and water: they don't mix. However, we must be clear that this isn't the only way of thinking about faith.

A famous definition of faith is found in the Christian New Testament: "faith is the assurance of things hoped for, the conviction of things not seen" (Hebrews 11:1, New Revised Standard Version). Focus on the second clause for a moment: faith is the conviction of things not seen. In Roman Catholic theology, Divine Faith is intellectual assent to truths that aren't evident to human reason or the senses but that are revealed by God. The intellectual assent that's part of Divine Faith is the result of an act of will that divine grace enables the believer to make. It can be compared to our accepting the authority of scientists, who tell us things that aren't evident to us. However, because the authority accepted in an act of Divine Faith is God, the authority is infallible. Indeed, in Catholic theology, faith is a form of *knowledge* rather than something contrary to knowledge.

A full exposition of this concept of faith is more than we can undertake here; it fits into a rich and complex **epistemology** of religious belief. The reader may want to look at the lucid 10,000-word entry on faith in the 1914 edition of the Catholic Encyclopedia. Here we will simply mention two challenges to this view.

One is that if faith is a matter of assent to revelation, we need knowledge of the God who reveals what faith assents to. Catholic tradition has a lot to say about this, some of which we have already discussed. But establishing this part of the account isn't trivial. This is exactly where the sort of person this chapter is concerned with will likely find himself intellectually unconvinced.

The other challenge is like the one that religious diversity posed for Alston's account of Christian Mystical Practice, as discussed in Chapter 6. Other religions can construct accounts that are broadly parallel to the Catholic understanding of faith, but the conclusions the believer is expected to accept will be very different. For someone who is not already convinced, the theory isn't likely to give him a reason to accept one set of doctrines by faith rather than another.

2 W. K. CLIFFORD AND THE ETHICS OF BELIEF

For the moment, we'll set aside the idea that faith might be a form of knowledge. We'll turn to the person who thinks that the objective grounds for religious belief aren't enough to make the case. Some such people believe anyway, using the word "faith" in what some might call the "vulgar" sense to describe their attitude. W. K. Clifford (1845–1879), known in some circles for his contributions to mathematics, is most famous for his bracing denunciation of faith understood in this way. As Clifford saw it, it's actually immoral to believe without adequate evidence.

Here's the scenario that Clifford presents us with in his essay, "The Ethics of Belief." Suppose a shipowner has a ship that he knows is old and quite possibly in poor repair. It's about to set sail carrying a group of emigrants to their newly-intended home. Rather than have the ship checked over, he persuades himself, without any real evidence, that the ship is fit to sail. It's not just that he decides he doesn't care; he actually lets himself come to believe that the ship is in good repair. Weeks later, it sinks at sea and all of the people on board drown.

Clifford says that the shipowner is guilty. He's morally responsible for the deaths of those passengers. He didn't have anything close to good evidence for thinking the ship was seaworthy, and so he had no right to believe it. But Clifford goes further. He says that even if the ship had made it safely to its destination, the shipowner would be just as guilty. Only luck kept his sloppy thinking from leading to disaster.

Suppose we grant Clifford his point: the shipowner is guilty in the moral sense, whether or not in the legal sense, and would still be guilty even if the passengers had survived. Is it his belief that makes him guilty? We might say that what matters isn't what the shipowner privately believed. What matters is what he did or failed to do.

Clifford agrees that to act on an ill-founded belief is even worse than to hold the belief but not to act on it. Nonetheless, he thinks that's not the whole story. We depend on one another in our beliefs. No one alone can do all the work of sifting the evidence we need to keep ourselves on track. By believing without evidence, we make ourselves gullible, we make it more likely that at some point we'll really foul things up, we make ourselves less reliable as a source of knowledge for others, and we weaken the common trust of beliefs that all of us need to depend on. Here's the consequence, according to Clifford:

> [I]t is wrong always, everywhere, and for anyone, to believe anything upon insufficient evidence (Clifford 2003 (1901), p. 367).

Of course, if this is correct, religious belief would be acceptable if there is sufficient evidence for it, but what if that's not so? Has Clifford really shown that religious faith is wrong?

2.1 Satisfying Clifford's Slogan

Suppose you ask a stranger on the street what time it is. She glances at her watch and says "3:15." Is that sufficient evidence? After all, you don't know this person, don't know how carefully she looked at her watch, don't know if the watch works correctly, and don't know if she set it properly. There is plenty of room for doubt. Should you refuse to believe? If so, then it may turn out that "sufficient evidence" is a rare thing. But it's hard to believe that we shouldn't take a stranger's word for the time of day. We don't have unlimited leisure to spend sorting out what is and isn't so. Isn't it plausible that in some matters it's not worth worrying too much about whether we get things right? Clifford would almost certainly agree that we should take the stranger's word, but whether he can provide a good account of this is another matter.

Also notice that Clifford's argument appeals to facts, and it's not clear that he's gotten them straight. Is it really true that people who are careless about some of their beliefs are likely to be careless when the truth really counts? Wouldn't showing that take hard scientific work? Clifford didn't do any studies; he just insists.

Actually, it's worse. It's not just that Clifford isn't true to his own dictum; his dictum applies to itself. Do we have sufficient evidence to believe that it's always wrong to believe without sufficient evidence? It's hardly clear that we do.

Finally, Clifford makes it sound as though there's only one value at stake in believing: the truth. That may well be wrong.

3 EPISTEMIC VS. NON-EPISTEMIC REASONS

When we think about reasons for believing, we usually think about reasons that bear on how likely the belief is to be true. But there are other sorts of reasons. Gilbert Harman offers a distinction. First, Harman's own way of putting it:

> *Epistemic reasons for belief*: R is an epistemic reason to believe P only if the probability of P given R is greater than the probability of P given not-R.
>
> *Non-epistemic reasons for belief*: R is a non-epistemic reason to believe P if R is a reason to believe P over and above the extent to which the probability of P given R is greater than the probability of P given not-R (Harman 1995, p. 183).

The language here is a little dense, so let's illustrate. The fact that George's fingerprints were found at the crime scene is an epistemic reason for thinking he was there. To use the language of Chapter 5, it's **relevant**. The **probability** that he was there is higher on the assumption that his fingerprints were found there than on the assumption that they weren't. However, the fact that you have a grudge against George isn't an epistemic reason for believing that he was at the scene. The probability that he really was there is the same whether or not you have a grudge.

Epistemic reasons are important, but whether believing something is reasonable isn't always just a matter of epistemic reasons. If a friend of yours has been accused of dishonesty, you might believe that he's innocent because you value being loyal to him. Harman points out that depending on the value of the friendship, this might not be unreasonable at all, even though your loyalty isn't an *epistemic* reason for believing him. Some studies suggest that people who are depressed actually view the world more realistically than people who aren't. But it may be that realism isn't good for the depressed person, and that he'd be better off if his glasses were a little rosier. If so, most of us have a non-epistemic reason for having optimistic beliefs.

It seems that reasonableness isn't entirely a matter of *epistemic* reasonableness. If that's correct, then religious belief could be reasonable in this broader sense even if it isn't based on epistemically relevant evidence.

Harman uses the term "non-epistemic reasons." It's not unusual to find the term **pragmatic reasons** used as a way of covering much the same territory. A pragmatic reason for believing is a reason that has to do with our well-being, broadly understood, rather than with the likelihood that the belief is true. We'll use this term interchangeably with "non-epistemic reasons."

4 PASCAL'S WAGER

The seventeenth-century French thinker Blaise Pascal agrees that there isn't sufficient evidence to justify belief in God on epistemic grounds. However, in his *Pensées* he argues that the non-epistemic reasons are overwhelming.

Pascal thinks of deciding whether believe in the existence of God as a sort of a gamble. You can believe in God, or not. Depending on whether God exists or not, certain consequences will follow. Think of a more ordinary wager. Suppose you can take the following gamble: you roll the dice. If they come up 2 (that is, each die comes up 1), you will win $35. If they come up anything else, you'll lose $1. Is this a reasonable bet? The chance that the dice will come up 2 is 1/36. This means that you would only win one time out of 36 but, on average, if you played often enough, you would break even. Rationality doesn't require you to take the gamble, but it certainly allows you to do so. However, suppose that the gamble was this: you roll the dice, and if they come up 2, you win $1000. If they don't, you only lose $1. In this case, the bet is so favorable to you that it almost seems unreasonable not to take it.

A concept called **expected utility** helps us think about this, and though Pascal didn't use the term, his wager argument is one of the sources for the idea. When we make a choice, we have alternatives. The outcome for us depends on which alternative we pick and on how things turn out in the world. If you bet on 2 and the dice come up 2, you win; otherwise, you lose. The **utility** of an outcome is its value to you. For winning at dice, it will usually be some amount of money. (On the relationship between money and utility, see the glossary.) For losing, the utility is negative—money lost. In other circumstances, the utilities might not be monetary. Having a good time on your vacation might be the outcome of a choice, and whatever value you put on that is the utility it has for you.

The idea of expected utility is to help us deal with uncertainty by asking on average how much we might expect to gain or lose by deciding in a certain way. The unrealistic game we've just described provides an illustration. Suppose you played the game many, many times. In 36,000 plays (about 25 a day for 4 years), you could expect to lose approximately 35,000 times. This would cost you $35,000. But you would expect to win 1000 times, and that would pay $1 million. Your total winnings would be $965,000 and your average win per game would be about $26.81. That average is the expected utility. The idea is that when choosing, you should pick the option with the highest expected utility.

What does all this have to do with God? Either God exists or he doesn't. Pascal assumes either you choose to believe he does or you don't. **Agnosticism** is still lack of belief. What should you do? Clifford would say: look at the evidence for God's existence. Pascal says: look at the potential gains and losses that go with believing or disbelieving. Let your reasoning about them decide what you choose to believe.

As Pascal sees it, we have no way to know whether God exists or not. At one point, Pascal talks about a coin toss at infinity, and this might suggest that it's a 50/50 chance whether God exists. The argument doesn't have to assume that probability, but let's begin this way. Suppose you decide to believe in God and, as the universe turns out, God really exists. Then your payoff is infinite bliss. Alternatively, suppose that you decide not to believe. Then you've gained whatever value there is in living as a non-believer but you've missed your chance at the infinite.

Now suppose you've decided to believe but God doesn't exist. Pascal says that this costs you nothing. We'll have more to say about this later but for now, suppose we disagree with Pascal and grant that there is some cost in avoiding the worldly pleasures that a life of religious devotion would leave behind. Likewise, we'll suppose that if no God exists and you don't believe, this gives you some advantage over the believer.

Here's one possible pay-off table:

	God Exists	*God Doesn't Exist*
Believe in God	∞	−10
Don't Believe in God	10	10

The numbers in the cells are the utilities or values of the four possible outcomes. As we'll see, nothing depends on the exact choice of the three finite numbers. All that matters is the infinite value in the first cell. (By the way, note that we've ignored the possibility of hellfire for not believing—more on that below. For now, we're staying close to the way Pascal actually presented his argument.)

What's the expected utility of believing in God? In the normal case, we need two kinds of information to figure that out: the utilities or values of the outcomes, and the probabilities of the facts at issue. In this case, the fact at issue is whether God exists. Let's use the probability of 1/2 that Pascal's comment about the coin toss suggests. To get started, we multiply the number in each box by the probability at the top of the column:

	God Exists (p = 1/2)	God Doesn't Exist (p = 1/2)
Believe in God	$\infty \times 1/2 = \infty$	$-10 \times 1/2 = -5$
Don't Believe in God	$10 \times 1/2 = 5$	$10 \times 1/2 = 5$

To find the expected utility of not believing, we add the results in the two "don't believe" boxes. Because 5 + 5 = 10, the expected utility of non-belief is 10. We do the same to get the utility of believing, but here we get a spectacular result: 1/2 of infinity is still infinity, and infinity minus 5 is still infinity. Even though there is a 50/50 chance that you'll end up a loser, the payoff is infinite if God exists, and you've chosen to believe he does. Therefore, the expected utility of believing in God is infinite. If this is correct, it would appear to be completely irrational not to believe!

So long as the probability of God's existence is greater than zero, we get the same result. But even if you think God's existence is very improbable, setting the probability at a flat zero seems extreme.

4.1 Some Preliminary Objections

In the next section, we'll discuss a major objection to Pascal's wager. Here we'll deal briefly with a number of smaller objections.

4.1.1 Does Expected Utility Apply?

First, we introduced the idea of expected utility by talking about what you would expect to happen on average if you repeated a gamble many times. That doesn't fit the problem we're dealing with, though. We don't get to try belief or non-belief over several lifetimes and let the average rack up. However, if we're thrown into a one-shot situation where we have no choice but to wager, it's not obvious that we have a better alternative than using expected utilities to decide. Let's assume this for argument's sake, even though there's actually plenty of room to argue.

Trying to apply the theory of expected utility when infinite pay-offs are part of the mix raises complicated technical questions. Sorting this out is beyond our scope. We'll assume that the difficulties can be resolved, but we can also add: if we replace the infinities with numbers that are very large compared to the probabilities, we can get the same conclusion without having to address the problem of infinite payoffs.

4.1.2 Can We Choose Our Beliefs?

Pascal assumes that we have a real option about what to believe, but it's not obvious that we can choose our beliefs. For example, we dare say that you can't choose to believe—really believe—that you are a poached egg. The brief reply is that in some cases, we do have some control, even if we can't just immediately decide what to believe. Pascal suggests that if you pray, start going to religious services, make friends with religious people, and so on, you will be able to come to believe.

This idea isn't crazy at all. It's often said during the first year of law school, you begin thinking like a lawyer. A person who has been part of the workforce and accepts an offer to join the management team is very likely to find that a lot of workplace issues come to look very different. If you move to a new culture, you're very likely to find your values and ways of looking at things gradually shifting. Our choices can influence our beliefs. It seems reasonable to assume that for many people who don't believe, picking religious companions and practices that suit their personalities might very well eventually bring them to believe in God.

4.1.3 The Possibility of Damnation

Yet another issue: we've assumed that even if a God does exist, the cost of being a non-believer is finite at worst. This overlooks the possibility of eternal damnation. We'll address this problem in the next section, but on the face of it, it helps Pascal's case: if damnation is a possibility, then non-belief, it seems, has infinitely negative utility.

4.1.4 Using the Wager is Cynical

One final preliminary objection: some people would say that deciding to believe based on calculating the payoffs is such a cynical choice that we couldn't expect God to reward it, assuming that God exists. However, George Schlesinger and William Lycan point out that even if you start out as a cynic, by doing the right things you can become a sincere believer, and that might be good enough.

4.2 The Many Gods Objection

If Pascal's argument is a good one, then even if there's no sufficient epistemic reason for believing in God, there's a pragmatic or non-epistemic reason so powerful that it's not clear how it could be rational to resist. In that case, Clifford is wrong with a vengeance. However, the story isn't quite this simple.

As we noted above, certain traditional views have the consequence that if God exists and you don't believe, then you're in for eternal damnation. In fact, this might have been what Pascal had in mind, though it's not easy to say for sure. In the simplest case, we get a table like the one shown, which you'll see in many presentations of the wager:

	God Exists ($p = x$)	God Doesn't Exist ($p = y$)
Believe in God	$\infty \times x = \infty$	$-10 \times y = -10y$
Don't Believe in God	$-\infty \times x = -\infty$	$10 \times y = 10y$

Here x can be any probability you like, except zero. The probabilities x and y add to 1 since God either exists or doesn't. The end result is that believing in God has infinite expected utility, but the expected utility of not believing is infinitely bad.

This appears to make the argument even stronger. However, assuming that damnation is a possible option makes one particular objection to Pascal especially powerful. That objection is called the *Many Gods Problem*. The problem comes up even if we leave out the possibility of Hell, but we'll include that worry in what we say from here forward.

Suppose that God exists but it's the God of traditional Christianity. According to many believers, that God will condemn us if we don't accept specifically Christian beliefs. However, suppose that you are considering converting to Islam. If you believe in Allah but don't believe in the Holy Trinity of Father, Son, and Holy Spirit, traditional Christians would say that you're damned all the same. Alternatively, perhaps the true God is not the God of Christianity but some other God who will condemn Christian believers to eternal torment. To get the correct expected utility, we can't avoid considering all these possibilities. That makes the utility table considerably more complicated than the simple version we have above. Minimally, it's more like this:

	God 1 Exists (prob = v)	God 2 Exists (prob = w)	God 3 Exists (prob = x)	God 4 Exists (prob = y)	No God Exists (prob = z)
Believe in God 1	$+\infty \times v = +\infty$	$-\infty \times w = -\infty$	$-\infty \times x = -\infty$	$+\infty \times y = +\infty$	$-10 \times z$
Believe in God 2	$+\infty \times v = +\infty$	$+\infty \times w = +\infty$	$-\infty \times x = -\infty$	$+\infty \times y = +\infty$	$-10 \times z$
Believe in God 3	$-\infty \times v = -\infty$	$+\infty \times w = +\infty$	$+\infty \times x = +\infty$	$+\infty \times y = +\infty$	$-10 \times z$
Believe in God 4	$-\infty \times v = -\infty$	$-\infty \times w = -\infty$	$-\infty \times x = -\infty$	$+\infty \times y = +\infty$	$-10 \times z$
Don't Believe	$-\infty \times v = -\infty$	$-100 \times w$	$-\infty \times x = -\infty$	$+\infty \times y = +\infty$	$-10 \times z$

Some gods might reward us only if we believe in them explicitly (God #3; look down the column under "God 3 Exists"). Some might reward us if we believe in them or in some "nearby" god, but not otherwise (God #1 and God #2). Some gods might reward us no matter what we believe or don't believe (God #4). Some gods see believing in certain other gods as worse than non-belief (God #2). Obviously, we've left out many, many variations, and the problem would still come arise even if we replaced all those negative infinities with finite numbers.

Is anything left to say? In the table above, we can see that some infinities cancel and some don't. We end up with these results:

Expected Utility of Believing in God #1	$-10z$
Expected Utility of Believing in God #2	$+\infty$
Expected Utility of Believing in God #3	$+\infty$
Expected Utility of Believing in God #4	$-\infty$
Expected Utility of Non-Belief	$-100w - 10z$

This might suggest a solution of sorts: do all the calculations and see which choices have the highest expected utilities. If there are ties, choose among the best as you see fit. For our table, that would mean believing in God #2 or in God #3. How should we choose at that point? William Lycan and George Schlesinger point out that even if two options have the same expected utility, the evidence for one might be better or theoretical considerations might favor believing in one sort of God over another. That might give us a reason for choosing, even if the infinities make the theory of expected utility unsuitable for seeing this.

The optimistic view is that we'll get a tidy table and we'll be able to find a clean way to make a decision. Unfortunately, the table might work out many, many ways and some of them are bound to be very untidy indeed. It's hard to know how we should even begin the reasoning once we get serious about the range of possibilities. As soon as we try to fill in the details, Pascal's wager becomes a very confusing bet.

5 WILLIAM JAMES AND THE WILL TO BELIEVE

Pascal's argument has problems, but perhaps its possible to show something weaker. Perhaps it can be shown that even if the evidence is poor, belief in God is rational, even though it may not be rationally required. This is what William James, the great early twentieth-century American pragmatist philosopher, argued in his essay, "The Will to Believe." He describes his argument as "an essay in justification of faith, a defense of our right to adopt a believing attitude in religious matters, in spite of the fact that our merely logical intellect may not have been coerced."

James argues that our passions can influence our beliefs, and that sometimes it's perfectly appropriate that they should. Here's his principle:

> Our passional nature not only lawfully may, but must, decide an option between propositions, whenever it is a genuine option that cannot by its nature be decided on intellectual grounds (James 1896, p. 200).

This is how James sees the religious case, but to understand him, we need to define some terms.

5.1 Options

First, an *option* between propositions is a choice about whether to accept one hypothesis or belief instead of another. In the case we're considering, the option is between accepting or not accepting a religious view of the world. Second, a *genuine* option is one that's living, forced, and momentous—more terms to define.

A *living option* is one in which both sides have some credibility for us. Even atheists are often able to take the possibility that a God *might* exist seriously. That said, probably none of us can take seriously the hypothesis that the Moon is made of green cheese or that the universe was created by an immaterial cockroach.

A *forced option* is one in which we don't have any additional alternatives. If we ask you to choose between believing that the next US president will be a Democrat or a Republican, you aren't forced to pick one of these choices. You could believe that it will be a third party candidate, or you could refuse to have a definite opinion at all. But if we ask you to choose between believing that a God exists or not believing, the option is forced. Even if you are an *agnostic*, that amounts to not believing that God exists.

A *momentous option* is one in which the stakes are extraordinarily high or where you are confronted with a unique and uniquely valuable opportunity. This isn't a precise idea, but James thinks that the decision to believe or not believe in God is momentous.

A genuine option then is a living, forced, momentous option. In the case of religious commitment, the option is at least partly a matter of accepting or not accepting certain hypotheses. Clifford would say that even in this case, we should only accept a hypothesis if the evidence warrants it. James disagrees, and we'll explain why below. Meanwhile, James insists that even if we follow Clifford's advice, we're letting our passions rule. How so?

5.2 Passion, Truth, and Error

We aren't robots. We have real intellectual commitments. What's clear in Clifford's case is that he was passionately committed to the proposition that we should never believe without sufficient evidence, and James diagnoses this passion as the desire to avoid error. However, James points out that many of us also have another passion—a passion to believe what's true. The trouble is that these two passions are sometimes in conflict. If we avoid believing something because believing it runs the risk of error, we are automatically running the risk of not believing some positive and possibly important truth.

In some cases, the truth we risk missing depends partly on what we believe. If you don't believe that people like you, James points out that this might make it less likely that they will like you. For at least some medical conditions, patients who are optimistic about their chances of recovery actually do better. The belief that they will get well plays a part in making it so. Especially in cases like this, James thinks it would be foolish to adopt Clifford's rule. Clearly, however, our beliefs about God doesn't make it a bit more likely that God exists. What does James's point have to do with God?

If the only religious issue were whether a certain kind of exalted being exists, the answer to the question of what our beliefs have to do with the facts would be "Nothing." But at the most general level, James thinks religions offer two ideas. The first is, as he puts it, "the best things are the eternal things." The second is that we're better off even in this mortal world if we believe the first thing.

Pascal would agree with this second point: the satisfactions of leading a religious life outweigh the pleasures that many non-religious people pursue. That's why Pascal thought that accepting the wager has no cost. We could add that some relevant **empirical** evidence seems to exist. Some studies suggest that believers are less prone to depression, alcoholism, high blood pressure, and various other maladies (for examples, see Matthews et al. 1998). Considerations like this could provide pragmatic reasons all by themselves for believing in

God but James goes further. As we already pointed out, a person who isn't prepared to trust others and meet them halfway may cut himself off from the rewards of friendship and human contact. But if there is a God, then we might have to meet God halfway by adopting a believing attitude to enter into a relationship with God. James goes farther. He writes,

> [A] rule of thinking which would absolutely prevent me from acknowledging certain kinds of truths if those kinds of truths were really there would be an irrational rule. (James 2003 (1896), p. 202)

6 MAKING CHOICES, SETTING LIMITS

Pascal's argument was intended to convince us that the pragmatic reasons for belief in God are overwhelming, but the argument assumes that we can compare some pretty inscrutable expected utilities, and the possibilities seem too complicated for that to be feasible. James's approach is less demanding. He points out that our commitments for or against religious belief reflect our passions either way. He adds that if we insist on giving priority to Clifford's passion for avoiding error, we do so without good reason, since doing that would inevitably cut us off from some possible truths that are deeply important if they are real. Believing in spite of the lack of evidence can be rational, even if it's not absolutely required.

Is this conclusion acceptable? It's hard to see how James could be completely wrong. In general, it's difficult to see that epistemic reasons for belief could be the *only* acceptable reasons. However, James's approach raises two problems.

The first is similar to a problem we encountered in our discussion of Pascal. There are many ways to be a believer. The choice is not just: believe in God or don't. For many people—especially in a world with no shortage of faiths on offer—more than one religious outlook will be tempting. James doesn't address the case where the genuine option that reason can't decide is a choice among three or more possibilities.

Because James isn't trying to show that belief is rationally required, he has a bit of room to maneuver. He needn't say that in picking a faith, we must pick the one that we think is most likely to be true, or that offers the greatest potential benefits. What James is saying is that when we're faced with a genuine option that the evidence can't decide, our passions may and must decide—*may* decide because a rule that tells us to play it safe is a rule that might leave us missing out on an important truth, and *must* decide because they're all that's left to settle our minds. James might well say: if reason can't settle things, let your heart be your guide. In practical terms, that might mean picking the option you are most drawn to. After all, James might say if a benefit is to be had in religious belief, you may not be able to gain it unless you can commit yourself whole-heartedly to some belief or other.

Perhaps this is a way for the Jamesian to cut the Gordian knot when deciding among a range of options that's wider than "believe/don't believe." However, we now face an urgent question about the limits of the sorts of reasons to which James appeals. Suppose someone is considering the prospect of accepting the religious worldview of Osama bin Laden and joining al Qaeda (a worldview, we hasten to add, that we do not take to be in any way a fair representation of Islam). For such a person, this is likely to count as a genuine option that can't be decided on intellectual grounds alone. It's also just the sort of case Clifford and his sympathizers would most worry about. We hope our readers are with us in saying to this person: please don't just follow your passion. Please stop and think.

Surely this isn't a case where exercising the will to believe would be wise. James's argument must have limits, but James doesn't tell us anything about what those limits are. Is there any principled way to grant James at least some of what he argues for while ruling out the terrorist?

In the case of the potential al Qaeda convert, consider this: if he accepts bin Laden's worldview and this view is wrong, then a great many people may suffer serious worldly harm without any eternal benefit. That suggests a significant limit on the role that the passions should play in settling our beliefs. Sometimes we should put a high premium on avoiding error because the cost of error is unacceptably high.

Whether that's enough to solve the problem isn't clear. The potential al Qaeda convert thinks that the cost is also high if bin Laden is right and he doesn't believe. What's at stake he'll say, is of cosmic significance. Both sides carry enormous risk.

Most people who are trying to decide whether to take a leap of faith aren't thinking about becoming terrorists. If the choice they're drawn to doesn't threaten any worldly harm, then perhaps we can allow that following James is acceptable. However, there's a lot of territory between complete worldly harmlessness and al Qaeda. What if someone is drawn to a faith that would have them withhold medical treatment from their children? Or would encourage them to keep women in a subservient position? Or require them to be complete pacifists no matter how evil the threat? Religious commitment very often has real-world consequences that go far beyond the fate of the believer's own soul; James has nothing to say about how these consequences enter into the believer's choice. Do we fall back on expected utilities? If so, James's position might not have any advantages over Pascal's. But if we don't, what do we do?

It's hard to give a good answer. Clifford's rule seems too strong. Are there cases where siding with James over Clifford is acceptable? The answer is probably yes. Is it easy to say in general which those cases are? Unfortunately, the answer seems to be no.

7 POSTSCRIPT: KNOWLEDGE, FAITH, AND THE HEART

James cites a famous quote from Pascal's wager argument in his own essay:

> *The heart has its reasons, which reason does not know.*

Whatever their differences, Pascal and James agreed on one thing: in some cases, following our hearts in deciding what to believe is the best thing we can do. We'll close this chapter by pointing to two other ways of thinking about the role of the heart in religious belief, both of which are rather different than the roles that Pascal and James had in mind.

7.1 Skeptical Faith?

One way is particularly friendly to skeptics. The Episcopal priest James R. Adams found himself troubled throughout his early career by the idea that "faith," as it was described to him, was supposed to be firmly holding beliefs that are "unsupported or even contradicted by empirical evidence." (Adams wasn't thinking about the Roman Catholic view discussed in Section 1 but, for better or worse, it's a fair bet that he wouldn't have found it convincing.) Then one day Adams heard a lecture by an Oxford theologian who was discussing a famous passage in St. Paul's Epistle to the Romans. The passage (Chapter 10, verse 9) asks the Christian to "believe in his heart" that God raised Christ from the dead. The speaker pointed out that the Latin word *credo*, usually translated as "I believe" and part of the traditional statement of the Christian creeds, comes from the Greek word for "heart." He suggested that for religious purposes, "I believe" might best be thought of as, "I set my heart."

Whatever we make of this bit of etymology, Adams found in it a way to express a different way of thinking about faith. In his view, faith is not a matter of intellectual assent—of believing *that* certain theological statements are true. It's a matter of believing *in* certain things. This point is not original to Adams; many people have commented on the difference between believing that—an intellectual matter—and believing in—a matter of trust, and believers have long debated over whether faith is best thought of simply as trust. (See the essay in the Catholic Encyclopedia noted in Section 1.) Adams' contribution was to see this "setting of the heart" as something that even a skeptic might be able to do. The skeptic might find that certain religious ideas express her heart's deepest longings, even if she can't just accept the corresponding statements as intellectual propositions.

Could Clifford go along with that? We doubt that he would, but it's not clear that it sins against his restrictions. The skeptical "believer" we've just described doesn't exactly believe at all. This might be an intriguing way to bridge the gulf between giving full weight to the evidence and acknowledging what is in one's heart. But for many religious people, it doesn't go far enough.

7.2 The Knowledge of the Heart

Our approach so far has been to assume that there isn't enough evidence to provide epistemic justification for believing in God and to ask whether non-epistemic reasons for belief could bridge the gap. A philosopher like Alvin Plantinga would say that this whole approach is based on a faulty assumption that we need to have evidence in the first place. Plantinga's approach is discussed at length in the chapter on reformed epistemology and we direct the reader who wants details to look there. In this final section, we want to isolate one point from Plantinga's discussion.

As Chapter 7 explained at length, philosophers like Plantinga think we could know that God exists if God reliably causes us to hold true beliefs. Arguments and explicit evidence wouldn't be part of the story. It might be something as simple as looking at the night sky and spontaneously being overwhelmed with the thought that God made all this. The further point relevant for our purposes is that even though emotion is often contrasted with reason, many philosophers think that's a mistake. Without question, our emotions can sometimes highjack our thinking, and to think we can always trust unexamined emotions would be foolish. However, we might add that a hyper-rationalism that simply ignores the emotions is almost as bad. Our emotions, like our senses, can bring us to realize that certain things are true. One's feeling of love for one's lover or spouse or child brings us to see how important these people are in our lives and what their loss would mean to us. Our sense of revulsion at some of the atrocities we read about in the news is part of our recognition of how wrong they are. Coming to recognize that someone is trustworthy is often something that we learn under the guidance of our emotions. Plantinga points out that even in science, the beauty of a theory is often taken as a reason for thinking of it as true. But perceiving beauty doesn't seem to be a matter for the head alone (Plantinga 2000, pp. 207–208).

More generally, to recognize certain truths our emotions might have to be in order, and our emotions might help guide us to right belief. If Plantinga is correct, this wouldn't amount simply to assessing reasons intellectually. It would be—at least in part—a matter of being guided aright by our hearts. If that's so, then Pascal's quote takes on a deeper meaning: the heart would indeed have reasons that purely intellectual reason wouldn't know. And although we've presented Pascal's argument as a pure intellectual exercise, no one who reads the *Pensées* could possibly take it that way. Pascal aims at our hearts even more clearly than James does.

This is a surprising development. What started out as a discussion of "pragmatic," "non-epistemic" reasons for belief might lead to an account of the heart's role in knowledge. (It also means, perhaps surprisingly as well, that after setting the view of faith sketched in Section 1 aside, we've found our way back to something that is like it in some important ways.) Intriguing as this may be, however, it leaves us with a problem that's not unlike the ones that plagued James and Pascal. In both cases, we saw that the variety of religious possibilities made seeing how their arguments could settle down on any one conclusion difficult.

In one way, that's not a problem for the longings of our hearts. If we find our hearts set in one way rather than another, then being guided by our hearts will let us set the competing views aside. If philosophers such as Plantinga are correct, the result might even amount to knowledge. The problem is that even if you find your heart set one way, you can well imagine that if things had been a little different, it might have been pointed another way entirely. That means that even if our hearts brings us to know the Heart of the world, it's quite another thing to know that we know this, and that kind of knowing may be beyond our means. For some, this might not matter; conviction will overcome epistemic fears. For others, the heart might find itself inclined in some way, but it may never cease to flutter.

AT A GLANCE: PRAGMATIC REASONS TO BELIEVE

1. Faith
   - Faith is sometimes opposed to knowledge.
   - Roman Catholic theology sees faith differently.
     1. In the RC view, faith is intellectual assent to divine revelation.
     2. Understood this way, faith is knowledge.
   - Our concern is with people who don't think knowledge of religious truth is possible.
2. W. K. Clifford
   - Clifford's maxim:
   - It is wrong always, everywhere, and for anyone, to believe anything upon insufficient evidence.
     2.1. Evaluating Clifford
       - Clifford's maxim may be too demanding to be realistic.
       - Clifford appeals to claims (about people who ignore his maxim) for which he doesn't offer evidence.
       - Clifford doesn't give evidence for believing that we should never believe without sufficient evidence.
       - Clifford assumes that the truth is the only relevant value in believing.
3. Non-Epistemic/Pragmatic Reasons
   - Epistemic reasons for a belief increase its probability.
   - Non-epistemic (pragmatic) reasons are reasons over and above epistemic reasons.
   - Examples of the distinction:

Belief	*Evidential Reason*	*Practical Reason*
The president is in the oval office juggling candy bars while riding a unicycle.	You saw him doing this.	A stranger pointed a gun at you head and told you to believe or he would shoot you.
A friend who is accused of dishonesty is innocent.	You have reliable testimony that they told the truth.	You value being loyal to them.
The optimistic view that everything will turn out all right in the end.	Your experience and others' testimony bears this out.	It contributes to your success and mental health to think this way.

4. Pascal's Wager

   a. If God exists, then the utility of believing that God exists is infinite, whereas the utility of disbelief is at most finite.

   b. If God doesn't exist, then the utility of belief is at most finitely negative and the utility of non-belief is at most finite.

   c. Therefore, the expected utility of belief in God is infinite, and the expected utility of disbelief is at most finite.

   d. Therefore, (pragmatic) rationality demands that we believe in God.

  4.1. Preliminary Objections

     4.1.1

- Objection: expected utility makes most sense as a decision method in cases where the situation will recur; belief in God is not like that.
- Reply: there may be no better way.

     4.1.2

- Objection: we can't choose our beliefs.
- Reply: we do have some influence over what we will come to believe.

     4.1.3

- Objection: we've ignored the possibility of eternal damnation.
- Reply: at least on the surface, this helps Pascal's case.

     4.1.4

- Objection: believing because of the Wager is cynical; God wouldn't reward cynical belief.
- Reply: even if the belief begins cynically, it could end up a sincere belief.

  4.2. The Many Gods Objection

- There are many possible sorts of gods who might reward or punish us in different ways. Which way affects what we should believe.
- Some strategies (e.g., theoretical considerations) might break some ties, but the prospects for a clean version of the Wager seem poor.

5. William James

- James argues that when facing a genuine option that can't be decided on intellectual grounds, our passions must decide.

  5.1. Options

- Option: a choice between hypotheses.
- Living option: an option where both sides have some credibility.
- Forced option: an option with no additional alternatives.
- Momentous option: an option with high stakes.
- Genuine option: a living, forced, momentous option.

5.2. Passion, Truth, and Error
- Two intellectual passions exist: believe truth, and avoid error.
- Too strong a passion for avoiding error might cause us not to believe important truths.
- In some cases (e.g., whether someone will like us), the truth depends on what we believe.
- This might also apply to religion; we might have to "meet the universe halfway."
- A rule that would absolutely exclude believing an important truth is a bad rule.

6. Limits
- James may have shown that deciding by our passions is sometimes acceptable.
- He has not told us what the limits are and, in some cases, this is a serious issue.

7. Reasons and the Heart
- A quote from Pascal: The heart has its reasons, which reason does not know.

7.1. Skeptical Faith
- James Adams argues that a skeptic may "set his heart" on a proposition even if he isn't intellectually convinced.

7.2. The Knowledge of the Heart
- If philosophers like Plantinga are correct, then properly functioning emotions might lead us to knowledge.
- This still leaves the problem of diversity: there are many potential ways for our hearts to set our beliefs.

WEB RESOURCES

Pascal's *Pensées* are online at http://philosophy.eserver.org/pascal-pensees.txt.

W. K. Clifford's "The Ethics of Belief" is online at http://ajburger.homestead.com/ethics.html.

William James's "The Will to Believe" is online at http://www.infomotions.com/etexts/philosophy/1800–1899/james-will-751.txt.

The Stanford Encyclopedia of Philosophy has an essay on pragmatic reasons for belief in God found online at http://plato.stanford.edu/entries/pragmatic-belief-god.

The 1914 *Catholic Encyclopedia* has a rich discussion of the Roman Catholic understanding of faith. It can be found at http://www.newadvent.org/cathen/05752c.htm.

CHAPTER 9

The Argument from Evil

Evil, especially in the form of suffering, has long been considered a problem for belief in God. Many atheists see suffering as evidence that God does not exist. Theists see it as a perplexing difficulty or a puzzle but not as a disproof of God's existence. We shall explore three types of argument from evil: the logical, inductive, and abductive. We'll examine and analyze the two basic responses to these arguments: theodicy and defense. Lastly, we'll look at how the problem of evil can legitimately be interpreted and understood differently by different people.

If God exists, why does he allow children to die of starvation? Why does he tolerate rape and let millions die at the hands of brutal dictators? Why does God permit suffering at all? Holocaust survivor Elie Wiesel tells of a hanging he observed while in a German concentration camp. The Nazis hanged two adults and a child. The two adults died quickly. However, the child took longer:

> For more than a half an hour he stayed there, struggling between life and death, dying slowly in agony under our eyes. And we had to look him full in the face. He was still alive when I passed in front of him. His tongue was still red, his eyes were not yet glazed. Behind me, I heard the same man asking: "Where is God now" (Wiesel 1992, p. 86).

If God is perfectly good, all-powerful, and all-knowing, why does evil exist? This question is so compelling that, as novelist Peter De Vries puts it, the question mark turns like a fishhook in the human heart (quoted in Yancey 1990, p. 20).

Atheists argue that suffering is powerful evidence that God doesn't exist. The argument from suffering against the existence of God typically takes three forms: logical, induction, and abduction.

1 THE LOGICAL ARGUMENT

Why do many think that suffering is a reason to doubt God's existence? Because it seems to involve an inconsistency. For instance, the atheist philosopher J. L. Mackie writes that the problem of evil "is a logical problem . . . there seems to be some contradiction" (Mackie 1992, p. 89). Traditionally, theists have believed the following set of propositions.

1. God exists.
2. God is **omnipotent**.
3. God is **omnibenevolent**.
4. God is **omniscient**.

According to Mackie, this set of essential theistic beliefs is logically inconsistent with:

5. Evil exists.

If God were all-powerful, he could destroy evil. If he were all-good, he would want to destroy evil. Because evil exists, either God is not all-powerful or he is not all-good, or he simply doesn't exist.

Mackie thinks that it is logically impossible for both God and evil to exist. Claiming that God and evil exist is like saying that square circles or married bachelors exist. As H. J. McCloskey puts it:

> Evil is a problem for the theist in that a contradiction is involved in the fact of evil on the one hand, and the belief in the omnipotence and perfection of God on the other. God cannot be both all-powerful and perfectly good if evil is real (McCloskey 1997, p. 203).

We can summarize the logical argument from evil this way:

Premise #1: Either God exists or suffering exists, but not both.
Premise #2: Suffering exists.
Conclusion: Therefore, God does not exist.

2 THEODICY

How might the theist respond to Mackie's and McCloskey's challenge? If someone claims that it's impossible for something to be both a square and a circle, an obvious response for one who thinks otherwise is to draw one. We know that's not really possible. But if someone *could* draw a square circle, it would refute the claim that square circles can't exist. The logical argument claims that God and evil can't both exist. The theist can undermine it by describing a scenario in which they do both exist.

How might such a description look? To be successful, it should describe a situation where God permits evil for a morally justified reason. Why? If God permits suffering for a morally justified reason, then suffering does not necessarily undermine his omnibenevolence. To see this, think about everyday examples.

A surgeon might permit a patient to suffer by refusing to perform surgery because the surgery is too risky. A lifeguard might let one person drown in order to save five children. It is regrettably that someone died but the lifeguard didn't do anything wrong by saving the other five swimmers. Instances occur everyday where people permit suffering and we don't think any less of them, morally. Likewise, if the theist can give reasons that morally justify God permitting suffering, she will undermine the logical argument from evil (we discuss this more in section 3.1). The project of offering these morally defensible reasons is known as **theodicy**. A theodicy is any response to the problem of evil that purports to tell us why God permits evil.

A very common theodicy is the punishment theodicy. For example, in the Bible we read of the sufferings of Job. He loses his entire family, all his property, and contracts a painful disease. His friends try to console him. One friend, Eliphaz, explains Job's suffering as punishment for sin (Job 4:7–9). Like Eliphaz, many theists believe that God is justified in permitting suffering as a punishment for sin.

The main criticism of this theodicy is that so many innocents suffer. It is hard to see what a baby born addicted to drugs could have done to deserve punishment. If suffering is punishment for sin, it stands to reason that it should be distributed proportionately to the sinfulness of the sufferer, but it isn't. Many basically good people suffer worse than many evil people. Rabbis at Auschwitz suffered more than Hitler. The people of Afghanistan or sub-Saharan Africa don't seem more sinful than the people of Switzerland, but Afghanis and Africans have suffered far more in the twentieth century than the Swiss.

The punishment theodicy also comes in a second form according to which disease, physical hardship, natural disasters, and death entered the world as a result of the sin of the first humans—Adam and Eve. According to this theodicy, the actual guilt for Adam's sin as well as a tendency to sin is inherited by every human. Even infants inherit the guilt of Adam's sin and so, strictly speaking, no one is completely innocent. This theodicy is subject to some of the same criticisms as its cousin mentioned above. Additionally, it depends on a particular view of the Bible and the history of humankind. If someone doesn't take the biblical account of the fall of man and original sin seriously, they won't find this theodicy plausible. Further, many people are bothered by the notion that someone can inherit the guilt of another.

A second theodicy is the counterpart theodicy. According to this theodicy, good and evil are **metaphysical** counterparts or compliments. One can't exist without the other. God is justified in permitting evil because without evil, there could be no good. This theodicy seems to limit God's power because even God cannot create good without also creating evil. It also assumes that if two properties or qualities are opposites, then one cannot exist unless the other does. But we find many properties in the world where the corresponding negative property isn't found. The property of being a non-unicorn is an example. Everything in the world has that property. This doesn't mean that its opposite, the property of being a unicorn, must be instantiated somewhere.

A third theodicy is the contrast theodicy. Whereas the counterpart theodicy makes a claim about the *world*, the contrast theodicy makes a claim about *knowledge*. According to this theodicy, if there were no evil to contrast with good, we wouldn't *know* what good is. This response limits God's power because it claims that even God cannot give us knowledge of good without permitting evil. Further, even if this is correct, surely we don't need so much evil to understand what good is. It's plausible that just a few instances of suffering would be enough to provide a basic contract between good and evil.

A fourth theodicy is the natural law theodicy. According to this theodicy, God created the world to work according to natural laws and rules. Much suffering, like drowning or falling from a cliff, is the result of these physical laws. Physical laws create the possibility of natural evil, but we need regular and systematic natural laws to farm, plan, build, and invent. The same water that quenches thirst also drowns. This theodicy also limits God's power by claiming that an all-powerful God couldn't create natural laws that do not result in suffering. What's more, surely God could intervene to prevent some suffering without making nature generally unpredictable.

The most popular theodicy is the freewill theodicy. According to the freewill theodicy, suffering is the result of people abusing their freewill. God is morally justified in permitting suffering because freewill is so valuable. There are three main objections to this theodicy. First, some say that it limits God's power. According to this objection, God should be able to create a world where people have freewill and always choose the good (but this objection is quite controversial). Second, some philosophers object to the freewill theodicy because they deny that humans have freewill. They think all the actions of an individual are determined entirely by their biology and environment. If this is true, then humans don't have **libertarian freedom**, and so the freewill theodicy is false. Third, it might explain moral evil but it doesn't explain natural evil. Moral evil is any suffering caused by a moral agent—murder, rape, theft, and so on. Natural evil is any suffering caused by non-moral things, like earthquakes and hurricanes. Freewill might be able to account for why people steal from each other but it can't explain why tornados kill people.

A fifth theodicy is John Hick's soul-making theodicy (Hick 1977). Hick thinks that God allows evil to promote moral and spiritual maturity. God wants us to develop character traits that suit us for a relationship with Him and others. We develop such character by making free choices in challenging situations. The world we inhabit is an environment designed to promote God's plan of soul-making. God permits evil in our environment because a world without suffering would not be conducive to spiritual growth.

There are several common objections to Hick's theodicy. First, it limits God's power because it says there is something God cannot do, namely, make spiritually and morally mature beings without permitting suffering. Second, even if suffering were necessary for spiritual maturity, surely the quantity of evil needed for spiritual growth isn't as much as the world actually contains. Third, many evils don't seem to contribute to soul-making. In fact, many have the opposite effect—they ruin character. Fourth, if theism is true, then God didn't become good. He has always been perfectly good, and so in principle, a being can be perfectly good without having to live in an environment like ours. Fifth, even if one grants Hick's theodicy, it can't explain the suffering of animals. Animals don't have any moral character to be improved.

Gottfried Wilhelm Leibniz (1646–1716) offers a sixth theodicy when he argues that this is the best of all possible worlds. God could not have created a better world than the actual world because no better world is possible. There are several standard criticisms of this theodicy. First, it implies that the world is incapable of improvement, but this just seems false. Second, it's not obvious that the reasons for thinking that God exists are better than the reasons to think that this isn't the best possible world. Third, it's not clear that there can be a best possible world. The concept of a best possible world might be like the concept of the tallest possible human. No matter how tall a human is, it is logically possible to add another inch. Thus, there can be no tallest logically possible human.

The last theodicy we will consider is the **disjunctive** theodicy. (A **disjunction** is an "or" statement). According to this theodicy, there's no *one* reason why God permits evil. A realistic theodicy links partially successful theodicies together with the disjunction "or." When the atheist asks why God allows suffering, the advocate of the disjunctive theodicy says it is as punishment for sin, *or* to provide a contrast with good, *or* because regular natural laws are necessary, *or* because of the freewill of men or demons, *or* to provide an environment for soul-making, and so on, where it's understood that several of these possibilities may apply. The disjunctive theodicy has two advantages. First, if successful it explains a broader range of evil than other theodicies. Second, it accords nicely with the intuition that if God has reasons for permitting suffering, they are likely to be complicated and might not be the same in each case.

Although each of the theodicies we discussed has objections that apply uniquely to it, they tend to run into one of two problems. They tend either to limit God's power or to make God less than morally perfect. A successful theodicy must explain the goods that morally justify God's permitting suffering and show that there can be no morally better way for God to achieve this good. God would not be perfectly moral if there were several ways to achieve a good, but he deliberately chose the more painful option.

What makes the project of theodicy so tricky is that God's omnipotence makes him capable of obtaining a good in any logically possible way. A cynic might put it this way: there's just not enough limits on God to find a good excuse for him. Theists have responses to these general criticisms as well as the specific one's we considered with each theodicy, but many philosophers of religion remain pessimistic about the prospects of theodicy.

3 DEFENSE

3.1 What is a Defense?

Many theists have been less than impressed with the classic theodicies and have turned instead to the project of giving a **defense**. A theodicy purports to tell us why God permits evil. A defense is any response to the argument from evil that tries to undermine the argument *without* telling us why God permits evil.

3.2 The Freewill Defense

Alvin Plantinga offers a defense that is widely regarded as one of the most important criticisms of the logical argument (Plantinga 1977, pp. 7–64). Plantinga's response has two stages. He first argues that atheists have yet to show that God and evil are logically incompatible. They claim both can't exist but haven't *demonstrated* this. Then he tries to actually show that they are logically compatible.

Recall that according to Mackie, the set of essential theistic beliefs is composed of these four propositions:

1. God exists.
2. God is omnipotent.
3. God is omnibenevolent.
4. God is omniscient.

This set is logically inconsistent with:

5. Evil exists.

Plantinga argues that if there is an inconsistency here, it isn't obvious. He distinguishes between three kinds of contradiction: explicit, formal, and implicit. An explicit contradiction is a pair of sentences that are the denial of each other—for example, "John is over six feet tall" and "John is not over six feet tall." (If we put these two sentences together with "and," that's another way of getting an explicit contradiction). Even a cursory glance at the list of five sentences above makes it obvious that no one sentence is the denial of any other. So, the set is not explicitly contradictory.

Perhaps the set is formally inconsistent. A set is formally inconsistent if one can derive an explicit contradiction from the set by making valid deductive inferences. For example, from (a) "John is in New

York," (b) "Mary is not in New York," and (c) "If John is in New York, then Mary is in New York," we can derive an explicit contradiction. Why? Because from (a) and (c), we can get "Mary is in New York" by an obvious inference called *modus ponens*, but that's exactly what (b) denies.

Looking at our set of five statements, they appear to lack the right kind of propositions to derive an explicit contradiction. If we added some propositions, we could get a contradiction. For example, if we added:

6. God is not omnipotent.

then statements (2) and (6) would explicitly contradict each other. The problem is that we can't add just any proposition.

What sort of propositions would be fair to add? Propositions that are essential to theism would be acceptable. After all, the point of the argument from evil is to show that theism can't be reconciled with the existence of evil, and so anything that's an essential part of theism can fairly be added to the argument. It's also legitimate to add propositions that are **necessarily true**. To see why, consider these two sentences:

John is a bachelor.
John is married.

Clearly, these two sentences contradict each other, but they are not explicitly or formally contradictory, and so there must be a third type of inconsistency. The two sentences above are inconsistent because there is a necessary truth that makes them inconsistent. It is necessarily true that:

All bachelors are unmarried.

Thus, if John is a bachelor and all bachelors are unmarried, then John is unmarried. This is inconsistent with John being married. Plantinga calls this type of inconsistency an implicit contradiction. A set is implicitly inconsistent if there's a necessary truth that, when added to the set, yields a set that is formally contradictory.

With these two constraints in mind, does some proposition exist that is either essential to theism or is a necessary truth that makes theism inconsistent with evil? Mackie offers two candidates:

There are no limits to what an omnipotent being can do.

and

A good thing always eliminates evil as far as it can.

It's not clear that either of these propositions is essential to theism. But are they necessary truths? Plantinga doesn't think so. Consider Mackie's first suggestion. **Omnipotence** means that God's power is unlimited. Some limits though are not due to a lack of power. For example, theists concede that God can't sin. This is a limit on God but they argue that it's not a limit due to a lack of power. They argue that God cannot sin because he is constrained by his moral character, and so this particular limit of God has nothing to do with power but is a limit nonetheless.

Theists also typically concede that even God can't make a square circle, not because he lacks power but because it's incoherent—it's a **pseudo-task**, as we said in Chapter 1. It's not true that if God had a little more power, he could make contradictions true. The first candidate doesn't seem to be a necessary truth. Plantinga thinks Mackie can avoid this objection by refining his claim like this:

> *There are no non-logical limits to what an omnipotent*
> *being can do.*

But notice that even if this is a necessary truth, it still does not yield a contradiction because there might be some *logical* limit preventing God from stopping evil.

Now consider Mackie's second candidate. There are times when a good person doesn't eliminate an evil that she can. For example, someone might be able to help a friend whose car broke down in bad weather but doesn't because she doesn't know about her friend's situation. Plantinga suggests modifying Mackie's original suggestion thus:

> *A good thing always eliminates evil that it knows*
> *about as far as it can.*

But this doesn't appear to do the trick either. Suppose a surgeon can eliminate the mild suffering of a knee scrape by amputating a leg. If she refused to alleviate the pain of the scrape, we wouldn't consider her immoral because doing so would bring about a greater evil.

Plantinga proposes still another modification to help Mackie. He does so by introducing the notion of properly eliminating an evil. An evil is properly eliminated when it is eliminated without bringing about a greater evil or eliminating a good state of affairs that outweighs the evil. So the modified candidate looks like this:

> *A good thing eliminates every evil that it knows about*
> *and can properly eliminate.*

Plantinga argues that even this modified form is not necessarily true. Suppose you come across two people rock climbing as a violent storm approaches. If they don't get down before the storm hits, they will fall to their deaths. Suppose that for whatever reason, they need help getting down and you only have enough time to save one before the storm hits. You can properly eliminate only one evil; you can't eliminate both. Suppose you help one and the other dies. According to the Mackie's modified principle, you are not perfectly good because you could have properly eliminated the death of the person who actually died.

The obvious objection to Plantinga's counterexample is that God, unlike us mere mortals, can save both rock climbers. So the proposition that must be necessarily true for God and evil to be logically incompatible is:

> *An omnipotent, omniscient, wholly good being can*
> *properly eliminate every evil.*

But is this necessarily true? If it is Plantinga doesn't think it's obvious. At any rate, he doesn't think any atheist has proven it to be necessarily true. Until this is shown, it can't be said that the atheist has *proven* that God and evil and incompatible.

So far, Plantinga has only argued that the atheist has yet to make a complete case. But just because the atheist hasn't demonstrated an inconsistency doesn't mean God and evil are compatible. Maybe they are inconsistent and atheists just haven't proven this yet. Plantinga realizes this, and in the second stage of his response to the logical argument, he endeavors to show that it is logically possible for both God and evil to exist.

He argues that the existence of God and evil are compatible by describing a possible state of affairs where God and evil both exist. Unlike the person offering a theodicy, Plantinga doesn't claim to know *why* God actually permits evil, but then he doesn't need to claim this. According to the logical argument, there is no *logically possible* moral justification for God to permit evil. All the theist must do to show that claim is false is describe a logically possible reason God could have for permitting evil.

To that end, Plantinga offers what he calls the "Freewill Defense." According to the Freewill Defense, it is logically possible that:

> A world containing creatures who are significantly free (and freely per-
> form more good than evil actions) is more valuable, all else being equal,
> than a world containing no free creatures at all (Plantinga 1977, p. 30).

Distinguishing the Freewill Defense from the Freewill Theodicy is important. According to the Freewill Theodicy, God permits evil because a world with freewill and evil is better than a world without suffering that lacks freewill. The Freewill Defense doesn't make any claims as to why God *actually* allows evil. It just gives one *logically possible* reason.

Like the Freewill Theodicy, a major objection to the Freewill Defense is that it cannot account for natural evil. Plantinga points out that it is logically possible that natural evil is caused by Satan or lesser demons. This might sound wildly implausible and even crazy, but remember that because Plantinga is giving a defense and not a theodicy, all he needs to show is that it is logically possible (i.e., involves no contradiction) that all natural evil is caused by malevolent spiritual beings. If he's right, the Freewill Defense accounts for natural evil by collapsing it into moral evil.

Plantinga's Freewill Defense is widely regarded as successfully undermining the logical argument from evil. For example, philosopher Paul Draper, who is a defender of atheism, agrees "with most philosophers of religion that theists face no serious logical problem of evil" (Draper 1996, p. 26).

4 THE INDUCTIVE ARGUMENT

Most of the recent discussion surrounding the argument from evil has focused on evidential or empirical versions. Rather than arguing that there *can't* be a morally sufficient reason for God to permit suffering, many atheists now argue that it is *unlikely* there is one.

The logical argument from evil is not strictly an *a priori* argument because the second premise is **empirical** (see the argument in premise form at the beginning of this chapter). However, the first premise is *a priori* because it involves a claim about the logical compatibility of two concepts—an omnipotent and omnibenevolent God and the existence of suffering. The second premise, that there is suffering, is not very controversial. The first premise is pulling all the weight in the argument, and so the logical argument from evil has an important *a priori* element that the other two versions of the argument from evil that we will consider don't have.

A priori knowledge is knowledge that is justified prior to and independent of experience. It's sometimes described as "armchair knowledge" because it can be justified without the need to get up from one's armchair to inspect the world. For instance, arithmetic is *a priori* knowledge because we can know that 1 + 1 = 2 just by reason alone. We don't need to look around the world or do an experiment to know it is true.

By contrast, **empirical knowledge** is gained through experience and observation. For instance, scientists gain knowledge by going into the field or lab and making observations about the actual world. Unlike the mathematician, the marine biologist can't study his subject matter just by thinking.

The logical argument is *a priori* because it doesn't depend upon an empirical inspection of the world. According to the logical argument, reasoning alone tells us that the five propositions we have been examining cannot all be true. In contrast, the evidential argument is empirical. According to the evidential argument, only upon inspecting the world do we see that much pain and suffering is pointless and unjustified. There are two forms of the evidential argument: **inductive** and **abductive**.

William Rowe offers an inductive argument from evil. Rowe's argument comes in two phases: The first phase is deductive, and the second is inductive. The deductive portion of Rowe's argument can be simplified as follows:

Premise #1: Morally unjustified, or pointless, suffering exists.

Premise #2: If God exists, no morally unjustified, or pointless, suffering would exist.

Conclusion: Therefore, God does not exist.

This argument is logically valid. If the both premises are true, the conclusion must be true. Premise #2 is true. If God permits evil that serves no purpose and is completely pointless, he is not completely good, and hence not the God of traditional theism. So whether Rowe's argument is successful or not depends on the truth of Premise #1.

Rowe gives several closely related arguments in support of Premise #1. We will focus on two. Both revolve around the following case:

Suppose in some distant forest lightning strikes a dead tree, resulting in a forest fire. In the fire a fawn is trapped, horribly burned, and lies in terrible agony for several days before death relieves its suffering. So far as we can see, the fawn's intense suffering is pointless. For there does not appear to be any greater good such that the prevention of the fawn's suffering would require either the loss of that good or the occurrence of an evil equally bad or worse (Rowe 1996b, p. 4).

If this is a case of pointless suffering, then Rowe's argument goes through. Rowe's first argument is that the suffering of the fawn is pointless, and so there is at least one case of pointless suffering. In that case, Premise #1 is true.

Rowe's second argument is inductive and amounts to a reply to anyone not convinced by his example. For a case of suffering not to be pointless, it would have to be justified by some greater good. For example, during the Civil War and before anesthesia, the suffering caused by a surgeon amputating a leg was morally justified because if the leg was not amputated, the soldier would most likely die from gangrene. The greater good of surviving an infection outweighed the suffering caused by amputation.

Rowe argues inductively for Premise #1 by arguing that no greater good justifies the kind of horrible suffering experienced by the fawn burned in the forest fire:

[W]e are justified in making this inference in the same way we are justified in making the many inferences we constantly make from the known to the unknown. All of us are constantly inferring from the A's we know of to the A's we don't know of. If we observe many A's and all of them are B's we are justified in believing that the A's we haven't seen are also B's (Rowe 1988, pp. 123–124).

Rowe's inductive argument looks something like this:

Observation #1: $Good_1$ does not justify the type of suffering experienced by the fawn.

Observation #2: $Good_2$ does not justify the type of suffering experienced by the fawn.

Observation #3: $Good_3$ does not justify the type of suffering experienced by the fawn.

Observation #4: $Good_4$ does not justify the type of suffering experienced by the fawn.

Observation #n: $Good_n$ does not justify the type of suffering experienced by the fawn.

Conclusion: Therefore, no good justifies the type of suffering experienced by the fawn.

5 WYKSTRA'S AND HOWARD-SNYDER'S DEFENSE AGAINST ROWE'S ARGUMENT

Does the inductive argument fare any better than the deductive argument? Rowe's argument tries to establish empirically what the defender of the logical argument couldn't establish *a priori*, namely, that God has no morally sufficient reason to permit suffering. As in the case of the logical argument, the theist has two general strategies he can employ to counter the inductive argument from evil—theodicy and defense. If the theist gives a theodicy, he is maintaining that God does in fact have a good reason to permit evil and that reason is spelled out by a theodicy. If the theist gives a defense, he is contending that even though he doesn't know why God permits evil, the empirical argument to establish that there is pointless suffering fails. We have already examined the standard theodicies. So let's see how a theist might undermine the inductive argument without saying why God permits evil.

Recall that Rowe offers two very closely related arguments in defense of the first premise of the deductive portion of his argument. First, he argues that the suffering of the fawn is pointless, so at least one case of pointless suffering exists. Second, he argues inductively that no observed good justifies the kind of suffering experienced by the fawn.

Both of Rowe's arguments depend on an inference of the following sort: it appears that there is no P, therefore there is no P. He argues that it *appears* that there is no good reason to let the fawn suffer, therefore there *is* no good reason to let the fawn suffer. Stephen Wykstra calls this type of inference a "*noseeum* inference" (pronounced, *noh-see-um*) because it moves from the fact that we "no see" P to the fact that there is no P (Wykstra 1996).

Sometimes *noseeum* inferences are legitimate and sometimes they aren't. To determine whether Rowe's *noseeum* inference is a good one, we must determine under what conditions *noseeum* inferences can properly be made and whether his inference meets those conditions. Suppose you walked into a classroom and the professor told you that for all he knows there could be a flea egg in the classroom. You are not allowed to search the room with a magnifying glass or by crawling around on your knees. You can only look around the room from your desk. Looking around the room, you do not see a flea egg. Clearly, you cannot legitimately infer that there is not a flea egg in the room just because you don't see one. It would be a mistake to make a *noseeum* inference in this case.

Now suppose you walk into a classroom and the professor informs you that a normal-sized adult elephant is in the room. You look around and you do not see an elephant. In this case, one can legitimately make a *noseeum* inference. The fact that you can't see the elephant is sufficient reason to think there is no elephant.

What's the difference between these two cases? If an elephant were in the room, we would see it. Because we don't, we're entitled to conclude that no elephant is in the room. If a flea egg were in the room, we wouldn't be in a position to see it. We can't tell just by casually glancing around the room that no flea eggs are found. These cases show us that inferences from "it appears that there is no P" to "there is no P" are good only when it's reasonable to believe that we would see P, if P were true.

We must ask whether we then would expect to know God's reasons for permitting evil. Rowe hasn't provided any reason to think that if God has good reasons to permit evil, we would be in a position to know them. At best, his argument is incomplete. Further, we do seem to have some reason to think that if God has good reasons for permitting evil, we would probably not know them.

Considering the enormous difference between how much we know and how much God knows, it seems unlikely that we would know His reasons for permitting evil. If he exists, God knows everything. What percent of everything do we know? Not much. The relationship between God's knowledge and our knowledge might be represented like this:

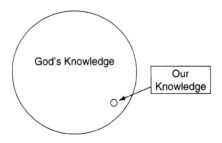

God knows everything we know and we know very little of what he knows.

Now suppose that the greater good that justifies God permitting evil is somewhere in the circle of God's knowledge. What is the likelihood that it is also in our little sphere of knowledge? To make an estimate, assume the drawing above represents a dartboard. If you randomly threw a dart at the dartboard, how likely is it that it would hit inside the smaller circle? It isn't very likely. Stephan Wykstra writes:

> [T]he outweighing good at issue is of a special sort: one proposed by the Creator of all that is, whose vision and wisdom are therefore somewhat greater than ours. How much greater? A modest proposal might be that his wisdom is to ours, roughly as an adult human's is to a one-month old infant's . . . that we should discern most of them seems about as likely as that a one-month should discern most of his parents' purpose for those pains they allow him to suffer—which is to say, it is not likely at all (Wykstra 1990, pp. 155–156).

Rowe's *noseeum* inference is akin to inferring that no intelligent extraterrestrial life exists because we have not seen any. Given the vast amount of space and the tiny sliver of the sky we have been able to examine, it is unlikely that we would have evidence of intelligent extraterrestrial life, if it exists.

The atheist has a reply here, though. It may be true that we only know a tiny portion of what an omniscient God knows but we know much of what he knows in certain domains. Consider arithmetic. We seem to know most about addition that can be known. We certainly know, at least in principle, how to solve any addition problem. So if God does know more about addition than we do, it isn't much. In the case of the inductive argument, the relevant domain is moral goods, not knowledge in general. It's open for the atheist to argue that our knowledge of goods is like our knowledge of arithmetic. If this is right, Wykstra's argument fails.

How much do we know about moral goods? This isn't entirely clear. To make a proper *noseeum* inference, it has to be reasonable to believe that we would see P, if P were true. If we don't know how much we know about moral goods, then it is not reasonable to believe that we would see P, if P were true.

In other words, there are two ways a *noseeum* argument can fail. We can be in a position similar to the one we're in the case of the flea egg, or we might not know which kind of position we are in. If we don't know whether our knowledge of goods is more like the case of the elephant or more like the case of the flea egg, we can't make a proper *noseeum* inference.

6 THE ABDUCTIVE ARGUMENT

Perhaps the most serious form of the argument from evil is the abductive argument. Abduction is inference to the best explanation. Abductive reasoning consists in coming up with a hypothesis that best explains some relevant data.

Paul Draper presents an abductive version of the argument from evil (Draper 1996). He argues that the facts about pain and suffering are better explained by what amounts to atheism (Draper uses different terms in different places) than by theism, and hence evil is abductive evidence against the existence of God.

Draper argues that all our observations about pain and pleasure can be reduced to three facts: first, moral agents experience pain and pleasure that we know to be biologically useful. Something is biologically useful if it is part of an organism (Draper says "biological system") and it contributes to the biological goals (i.e., survival and reproduction) of that organism. A moral agent is any being that is morally responsible for his actions. What makes someone a morally responsible agent is something like the ability to understand moral reasons and to control one's behavior in light of those reasons. A typical adult is a morally responsible agent, but a newborn infant isn't.

Second, sentient beings that aren't also moral agents experience pain and pleasure that we know to be biologically useful. A sentient being is any being that is capable of conscious experience. All moral agents are sentient beings, but not all sentient beings are moral agents. A typical adult is a moral agent and a sentient being. A dog is not a moral agent, but is a sentient being because a dog is capable of sensory experiences. Third, moral agents and sentient beings experience pain and pleasure that we do not know to be biologically useful.

Draper argues that each of these three observations is less surprising if atheism is true than if theism is true. Thus, the facts about pain and suffering are strong evidence for atheism over theism. We can summarize his argument thus:

Observations of Pain and Pleasure:

> *Observation #1*: Moral agents experience pain and pleasure that we know to be biologically useful.

Observation #2: Sentient beings that are not also moral agents experience pain and pleasure that we know to be biologically useful.

Observation #3: Moral agents and other sentient beings experience pain and pleasure that we do not know to be biologically useful.

Conclusion: Therefore, God does not exist.

Let's consider each observation in its turn. First, Draper argues that if there is no God, it's not surprising that moral agents experience biologically useful pain and pleasure. Independent of our observations about pain and pleasure, we know that moral agents, like humans, are organisms that have biological goals like survival and reproduction. The various parts of those organisms—like kidneys, lungs, and the reproductive system—contribute to those goals. It shouldn't be surprising, then, that the part of the organism responsible for pain and pleasure also contributes to survival and reproduction.

Given theism, though, it would be surprising that pain has biological utility. An omnipotent God could create beings that survive, reproduce, and even thrive without using pain. This is because God is all-powerful and all-knowing, and could have created us so that we knew to avoid touching excessively hot objects without having to experience the intense pain associated with burns. If God could create moral agents who achieved their biological goals without experiencing pain, he would do so because he is completely good. All things being equal, only a cruel person would see two equally effective ways to teach someone not to touch hot objects and purposely choose the one that involves the most pain. So Observation #1 seems to be evidence against the existence of God because it is surprising on theism but not on atheism.

Second, sentient beings that aren't moral agents are biologically very similar to moral agents. This, he maintains, gives us reason to predict that in an atheistic universe, sentient beings would experience pain and pleasure that we know to be biologically useful. Any reason we have to expect that moral agents would experience biologically useful pain and pleasure also gives us reason to expect the same of sentient beings in general.

He contends that if theism is true, we have two reasons to be surprised if sentient beings experienced biologically useful pain. First, we have the same reason in this case as in the case of moral agents. If God is all-powerful, he could create sentient beings—say, dogs—that survived and reproduced without experiencing pain. If God is moral, he would create dogs that way. Imagine a dog owner who could teach his dog to behave either by kicking it senseless when it disobeyed or by rewarding it when it obeyed. Suppose both methods were equally effective. If he chose the kicking method, he would not be a very good person. Second, the case of sentient creatures that aren't moral agents seems to bode even worse for the theist because in the case of moral agents, pain and pleasure might play a moral role in addition to a biological one. If a sentient being isn't a moral agent, pain can only play a biological role. So Observation #2 seems to be more surprising on theism than atheism.

Third, Draper argues that if there is no God it should not surprise us that both moral agents and other sentient beings experience pain that does not contribute to survival or reproduction. Given what we know about the world, biologically useless pain is unsurprising because we would expect that the processes that brought about our nervous system would not be perfect. The same pain that teaches us to avoid a hot stove continues to hurt days after we remove our hand. This pain doesn't contribute to our survival or reproduction—it just makes us miserable. This lack of fine-tuning of our nervous system is not surprising given atheism. But if we were created by an omnipotent and wholly good God, we would expect all biological pain to be perfectly fine-tuned. This is even more surprising in the case of merely sentient beings.

Thus, Draper concludes that our observations about evil would be more suspiring if theism were true than if atheism were true. Evil seems to provide strong abductive evidence for atheism rather than theism.

7 DEFENSES AGAINST DRAPER'S ABDUCTIVE ARGUMENT

How might the theist respond to the abductive argument? Against Draper's specific argument, Plantinga contends that it isn't clear that atheism explains evil better than theism. If atheism is true, should we really expect pain and pleasure to be biologically useful? Many areas of human life—like morality and altruism—don't play much of a biological role, so why shouldn't pain and pleasure be like them? As Plantinga puts it:

> There are many other characteristically human activities and phenomena that apparently do not (or do not apparently) contribute to those biological goals. Literature, poetry, music, art, mathematics, logic, philosophy,

nuclear physics, evolutionary biology, play, humor, exploration, and adventure—these are phenomena of enormous significance in human life. Indeed they are among the most important and significant of all things we human beings do. But again, they don't seem in any direct way to contribute to survival and reproduction (Plantinga 1996, p. 253).

Shouldn't we expect pain and pleasure to be like much of human life and lack biological utility as well? Of course, some people argue that those endeavors do contribute to survival and reproduction but Plantinga responds that evolutionary explanations of morality, altruism, and art, for example, are speculative at best (Plantinga 1996, p. 253).

Given the nature of the abductive argument, the theist has five general strategies available to him for criticizing the abductive argument. The theist can argue that:

1. Atheism doesn't explain suffering as well as one might expect.
2. Theism can explain suffering better than one might expect.
3. There is other relevant evidence that theism explains better than atheism, and it explains that evidence better than atheism explains suffering.
4. Contrary to initial appearances, we are not in a position to judge whether atheism or theism explains suffering better.
5. Theism is not a bad explanation of suffering because it is not an explanation at all.

The first option is the most difficult and least promising. One criticism in this vein is the sort offered by William Alston. He thinks that theism and atheism are just too general to explain much. Theism is the view that God exists; atheism is the view that God does not exist. How does either of these views explain why there is suffering in the world? As Alston points out, saying that theism explains suffering is like saying that the Sun explains the growth of plants. It is just too general to illuminate or explain much. Atheism is in a worse situation because it just tells us what doesn't explain suffering, namely, God (Alston 1996, p. 329). So according to Alston, atheism doesn't explain suffering as well as one might expect because it isn't clear that it explains suffering at all.

The second strategy is the project of giving theodicies. The goal of a theodicy is to tell a story that, if true, makes suffering less surprising given theism. We quickly reviewed the nine most common theodicies earlier. We leave for the reader to decide how well they fare.

The third option involves giving stronger reasons to think that God exists than suffering provides reason to think he does not exist. If the evidence for the existence of God outweighs the evidence against the existence of God, then the total evidence favors the existence of God. Any proper abduction is made from all relevant evidence.

Broadly speaking, the evidence for the existence of God can be divided into two sorts: non-propositional and inferred evidence. Inferred evidence includes the ontological, cosmological, teleological, and moral arguments. Non-propositional evidence includes things like religious experience. Suppose we knew that nine out of ten Germans cannot swim. This piece of evidence would make it unlikely that Fritz, a German, can swim. Now, suppose we see Fritz swim. Seeing Fritz swim justifies our belief that he can swim despite some propositional evidence that makes Fritz's being able to swim unlikely. It doesn't do so indirectly through reasoning, inference, or argument, but directly. Upon seeing Fritz swim, we immediately form the belief that he can swim. Religious experience and related grounds, like those urged by Reformed epistemologists, can provide reason to believe in God despite other facts that make it unlikely that God exists.

Peter van Inwagen employs the fourth strategy. He thinks evil is not all that surprising given theism because we aren't in a position to know what to expect if theism is true. He contends that to make a good abductive inference from evil, we have to make certain judgments that we aren't in a position to make. To decide how likely evil is if God exists, we must be able to make three types of judgments **probability, modality** (possibility and necessity), and morality.

Van Inwagen argues that we can make these kinds of judgments reliably about situations that don't stray too far from everyday life but not when they are distant and removed from our ordinary environment. For example, we know that if you flip a coin it's unlikely to land on its edge rather than on either flat side. We know whether a table can be a different shape or a different color is possible. We know that the act of helping an old lady across the street is morally better than murdering an innocent child. Our cognitive abilities serve us well when applied to the medium-sized dry goods we encounter in everyday life. But when we start making abstract probability, modal, and moral judgments far removed from our ordinary environment—about distant possible worlds or the value of highly abstract and removed goods—our cognitive abilities fail us. And it is precisely these remote judgments that we need to be able to make in order to know what to expect if God exists (Van Inwagen 1996).

Fifth, the theist can argue that theism is not a bad explanation because it is not an explanation at all and shouldn't be viewed as one. Theists don't typically think of belief in God as some explanatory hypothesis competing with rival scientific hypotheses to account for aspects of the natural world. People don't believe in God because they think theism explains the world better than other theories. Some theists argue that it seriously misconstrues belief in God to understand it as an explanatory hypothesis. Even worse is to then turn around and criticize it for not being a good one.

8 CONCLUSION

We have seen that the logical argument from evil is flawed, but what of the inductive and abductive arguments? They are serious challenges to theism and may rationally justify atheism. On the other hand, they are not so strong that they rationally compel a believer to give up belief in God's existence. It's not hard to see how evil might justify atheism but how might a rational theist take the argument from evil seriously without being giving up belief in God?

There are two ways to ask why God permits suffering: from faith or from unbelief. Theists typically ask because they genuinely want to know why God permits suffering. Atheists ask to challenge the rationality of belief in the existence of God. These two approaches reflect two ways to view any argument that leads to a controversial conclusion from plausible premises. One can accept that the argument is good and acknowledge the truth of the conclusion, even though it is surprising. Or one can reject the conclusion and be left with the problem of explaining how the plausible premises that lead to that conclusion are, in fact, mistaken. The difference of approach is the difference between seeing an argument as a disproof and seeing it as a puzzle.

The history of philosophy affords many examples of these kinds of arguments: **Zeno's paradoxes**, the **problem of induction, skeptical arguments** against the existence of the physical world, the **problem of other minds**, and so on. In each case, philosophers have taken both approaches. Some have accepted the counterintuitive conclusions and rejected motion or the existence of the physical world. Most, though, have seen these arguments as creating puzzles to be solved with careful philosophical analysis. Indeed, some of the best philosophy has been produced by efforts to diagnose where these arguments go wrong. A theist may acknowledge the problem generated by suffering and see it as puzzling rather than proof that God doesn't exist.

Notice that both of the evidential arguments depend upon certain probability, modal, and value judgments. Whether they constitute evidence against God depends upon the plausibility of the relevant judgments. The plausibility of these judgments in turn depends upon the epistemic situation of the individual assessing the evidence.

Suppose you are playing spades with a standard 52-card deck. If you wanted to know the probability that you would be dealt the ace of spades from a randomized deck, you conclude it is one in four (spades has four players and the whole deck is dealt, so each player receives one-quarter of the deck). Suppose that you were the first person to the left of the dealer and saw the dealer mistakenly flash the top card. No one besides you—including the dealer—saw the card and that it was an ace of spades. You would judge your chances of getting the ace of spades as 100%, whereas the others would judge it to be one in four. Your probability judgment differs from that of your fellow card players because you have different background beliefs than they do.

The theist and atheist are likewise in different epistemic situations. They believe different things. They have different experiences and background knowledge. This results in them making different judgments about what is probable, possible, and valuable. If the theist has reason to think God exists based on religious experiences, then the problem of evil might generate a puzzle for her, not a disproof of theism.

It would still be a difficulty for the theist because it really is hard for her to understand why a good God permits many instances of suffering. As Marilyn Adams points out, taken this way "the argument is constructive: it is an invitation to probe more deeply into the logical relations among these propositions, to offer more rigorous and subtle analyses of the divine perfections" (Adams 1999, p. 8).

The atheist might make different judgments based on their background beliefs. If the atheist has no reason to believe that God exists, she might be justified in making different probability, modal, and value judgments than the theist. It may be reasonable for her to take evil as evidence against God. We can then ask: Is evil proof that God doesn't exist, or is it a puzzle that is difficult to understand and explain? The answer is that it provides some rational support for the atheist but is not so strong as to compel the theist to abandon their belief in God.

It's important to note that these same observations about evidence can be made about the arguments for the existence of God. At best, some of these arguments might be sufficiently strong to contribute rational support to a theist's belief in God. None of them, however, are strong enough to rationally compel some into believing in God. For those who find some bit of evidence for God appealing, it is important to keep in mind that others might look at the same evidence and legitimately make different probability, modal, and value judgments.

AT A GLANCE: THE ARGUMENT FROM EVIL

Three Arguments from Evil (from the Introduction)

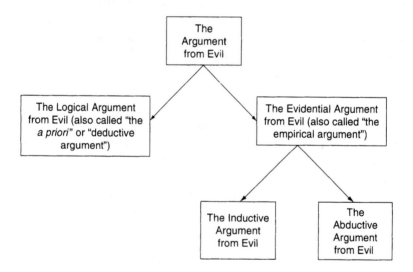

1. The Logical Argument
   1.1. The Argument

   > *Premise #1*: Either God exists or evil exists, but not both.
   > *Premise #2*: Evil exists.
   > *Conclusion*: Therefore: God does not exist.

   1.2. Defense of Premise #1

   - It follows from our concepts of "completely good" and "all-powerful" that (1) a completely good being would want to prevent all suffering; and (2) an all-powerful being could prevent all suffering. Because evil exists, either God is not all-powerful, or he is not all-good, or he simply does not exist.

1.3. Defense of Premise #2: The evidence that suffering exists is overwhelming and hardly needs defending.

2. Theodicy
   - A *theodicy* is any attempt to undermine the problem of evil that tells us why God permits evil.

Theodicy	God is justified in permitting suffering because . . .	Proponent(s)	Criticisms
Punishment Theodicy	. . . suffering is a punishment for sin.	Eliphaz (Job 4:7–9)	Suffering of innocents; suffering disproportionate to sin; suffering of non-moral agents like animals
Counterpart Theodicy	. . . good cannot exist without evil.		Limits God's power; assumes dubious metaphysical principle
Contrast Theodicy	. . . we couldn't know good without evil.		Limits God's power; don't need much evil for the contrast; we could learn from novels, movies, and so on
Freewill Theodicy	. . . freedom is so valuable despite its potential for abuse.	St. Augustine; Richard Swinburne	Limits God's power; doesn't explain natural evil; assumes freewill exists;
Natural Law Theodicy	. . . laws of nature are necessary and create the possibility of suffering.	Natural Law Theodicy	Limits God's power; doesn't explain moral evil; God could reduce suffering without making world too unpredictable

(continued)

Continued

Theodicy	God is justified in permitting suffering because ...	Proponent(s)	Criticisms
Soul-Making Theodicy	... it promotes moral and spiritual maturity.	John Hick	Limits God's power; empirically false: man is not getting better; quantity not necessary; much suffering doesn't seem to contribute to soul-making; some suffering seems to ruin character; God has good character without suffering; suffering of non-moral agents like animals
Best-Possible-World Theodicy	... this is the best possible world.	Gottfried Leibniz	Limits God's power because it says something exists that God cannot do, namely, make a world without suffering; there is reason to doubt that the world we live in is the best God could have created; implies our world is not capable of improvement; concept of best possible world may be incoherent (e.g., highest prime number); perhaps no world at all is better than this world
Disjunctive Theodicy	... there is no single reason why God permits evil (multiple reasons exist).	John Hare	Leaky buckets objection

3. Defense
   3.1. A *defense* is any response to the argument from evil that tries to undermine the argument without telling us why God permits evil.
   3.2. The Freewill Defense: That a world containing creatures that are free is more valuable than a world containing no free creatures at all is logically possible, and for God to create free creatures and guarantee they only chose to use their freedom for moral purposes is not logically possible.

4. Rowe's Inductive Argument from Evil
   4.1. The Deductive Portion

   Premise #1: Instances of intense suffering exist that an omnipotent, omniscient being could have prevented without thereby losing some greater good or permitting some evil equally bad or worse.

   Premise #2: An omniscient, wholly good being would prevent the occurrences of any intense suffering that it could, unless it could not do so without thereby losing some greater good or permitting some evil equally bad or worse.

   Conclusion: An omnipotent, omniscient, wholly good being does not exist.

   Defense of Premise #2

   • The theist already concedes that an omnipotent, omniscient, wholly good being would not permit evil unless he had to acquire a greater good or to prevent a worse evil.

   4.2. The Induction Portion
   Two Defenses of Premise #1

   • The first way Rowe argues for Premise #1 is by an existential generalization inference. He argues that the suffering of the fawn is pointless, so at least one instance of suffering exists that is pointless.
   • The second way Rowe argues for Premise #1 is by an inductive inference. For an instance of suffering to not be pointless, there would have to be some greater good that justifies it. So he argues inductively that no greater good justifies the type of horrible suffering experienced by the fawn burned in the forest fire.

   Observations of Goods:

   Observation #1: $Good_1$ does not justify the type of suffering experienced by the fawn.

   Observation #2: $Good_2$ does not justify the type of suffering experienced by the fawn.

   Observation #3: $Good_3$ does not justify the type of suffering experienced by the fawn.

> *Observation #4*: Good$_4$ does not justify the type of suffering experienced by the fawn.
>
> *Observation #n*: Good$_n$ does not justify the type of suffering experienced by the fawn.
>
> *Conclusion*:   Therefore, no good justifies the type of suffering experienced by the fawn.

5. Wykstra's and Howard-Snyder's Defense against Rowe's Argument
   5.1. Diagnosis of Rowe's Argument
   - Howard-Snyder argues that Rowe's defense of Premise #1 depends on an inference of the following type: it appears that ~P, therefore ~P (i.e., it *appears* that there is no good reason to let the fawn suffer, therefore there *is* no good reason to let the fawn suffer). He calls this type of inference a "*noseeum* inference."

   5.2. When Are *Noseeum* Inferences Legitimate?
   - Howard-Snyder points out two types of *noseeum* inferences:
     1. Illegitimate cases (flea egg in room).
     2. Legitimate cases (elephant in room).
   - The differences between these types of cases suggest that inferences from it "appears that ~P" to "~P" are good only when it is reasonable to believe that we would see P, if P were true.

   5.3. Rowe's *Noseeum* Inference
   - Rowe's *noseeum* inference does not meet this condition, and hence is a bad inference.

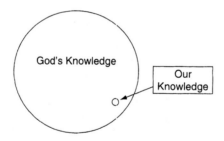

   - Some have argued that we have good reason to think that we would not see the truth of P. Consider:
   - However, Howard-Snyder argues that Rowe's *noseeum* inference fails because we have good reason to doubt that we would not see the truth of P.

6. Draper's Abductive Argument
   6.1. Draper's Basic Contention
   - He argues that the facts about pain and suffering are better explained by the hypothesis of indifference than by theism, and therefore evil is abductive evidence against the existence of God.

6.2. Draper's Argument

> *Observation #1:* Moral agents experience pain and pleasure that we know to be biologically useful.
>
> *Observation #2:* Sentient beings that are not also moral agents experience pain and pleasure that we know to be biologically useful.
>
> *Observation #3:* Moral agents and sentient beings experience pain and pleasure that we do not know to be biologically useful.
>
> *Conclusion:* Therefore, God does not exist.

7. Defense against Draper's Abductive Argument
   7.1. Plantinga #1: That atheism explains evil better than theism does isn't clear. If atheism is true, should we really expect pain and pleasure to be biologically useful? So many areas of human life—like morality and altruism—don't play much of a biological role, so why shouldn't pain and pleasure be like them?
   7.2. Plantinga #2: Even if suffering is evidence against God's existence, that we should disbelieve God exists doesn't follow. There may be much stronger evidence for God, particularly non-propositional evidence (see Chapters 6 and 7).
   7.3. Alston: Theism and atheism are just too general to explain much. Saying that theism explains suffering is like saying that the Sun explains the growth of plants. It is just too general to illuminate or explain much.
   7.4. Van Inwagen: Given our cognitive limitations, we are not in an epistemic position to judge whether theism of atheism is more likely given suffering.

FURTHER READINGS

Adams, M. M. (1999). *Horrendous Evils and the Goodness of God.* Ithaca, NY: Cornell University Press.

Hick, J. (1977). *Evil and the God of Love.* New York: Harper and Row.

Howard-Snyder, D. (Ed.). (1996). "The Evidential Argument from Evil." In *The Indiana Series in the Philosophy of Religion.* Bloomington, IN: Indiana University Press.

Mackie, J. L. (1955). "Evil and Omnipotence." *Mind* 64:200–212.

Plantinga, A. (1977). *God, Freedom, and Evil.* Grand Rapids, MI: William B. Eerdmans Publishing Co.

Rowe, W. (Ed.). (2001). "God and the Problem of Evil." In *Blackwell Readings in Philosophy.* Malden, MA: Blackwell Publishers.

CHAPTER 10

God and Morality

Many people believe that things are right and wrong because of what God commands or forbids. This view is called the Divine Command Theory, but there are believers and non-believers who think that it gets the relationship between religion and morality wrong. We examine the strengths and weaknesses of several versions of the Divine Command Theory.

It's almost impossible to imagine what it must have been like for that man, bringing his son to that remote place, binding him up like a trussed animal and standing over him with the knife. Nothing the boy had ever done could have called for what was happening to him. The father loved the boy and our hearts ache when we try to imagine the ache in his heart. But it had to be done. God had commanded it, and if God had commanded it, it had to be right.

Or so it must have seemed to Abraham as he stood ready to sacrifice his son Isaac at what he took to be God's command. The story has a happy ending: at the last minute, God told Abraham to free Isaac and instead to sacrifice a ram that was caught in the bushes. But what are the lessons of this strange tale?

1 MORALITY AND GOD'S COMMANDS: THE PROBLEM

Perhaps the story of the binding of Isaac occurred just as reported in Genesis, or perhaps it's religious fiction. For our purposes, it doesn't matter. The story raises thorny questions. What, if anything, would

229

make it right for Abraham to kill his son? Would the fact that God commanded it be reason enough?

Suppose there's a God who sometimes gives commands. We could wonder if what God commands has to be right at all, and later on we will. For the moment, suppose that whatever God commands really is morally required. We can ask why. Does God command things because they're right? Or is what God commands right because God commands it? It's worth being clear about the difference.

Imagine a country whose laws are determined by a legislature. In this country, there is a Chief Judge. She never makes legal mistakes, and she never bends or breaks the law. Sometimes she issues certain orders. Because her command of the law is so flawless, we can say: if the Chief Judge orders something, then it's obligatory; it's the law.

Now imagine a different country, run by an absolute monarch. Laws are determined and changed by the monarch's decrees. In this second country, we can say: if the monarch commands something, then it's obligatory; it's the law. Still, there's an important difference between the judge and the monarch. The judge commands things because they're the law. Her orders don't make things required independently of the existing law. Even though she has never made a legal error, it could still make sense to wonder in a particular case whether she got things right. The monarch, on the other hand, makes the law. The reason his commands are legally binding is that in his country, that's what the law is. Things like slips of the tongue aside, it makes no sense to wonder whether he has made a mistake about the law. What he commands is the law *because* he commands it.

When it comes to the law, there's a difference between something's being required because it's commanded—the case of the monarch—and being commanded because it's required—the case of the judge. We can raise much the same issue about morality, and the origins of the issue go back to Plato. In his dialogue *Euthyphro*, Plato depicts an encounter between Socrates and a man named Euthyphro, who is prosecuting his own father for murder. The charge seems flimsy and Plato clearly wants us to feel uncomfortable about what Euthyphro is up to, but Euthyphro insists that he's doing what piety demands. Socrates asks what piety is. At first, Euthyphro maintains that piety is what the gods hold dear, but Socrates persuades him that even if the gods approve of whatever is pious, they approve of it because it's pious and not the other way around.

Now piety isn't the same thing as morality. Still, we can ask: are things morally right because God commands them? Or does God command things because they're right? The view that God's commands are what make things morally right or wrong is called the **Divine Command Theory** and superficially, our analogy with the law might seem to favor it. God we might say, is like the absolute monarch; moral requirements are God's laws. Because God is the supreme lawgiver, if God commands or forbids something, that makes it right or wrong and unless God commands it or forbids it, it isn't right or wrong.

A little thought makes clear that things can't be quite this simple. The monarch may be able to make something a law by commanding it, but that isn't enough to make it a moral requirement. Suppose the monarch commands that no family shall have more than two children, and that any further children born into a family are to be put to death. This might be the law but most of us would think that it's an outrageous and deeply immoral law.

This sharpens the issue. Someone might say: the world is God's kingdom, and as the most Absolute of Monarchs, God's commands settle the law for the kingdom that we call the world. But can't we ask if the Divine Law meets the demands of morality? And in asking that, aren't we presupposing that there's a difference, at least in principle, between what God commands and what's morally right? Aren't we presupposing that morality is independent of God's will?

It's in the nature of morality that what's right and wrong isn't just arbitrary. Torturing innocent people is wrong; being kind to children isn't. Stealing is wrong; giving birthday presents is not wrong. It's hard to find anyone who seriously thinks that stealing could have been right and gift-giving wrong, torture right and kindness wrong. The implication seems clear: if God's commands are morally right, then this is so not simply because God gave the commands. Otherwise, no matter what God commanded and no matter how outrageous or perverse it seemed, it would be right. If the Divine Command Theory of morality allows that, then the Divine Command Theory is wrong.

2 SOME OBJECTIONS

It's not unusual for people to resist this conclusion. Let's look at some reasons why.

232 ◇   *Chapter 10: God and Morality*

2.1 Objection #1: God Would Never Command Evil

One reason for resisting the conclusion that the divine command theory fails is that people can't imagine God commanding anything evil. However, this misses the point. Opponents of the Divine Command Theory might agree that as a matter of fact, there's a God who never commands anything wrong. Their point is that this means that God meets some objective, independent standard. If God is perfectly good, then it would be no surprise that whatever God commands is right. God has the moral wisdom to know what's right and the goodness to command it. But in that case, God commands things because they're right and not the other way around.

2.2 Objection #2: God Is the Creator

A second reason for doubting that morality is independent of God's will insists that we're ignoring something important. After all, if God exists, God isn't a mere earthly monarch. God is the creator of all there is. Doesn't that give divine commandments a special status? As creator, the story would go, God can command as God will and we're obliged to obey. What would give the creature the right to rise up against the creator?

The answer is that it depends on what the creator is like. Imagine a universe made by a deity who is perfectly powerful but perfectly cruel. Sometimes this god commands horrible things out of sheer perversity. It might be smart to go along but it certainly wouldn't be morally required. In fact, in a universe like that, the noblest and most moral act imaginable might be to rebel against the cosmic sadist who assembled the whole sorry scheme to begin with.

Someone who believes that the world was made by an evil being may be wrong, but we can at least imagine what it would mean for her to be right. In a world like that, the fact that the creator commanded something wouldn't make it moral. And so if our world was made by a God whose commands are morally binding on us, the binding force isn't simply because God is the creator.

2.3 Objection #3: Morality Needs Religion

A third reason why people resist the objections to the Divine Command Theory is a worry about what happens to morality if we don't yoke it to religion. As Dostoevsky's Ivan Karamazov never quite put it, the point is that if there's no God, then everything is permitted. In other words, some people think that if no God exists, then we don't have any moral obligations at all. That's a view that many of us would like to avoid.

Why think this way? Some people would say that unless there's a
God to threaten punishment, no one could ever have a reason to act
morally. This seems wrong, as we'll explain in a moment. It's also
morally confused. If someone does the "right" thing just because he's
afraid of being punished, he isn't acting for moral reasons at all. However, let's turn to the main complaint that unless a God exists, there's no
basis for morality. Plenty of thoughtful, philosophically sophisticated
atheists believe that there's a real difference between right and wrong.
For example, plenty of atheists would agree that stealing from someone
for no better reason than because you want what they have is just plain
wrong. In fact, most of us—atheists or not—can give reasons for our
moral beliefs that don't appeal to religion at all. Why shouldn't I steal
your purse? Because it would cause you a lot of trouble, because I would
be upset if anyone stole my wallet, and because I have no basis for thinking it would be right for me to steal from you but not right for you to
steal from me. Atheists can reason this way just as well as theists can, and
they can be just as motivated to act accordingly.

2.3.1 The "Queerness" Problem

Does this sort of reasoning prove that we have moral obligations?
Perhaps not. What we've pointed to are various non-moral facts—facts
about what would cause you trouble, about how I would feel if the
tables were turned, and about my inability to come up with an argument
for making a special case of myself. Most of us find these sorts of facts
morally relevant, but there seems to be a logical gap between them and
the existence of an objective moral obligation not to steal. Philosophers
have sometimes phrased the difficulty by saying that you can't derive an
"ought" from an "is." This raises a puzzling theoretical issue. Moral
truths don't seem like what we ordinarily call "facts." They don't just
tell us how things are. C. S. Lewis puts it this way:

> You have the facts (how men do behave) and you also have something
> else (how they ought to behave). In the rest of the universe, there need
> not be anything but the facts (Lewis 1949, pp. 17–18).

J. L. Mackie saw this difference as fodder for what he called the
argument from queerness. "If there were objective values, then they
would be entities or relations of a very strange sort, utterly different
from anything else in the universe" (Mackie 1977, pp. 38). Accordingly,
the way we know them would have to be completely different from the

way we know other sorts of facts. Mackie uses the phrase "objective values," which is broader than the idea of obligation, but part of what puzzles Mackie is the "action-guiding" character of these facts. In any case, when we use the phrase **"queerness problem"** here, we will mean the problem of understanding how there could be such a thing as moral obligation.

There's a deep puzzle here. How could moral obligation rest on what we usually think of as the facts? Superficially, this makes it easy to see a point in Ivan Karamazov's slogan. If no God exists, all we seem to have are the facts. In that case, or so the argument goes, there aren't any moral obligations. If God determines morality by issuing commands, the thought might go, the "queerness problem" goes away.

This thought may seem compelling at first, but we can wonder how good it really is. Suppose God gives a command. As we already saw, even if a supernatural creator commands something, that wouldn't automatically make it morally right. The fact that God commands something is just another fact—a striking fact, to be sure, but one more fact.

We'll have more to say later about the queerness problem. In the meantime, a good many philosophers who are aware of the problem still think there's a real difference between right and wrong. Perhaps that's a mistake, but let's proceed on that assumption for the time being.

3 PHILIP QUINN: DIVINE COMMAND ETHICS FOR THEISTS

So far, things don't look good for the Divine Command Theory, but in recent years philosophers have offered newer, more sophisticated versions. An ambitious divine-command theorist might try to convince philosophers in general that morality requires religion. However, as Philip Quinn points out, a less ambitious goal might be to develop divine command theories from within a religious framework and not to worry about whether religious skeptics will be convinced (Quinn 1990, p. 345). In Quinn's view, divine command theories are the most plausible way for theists to look at morality (Quinn 1992, pp. 493–513).

3.1 Three Reasons

Quinn's first argument appeals to the notion of divine sovereignty. Many theists maintain that God is sovereign over creation. Part of what they mean is that God's will is completely effective: what God wills must come to pass. If that's so, they claim then moral truths in particular should be up to God.

Quinn's second reason for saying that theists should accept the Divine Command Theory is the so-called "immoralities of the patriarchs." This second argument only applies to theists who grant authority to the Hebrew Bible (which Jews call the Tanakh and Christians call the Old Testament). There are several points in the Hebrew Bible where God apparently commands things that violate biblical commandments. God orders Abraham to sacrifice his son Isaac, but this violates the commandment against killing (Genesis 22:1–2). God apparently orders the Israelites to plunder the Egyptians (Exodus 11:2), though the meaning of the verse is not entirely clear. This seems to violate the commandment not to steal. God also orders Hosea to have sex with a prostitute (Hosea 1:2 and 3:1), in what some say amounts to a violation of commandments against adultery or fornication. Quinn's idea is that unless God had commanded these things, they wouldn't have been right.

The third argument is based on the role of love in Christian ethics. Quinn takes Matthew 22:37–40 as his text:

> You shall love the Lord your God with your whole heart, with your whole soul and with all your mind. This is the greatest and first commandment. The second is like it: you shall love your neighbor as yourself. On these two commandments the whole law is based, and the prophets as well.

Quinn points out that elsewhere (John 15:17) Jesus commands us to love: "the command I give you is this: you shall love one another."

This ideal of love isn't unique to Christianity; we can find similar themes in other religions. Quinn might well agree with this, but his thought is that the love Jesus has in mind is profoundly unnatural for human beings. It tells us to treat everyone as our neighbor and tells us to love everyone as much as we love ourselves. Erotic love, love of friends and family—all of these are partial and are based on special circumstance or special facts about the loved one. As Quinn puts it, "only a dutiful love can be sufficiently extensive in scope to embrace everyone without distinction" (Quinn 1992, p. 507). None of us ever succeeds completely in this dutiful love, but Quinn says, "loving everyone as we love ourselves is . . . obligatory in Christian ethics, and it has this status, as the Gospel indicates, because God has commanded this all-inclusive love."

3.2 Three Reasons Challenged

Quinn claims that these three reasons give theists a strong argument for accepting a Divine Command Theory, whatever non-believers might think. Should the theist be convinced?

There's an obvious objection to the argument from God's sovereignty: there are some things that even God isn't sovereign over. As Quinn himself points out, there's lots of room to doubt that God is sovereign over **necessary truths** such as 2 + 3 = 5. Quinn considers a suggestion that necessary truths are determined by what God strongly believes, but most philosophers are likely to think that God "strongly believes" that 2 + 2 = 5 because it's necessary rather than the other way around.

It's plausible that moral truths are necessary truths. Technical language aside, it's even more plausible that there are certain things God couldn't make right. What would it mean to for vicious cruelty to be right? Wouldn't a god who commanded it be like the evil creator we imagined above? In Chapter 1, we already saw that God's omnipotence doesn't have to mean that God can do absolutely anything. Why think that God's sovereignty calls for a mysterious "ability" to make things that seem patently evil morally required?

What about the immoralities of the patriarchs? The examples are supposed to show that God can override the usual moral rules, but suppose God had commanded the Israelites to torture as many innocent Egyptian babies as they could. Would this have been right? If the answer is no (as we suspect most people would agree), then there are limits to how far God could go in overriding moral rules.

Beyond that, moral principles often allow for exceptions, and it doesn't take a Divine Command Theory to see this. For example, usually we shouldn't lie. But imagine someone during the Second World War who was hiding Jews from the Nazis. The storm troopers come to the door. They ask if there are any Jews in the house. Most of us think this situation would call for setting aside the usual rule against lying.

A theist who doesn't accept the Divine Command Theory can point out that in the case of the plundering of the Egyptians, God could have had very good reasons for commanding the plunder. After all, the Egyptians had enslaved the Hebrew people and the Pharaoh had consistently refused the just demand to let them go. God may have commanded the "plunder" as a way of extracting just reparations. A theist could say very plausibly: it was those reasons, and not the mere fact that God gave a command, that made the command morally acceptable. As for Hosea, he *married* Gomer; he didn't just have sex with her. It's not clear that any moral rule got broken to begin with.

The case of Abraham and Isaac is tougher. Isaac hadn't done anything to deserve to be killed, and so the familiar exceptions to the rule against killing don't apply. The story is usually read as a test of Abraham's willingness to trust God. Understood in that way, it's important to keep in mind that God didn't make Abraham go through with the sacrifice: Abraham's trust was well-placed. But what if the story had ended differently? What if God had sat back while Abraham went through with it, plunging the knife into his son and then burning the body as a sacrifice?

It's hard to know the answer to this sort of hypothetical because so much depends on the details. However, taking the story at face value, Abraham knew some very important things. One is that God is almighty and so can bring good out of any situation. Another is that all of Abraham's experience showed God to have been completely and utterly trustworthy in the past. Remember also that on the concept of God that Jews, Christians, and Muslims share, it's within God's power to take care of Isaac even in death.

Abraham could have trusted that God had a good reason for this command—a reason that if he only knew it, would convince him that carrying out this order would be for the best. But once again, in that case it would be the reasons that made the act acceptable and not God's mere command. If that's so, the so-called "immoralities of the patriarchs" don't really support a Divine Command Theory because in none of these cases would God's mere commands be what made it right to do what was done.

Turn now to the case of commanded love. This example also has a limitation. The most it could show is that God's commands can add to the requirements of ordinary morality, making it our duty to do things that most people would see as beyond the call of duty. This wouldn't show that there's no morality independent of God's will; it wouldn't show that ordinary moral reasoning can't provide the basis for countless real obligations.

The example also raises a question of interpretation. Just what is this "commanded love?" Is it the same as the Golden Rule—do unto others as you would have them do unto you? In that case, we have a principle that's very widely accepted, even by non-believers. In fact, some people would say that this principle is part of any acceptable system of morality. However, let's suppose that this commanded love calls for something much more extensive—a kind of care for one's neighbors that many decent people would see as beyond anything that ordinary moral reasoning could require. If that's what's at stake, just how does the example support the Divine Command Theory? It's not exactly clear that it does. First, we can find a call to this kind of compassion outside the theistic traditions. The Mahayana Buddhist idea of compassion evokes a concern for our fellow beings that is at least as extensive as what Jesus demands. However, for the Buddhist the basis for compassion isn't the commands of a deity. It's something that the Buddhist believes expresses our own deepest nature.

However, suppose that God does command this sort of love. Within ordinary moral thinking, there's a way of understanding why the believer might feel compelled to obey. Start with a simple case. Suppose you and your best friend are sitting in a room reading. You have your favorite CD on in the background and your friend asks you to turn down the volume. This is the sort of request you ought to go along with even if the person in the room with you had been just a stranger. But the fact that it's your friend gives you a reason all by itself to do what she asks, and this is something that ordinary moral reasoning accepts.

Now change the example slightly. Suppose your friend is filling out her tax returns and gets stuck on some complication. She feels confused, so she asks you for help. (We'll suppose you're good at this sort of thing.) Most people would agree that unless you're doing something really important, you should help. Most people would also agree that if she wasn't your friend but just someone who happened to be in the room, then it would be very nice of you to go along, but you wouldn't be obliged to.

Special relationships create special obligations, and we don't need a Divine Command Theory to see this. Most of us think that we have special obligations to our parents and to our children. Many of us believe that we have special obligations to our friends or our co-workers or our fellow citizens. These special obligations don't lower the bar on what we owe to other people, but they raise the bar for how we treat the people we're specially related to. More important, these special relations sometimes mean that we should treat the wishes and even commands of these other people as giving *us* reasons to do as they say. [Thanks to Chris Morris for useful discussion of this point.] Ordinary morality makes room for the idea that in certain special cases, what other people ask of us can give rise to moral obligations.

A theist who rejects the Divine Command Theory can use this idea to explain why we should do what God wills. If you're a theist, then you believe that your relationship with God is absolutely unique. Without God, none of the goods in your life would be possible. Without God, you wouldn't even be! No one cares for you more than God, no one is more faithful to you than God, and no one—including you—understands your needs better than God. God is so wise, so faithful to you, and so loving toward you the thought would go, that all by itself this explains why you should do as God wills. This explanation doesn't appeal to the Divine Command Theory. It appeals to two things: the familiar idea that special relationships create special obligations, and the extraordinarily special character of your relationship with God.

Now bring this around to the particular case Quinn has in mind: loving your neighbor as yourself. Suppose that ordinary morality by itself doesn't require this. However, the argument would go, if the God who creates us, sustains us, and loves us wills this love, then what reason could we possibly have for saying no? Refusing the request would be wrong because it would not do honor to our extraordinary relationship with God.

If we focus on our special relationship with God, the divine-command theorist gets at least some of what he wants: God's commands make a moral difference. We can be obliged to do things that we wouldn't be obliged to do unless God commanded them. Nonetheless, we haven't reduced morality to divine commands. First, we can appeal to ordinary moral ideas to explain why God's commands might make a difference. Second, there seem to be many things we're morally obliged to do whether or not God commands them.

4 GOD, LOVE, AND MORAL OBLIGATION

Robert Adams has offered a version of the Divine Command Theory that attempts to tighten the connection between moral obligation and what God commands—at least, for theists. Adams points out that for believers, talk of what we should do is pretty much interchangeable with talk of God's will. Believers who are trying to solve a moral dilemma often describe themselves as trying to figure out God's will. This suggests that believers mean the same thing by "what's morally right" and "what God wills." If Adams is correct, for believers these two phrases are two different ways of saying the same thing.

However, there's an important limitation. Adams agrees that we can imagine—as a bare possibility—that God might command cruelty for its own sake. If that happened, believers would no longer see what's right and God's will as the same thing. That's because a crucial presupposition of how believers think about God would have failed. Theists of the sort Adams has in mind believe that God is perfectly loving, and if they didn't believe that, they wouldn't equate what's right and wrong with what God commands and forbids.

The opponents of divine command ethics won't be satisfied. "What if there was no loving God?" they'll ask. "Would there be no such thing as morality?" Adam's answer is complicated but it boils down to this: the nature of what "right" and "wrong" refer to depends on the nature of reality—just as the nature of what the word "water" refers to depends on the nature of reality.

Assuming a loving God does exist, Adams thinks the best theory of the nature of right and wrong equates them with what God wills and forbids. However, if there were no God, there might still be a practice like what we call morality and some other, non-theistic theory might give the best account of what terms like "right" and "wrong" refer to. Assuming that God does exist, Adams thinks that God's will is the crucial part of reality that underpins the nature of right and wrong.

It's not immediately clear why we should think this. Consider Adams's own caveat: if God were to command cruelty, the believer would no longer think that what's right is what God wills. But it's plausible that we can go even further: cruelty is wrong, period—whether a God exists or not. It's plausible, in other words, that we're back to the Euthyphro argument: cruelty isn't wrong because a loving God forbids it. A loving God forbids cruelty because it's so clearly wrong.

What about the fact that many believers seem to see deciding what's right as discerning God's will? By itself, this won't settle the matter. If it's part of God's very nature that God is perfectly loving and good, then necessarily what God wills would be right. This would mean that discerning God's will really would be discerning what's right because the two couldn't differ, even though God wills things *because* they're right and not the other way around. Moreover, if the believer loves God, then the believer wants to do God's will not just as a way of doing right but also as an expression of that love. The fact that believers talk in the way that Adams says they do may not provide a very strong reason for saying—as theists need to say—that divine commands are what make things right or wrong.

5 NATURAL LAW THEORIES

Even if what's right isn't simply determined by God's commands, a God of the sort that the major theistic traditions conceive of isn't morally irrelevant. We've already seen some reasons for saying that. However, so far we've said nothing about a very important tradition of thinking about the relationship between morality and God. This is the **natural law** tradition, whose most important advocate was St. Thomas Aquinas (C. 1225–1274). Our discussion here is indebted to the very useful essay on natural law theories by Mark Murphy in the *Stanford Encyclopedia of Philosophy*, though it offers a particular take on natural law that Murphy might not accept.

5.1 Providence

At the root of natural law theories is the idea of divine Providence. God has arranged the world according to a plan—a plan that's wise and good. This plan includes a harmonious relationship between our needs and desires. For example, our desire for food serves our need for nutrition. Gluttony thwarts that natural ordering. Given the existence of this plan, certain things are objectively good for us and are objectively good ways of behaving. Furthermore, according to natural-law theorists, we come equipped by nature with the ability to tell the good from the bad. This isn't to say that every case is clear, but it is to say that for what we might call the straightforward cases, we can know if what we are doing is good or bad—if it accords with the providential design of the universe.

As for right and wrong, they depend on good and bad for natural-law theorists, though there are different ways of working out the connection. The point is that for the natural-law theorist, not just anything can be morally required. It depends on what's good and what's bad.

Whatever we make of natural law theories in detail, it seems reasonable to say that what's good and bad depends in part on how the world is organized. For example, the fact that something is poisonous—and therefore bad for us—depends on how our biology actually works. If nature at large is organized according to a providential design, that will make a difference for good and bad, and therefore for right or wrong. This is another way in which God can make a difference for right and wrong, even from the point of view of someone who rejects the Divine Command Theory. And for reasons that we've already explored, God's will could create special obligations for us because of our special relationship with God. Taking all this into account, a theist who rejects the Divine Command Theory will have to concede that what God has done and what God wills makes a significant moral difference. And a non-theist will also have to concede that if a God did exist, it would matter morally. All in all, we see again that it's possible for a theist to defend a good deal of what the divine-command theorist wants without simply accepting the Divine Command Theory.

*6 GOD, OBLIGATION, AND THE "QUEERNESS PROBLEM"

In this somewhat more advanced section, we turn to a problem that we raised earlier but set aside, the so-called "queerness problem." The facts deal with how things are. But moral claims deal with how things ought to be. What makes a statement like "birds aren't mammals" true is something about the way that things are arranged in space and time. But what makes a statement like "stealing is wrong" true? In this section, we explore a possible way of addressing that question.

*6.1 Value

Start with the distinction between value and obligation—between good versus bad, and right versus wrong. Other things being equal, happiness is good and depression is bad; health is good and illness is bad. However, to say something is good isn't the same as saying that it's obligatory. It might be a good thing if Cecilia Bartoli recorded a new CD. That doesn't mean she's obliged to, nor that she would be acting wrongly if she didn't. Showing courage when you're in serious danger might be a good thing. If you don't, that doesn't automatically mean you failed to do something you were obliged to do; maybe the level of courage called for was too much to ask.

People can also be good and when we say that they are, we don't have to mean that they do what's right or wrong. A loving, thoughtful, considerate person is a good person, at least in the sense that she makes the world a better place—whether or not we think it makes sense to talk about moral obligation.

Some people think that the idea of goodness itself is puzzling. Perhaps those people are right, although most of us aren't puzzled by the idea that happiness is good and unhappiness isn't, for example. For many people, right and wrong are murkier. For example, even if we can agree that happiness is generally a good thing, showing that anyone is obliged to promote your happiness is a different matter.

*6.2 Legal Obligation, Moral Obligation, and Legitimate Lawgivers

How could bringing God into the picture help? Our discussion owes a debt to an essay by Jeffrey L. Johnson (Johnson 1994, p. 39–55), though what we describe is not a view that he would accept, nor is it exactly the one he discusses. Start with the queerness problem: it's difficult to see what sort of facts moral facts could because they seem so different from ordinary facts. In particular, it's hard to see what sorts of facts "oughts" or moral obligations are. But now think about legal obligation. Legal obligation is like moral obligation in many ways but it seems much less mysterious.

Legal obligations come from legal authorities—from lawgivers, as we'll say. (These might include monarchs, legislatures, or even common-law traditions.) A bad way of proceeding would be to argue that all obligations must come from a lawgiver. That would be a bad way to proceed because some obligations don't seem to work that way. For example, if you believe some statement—say, "Ishmael is in Nantucket"—then you shouldn't also believe its denial—"Ishmael isn't in Nantucket." But that rule (a rational principle, if you will) doesn't seem to come from a lawgiver. However, talking about lawgivers can cast light on at least some kinds of obligations.

As we noted, ordinary laws can't exist without a lawgiver or legal authority of some sort. It might be a good thing if there were a law that made selling cars that get less than 10 miles to a gallon of gas illegal, but unless the legislature or the ruler or some other appropriate authority makes it a law, it isn't one. And once we have a lawgiver, we usually don't think legal obligation is mysterious. (Perhaps we should, but for the moment, we'll stick with our usual reactions.) Laws become "real" because people accept or "recognize" this source of authority. And at this point, we might add that laws are legitimate if they come from an authority that we not only accept but that's overall good enough to deserve our respect. (Johnson's discussion of the point is much more sophisticated.)

All of this is complicated. For example, what counts as law isn't a matter of each and every person agreeing that the legal authority is legitimate.

If some resident of Baltimore says, "I think the laws of the State of Maryland are a bunch of hogwash," that doesn't mean those laws don't legitimately apply to him. Spelling out a full theory of legal authority is a very big job and is well beyond our expertise. But let's suppose that the notion of legal authority makes sense.

*6.3 Divine Obligation

Someone who holds a Divine Command Theory may think that just as a legal requirement—a civil or criminal law—must be backed by a legal authority, so a moral requirement—a moral law, if you will—must be backed by a moral authority. However, there is another approach. Perhaps moral obligation can be explained without having to invoke the idea of a moral authority, but the search for a suitable theory hasn't produced much agreement. However, the theist can say this: if the God of classical theism exists, then it would be entirely rational to treat God as the ultimate lawgiver, whether we use the word "morality" to describe God's laws or not. After all, God would be perfectly good and perfectly wise. To submit to God's authority could hardly be less reasonable than to the authority of an earthly lawgiver. And in fact, it's difficult to see how it could be rational not to submit to God's authority.

Call the kind of obligation we're under if we grant authority to God *divine obligation*. The theist we're imagining says this: anyone who grants God's existence should, in all rationality, recognize God's authority—treat God as the ultimate lawgiver. Divine obligation would be no more mysterious than ordinary legal obligation, but it would have an advantage over legal obligation. Suppose there is some other way of making sense of moral obligation—of solving the queerness problem. Given God's wisdom and goodness, it's difficult to see how fulfilling our divine obligations could ever conflict with the demands of morality. We can't say this about ordinary legal obligation because the best earthly lawgivers are inevitably flawed. However, if solving the queerness problem by other means proves impossible, divine obligation would be a genuine kind of obligation that could do the job that we wanted moral obligation to do.

Isn't this really just a version of Adams' theory? That is, doesn't it simply amount to saying that the nature of what's right is that it's what God wills? Not really. Our theist's point is that thinking about legal obligation gives us a way of understanding how a sort of all-encompassing obligation could exist—like legal obligation, but vastly more powerful. Perhaps divine obligation is moral obligation, or perhaps it's the perfect substitute for moral obligation. Our theist can insist that he don't have to decide.

*6.3.1 Objections and Replies

A critic might say that moral requirements don't have to be backed by a moral authority. Our theist would reply that maybe the critic is correct. But even so, accepting divine authority would never lead to conflict with genuine moral requirements. And if the critic is wrong—if moral obligation doesn't make sense without a moral authority who imposes the obligation—divine authority provides us with all we could ever need or ask. What our theist wants to stress is the way that theism can leverage the idea of legal authority into something more all-encompassing.

A critic might say that the decision to recognize God's moral authority is already a moral decision—the decision that one ought to obey the commands of a perfectly good and loving God. The believer would say that it's certainly a *rational* decision. Assuming that God exists, there is no reason why we shouldn't grant God ultimate authority over our actions. Whether it's "already" a moral decision is more-or-less beside the point.

Of course, all this applies only if theism is correct. And even if it is, we will see in the next section that difficult problems remain.

7 KNOWING WHAT TO DO

For the divine-command theorist, God's will is the source of moral obligation. For the person we described in Section 6—the one who grants authority to God and accepts divine obligation—God's will is an ultimate source of obligation whether or not we call this obligation "moral." We've also seen that even for theists who favor ordinary understandings of morality, our special relationship with God provides the basis for special obligations. It's hard to see how theism can fail to grant very significant authority to God's will. But now an obvious problem arises: how should the theist decide what counts as the will of God?

Clearly, this isn't a problem for the non-theist. The non-theist obviously won't grant authority to God's will. And though there are serious considerations in favor of theism, serious considerations are also found on the other side. But let's return to the theist for the moment.

The natural-law theorist thinks that everyone has a basic knowledge of right and wrong, but that won't settle the difficult cases in any simple way. For example, Catholic moral theology provides arguments based in natural law for saying that homosexual relations and birth control are wrong. Many atheists disagree, but some theists also disagree. With questions like this, sorting out just what the providential order really is and what it obliges us to do or not do is highly controversial.

More generally, many things done in the name of God have serious consequences, and if they aren't God's will, they may be very wrong indeed. If you kill your son under the false impression that it's God's will, then you've committed a horror. Abraham might have been so intimate with the Almighty that he couldn't mistake God's will. Most of us aren't in that position. Worse, we live in a world with plenty of false prophets. Separating true revelation from crackpot delusion is a serious issue.

The theist has some guidance. On the sort of theories we've been considering, if God weren't loving we wouldn't be obliged to do God's will. That gives the theist a test: is this supposed divine command the sort of thing a loving God would will? If not, that's a reason for thinking that it's not a real revelation.

7.1 What Would God Want?

Here something is worth noticing: asking in a purely hypothetical spirit, "what would a perfectly loving, perfectly knowledgeable God want us to do?" might be morally useful for believers and non-believers alike. It might force us to ask good questions about the facts as best we can ascertain them, and about what real, deep sympathy toward our fellow creatures calls for. Thinking hypothetically about God's will might be a useful tool for solving actual moral problems more-or-less independently of what we take the foundations of morality to be—and independently of whether we think God exists.

7.1.1 Revelation vs. Moral Reasoning?

Of course, the theist believes that there have been genuine revelations, and the theist cares about what God actually wants. So imagine that Sarah, a believer, is faced with a serious moral dilemma. She reasons to the best of her ability in a hypothetical way, asking what would a good and loving God tell her to do. But members of her church tell her that God has provided a revelation on the question she's facing, and wants her to do something very different from what her hypothetical reasoning has led her to think is right. What should she do?

If the revelation is accompanied by some reasons, Sarah might revise her own views about what a good and loving God would want. But what if the supposed revelation isn't accompanied by reasons? If the "revelation" isn't a real revelation, it could lead Sarah to do something very wrong. How should she decide?

This is not a simple question. Return once again to the questions of homosexuality and birth control. If, as some liberal theists believe, birth control and homosexual relations do not violate the providential plan, then heaping shame upon or passing laws against people who engage in either practice increases the sum total of the world's misery for no good reason. Needless to say, the more conservative theist will argue that the stakes are at least as high in the opposite direction. Reasoning about what a good and loving God would want us to do only gets us so far—especially because the reasoning may depend on how we assume this God designed the world, and with what grand plan.

7.2 Coda

For the believer, there's no simple answer. A mere appeal to revelation won't do. If the source of the revelation seems trustworthy enough, the believer might set any qualms aside. But how trustworthy is trustworthy enough? When would setting ordinary moral reasoning aside and replacing it with appeal to moral revelation be appropriate? For the non-believer, the question doesn't come up. For the believer, the question can't be avoided—even if the answer is formed in fear and trembling.

AT A GLANCE: GOD AND MORALITY

1. Morality and God's Commands: the Problem
   - Suppose what God command is in fact morally right.
   - We can ask: Does God command things because they're right? Or is what God commands right because God commands it?
   1.1. The Divine Command Theory
      - The Divine Command Theory says that things are right or wrong because God commands or forbids them.
      - Problem: Morality is not arbitrary. If God commanded cruelty, it would still not be right.
      - Implication: The Divine Command Theory is wrong; if God's commands are morally right, then it's not simply because God gave the commands.

2. Some Objections
   2.1. Objection #1: God Would Never Command Evil
   - Reply: this misses the point. The question is whether things are evil because God forbids them or whether God forbids them because they are evil.
   2.2. Objection #2: God Created Us, Therefore We're Obliged to Obey
   - Reply: we can imagine an evil creator whose commands were morally abominable.
   2.3. Objection #3: Morality Needs Religion
   - Reply: it's not difficult even for atheists to give good reasons for saying that, e.g., stealing is wrong.
     2.3.1. The "Queerness Problem"
     - Moral facts seem "queer": if moral facts existed, they would apparently be different from all other sorts of facts.
     - It's difficult to see how moral obligation could rest on non-moral facts.
     - Apparent solution: let God's commands determine right and wrong.
     - Problem: God's commands would simply be further facts.

3. Philip Quinn: Divine Command Ethics for Theists
   - Quinn argues that the Divine Command Theory is the best way for theists to understand right and wrong.
   3.1. Three Reasons
   3.1.1. Sovereignty
   - If God can't make things right or wrong, then God isn't completely sovereign.
   3.1.2. Immoralities of the Patriarchs
   - In the Bible, God commands things that violate usual moral rules.
   - Therefore, God must have the power to make things right or wrong.
   3.1.3. Commanded Love
   - The commandment to love your neighbor as yourself goes beyond any ordinary human love.
   - It is a duty for Christians.
   - But it could only be a duty because it's commanded by God.
   3.2. Three Reasons Challenged
   3.2.1. Sovereignty and Necessary Truths
   - Moral truths are arguably necessary truths.
   - It's doubtful that God is sovereign over necessary truths.
   3.2.2. "Immoralities of the Patriarchs?"
   - It's not difficult to imagine good moral reasons for commanding the Hebrews to plunder the Egyptians. And Abraham:

        i. Knew that God could take care of Isaac even in death, and

        ii. Could have had excellent reasons to trust God.

   3.2.3. Commanded Love

- The most this example could show is that God can require things that go beyond ordinary duty.
- Ordinary morality can account for special obligations in cases where special relationships exist.

4. Robert Adams

- Adams thinks that for believers, "what's morally right" and "what God wills" mean the same thing.
- Caveat: this is on the presumption that God is loving; if God commanded cruelty, believers would abandon this view.
- Reply: cruelty is wrong, period. This suggests that God forbids cruelty because it's wrong. No need for Divine Command Theory.

5. Natural Law Theories

- Natural law theories offer another way of thinking about how God might be relevant to morality.

   5.1. Providence

- Natural law theories assume divine Providence: God has ordered the world in a wise and good way.
- Natural law theories assume that we have a basic ability to tell right from wrong.
- Right and wrong depend on good and bad.
- Other theorists can agree: if a providential order does exist, it makes a moral difference.

6. God and Obligation

- Question: could appealing to God's will help solve the "queerness problem"?

   6.1. Value

- We can distinguish between value (good and bad) and obligation (right and wrong).
- Good and bad are (arguably) less puzzling than right and wrong.

   6.2. Legal Obligation and Moral Obligation

- Legal obligations don't exist without lawgivers.
- Legitimate laws come from legitimate authorities—authorities good enough to deserve our respect.

   6.3. Divine Obligation

- Call "divine obligation" the kind of obligation we would be under if we submitted to God's authority.
- If God exists, then it would be perfectly rational to submit to God's authority.
- Recognizing divine obligation would never conflict with any genuine moral obligations there might be.

- Divine obligation would be no more mysterious than legal obligation.
- The theist need not decide whether divine obligation is moral obligation or is simply the perfect surrogate for it.

7. Knowing What to Do

- If the God of classical theism exists, then God's will makes a moral difference—whether or not we equate morality with God's will.
- For the theist, this raises the problem of knowing God's will.
- Mistakes about this—or mistakes about the nature of the providential order—could have serious consequences.

7.1. Hypothetical Reasoning

- Reasoning hypothetically about what God would want could be useful for moral reasoning whether or not we think God exists.

7.1.1. Reason vs. Revelation

- The theist faces a potentially difficult problem: the results of this kind of hypothetical reasoning could conflict with supposedly genuine revelations.
- There may be no easy way for the theist to solve this problem.

7.2. Coda

- The non-believer doesn't have to try to solve conflicts between moral reasoning and revelation.
- The believer has no way to avoid the problem.

WEB RESOURCES

You can read Plato's *Euthyphro* online at http://classics.mit.edu/Plato/euthyfro.html.

On the fact that not all obligations must come from a lawgiver, see "Moral Arguments for the Existence of God," Section 1.1 in the *Stanford Encyclopedia of Philosophy*, found online at http://plato.stanford.edu/entries/moral-arguments-god.

For more on natural law from the Roman Catholic perspective, go to http://www.newadvent.org/cathen/09076a.htm.

CHAPTER 11

Religious Diversity

*There are Scores or even hundreds of religions, and their
doctrines often differ sharply. However, most people stick
with the religion they were born into. What should a reasonable person's reaction be to the diversity of world religions?
We discuss several possible answers.*

"Jesus never offered opinions," or so the signboard said. "He spoke the
truth." Perhaps so. No doubt Muslims would say the same about
Mohammed after he received the Koran, as would Buddhists about
Siddhartha Gautama upon his enlightenment. Why should we believe
Jesus rather than the Buddha? Or Mohammed rather than Guru
Nanak?

The world is awash in an alphabet soup of religions, from the now-
defunct Abecedarian Anabaptists to the 150,000 or so Zoroastrians, and
these many faiths disagree about a great deal. The term "religious diversity" refers to this welter of religious outlooks. Our task in this chapter
is to explore the issues that religious diversity raises for religious belief
and religious commitment.

1 INTELLECTUAL RESPONSES TO RELIGIOUS DIVERSITY

Deciding how to respond to religious diversity isn't just an intellectual
question, but having some concepts for sorting through the issues is
helpful. We'll begin by identifying some of the major views.

1.1 Skepticism

A nonreligious observer might offer the following thoughts: Several religions seem roughly equal in terms of evidence and philosophical credentials, but figuring out which, if any, is true seems hopeless. Therefore, a careful thinker will refuse to believe any of them; he'll be a religious skeptic.

We'll have more to say below about this sort of reasoning, but we agree that refusing to hold any religious beliefs is a defensible option. That being said, we take for granted for purposes of this chapter that religious belief is also a defensible option. Furthermore, there are interesting questions about the religious responses to religious diversity. That's what we'll focus on in what follows.

1.2 Exclusivism

Some believers take a dim view of other faiths. The broad label is *exclusivism*, but we need to distinguish two versions.

Doctrinal exclusivism is the view that the doctrines of one's own religion are true, and that where other religions disagree with one's own, they're mistaken. **Salvific exclusivism** focuses on the believer's ultimate fate. The word "salvific" comes from "salvation," a term mainly associated with Christianity. Unfortunately, no widely accepted neutral term is available. We'll sometimes use John Hick's "salvation/liberation," and at other times, we'll talk about the Ultimate Good.

Salvific exclusivism is a special case of doctrinal exclusivism. Christian salvific exclusivists don't just think that the doctrines of Christianity are true. They also think that unless you believe them explicitly, you won't get the Ultimate Good. There is a strong historical association between Christianity and salvific exclusivism, most likely because of sayings like this one, attributed to Jesus in the Gospel of John.

> I am the way, the truth and the life. No one comes to the father except that he comes through me (John 14:6).

If the arguments for salvific exclusivism come from scripture, the arguments against it are more general. One problem is that the doctrine seems to cast God in a harsh light. Suppose we grant that we're all sinners, as Christianity claims. If two people are equally sinful but also equally decent and pious, and one belongs to the "wrong" religion, why would God save one but not the other? Why would God care so much about whether people have correct views on hard questions about the deepest nature of reality?

Theologians have wrestled with that question but whatever the answer, not all Christians are salvific exclusivists. Here's a view that's been part of Catholic thought since *Vatican II*:

> Concretely, it will be in the sincere practice of what is good in their own religious tradition and by following the dictates of their conscience that the members of other religions respond positively to God's invitation and receive salvation in Jesus Christ, even while they do not acknowledge or recognize him as their savior. (From the Vatican document "Dialogue and Proclamation: Reflections and Orientations on Interreligious Dialogue and the Proclamation of the Gospel of Jesus Christ," and quoted almost verbatim in an address by Pope John Paul II on September 9, 1998.)

On this view, non-Christians may be responding to Christ even though they can't properly name what they're responding to. A secular analogy: someone could be cured of an illness even though they have a mistaken idea about what actually caused the cure.

Even though the quote from John Paul II is stated in Christian terms, there's a more general idea here that believers in other faiths could appeal to in stating their own views on the Ultimate Good. Even if one religion has the correct view about the source of salvation/liberation, people who belong to other faiths might be able to get the benefits of that source even though they have the wrong theory about its nature.

1.3 Inclusivism

Our description of exclusivism shaded off into a sketch of *inclusivism*. An inclusivist is someone who thinks that only her own religion is true but that people who have false religious beliefs can still be saved/liberated. Inclusivism is doctrinal exclusivism that rejects salvific exclusivism. Inclusivism can be more-or-less broad. For example, someone might think that only **monotheists** can be saved. Other inclusivists might have a very wide view of who is eligible for salvation/liberation—in some cases, broad enough even to include non-believers.

1.4 Pluralism

The fourth major response to religious diversity is **pluralism**. Like inclusivists, pluralists think that people from different religions can attain the Ultimate Good. Where pluralists and exclusivists differ is on the matter of truth. The inclusivist thinks that one religion (theirs) tells the truth about religious questions. The pluralist thinks that none of the religions gets things literally right.

John Hick offers the most important contemporary defense of pluralism. Hick thinks that a **transcendent** reality exists, which he refers to as The Real. He argues that The Real is beyond our comprehension and that no religion manages to describe it correctly. It might help to remember the old parable of the blind men and their first encounter with an elephant. One of them falls against its side and concludes that an elephant is like a wall. One grabs its tail and decides that an elephant is like a rope. Another feels its ear and thinks an elephant is like a fan. The American poet John Godfrey Saxe (1816–1887) set this tale to verse and offers the following moral:

> So oft in theologic wars,
> The disputants, I ween,
> Rail on in utter ignorance
> Of what each other mean,
> And prate about an Elephant
> Not one of them has seen!

Hick isn't cynical in the way Saxe is, but his idea isn't so very different. We can make some sort of contact with The Real but when we do, our contact is filtered though our cultural symbols, our traditions, and our finite minds; we never get the whole picture. Fortunately, we don't need to grasp the correct metaphysics to be saved/liberated. Very different religions might be equally good at moving us along toward the Ultimate Good.

Hick isn't saying that we know nothing about The Real. For one thing, we know that it leads people away from self-centeredness and toward "reality-centeredness." Still, if we try to describe The Real as it is in itself, our human concepts won't apply. Nonetheless, we can make negative claims: The Real is not finite. It's not an ordinary physical object. And needless to say, it's not any ordinary human being. Furthermore, pluralism doesn't put all religions on a par. Kevin Meeker points out that there once was a Hindu sect called the Thugs, whose members were devoted to the goddess Kali and saw it as their religious duty to commit brutal murders (Meeker 2003). Hick's pluralism doesn't stretch far enough to include the Thugs, but that still doesn't make him a doctrinal exclusivist. An exclusivist thinks that some single historically situated religion is privileged; Hick would disagree.

1.5 Summing Up the Responses

We've now described several positions on religious diversity. Organizing them into a table might help clarify things:

Position on Diversity	View on Truth	View on Salvation/Liberation
	Only One True Religion	Only One Religion Leads to Salvation
Salvific Exclusivism	Yes	Yes
Doctrinal Exclusivism	Yes	Not necessarily
Inclusivism	Yes	No
Pluralism	No	No

Keep in mind that when we use the term "exclusivist" without any qualifier, we mean a doctrinal exclusivist. That means the person may or may not be a salvific exclusivist.

2 DO THE FACTS OF DIVERSITY RULE OUT EXCLUSIVISM?

In the introduction to *An Interpretation of Religion*, John Hick writes:

> For it is evident that in some ninety-nine percent of cases the religion which an individual professes and to which he or she adheres depends upon the accidents of birth. Someone born to Buddhist parents in Thailand is very likely to be a Buddhist, someone born to Muslim parents in Saudi Arabia to be a Muslim, someone born to Christian parents in Mexico to be a Christian, and so on (Hick 1989, p. 2).

If religious beliefs depend largely on accidents of birth, then a critic might doubt that we're really entitled to those beliefs. That's not what Hick is saying, but it may be the most popular reason for rejecting exclusivism. Can we this thought into a serious argument? Two prominent philosophers of religion don't think so.

2.1 Van Inwagen on Accidents of Birth

Suppose you point out to someone—say, a convinced liberal Democrat or conservative Republican—that if he had been born to non-Jewish parents in Nazi Germany, he might have ended up joining the Hitler youth. Peter van Inwagen thinks that the correct response would be, "So what?"

> No one I know supposes that the undoubted fact that one's adherence to a system of political thought is conditioned by one's upbringing is a reason for doubting that the political system one favors is—if not the uniquely "correct" one—clearly and markedly superior to its rivals (Van Inwagen 1995, p. 238).

This misses the point. The question isn't whether we've been influenced by our upbringings, but how. Most of us know that some parts of our upbringings could get in the way of thinking well. For example, our parents or community might have been given to irrational fears and prejudices. If tendencies like that rubbed off on us, our upbringings will interfere with the reasonableness of our beliefs. To put it mildly, Nazi Germany in the 1930s and 1940s wasn't a good place for thinking well about politics. That's why van Inwagen's comment about the Hitler Youth seems beside the point: people in Nazi Germany faced an intellectual disadvantage that, thankfully, most of us don't have to face.

2.2 Plantinga on Accidents of Birth

Alvin Plantinga also thinks that Hick's observation doesn't make difficulties for exclusivism. Here's what he says:

> No matter what philosophical and religious beliefs we hold and withhold (so it seems), there are places and times such that if we had been born there and then, we would not have displayed the pattern of holding and withholding of religious and philosophical beliefs we do display (Plantinga 1995, p. 212).

This is true but, once again, it seems to miss the point. What's striking about Hick's observation is that if he's correct, religious belief doesn't just occasionally depend on the believer's background; it seems to be largely determined by it. The critic's point is that if this is correct, then religious belief doesn't seem to be a response to the truth about the world; it seems to be a response to what people around us happen to believe, whether or not their beliefs are true.

In Plantinga's vocabulary, the question is whether the process that produces religious belief is **reliable**. Using our eyes is normally a reliable way of finding out what's around us; it generally leads to true beliefs. As far as we know, consulting a Ouija board isn't a reliable way to discover things about the world. What about religious belief? Should Hick's observation convince us that it's produced by an unreliable process?

2.3 Reliable and Unreliable Belief-Forming Processes

Plantinga points out that no one process produces religious beliefs. For all Hick's quote tells us, one group of people (Christian believers, in Plantinga's view) could come to believe what they do because they are directly inspired by God. In that case, Plantinga insists, their beliefs would be perfectly reliable.

This should sound familiar to readers who recall the chapter on Reformed epistemology. The question some philosophers will have is whether it solves the problem. Suppose scientists put drops in the eyes of a group of experimental subjects, drape each with a head-to-toe robe, take them to a room they've never been in, and open a slit in the robe just big enough to see through. (This keeps you from seeing your own skin, for example.) You're one of the subjects. You know that most or maybe even all of the drops distort color vision, but some of them may just be distilled water. You're asked to describe the colors you see in the room.

Your visual system *may* be functioning perfectly. The colors you see may be the ones that are really there. But you know three things: the first is that most of the people in the room have malfunctioning color vision systems. The second is that simply checking your own impressions won't settle anything. And the third is that even if some of the subjects agree with your color perceptions, this doesn't solve anything, particularly if other groups of people agree among themselves and disagree with you and your new-found friends.

Here's the point of the analogy for a critic of exclusivism: some of the experimental subjects might be in touch with the visual facts, but most aren't. Likewise, even if some believers are directly in touch with The Real, most aren't. (After all, there's no majority religion.) The critic would say that without some other way of checking or some other reason for believing that your view is more likely to be right, you have no basis for thinking you're in the privileged group.

2.4 A Biblical Analogy

Plantinga replies to a similar criticism by way of a biblical story. King David lusted after Bathsheba, the beautiful wife of Uriah. David seduced Bathsheba and made her pregnant. He tried to trick Uriah into thinking he was the father, but when that didn't work, David made sure Uriah died in battle. God sent the prophet Nathan to confront David with what he had done, and David came to see how utterly despicable his actions were.

Plantinga agrees with David's own judgment: what David did was deeply wrong. He admits that there might be people who disagree, whom he couldn't argue out of their views and whose moral emotions, sense of conviction, and so on might be as strong as his own. But he still thinks David's actions were heinous and doesn't think he should give this belief up just because other people see things differently.

We agree with Plantinga: what David did was detestable. Plantinga suggests that people who think otherwise have a blind spot and that the rest of us are seeing something they aren't. That seems right. Plantinga suggests that the Christian believer can say much the same thing about the convictions of Buddhists or Hindus. Let's explore this idea by going back to the case of David and Bathsheba.

Some people think that there's no such thing as right and wrong, but we'll ignore this broad kind of ethical skepticism; dealing with it would take us too far afield. The more interesting case is the person who thinks David didn't do anything wrong but who isn't a moral skeptic. Assume he agrees with us about things like this: David acted out of greed and lust; David tried to trick Uriah simply to cover his own tracks; David didn't show any concern for Uriah's well-being; Uriah had done nothing to deserve what David did to him; David treated Uriah in a way that he wouldn't agree to be treated and with which he couldn't possibly have expected Uriah to go along.

If all this is so, it's no mere assumption that the person is missing something. He lacks empathy with Uriah, lacks an appreciation for the shock that David himself felt when he was confronted with his own behavior, and perhaps most importantly, he lacks any sense of how good moral thinking actually proceeds. There's every reason to think that there is a deep asymmetry between Plantinga and the person who thinks David did no wrong. To put it bluntly, the person who thinks that David didn't do anything wrong is a moral incompetent. There's every reason to think that Plantinga sees something he doesn't and that the reverse isn't true.

Now take the case of a Muslim, who doesn't hold Plantinga's religious beliefs. Is the Muslim missing something? Quite possibly so. It might be the power of the Gospel stories or the depths of the **Eucharistic** ritual. The Muslim is certainly missing Plantinga's sense of conviction that Jesus is the Son of God. But is Plantinga missing anything?

The Muslim would say yes: he's missing the glory of the Koran. He's missing the particular sense of surrender to God that comes from following the Muslim rituals of prayer. He's certainly missing the Muslim's conviction that God is absolute Unity and that Mohammed was the Seal of the Prophets. In the religious case, the asymmetry that we saw in the previous example is replaced by an apparent symmetry. Plantinga, or the Muslim, or both may be mistaken. There's no reason to think that either of them is a religious incompetent.

Of course, this may not help the critic of exclusivism as much as might appear. After all, Plantinga might say that we have similar symmetries in philosophical, ethical, and political disagreements. That doesn't mean we should give up our views in those areas.

Quite so, and we'll return to this point in Section 5. Meanwhile, all of this began with Hick's comments about the way in which most people's religious beliefs seem to be determined by their backgrounds. When we introduced Hick's observation, we pointed out that he wasn't trying to talk people out of their beliefs. To understand this, we need to look at pluralism more closely.

3 PLURALISM AGAIN

Hick thinks the world is religiously ambiguous. That means skepticism is a legitimate option, but Hick accepts something like the **Principle of Credulity** that we discussed in the chapter on religious experience. He insists that people are entitled to trust their religious experience—for example, their sense of God's presence—unless there's a good reason not to. He goes further: if someone's religious experience is best expressed in Christian or Muslim or Hindu terms, they're entitled to trust that experience and talk about it in the terms that seem to them to fit. Hick is not telling the Christian to stop being a Christian or the Hindu to stop being a Hindu.

So what is he saying?

Pluralism isn't a religion but in Hick's version, it *is* a religious hypothesis. It assumes the existence of a transcendent Real as a way to make sense of religious diversity. However, Hick insists that The Real is ultimately beyond our grasp. This theme shows up in most religious traditions. The *Tao Te Ching* begins with these words:

> The Tao that can be spoken of is not the eternal Tao;
> The name that can be named is not the eternal name.

Many people believe that Asian religions tend to treat The Real as a mystery, but there's a rich sense of divine mystery in such Christian mystics as St. Teresa of Avila, in Jewish Kabbalism, and in Islamic Sufism. "My thoughts are not your thoughts, and my ways are not your ways," says God in the book of Isaiah. Believers may differ about exactly what and how much we know about The Real, but most mature believers agree that there's an infinity that we don't know.

On Hick's hypothesis, people with very different beliefs can still come in touch with Ultimate Reality and make their way toward salvation/liberation. The explanation for the fact that different traditions offer such different accounts is that even though The Real is the source of authentic religious experience, the only way we can approach The Real is through the conceptual and symbolic means that our traditions make available to us. In Hick's view, none of the religions gets things literally right but many of them provide means that can bring us closer to the Ultimate Good.

3.1 Metaphors for Pluralism

Consider this philosophically famous figure:

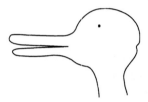

Duck or rabbit? It depends on how you look. Hick asks us to imagine two societies. In one, rabbits are plentiful but ducks are scarce. In the other, it's the other way around. People in the first society might find it very hard to see the figure as a duck; people in the second society might have trouble seeing it as a rabbit. Both descriptions are faithful to the figure in a way that describing it as a hippo wouldn't be. But neither description is The Truth, and neither is fully adequate.

Hick offers another metaphor, this one from quantum theory. Depending on the experiment we perform, light can seem to be a particle or wave. Nonetheless, neither description is fully accurate, and if we're in a situation where one description seems to fit, then the other won't.

The point the duck-rabbit image makes is that in some cases, two people might see one and the same thing in different and seemingly contradictory ways without either of them simply being wrong. The quantum analogy may be even more adequate, but it's also trickier; quantum theory has been used for a lot of dubious intellectual ends. What's useful about the quantum metaphor is that on one important understanding of quantum mechanics, we can't "add up" the results of different measurements to get a more and more exhaustive picture of a quantum entity. Quantum reality is somehow too complex for that. On this view, the wave and particle natures of a quantum system are "complementary," to borrow the term that the physicist Neils Bohr used. They can't be fitted together into a comprehensive true description. Still, when we perform an experiment or make a measurement on an electron, we really are finding out something about the electron itself.

The quantum metaphor is only a metaphor, but it's not hard to see its appeal for Hick. Consider the question of whether The Real is personal. If one faith sees The Real as a personal God and another sees it in terms of impersonal Nirvana, it might be difficult to imagine how the two descriptions could be equally valid. But ask yourself: does God think thoughts in sequence, as we do? Does God feel pain? What would it be like to be aware of everything at once? The point is that even if the term "person" fits The Real in some ways, God is a lot different from an ordinary person. If Hick is right, then the truth can't be fully captured by calling The Real personal *or* impersonal. Sometimes The Real might reveal itself in ways that seem more adequately described in personal language and other times in ways that this language doesn't seem to fit.

Here's another metaphor, though not one that Hick offers. Pick two similar-looking bits of the image below—say, two small black blobs that look the same and are near to one another. While you look at the figure below, let your eyes relax as though you were looking through the page. Relax your focus (don't cross your eyes) until the two black blobs overlap, and then see what, if anything, emerges:

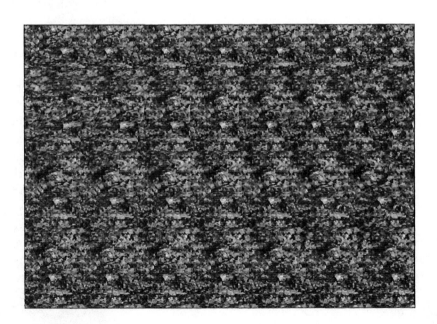

Some of you—anyone without binocular vision—won't even be able to try this. Others will try but will never see anything other than a jumble. But some of you will see a three-dimensional shape that—especially in the context of this chapter—you should recognize. There will be differences even among those who succeed. The figure will be very stable for some people. For others, it will flicker in and out of view.

It's important for the point of the illustration to recognize that the figure is not only difficult to see but also ambiguous. (Yes, it's the duck-rabbit.) And even people who see some three-dimensional image may have relaxed their focus too much and not see what's intended. For them, the image that emerges might simply look bizarre.

Of course, all this is just a metaphor; it can't prove anything. However, as a metaphor it may be particularly useful for getting Hick's idea across. Its message to the skeptic is that just because you can't see something doesn't mean it's not there. To the exclusivist, the message is that what's really there may be capable of being seen in very different but equally legitimate ways.

4 PLURALISM'S PROBLEMS

Hick's theory offers the exclusivist a compromise. On the level of religious practice, Hick thinks it's perfectly legitimate that the Christian should approach The Real as a Christian, the Buddhist as a Buddhist, and the Jew as a Jew. The pluralistic hypothesis isn't a recipe for conducting your religious life; it's a second-order interpretation of religion, but one that takes first-order religious practice seriously.

Traditional believers might not be satisfied. After all, if Hick is correct, their beliefs are false. Perhaps Hick could answer this way: consider the difference between the way we normally think about the world around us and the way we think about it for certain scientific purposes. If science is right, then the physical world is intrinsically a very different place than it appears to be. The chair you are sitting in is mostly empty space; the colors you see aren't out there in the objects in the way they appear to you in experience. However, realizing that doesn't tempt you to give up your ordinary way of talking and thinking about the world, and it doesn't mean that everything you see is simply an illusion. Likewise, Hick might say, the fact that ultimately, things aren't the way our creeds literally say they are doesn't mean that we must give up thinking in terms of those creeds. (The reader might recall the discussion of religious instrumentalism in Chapter 6.)

Perhaps that helps, but it only goes so far. Consider Jesus from the perspectives of Islam and Christianity. For Christians, the idea that Jesus of Nazareth really died on the cross and was resurrected is absolutely central. For Muslims, it's a fundamental belief that the Koran is completely reliable, because Mohammed received it from the angel Gabriel. The problem is that the Koran teaches that Jesus didn't really die on the cross. It's difficult to see how pluralism can bridge this gap without one group or the other having to grant that they are deeply wrong about something they care about deeply.

Hick's compromise depends on distinguishing pluralism from first-order religion, but it's not clear that this can be done. According to Judaism, one God exists—a personal being who created the heavens and Earth. According to pluralism, there is a protean Real that manifests itself in a dazzling array of guises. Why aren't these just straightforwardly conflicting religious doctrines?

Hick might reply that religion is a lot more than doctrines and that even if there is a metaphysical dispute between him and die-hard exclusivists, that doesn't make pluralism a religion. The exclusivist's answer would most likely be that even if religion is not just doctrine, doctrine is a critical part of his religion, and giving it up for pluralism is a bad bargain.

5 RELIGIOUS VS. NON-RELIGIOUS DIFFERENCES

It's time to face a question that the exclusivist will think has been postponed far too long. Exclusivists from different religions disagree, but no one is tempted to think that people who believe in free will are committing some sort of intellectual sin just because other people think free will doesn't exist. No one is tempted to think that people who favor abortion rights are misguided simply because some people oppose them. Why treat religious disagreements any differently?

From one perspective, there's no reason. Religious claims can be treated as philosophical theses and debated in the way that people debate about philosophy. Apologists for various religions offer arguments and evidence on behalf of the religion's central claims. There are arguments for the existence of God, and arguments for various more specific theological claims. For example, some Christian thinkers have argued in detail that the best explanation for a whole range of reports and events after the death of Jesus of Nazareth is that Jesus really did rise from the dead. Insofar as people hold their religious exclusivism in the way that people hold controversial philosophical positions—that is, as a matter that's open to debate—there's no basis at all for treating an exclusivist any differently from someone whose philosophical commitments include a commitment to the existence of free will.

However, the fact of the matter is that relatively few people look at their religious beliefs this way, and according to philosophers like Plantinga, they don't need to. Differences about religion could proceed in the way that philosophical disagreements do, but for most people, they don't. Accordingly, the rest of what we say in this section deals only with the situation of this more typical believer.

Suppose someone is in favor of abortion rights but has no serious knowledge of what people opposed to abortion have to say, shows no interest in finding out, and when faced with thoughtful anti-abortion arguments, feels no need to reply in any deeper way than by saying, "Well I think you're wrong!" We don't think this person should be forced to give up his view or hauled off to jail for expressing it; in that sense, he's entitled to his opinion. But in an obvious sense, he hasn't earned the right to his view at all.

We've talked about what we're "entitled" to believe but the point could be made in other ways. We might say that this particular abortion-rights advocate is unreasonable, or not intellectually serious, or perhaps arrogant or stubborn or uncritical. Whatever terms we ended up settling on, clearly we'd find some serious fault with the thinker. (We hope it's understood that in saying this, we aren't taking a stand one way or another on the issue of abortion rights.) The same goes for the other disagreements we've noted. At a minimum, we generally think that to have earned their views on controversial topics, people on either side must make some effort to understand and respond to the opposition.

In the case of religious commitment, many people don't see it this way. A sizeable number of believers have no serious understanding of the religions they reject and aren't inclined to do anything about that. In fact, many believers consider it a virtue to hold their beliefs on "faith," as they might put it, by which they mean in part the steadfast refusal to consider any objections. This looks arbitrary to the non-exclusivist in at least two ways. It looks like a case where believers single out their own beliefs as privileged without any basis other than their own sense of conviction. It also looks arbitrary because it's a departure from the standards we assume in other domains where's there is serious controversy with sane people on all sides.

We can ask: why the difference? Notice that there are two ways to read this question. One is as a request for an explanation: what factors, psychological or otherwise, lead people to treat religious belief in this way? The other way to read the question is as a request for a justification, an account that would make it reasonable for people to hold their religious beliefs to a different standard than they might hold, for example, their political beliefs. We could offer all sorts of psychological hypotheses about why so many people hold their religious beliefs much more immune from criticism than other beliefs, but our speculations don't carry any special weight. Instead, we'll look at a reason that might function both as an explanation and as a justification. This isn't a reason most people would actually give, but it could be a genuine reason for all that.

Imagine a man who's thinking about getting married. He could spend endless amounts of time debating with himself and discussing with others whether his prospective mate really is the best person for him, or whether he really knows this person well enough to make the commitment. A certain amount of that sort of questioning might even be healthy. However, after a while the internal debate would start to seem unseemly. Furthermore, once our hypothetical suitor has made his commitment, it would be even more unseemly to revisit it constantly.

Unseemliness isn't the only issue. Treating an intimate relationship as though it were an intellectual puzzle is a good recipe for unhappiness. If we found one of our friends doing this, we would try to persuade him that it's bad idea. Treating questions about intimate relationships as subjects for continual debate and verification is positively unreasonable.

The analogy between faith and intimate relationships will ring true for believers in many ways. It's not just a question of a relationship with an Ultimate Being, but with a tradition, with fellow believers, and with a way of life. Arguably, even the earthly comforts of religion call for making a leap into a particular way of being religious.

This reason for why people often treat their religious beliefs differently than their political beliefs straddles the fence between being an explanation—they do it to get the potential benefits of religious belief—and a justification—sometimes to hold beliefs for what we called pragmatic reasons in Chapter 8 is reasonable. We've taken something like William James's "will to believe" and applied it to choosing among possible faiths. On this approach, choosing a faith without thoroughly considering all the alternatives could be reasonable, and staying committed without feeling the need to engage in an ongoing debate could also be reasonable. The reasons don't have to do with evidence. The point is that engaging in endless argument and evidence-gathering runs the risk of passing up a chance at great rewards. To use a gaming analogy, there may be better and worse ways to play a game, but you might not have the luxury of figuring out the best strategy. If you waste your time worrying about it, you won't get in the game at all.

This approach won't appeal to anyone who isn't attracted to religion in the first place, but this chapter is intended mainly to deal with religious responses to religious diversity. The suggestion we've just made is that some of the issues look different if we consider them from a pragmatic, non-epistemic point of view. However, the sorts of questions we raised in Chapter 8 don't just go away. Religious beliefs have consequences for how people act, as anyone who lives in a post-9/11 world knows only too well, and we don't need to rise to the level of mass terrorism to find examples. Suppose you make your stand inside a faith that says it's wrong to treat illness in any way except with prayer. You refuse to take your sick child to the doctor and she dies of a burst appendix. If your religious beliefs are wrong, then your stand has come at a high cost. We can ask whether pragmatic reasons could ever outweigh the moral risks in a case like this. The fact that a leap into a particular form of faith *might* be reasonable, all things considered, doesn't guarantee that it *is* reasonable, and it doesn't relieve you of the obligation to take the moral risks into account before your feet leave the ground. Pragmatic reasons have their limits.

6 A MODEST PROPOSAL?

A few people may have carefully weighed their beliefs against the claims of other traditions and have concluded that the balance of reasons is on their side. That description doesn't come close to describing even most sophisticated believers. One way to read the preceding section is as a "pragmatic" argument for being a doctrinal exclusivist, but there's another way to look at things.

As we pointed out earlier, even if some believers are in a good position to believe that members of other traditions are missing something that they see, they almost certainly are *not* in a good position to think that they aren't missing something that the other traditions see. Put less obscurely, for all they know, there's some genuine truth that other sorts of believers see that they aren't well-positioned to see themselves.

This isn't a positive argument for thinking that pluralism is true. It's a negative argument for saying that perhaps none of us is in a position to say that it's false. More generally, whatever the truth about The Real might be, you don't have to be a pluralist or even a mystic to think that it's not that easy to get it right. Even the family disputes within a single religion should make this clear. Are people converted by reformed rabbis really Jews? Does the bread and wine in the Eucharist really become the body and blood of Christ? Was Ali the last rightful successor to Mohammed? When we come to the differences between religions, we could imagine a serious person blushing at the thought that she really knows how to sort out the ultimate truths. This includes the serious person whose faith has the sort of William James-like quality we described in the previous section.

All of this has an upshot. Skeptics have a solution to our problem, and as we've said, religious skepticism is a legitimate point of view. But what of believers? Believers might vacillate between doctrinal exclusivism and pluralism, but perhaps there's another approach: a kind of intellectual and spiritual modesty. It would offer two bits of advice. First, believe if you are so inclined, but when it comes to the deepest puzzles of the universe, believe with a certain lack of grasping. Don't be too sure you've gotten everything right. This may sound like a mere platitude, but when it comes to religious beliefs, many people find it remarkably hard to take this point of view. Second, unless they're acting crazily or dangerously (a standard that also applies to your own case), don't worry too much about whether other sorts of believers are wrong. One way to start following the first bit of advice is to accept that you already can be quite sure that you haven't gotten everything right. A proper modesty about your relationship to whatever the ultimate truths may be ought to make that plausible. As for the second suggestion, a quote from one of the Gospels may be apt: "The wind blows where it will, and you hear the sound of it, but you do not know where it comes from or where it goes."

AT A GLANCE: RELIGIOUS DIVERSITY

1. Intellectual Responses to Religious Diversity
   1.1. Skepticism
   - Religious diversity provides reasons for doubting that any religion is true or leads to salvation.

1.2. Exclusivism

- *Salvific Exclusivism*: only one religion is true and that is the only religion that leads to salvation (enlightenment, Nirvana, and so on).
- *Doctrinal Exclusivism*: only one religion is true. Doctrinal exclusivists come in two forms: those who don't think those of other religions will attain salvation (salvific exclusivists) and those who do think those of other religions will attain salvation (inclusivists).

1.3. Inclusivism

- The view that while there are many different paths to salvation, only the teachings of one religion can be true.

1.4. Pluralism

- The view that many religions lead to salvation but none are literally true.

1.5. Summary

Position on Diversity	View on Truth	View on Salvation/ Liberation
	Only One True Religion	Only One Religion Leads to Salvation
Salvific Exclusivism	Yes	Yes
Doctrinal Exclusivism	Yes	Not necessarily
Inclusivism	Yes	No
Pluralism	No	No

2. Do the Facts of Diversity Rule Out Exclusivism?

- Hick says that in most cases, a person's religious preference is determined by accidents of birth.
- Hick does not infer that people aren't entitled to their religious beliefs.
- This conclusion might seem to follow nonetheless.

2.1. Van Inwagen

- "Hitler youth" analogy intended to show that even though our views are "conditioned" by our upbringing, this isn't a reason to doubt them.
- Response: Van Inwagen fails to distinguish between influences that are neutral or helpful and influences that undermine rationality.

2.2. Plantinga

- For any philosophical view we hold, there are times and/or places such that if we had been born then or there, we wouldn't have held the view we do now.
- Response: Hick's observation suggests that religious belief isn't just influenced by upbringing but seems largely determined by it.
- Issue: is religious belief the result of a reliable process?

2.3. Reliable and Unreliable Belief-Forming Mechanisms
- Members of one religion could be directly inspired by God.
- Problem: even if this is true, members of that group have no basis for thinking that they are the privileged ones.

2.4. A Biblical Analogy
- Plantinga imagines someone who honestly thinks that what King David did to Uriah was not despicable.
- The existence of such people would not be a reason for us to doubt our own moral judgment.
- Reply: this is not a good analogy. A person like that would be clearly morally incompetent. Members of one religion usually have no reason to think that members of other religions are incompetent.

3. Pluralism
- Hick thinks people are entitled to trust their religious experience.
- He views pluralism not as a religion but as a religious hypothesis intended to make sense of religious diversity.
- The Real is beyond our grasp, but different religions can bring us into partial contact with it mediated through the symbols and concepts we have available.

3.1. Metaphors for Pluralism
- The duck-rabbit.
- Quantum theory and wave-particle duality.
- The stereogram.
  a. To the skeptic: the fact that you can't see something doesn't mean it isn't there.
  b. To the exclusivist: there may be more than one legitimate way to see something.

4. Problems for Pluralism
- Pluralism is more like a religion than Plantinga admits: it offers a particular and contentious view of the divine.
- Hick might reply that religion isn't just doctrine.
- The exclusivist might answer that doctrine still matters.

5. Religious and Non-Religious Differences
- Deep differences in philosophy don't usually persuade us to abandon our positions. Why should religions be different?
- Answer: it doesn't have to be, but for most people, religious beliefs aren't held on philosophical grounds.
- Usually (e.g., in the abortion debate), intellectual responsibility calls for thinking about other people's views and considering their arguments.
- People usually don't approach inter-religious difference this way.
- This may have a pragmatic justification.

6. A Modest Proposal
   - Believers are seldom in a position to be sure that they aren't missing something that members of other faiths see.
   - Getting religious truth right is likely to be difficult.
   - One can hold religious beliefs in a non-grasping way.
   - One can have religious beliefs without being too concerned about whether people who disagree are wrong.

FURTHER READING AND WEB RESOURCES

There is a great deal of statistical information about various religions at http://adherents.com.

One of the largest sites on the internet for the discussion of religious and interfaith issues is http://beliefnet.org.

John Hick has his own website at http://www.johnhick.org.uk.

S. Mark Heim explores the view that there may not be just one Ultimate Good in his book, *Salvations: Truth and Difference in Religion* (Maryknoll, New York: Orbis Books, 1995).

CHAPTER 12

God and Language

Some philosophers argue that language provides fertile ground for criticizing religious belief. In this chapter, we will look at three different problems for religious belief based upon considerations of language. Two of these problems are less serious than they seem, while the third seems difficult to the point of intractability.

On June 22, 1936, a professor at the University of Vienna in Austria was making his way to class to deliver his lecture. While ascending the stairs of the building where his class was to be held, the professor was confronted by a former student. The student pulled out a gun and shot the professor in the chest. The student was a Nazi sympathizer and future member of the Nazi Party. The murdered professor was the well-known philosopher, Moritz Schlick. Whether Schlick was a martyr for his views or whether his deranged assassin had simply been triggered by an academic slight is not easy to say. But Schlick's philosophical views, if correct, had potent consequences.

In the 1920s, a group of philosophers, scientists, and mathematicians led by Schlick had begun meeting regularly in Vienna to discuss issues involving **epistemology**, the **philosophy of science**, and language. This group of thinkers was known as the Vienna Circle. The Vienna Circle included some of the most famous and important philosophers of the twentieth century, including Rudolf Carnap, Herbert Feigl, Kurt Gödel, and Otto Neurath. The school of philosophy that originated with the Vienna Circle was **logical positivism**.

271

One topic of discussion among the logical positivists of the Vienna Circle was the lack of progress in disciplines like **metaphysics, ethics,** and religion. They watched scientific knowledge grow at a remarkable rate. While nonscientific disciplines like metaphysics, ethics, and religion appeared to stagnate over the last few hundred, or even thousand, of years.

For example, compare medicine and ethics. Our knowledge of how the human body, bacteria, and viruses work has increased tremendously since the time of the famous Greek physician Galen (c.130–c.200 BCE). But although we now know far more about medicine than Greek or Romans physicians did, we don't appear to have made comparable progress in our understanding of ethics. Has ethics really advanced all that much since Aristotle (384 BCE–322 BCE)? Some philosophers don't think so. Even ethical theories that came on the scene after Aristotle seem to have rough equivalents in the ancient world. It just isn't obvious that philosophical progress in ethics comes close to scientific progress in medicine.

Religion seems to be in an even worse state as a discipline of human knowledge. Has our knowledge of God increased and progressed in the last several hundred or thousand years? Consider monotheistic religions. Is Christianity an improvement on Judaism? Is Islam an improvement on Christianity? Is the Baha'i faith the culmination of Western monotheism? These would be hard cases to argue. Just because one religion comes after another religion doesn't mean it advances knowledge of God. So the question remains: Why has science progressed while metaphysics, ethics, and religion have remained relatively stagnant?

The members of the Vienna Circle answer that disciplines like metaphysics and religion fail to progress because the language they use is meaningless—it doesn't amount to much more than gibberish. It shouldn't be surprising that disciplines comprised of babble do little more than spin their wheels.

We'll give a more detailed explanation of logical positivism in the next section of this chapter. It suffices for now to say that at the heart of positivism is **empiricism,** the view that we can only know what we can detect with our five senses. This means that the philosophy of the Vienna Circle was anti-superstitious and anti-metaphysical; on this point, it ran afoul of the Nazi Party. Logical positivism didn't fit well with either the mystical and mythical worldview, or the occult elements of Nazism. The rise of Nazism in Austria caused many members of the Vienna Circle to flee to the United States and the United Kingdom. Moritz Schlick stayed in Austria and, unfortunately, paid the price for it. Schlick's murderer was paroled shortly after his conviction. Suspicion about positivist philosophy became entwined with strong anti-Semitic sentiments on the rise in Vienna—despite the fact that Schlick was not Jewish.

In this chapter, we will look at objections to religion that, like the Vienna Circle's, are based on considerations of language.

1 THE OBJECTION TO RELIGION BASED ON VERIFICATIONISM

Logical positivism was a complex movement and its development gave rise to some very sophisticated philosophy. What follows is a simplified account, intended to capture the gist of an important kind of objection to religious statements.

1.1 How Language Can Lead to Philosophical Mistakes

Language can be philosophically misleading. In particular, it can mislead us to think that some sentences are meaningful when they really aren't. In order to understand the logical positivist's objection to religion, we need to consider how language can distort our thinking and lead to philosophical mistakes.

Suppose, for example, that a person who is very ignorant of how cars work owns a car that has a top speed of 100 miles per hour. He wants his car to have a greater top speed and so he brings it to a mechanic. When he returns to pick up this car, he asks the mechanic to give him the old parts (to make sure that he hasn't paid for a part that wasn't actually installed). The customer sees his car's old pistons, spark plugs, and the like, but doesn't see the old top speed. The mechanic assures the customer that the car was really given a new top speed, but the customer, worried he has been ripped off, demands to see the old top speed. The mechanic explains to the customer that a car's top speed isn't a part of a car in the way that a tire or steering wheel is. It's a complex property, not a physical object one can hold in one's hand, says the mechanic (who used to be a philosophy major).

The scenario described above is not very realistic because no one is *that* ignorant of how cars work. But our story illustrates one way in which language can mislead. "The car's top speed" is a noun phrase—like "the car's steering wheel," but one is an object and the other isn't. While no one is really likely to be confused in this kind of case, there are more philosophically loaded and problematic cases.

Let's consider an example from the history of philosophy. Gilbert Ryle (who was influenced by the logical positivists) and Ludwig Wittgenstein argue that language has misled many of us about the nature of the mind. In particular, some philosophers, like René Descartes (1596–1650), hold a **dualist** theory of the mind, according to which the mind and body are two separate entities, one immaterial and the other physical. Ryle calls dualism the "ghost in the machine" view of the mind because it pictures the mind as some sort of immaterial ghost located in the body and operating it like a machine. He thinks this mistaken picture of the mind is a result of misleading language. Ryle offered an analogy: suppose someone visiting Oxford University is shown colleges, libraries, playing fields, museums, academic departments, and administrative offices. At the end of this tour, the visitor asks, "where is the university?" As Ryle puts it, the visitor's mistake:

> lay in his innocent assumption that it was correct to speak of Christ Church, the Bodleian Library, the Ashmolean Museum and the University, to speak, that is, as if 'the University' stood for an extra member of the class of which these other units are members. He was mistakenly allocating the University to the same category as that to which the other institutions belong (Ryle 1949, p. 17–18).

Ryle believes that dualists make the same mistake regarding the mind. A body is a thing; no doubt about that. But Ryle argued that talking about "the mind" is not a matter of talking about some entity. In his view, speaking of "the mind" is a way of speaking about the way people behave and are disposed to behave. Ryle's specific **behaviorist** view is no longer accepted. But the idea that when we talk about "the mind"—grammar notwithstanding—we aren't actually talking of some ghostly entity, is something that most contemporary philosophers would still accept.

Like Ryle after them, the positivists thought that language can mislead us philosophically. More specifically, the positivists thought that we were misled by language into thinking that theological discourse is meaningful when it isn't.

1.2 Verificationism

The positivists noticed that what seems to separates science from religion is that scientific statements can be checked empirically, while, as they saw it, religious statements can't. This suggested a general theory of meaning: a statement is meaningful only if it can be empirically checked out or verified. This theory of meaning is known as **verificationism** or the verifiability criteria of meaning.

The positivists understood that *some* sentences are meaningful even if they can't be verified empirically. They argued, though, that such sentences were limited to a very specific type: statements whose truth or falsity could be established by logic and mathematics—for example, "It's raining or it's not raining," or "2 + 2 = 4." Clearly both are meaningful and, in fact, both are true. But we don't know they are true by an empirical investigation of the world. That's obvious in the case of, "It's raining or it's not raining." This statement doesn't tell you anything about the actual weather. It's true because of how the words "or" and "not" work.

The arithmetic case is less obvious. You could put two sticks on the ground and set two more next to them and see that you have four sticks. That might seem to be a way to verify the statement that 2 + 2 = 4. Of course, if you put two drops of water beside two drops of water, you might end up with one big drop. Arithmetic isn't about what happens when we perform various physical operations. Very roughly, it's a framework that fixes what we mean when we apply numbers to the world. A physical operation that seems to violate the rules of arithmetic simply doesn't count as counting.

Verificationists often explain this distinction by differentiating between **analytic** sentences and **synthetic** sentences. Here's how this works for subject-predicate sentences—sentences like "John is running" or "Bachelors are happy." Immanuel Kant (1724–1804) pointed out that in some sentences, the subject word (or phrase) seems to completely contain the information found in the predicate. Consider the sentence, "All bachelors are unmarried." The subject "bachelors" already has built into it the concept "unmarried" because what it *means* to be a bachelor is to be an unmarried male of marriageable age. The subject already "contains" the concept included in the predicate. And notice, "All bachelors are unmarried," tells us nothing about the observable world. It merely reflects the definition of the word "bachelor."

If a statement like "All bachelors are unmarried" is analytically true, then "Not all bachelors are unmarried" is analytically false. It also counts as meaningful, and we'll use the term "analytic" to mean any statement whose truth or falsity can be established by logic, mathematics, and definitions.

Whether or not all true mathematical statements are analytic, simple arithmetic statements at least seem to fit this mold. Consider 2 + 2 = 4.

It's a matter of how the concepts of "2" and "+" work that 2 + 2 equals 4, or so the argument would go. (Here we have to add a disclaimer: the thesis that mathematics consists entirely of analytic statements is very controversial.)

Now consider the sentence, "This raven is black." Does the subject contain the predicate? Does the idea of a raven have built into its very definition that it is black? Not at all. Ravens are black, but we know this based on observation. You can at least imagine finding an albino raven. And so the sentence, "All bachelors are unmarried," is analytic whereas the sentence, "This raven is black," is synthetic.

David Hume used different words to explain what we've been calling the analytic/synthetic distinction. Hume understands what we've been calling analytic statements in terms of "relations of ideas" and he understands synthetic statements as "matters of facts." The sentence, "2 + 2 = 4," is arguably true as a matter of relations among ideas or concepts. Matters of fact are sentences about the actual world, not merely the world of ideas or concepts.

Analytic Sentences (Relations of Ideas)	Synthetic Sentences (Matters of Fact)
All bachelors are unmarried.	This raven is black.
2 + 2 = 4	The Sun is 93 million miles from Earth.
A tall man is tall.	Dirt is brown.
A woman is female.	George Washington was the first president of the United States.

According to the positivists, analytic sentences have meaning but synthetic sentences only have meaning if they can be checked out in the real world. That's because synthetic statements are about the world and not merely how ideas, concepts, and definitions relate to each other. Putting it more formally:

> *Verificationism*: A sentence is meaningful if and only if
> (i) it is analytic or (ii) it is synthetic and can be verified
> by experience.

It's important to understand that the positivists aren't making a claim about all types of linguistic meaning. The command, "Clean your room!" and the question, "Do I have to eat my peas?" are both meaningful sentences, but neither is the kind of meaning the positivists are interested in. They are concerned with the kind of meaning that factual claims have, sentences like, "George Washington was the first president of the United States." They called this kind of meaning **cognitive meaning**. Verificationism is a theory of cognitive meaning because it's concerned with statements of fact rather than commands, questions, expressions of emotion, or lines of poetry.

Sentences that Have Cognitive Meaning	*Sentences that Have Non-Cognitive Meaning*
Thomas Jefferson signed the Declaration of Independence.	Go to your room!
2 + 2 = 4	What is your favorite color?
This raven is black.	Yuck, spinach!
All bachelors are unmarried.	Between melting and freezing, the soul's sap quivers.

Logical positivists understood that there are many statements of fact that we can't check simply because we lack the practical ability to do so. Consider the statement that water exists on planets outside of our galaxy. This statement of fact is synthetic, but it can't be checked out because we don't yet have the means to investigate it. When the verificationists say that synthetic statements must be able to be checked out in the real world, they mean that that they have to be able to be checked out *in principle*, not necessarily in practice. In light of that, we can clarify:

> *Verificationism*: A sentence is cognitively meaningful if and only if (i) it is analytic or (ii) it is synthetic and can, at least in principle, be verified from experience.

Why think that an apparent factual claim is meaningful only if it can be verified? Suppose someone giving a talk says, "The irresolute is unencumbering itself." You quiz the speaker during the question period, trying to figure out what in the world he means. You get vague replies. Finally you ask whether there would be any difference in the world that anyone could detect, even in principle, depending on whether this statement were true or false. The speaker finally agrees that there wouldn't be. Isn't that reason to think that you haven't actually been told anything meaningful? The statement gives the appearance of providing information but it does no such thing. Whatever function this bit of language might be serving, the positivists would say that it is cognitively meaningless.

1.3 The Objection: Religious Claims Are Meaningless

We are now in a position to understand the positivists' objection to religious claims more fully. They contend that religious claims are cognitively meaningless because they purport to be synthetic statements—i.e., statements of fact about the world—but they can't be verified by experience, even in principle. Stated as an argument, the objection is this:

> *Premise #1*: A sentence is cognitively meaningful if and only if (i) it is analytic or (ii) it is synthetic and can, at least in principle, be verified from experience (verificationism).
>
> *Premise #2*: Religious and metaphysical statements are not (i) analytic nor (ii) can they be, at least in principle, be verified from experience
>
> *Conclusion*: Therefore, religious and metaphysical statements are not cognitively meaningful.

If the positivists are correct, we have been misled by language into thinking that religious statements are meaningful. They might look meaningful but they only pretend to make genuine claims about the world because the claims can't be checked out, even in principle. If we accept the positivists' view of language, this makes religious statement meaningless.

David Hume made a similar point over two centuries earlier:

> If we take into our hand any volume; of divinity or school metaphysics, for instance; let us ask, Does it contain any abstract reasoning concerning quantity or number? No. Does it contain any experimental reasoning concerning matter of fact and existence? No. Consign it then to the flames: For it can contain nothing but sophistry and illusion (Hume 1975 [1784], Section 12, Part 3).

This objection to religion does not claim that religion is false or that God doesn't exist. According to the positivists, theists, atheists, and agnostics are all confused because they all think that "God exists" is meaningful. They just disagree over whether it's true. A. J. Ayer, a famous logical positivist, puts it this way:

It is important not to confuse this view of religious assertions with the view that is adopted by atheists, or agnostics. For it is characteristic of an agnostic to hold that the existence of a god is a possibility in which there is no good reason either to believe or disbelieve; and it is characteristic of an atheist to hold that it is at least probable that no god exists. And our view that all utterances about the nature of God are nonsensical, so far from being identical with, or even lending any support to, either of these familiar contentions, is actually incompatible with them. (Ayer 1946, pp. 115–116).

1.4 Replies to the Objection from Verificationism

What are we to make of the objection to religion based on the verifiability theory of meaning? The verificationist's argument is logically **valid**. If the two premises are true, the conclusion must be true. The first premise just asserts the verifiability theory of meaning. The second premise claims that religious belief runs afoul of that theory of meaning. Are the premises true? Let's examine them in reverse order.

The second premise claims that religious assertions are neither analytic nor synthetic statements that could be empirically verified in principle. Let's assume for now that the verifiability theory of meaning is correct and ask whether religious statements fail to meet that criterion of meaning.

Are religious statements analytic? We might be able to make that case for some of them but, for the most part, religious statements aren't even intended to be analytic. A statement like, "God led the Israelites out of Egypt," isn't a matter of how concepts or ideas are related. It's meant to tell us something about the world.

The claim that God exists is an interesting case because on one way of looking at the **ontological argument** (see Chapter 4), the statement "God exists" *is* analytic. The concept of God is supposed to include the idea of necessary existence. Suffice it to say for now that those who think that "God exists" is analytic are in a very tiny minority, even among theists.

Let's take for granted what seems apparent to most philosophers, that "God exists" is intended to be a synthetic statement. Does it follow that it can't be empirically verified? The philosopher John Hick doesn't think so. He argues that religious beliefs can be verified—in the afterlife.

You might immediately object that there is no afterlife. Recall, however, that a claim need only be able to be verified *in principle*. If a religion has a theology of the afterlife where the individual survives death and comes into the fullness of God's presence as in Christianity and Judaism, then Hick would say that it's possible *in principle* to verify God exists.

Hick calls this **eschatological** verification. Notice there is a sort of asymmetry here. If Christianity, for example, is true, then it can be verified. If it is false, it can't be disconfirmed.

Several criticisms have been lobbed at Hick's suggestion. First, positivists would subject theistic pictures of the afterlife themselves to the verifiability theory of meaning. For eschatological verification to be possible, all sorts of other metaphysical claims must be true. For example, we must be able to survive bodily death. Not all philosophers agree that this makes sense (see Chapter 13 for relevant discussion).

Second, even if one grants the possibility of the afterlife, what sort of experience in the afterlife would count as experience verifying the existence of God? Would we see God with our eyes? Or would we "see God with our heart?" How would the verification work? As Hick himself says, it's logically possible for an atheist and a theist to both be resurrected after this present life and live together on a new earth. If so, what evidence in that resurrected world could the theist appeal to as an empirical observation of the existence of God? Eschatological verification doesn't seem to buy much in the way of empirical confirmation.

There are various moves the theist could make here. For example, we never see electrons directly, but we know that they exist because we can verify this indirectly, by the empirical consequences that their existence entails. We **abductively** infer electrons from other more direct empirical observations; electrons seem to be the best explanation for various observable phenomena. Theists, like Richard Swinburne, argue that God's existence is subject to the same sort of indirect verification. The strongest version of the verification principle calls for direct, conclusive verification, but that is asking too much.

A philosopher like William Alston would make a more radical reply. As we saw in Chapter 6, Alston argues that it's possible to perceive God. We can verify God's existence in the same sort of way that we verify the existence of the Eiffel Tower. But these claims are controversial, so for the moment, let's assume that Premise #2 stands. The most serious criticisms of the positivist objection are leveled at Premise #1.

First, some philosophers contend that verificationism was not so much argued for as merely asserted. For example, Alvin Plantinga contends that:

> the Verificationists never gave any cogent arguments; indeed, they seldom
> gave any arguments at all. Some simply trumpeted this principle as a great
> discovery, and when challenged, repeated it loudly and slowly; but why

should that disturb anyone? Others proposed it as a definition—a definition of the term "meaningful." Now of course the positivists had a right to use this term in any way they chose; it's a free country. But how could their decision to use that term in a particular way show anything so momentous as that all those who took themselves to be believers in God were wholly deluded? If I propose to use the term 'Democrat' to mean 'unmitigated scoundrel,' would it follow that Democrats everywhere should hang their heads in shame (Plantinga 1984)?

Second, it isn't clear that verificationism meets its own standard of meaningfulness. It isn't analytic, so it must be synthetic. Because it's synthetic, it must be capable of being verified experientially. What specific observations would count as verifying the truth of this theory of meaning? If there's an answer to that question, it certainly isn't obvious. If verificationism can't meet its own standard for meaningfulness, then it is self-refuting.

Third, the most serious problem for verificationism is that it's hard to formulate it in a way that rules out what the positivists want to rule out, but allows as meaningful all that they want to allow in. Theoretical statements in science are an important case in point. As we already noted, we don't see electrons directly. But the positivists think scientific statements are meaningful. That means that the crude form of the verification principle isn't right. Telling the story of how positivism developed to meet this objection would take us far afield. Suffice it to say that more subtle ways of formulating the criterion of meaningfulness will not neatly exclude religious statements while including scientific statements, especially once we take seriously the idea of indirect verification. Verificationism is difficult to formulate in a fine-tuned enough way for it to do the work the positivists had in mind for it.

Although a few philosophers still defend something like it, old-fashioned verificationism has seen its heyday come and go. If verificationism is false, or at least mired in very serious difficulties, then so too is the objection to religion based on it. If Premise #1 of the objection is false, then the argument is unsound.

2 THE OBJECTION TO RELIGION BASED ON FALSIFIABLITY

Although the objection to religion based on verificationism collapsed, this didn't mean that positivists weren't on to something. To many, some important connection seemed to exist between meaningful factual statements and our ability to observe whether they are true. In the 1950s, the British philosopher Antony Flew offered a new objection to religion rooted in this concern about meaning and observation.

Flew argues that religious people don't typically allow anything to count as evidence against the existence of God. Take the belief that God loves children. When a child suffers from the pain of cancer and dies without intervention from God, this is—at least on the face of it— evidence that God doesn't love that child. After all, if God truly loved that child as much as religious people claim, how could God stand to watch the child suffer so much when a snap of the divine fingers could stop it? But religious people don't take the child's suffering as evidence, even on the surface, that God doesn't love that child.

Flew argues that what they do is subtly change their claim so it avoids counterevidence. Religious people qualify their understanding of God's love so that cases like the child's death no longer count as evidence against God's love. They might say that God's love is different than ours. God's ways are beyond our ways. God's love is higher than our love and is inscrutable to us. Human love might not let a child die this way but divine love is different. It is somehow better but more difficult for us to comprehend.

This leaves Flew scratching his head and wondering what evidence would count, even in principle, as evidence against the existence of God. No matter what you point to, the theist seems to always subtly qualify or change the claim to inoculate theism from criticism. Theism, Flew argued, is **unfalsifiable**. No evidence whatsoever is allowed to count against it.

To make his point more clearly, Flew retells a story by the philosopher John Wisdom:

> Once upon a time two explorers came upon a clearing in the jungle. In the clearing were growing many flowers and many weeds. One explorer says, "Some gardener must tend this plot." The other dis- agrees, "There is no gardener." So they pitch their tents and set a watch. No gardener is ever seen. "But perhaps he is an invisible gardener." So they set up a barbed-wire fence. They electrify it. They patrol with bloodhounds. (For they remember how H.G. Well's *The Invisible Man* could be both smelt and touched though he could not be seen.) But no shrieks ever suggest that some intruder has received a shock. No move- ments of the wire ever betray an invisible climber. The bloodhounds never give cry. Yet still the Believer is not convinced. "But there is a

gardener, invisible, intangible, insensible, to electric shocks, a gardener who has no scent and makes no sound, a gardener who comes secretly to look after the garden which he loves." At last the Sceptic despairs, "But what remains of your original assertion? Just how does what you call an invisible, intangible, eternally elusive gardener differ from an imaginary gardener or even from no gardener at all?" (Flew, Hare et al. 1955, p. 266)

The parable tells the story of a believer and a skeptic. The believer asserts the existence of an invisible gardener. But every time the skeptic points to evidence that indicates no invisible gardener exists, the believer modifies or qualifies their claim about the gardener to inoculate it from the contrary evidence. Eventually, the believer's claim is so qualified and inoculated that no evidence at all is allowed to count as evidence against the existence of the gardener. The belief in the invisible gardener is unfalsifiable.

Flew thinks that religious belief works the same way. No evidence is allowed to count against it. It is unfalsifiable. He thinks this is reason to believe that religious claims are meaningless. They are not genuine assertions of fact. As Flew puts it:

And if there is nothing which a putative assertion denies then there is nothing which it asserts either: and so it is not really an assertion. When the Sceptic in the parable asked the Believer, "Just how does what you call an invisible, intangible, eternally elusive gardener differ from an imaginary gardener or even from no gardener at all?" he was suggesting that the Believer's earlier statement had been so eroded by qualification that it was no longer an assertion at all (Flew, Hare et al. 1955, p. 268).

Of course, one might object that if the believer really believes God exists, then she doesn't think that there actually is good evidence against the existence of God. Naturally, since the theist believes that God exists, she won't concede that it is false. What could be more obvious?

This misses Flew's point. His argument is that no evidence, *even in principle*, is allowed to count against the existence of God. Take our belief that George Washington was the first president of the United States. We don't think any actual counterevidence is sufficient to undermine our belief in this claim. But our belief is not unfalsifiable because there is evidence, in principle, that could count against it.

Suppose new and powerful evidence was found that someone else was the president. (Obviously, it would have to include an explanation of why we've all been mistaken for so long.) Suppose this evidence was so convincing that a strong consensus formed among historians who specialize in American history that Washington was not the first president. In principle, we would be prepared to give up our belief. Our belief that Washington was the first president is not false but it is falsifiable. Flew thinks this cannot be said of religious belief. Religious people won't allow any evidence, even in principle, to count against their belief, so it is unfalsifiable.

We can sketch Flew's argument this way:

> *Premise #1*: If a claim is unfalsifiable, then it is not a genuine assertion and is meaningless.
> *Premise #2*: Theism is an unfalsifiable claim.
> *Conclusion*: Therefore, theism is not a genuine assertion and is meaningless.

2.1 Replies to the Objection to Religion Based on Falsifiablity

Flew's objection is logically valid. That means that any criticism must focus on the truth of the premises. One radical response was made immediately by the well-known moral philosopher R. M. Hare. Hare contended that Premise #2 is false because theism is not a claim or assertion at all, let alone an unfalsifiable one. Instead, it's a "**blik**." What is a blik? A blik is a point of view. It's a lens through which we view and judge assertions, though it's not an assertion itself. Why the funny word for a point of view or worldview? Some have speculated that Hare coined the term "blik" based on the German word *blickpunct*, meaning "viewpoint." Hare later denied this.

Regardless of the origin of the term, if Hare is correct then theism is a blik, a point of view, a perspective, a lens we use to judge assertions, but not an assertion itself. Hare illustrates his point with the following story:

> A certain lunatic is convinced that all dons [professors] want to murder him. His friends introduce him to all the mildest and most respectable dons that they can find, and after each of them has retired, they say, "You see, he doesn't really want to murder you; he spoke to you in a most cordial manner; surely you are convinced now?" But the lunatic replies, "Yes, but that was only his diabolical cunning; he's really plotting against me the whole time, like the rest of them; I know it I tell you." However many kindly dons are produced, the reaction is still the same (Flew, Hare et al. 1955, p. 268).

Nothing the dons do is counted as evidence against the lunatics' view that they want to kill him. Hare points out that the lunatic has an insane blik. It is crucially important for Hare that we understand that we have a blik, too. Ours is a sane one. It's not that we have no blik at all. Why is that important to Hare?

Hare's point is that Flew's analysis of the believer and the skeptic is too simple. Flew's account only includes assertions. It does not include the important element of perspectives, or bliks, through which we judge the evidence. If we add this to our account of how people judge evidence and theories, Flew's criticism falls apart. Flew is wrongly identifying theism as an assertion rather than a blik. If we identify it as a blik, it is no objection to claim that bliks are unfalsifiable. That would be like criticizing musical notes for not having color. Musical notes are not in the category of things that have colors and bliks are not in the category of things that are falsifiable or unfalsifiable.

Unfortunately, it's not clear that Hare's point of view on points of view is consistent. He wants to say that bliks are unfalsifiable but, as the example of the don-fearing student makes clear, he also thinks that some are better or worse than others. But in that case, there must be a basis for judging between bliks. If so, then bliks are subject to judgment and criticism just like assertions. That makes it sound as though they are falsifiable after all, and if so, Flew would ask Hare once again: what would count against theism? Hare might reply that what Flew is really looking for are empirical consequences. Bliks may be subject to criticism and revision, but unlike assertions, not on the basis of empirical consequences. The sorts of standards we apply to bliks aren't like that.

A more important criticism of Hare is that even if he thinks of theism as a mere point of view, that's not how most theists—including many sophisticated theists—see it. When Plantinga says that God exists, he would emphatically deny that all he's doing is adopting a perspective or a point of view. He intends to be telling us something about the universe and what it contains.

There are other important criticisms of Flew's argument. Premise #1, for example, seems to fall victim to some of the same types of criticisms that verificationism did. Is Flew's claim about the necessity of falsifiablity itself falsifiable? It isn't obvious that his assertion meets its own standards.

Turning to Premise #2, is it true? Is theism unfalsifiable? Flew seems to be confusing the content of a belief with the way a belief is held. The story of the invisible gardener could be read as a story of a closed-minded person—a person who will not let anything count against his belief because he is dead set on believing it. But is the *way* a belief is held (close-mindedly) a legitimate criticism of whether the *content* of the belief is a genuine claim? Or is it merely a criticism of the person who holds it?

It is true that some religious people are closed-minded and won't allow any evidence to count against belief in God. However, this isn't a criticism of *theism* but of some *theists*. Because some people hold their beliefs in a closed-minded way doesn't mean the content of their belief is unfalsifiable. In fact, many religious people have given up their religious beliefs. Some have become atheists, others have become agnostics. In these cases, clearly evidence was allowed to count against religious belief. So it was not only falsifiable but was, as far as these converts are concerned, actually falsified. Those who still hold to religious beliefs also change those beliefs in light of reason, arguments, and evidence. It's not uncommon for people to change religions, change denominations, or change their theology based on evidence and reflection.

Consider also the debate over suffering and the problem of evil. If theists will not allow any evidence—even in principle—to count against theism, why do they seem so concerned about the argument from evil against God? They are concerned because *they think* suffering is *prima facie* evidence against the existence of God, even if they do not think it is sufficient to overturn their religious convictions at the moment. So, many religious people do hold theism in a way that is falsifiable, in principle. Flew's claim seems false.

3 DO WORDS HAVE MEANING WHEN APPLIED TO GOD?

3.1 God Is So Different that Words Don't Have Their Ordinary Meaning

So far, we have examined two objections to religious belief based on language. Both objections have serious flaws. There is, however, a worry about religious language that has more teeth. The concern is whether words have the same meaning when used of God as they do when they are used of us. Consider the following two sentences:

John sees Mary.
God sees Mary.

Does the verb "sees" in both sentences have the same meaning? When we say that John sees Mary, we mean something like this: light reflecting from Mary's body has reached John's eyes and resulted in a nerve signal being sent along the optic nerve to the John's brain, where it causes John to experience an image of Mary.

When we say that God sees Mary, we don't mean anything like that. God doesn't have physical eyes, an optic nerve, or a brain. We know what it means for one physical being to see another but what does it mean for a nonphysical being to see a physical being? Whatever it means, we know it means something different than it does for us because in our case, the language has its original meaning and in the case of God, it must have some other, as yet unspecified meaning.

Think about the problem this way. For most English words, there are several meanings. Look a word up in a dictionary and you will see several numbered entries, each a different meaning of the word. The definition of "sees" in the sentence involving John and Mary would be listed in the dictionary entry for "to see." The sense of the word "see" in the sentence involving God and Mary might be in the dictionary—it might have a definition—but it would not be same exact numbered entry.

But would an entry be found at all for "sees" in the sense that God sees Mary? Is it really meaningful to talk of God seeing at all? If it is, would we know what the word means or would the numbered definition have an empty space after it? Maybe the dictionary entry for "divine seeing" would just consist of the variable "X" standing for some meaning that we don't have access to—a mystery meaning. The problem is that we say things about God in human languages. We know what "sees" means when it's one human seeing another. If that is a different sense of "sees" than when God sees us, just what is that second sense, if there is one at all?

In the case of God "seeing" Mary, we might be tempted to say that there's no need to insist on this statement literally in the first place. We could say that when we say that God sees Mary, what we really mean is that God is just aware of Mary. But that just pushes the problem back one step. Given that God is so radically different from us, it's not obvious that we understand what it means to say that God is aware of Mary. The problem then is this: we don't really know what it means to say that God sees Mary. More generally, we don't really know what any words mean as applied to God because God is so different from us. God-talk, then, is meaningless.

288 ◆ *Chapter 12: God and Language*

3.2 One Suggested Solution: Analogy

One solution to this problem was offered by the medieval theologian St. Thomas Aquinas (1224–1274). Aquinas concedes that words have different meanings when applied to God than they do to humans. This raises the problem above: how do we know what language means as it applies to God when the only language we have to work with uses the words radically differently? Aquinas' suggestion for dealing with the problem is to argue that although the words have different meanings, those meanings are analogous.

Aquinas distinguished between three kinds of meaning: univocal, equivocal, and analogous. A word is used univocally when the same word has exactly the same meaning. A word is used equivocally when the same word is used in two or more completely different senses. A word is used analogously when the same word is used in two different senses but those senses are analogously related.

With this distinction in mind, let's return to what it means to say God "sees" or "is aware of" someone. Consider the two sentences, "John is aware of Mary" and "God is aware of Mary." John's awareness requires the use of his senses; it depends on his body. That's not true for God's awareness of Mary. This suggests that the phrase "is aware of" isn't univocal in the two sentences. However, the two uses aren't equivocal either because they are not entirely different senses. It's not as if the phrase "is aware of" in the sentence about God is completely different from human awareness. Aquinas would argue that the senses of "is aware of" in the two sentences are different but analogous.

Philosophers in Aquinas's time distinguished different senses of analogy. For simplicity's sake, we will only discuss one. Consider the word "healthy." We can talk about a healthy animal and when we do, we're using the word in its primary sense. But we can also talk about healthy food. In Aquinas's time, an animal's urine was used to diagnose its health, and so we can also talk of "healthy urine." Strictly speaking, though, neither food nor urine actually have health. We call food "healthy" when it is the kind of food that contributes to an animal's health. We call urine "healthy" because it is a sign of a healthy animal.

The word "healthy" here is not used equivocally because the meaning of "healthy" when applied to food or urine is not *completely* different than it is when applied to an animal. Aquinas thinks that the meaning of "healthy," in these cases, is analogous to the primary meaning. What does it mean that the meanings are analogous? Notice that there is a *causal connection* between the healthy animal, on the one hand, and the healthy food or urine, on the other. Healthy food *causes* an animal to be healthy and a healthy animal *causes* urine to be healthy. So, analogous meaning involves a causal connection between something that literally has some property (e.g., healthy) and something that has it in a derivative sense.

Let's apply this to God. Aquinas claimed that in statements like "God is good" and "John is good," the word "good" in the two sentences doesn't have the same meaning. The meanings are not univocal. Neither are they equivocal because the meanings are not completely different. Rather, they are analogous because there is a causal connection between the thing that is good in the primary sense (i.e. God) and the thing that is good in a derivative sense (i.e. John). God, who is Goodness itself, causes John's goodness. For Aquinas, the primary meaning of "good" is in its application to God rather than to humans. Whatever goodness John has is derived from God. Further, John's goodness is less than God's. "Good" as applied to humans is, as it were, proportional to human nature.

3.3 Speaking Literally of God

Perhaps we can use Aquinas's idea of analogy to make sense of statements like "God is aware of Mary," though this isn't immediately obvious. However, William Alston would argue that the discussion has gotten off on the wrong foot. We've been assuming that the difference between us and God means that we can't speak literally of God at all. Alston isn't impressed. He thinks the arguments for saying we can't speak literally of God are not good.

We'll illustrate by considering a problem that Alston tackles in an essay called "Speaking Literally of God" (Alston 1981). According to **classical theism**, God doesn't have a body—God is incorporeal. Nonetheless, most theists want to say that God can act. But what could it mean for this to be literally true? Doesn't action require a body? After all, when we act we do so by using our bodies. What could it possibly mean to say that a bodiless being acts? Doesn't part of the very concept of an action—the very meaning of the word "action"—involve bodily movements?

What follows compresses a complex philosophical story, but it should serve to get across the main idea. First, we need to mark the difference between actions and mere bodily movements. Actions require intentions—special states of mind. An involuntary tic isn't an action. But now we seem to have two problems. It's not just that God doesn't have a body. It's that we may be puzzled about what it would mean for God literally to have states of mind. Let's start there.

According to one view, states of mind are the sorts of things we come across when we introspect—when we turn our attention inward. On this way of understanding them, states of mind have a certain "feel" to them. Alston thinks that theologians are wise not to try to figure out what being God feels like. However, the "feeling" aspect might not really be crucial to states of mind to begin with.

Think about knowledge. Suppose someone knows that Beethoven was born on December 16th. That bit of knowledge doesn't amount to an inner feeling. The person knows this fact even when it's very far from their consciousness. The same goes for beliefs. You no doubt believe that water quenches thirst, even though nothing like that was on your mind a moment before you read this sentence. States of mind can be found that don't have feelings going along with them.

We can even say more. What does believing that water quenches thirst mean? One important view (called **functionalism**) would say that believing something amounts to having certain tendencies to act in certain ways. Suppose we see Vandana walk to the water cooler, fill up the paper cup, and drink deeply. Why did she do that? Here's a plausible story. She was thirsty and wanted to quench her thirst. She believed that water can do that, and that she could get water from the cooler. That's a pretty good rough sketch of an explanation for why Vandana went to the cooler and got a drink. Her belief that water quenches thirst—even if it didn't come consciously to mind—was part of what led her to undertake a certain action: going to the cooler and getting water.

Notice that this story doesn't call for any particular view of what a mind is made of. It works whether a mind is physical or nonphysical. It works even if we think of minds as like computers. But it does leave one piece dangling: it talks about tendencies to behave and act. But that's where we began—we were puzzled about what would be meant for an incorporeal being to act.

In fact, this might not be as puzzling as it seems. Start with something a little far-fetched: psychokinesis—the psychic power to make things happen just by an act of will. Someone with this ability (if anyone had it) could make a cup of coffee spill just by willing it. No need to reach out and knock it over, no need to shove against the table or throw something. Suppose you're sitting in a restaurant with your psychokinetic friend Kareem. A commotion is heard at the next table and Kareem chuckles. "I just made her pickle jump off her plate," he says. That would be an action—something Kareem did intentionally by causing something to happen. It is an action, regardless of how psychokinesis works (assuming it ever does!) and whether or not Kareem moved his body. This, admittedly implausible example, tells us something about our concept of an action. Actions don't necessarily require bodily movements.

Further, scientists are figuring out how to implant electrodes in the brains of paralyzed people that will allow them to send radio signals to muscles or to control external devices like computers. This would mean that a human being could perform an action like moving an on-screen cursor without moving their body. It seems that bodily movement is not necessarily part of the very concept of an action—even in the case of human actions. Rather, the basic concept of an action seems to be of intentionally causing something to happen.

If this makes sense, we might be able to make sense of an incorporeal God performing actions. God would perform actions by directly causing something to happen. The things God causes to happen would express the divine will. They would be actions. Alston thinks that if objections to speaking literally about God's actions are weak, then we might well be able to make literal sense out of many other things we say about God.

4 CONCLUSION

There are several difficult questions about what religious language can mean and how we can apply language to God. We briefly examined two objections: that religious claims are unverifiable and that they are unfalsifiable. We argued that neither issue is particularly troubling. The third problem, involving our understanding of everyday terms as they apply to God, is far more serious. There may be something to Aquinas' broad suggestion that meaning in this case works by analogy, but the specific way he develops this response is limited at best.

Alston's approach to making sense of literal talk about God avoids some of these difficulties. That said, it would be a mistake simply to dismiss the whole problem. If God is outside time, for example, then even the "functionalist" view of the mind that we sketched above doesn't make immediate sense of what it would mean for God to believe, or want or know. And when we come to the specific claims of some religions, the problems are even more difficult. For example, the Christian doctrine that God is three persons in one being is notoriously difficult to state coherently.

We are faced with a double-edged sword here. The idea that God's nature could be described in straightforward prose is one that many believers find religiously repugnant. These believers would say that God is ultimately a mystery to be contemplated rather than a puzzle to be solved. But if mystery degenerates into meaninglessness, the believer is hardly better off. The philosophical and theological challenge is to find a way to respect the mystery without sacrificing the meaning.

AT A GLANCE: GOD AND LANGUAGE

1. The Objection to Religion Based on Verificationism
    1.1. How Language Can Lead to Philosophical Mistakes
        - We can be misled to think that a car's top speed is a physical part of the car rather than a property of the car. "The car's top speed" is a noun phrase, like "the car's steering wheel." But one is a thing and the other isn't.
    1.2. Verificationism
        - The analytic/synthetic distinction is crucial to understanding verificationism. An analytic statement is any statement where the concepts in the predicate are already contained in the concepts of the subject. A synthetic statement is one where the concepts of the predicate are not contained in the subject.

Analytic Sentences (Relations of Ideas)	Synthetic Sentences (Matters of Fact)
All bachelors are unmarried.	This raven is black.
2 + 2 = 4	The Sun is 93 million miles from Earth.
A tall man is tall.	Dirt is brown.
A woman is female.	George Washington was the first president of the United States.

- The concept of cognitive meaning is also crucial to understanding verificationism. Cognitive meaning is the type of meaning that factual statements have, as opposed to questions, commands, expressions of emotion, and poetry.

Sentences that Have Cognitive Meaning	Sentences that Have Non-Cognitive Meaning
Thomas Jefferson signed the Declaration of Independence.	Go to your room!
2 + 2 = 4	What is your favorite color?
This raven is black.	Yuck, spinach!
All bachelors are unmarried.	Between melting and freezing the soul' sap quivers.

- With these distinctions in hand, we can define verificationism this way:
  - *Verificationism*: A sentence is cognitively meaningful if and only if (i) it is analytic or (ii) it is synthetic and can, at least in principle, be verified from experience.
- The Objection to Religion Based on Verificationism

  Premise #1: A sentence is cognitively meaningful if and only if (i) it is analytic or (ii) it is synthetic and can, at least in principle, be verified from experience (verificationism).

  Premise #2: Religious and metaphysical statements are not (i) analytic nor (ii) can they, at least in principle, be verified from experience.

  Conclusion: Therefore, religious and metaphysical statements are not cognitively meaningful.

- Replies to the Objection from Verificationism
  a. Pointing to the ontological argument, some argue that the existence of God is an analytic truth. If it is, then it is cognitively meaningful.
  b. John Hick argues that the existence of God is synthetic but that it can be eschatologically verified— i.e., verified in the afterlife.
  c. Some critics point out that verificationists think of empirical verification in a much too narrow fashion. We never directly see electrons, either. We infer them from other empirical observations. Philosophers like Richard Swinburne argue that we can likewise abductively infer the existence of God from other empirical observations.
  d. Philosophers like William Alston argue for the even more radical claim that we can, contrary to the verificationist, perceive God.
  e. Some philosophers like Alvin Plantinga point out that verificationism is asserted but rarely argued. At most, it is expressed as a definition. This counts against it because controversial and nontrivial claims should be held for good reason.
  f. Others point out that verificationism doesn't meet its own standard of meaningfulness. It isn't analytic but neither is it capable of being empirically verified, at least not obviously so.
  g. Lastly, verificationists were never able to successfully formulate their theory in a way that rules out what the positivists want to rule out, but allows as meaningful all that they want to allow in. They either

define it too broadly, allowing metaphysical claims to be counted as meaningful, or they defined it too narrowly, excluding some scientific statements as meaningful. They could never find a precise enough formulation to do the trick.

2. The Objection to Religion Based on Falsification
   • The objection from falsification:

   Premise #1: If a claim is unfalsifiable, then it is not a genuine assertion and is meaningless.
   Premise #2: Theism is unfalsifiable claim.
   Conclusion: Therefore, theism is not a genuine assertion and is meaningless.

   • Replies to the objection from falsification:
     a. R. M. Hare argued that religious views are "bliks," or perspectives, not propositions. By their very nature, bliks are not the type of things that can be falsified, so it is no objection to fault them on those grounds.
     b. Flew confuses a closed-minded person with a faulty belief. Just because a person holds a belief in a closed-minded way doesn't mean the belief itself is faulty.
     c. Many theists do hold their beliefs in a way that allows them, in principle, to be falsified. Some theists have become atheists. Theists convert from one religion to another and they change their beliefs about God all the time.
     d. The energy with which theists defend against the problem of evil shows that they think theism can, in principle, be falsified. If they really believed that nothing would count as evidence against the existence of God, then they would not respond the way they do to the challenge from suffering.

3. Do Words Have Meaning When Applied to God?
   3.1. The Problem: God is so different that words don't have their ordinary meaning.
     • For example, the word "see" can't have the same meaning for God as it does for us. When we say that John sees Mary, we mean something like light reflecting from Mary's body has reached John's eyes and resulted in a nerve signal being sent along the optic nerve to John's brain, where it causes John to experience an image of Mary. When we say that God sees Mary, we don't mean anything like that. God doesn't have physical eyes, an optic nerve, or a brain.

   3.2. One Suggested Solution: Analogy
     • St. Thomas Aquinas argued that terms applied to God are used analogously. They do not have the same exact meaning, but neither do they have an entirely different meaning. The terms are analogous.

   3.3. Speaking Literally of God
     • William Alston contends that we can speak literally of God, at least sometimes. If this is true, then the original worry about the meaning of terms when applied to God is, at best, exaggerated.

FURTHER READINGS AND WEB RESOURCE

Alston, W. (1981). "Can We Speak Literally of God?" In *Is God GOD?* Steur, A. D. and Mclendon, J. W. (Eds). Nashville, TN: Abington Press.

Ayer, A. J. (1946). *Language, Truth, and Logic*. New York: Dover Publications.

Flew, A., Hare, R. M. et al. (1955). "Theology and Falsification." In *Philosophy of Religion: Selected Readings*. Rowe, W. and Wainwright, W. (Eds). Chicago: Harcourt Brace Jovanovich Publishers.

Ryle, G. (1949). *The Concept of Mind*. London: Hutchinson and Company.

On attempts to connect brains to computers to help the disabled, see http://www.sciencedaily.com/releases/2005/01/050106115859.htm.

CHAPTER 13

Life After Death

The idea of life after death is intriguing but problematic. What could it mean? Would it be a good thing? Do we have reason to believe it? And are any alternative possibilities worth considering? In this chapter, we explore these questions.

We may face death with differing attitudes—resignation, dread, bewilderment, hope. It's both too hard and too easy to imagine our own non-being. For many, the main comfort that religion offers is the promise that this life is not the end. But life after death isn't a simple idea.

1 LIFE AFTER DEATH: A PUZZLING POSSIBILITY?

Suppose that Heaven exists. Long after the death of your body, a person very much like you ends up in Heaven. If there are bodies in Heaven, this person looks like you and talks like you. This heavenly being has your personality traits (except, perhaps, the bad ones), all of your memories, and think the way you think. We could ask if there's any good reason to believe that such thing will happen but before we do, we need to ask a different question: who is this person? They seem to be you, but are they?

Because this is a made-up story, you might say that we can decide as we like. But suppose we "decide" to tell our story so that this being in Heaven is you. Exactly what have we decided? What makes them you?

Puzzled? Here's a different story. In this story, the God of classical theism doesn't exist. Instead a Deity exists who doesn't actually bring people to paradise but makes perfect duplicates of the earthly people and populates Heaven with replicas. In this second story, once you die you stay dead. But for whatever comfort it offers, a copy of you will carry on in the Deity's presence.

These seem to be two different possibilities. In one of them, you survive and in the other, you don't. The outward appearances are the same. What would the difference amount to?

2 SUBSTANTIAL STORIES: BODY AND SOUL

One way to think of life after death is by way of the idea that some *thing* is what survives. Sometimes when people talk about life after death, they talk about the resurrection of the body. According to this view, the person survives because the body has survived and been rejuvenated. Other people prefer to talk about the soul—a very different sort of thing than the body. What these two approaches have in common is that they identify some *thing* that's essential to what the person is, and that's crucial for personal survival. Let's start with the bodily story.

2.1 Bodily Resurrection

In the early days of the Christian church, theologians spent a good deal of time trying to understand the idea of the resurrection of the body. In the case of the Resurrection of Christ, the story at least begins with an intact body. In most cases, that won't be so. When we die, sooner or later our bodies disintegrate. Chemical compounds break down; we become one with the earth and eventually most of us will be recycled, with parts of the matter that made us up becoming part of other organisms. It's entirely possible that as a result of this recycling, some of us have eaten food that contains matter that once was part of some other human body. And if the breakdown is complete enough, questions about what matter belonged to what body get fuzzy; at the subatomic level, saying that this particle now is the same one as that one then doesn't always make sense. But leave fancy physics aside. Suppose that God gathered up all the matter that used to be part of your body, put it back together, and reanimated it. Would that be you?

It's not obvious. Here's an example based on one from Peter van Inwagen (1978, p. 118). Suppose little Jack builds a house out of blocks. You stumble into the room and knock his creation down, scattering the blocks all over the room. Feeling guilty, you put the blocks back the way they were. Is it the same house? Or is it just *like* the original? If you think it's the same house, suppose Jack himself had knocked the house down on purpose and later Sally, who never saw what Jack did, put the same blocks together in the same arrangement by sheer coincidence. Would that be the same house? Its connection to the house that Jack built is completely accidental. For many philosophers, that makes doubtful that your deliberate re-creation was the same house.

Maybe in the case of building-block houses, it doesn't matter. Maybe we can make up the rules as we like. But that doesn't seem so plausible when talking of life after death. Put roughly, you want your consciousness to continue on in the future, and whether that really happens or not doesn't seem to be the sort of thing we can settle simply by deciding how to use our words. There's a real question about whether reassembling the matter of your body, after it's been broken down and scattered to the four winds, would be a way to bring your consciousness back into being.

We can look at bodily resurrection in another way. Van Inwagen imagines that at the moment of your bodily death, God took your very body, leaving behind an indistinguishable replica for the sake of the people who grieve for you. Then perhaps after a period of storage during the pre-Judgment Day wait, God whisked your body off to Heaven and brought it back to life. In this case, it pretty clearly seems to be you who ends up in heaven.

This might show that bodily resurrection is at least possible (assuming a God exists who can do what was just described), but it doesn't help much with the probability question. Our guess is that few believers think that anything like this actually happens.

2.2 The Soul

For many people, what really matters about surviving death is having consciousness continue. On that way of thinking about it, worrying about our bodies is worrying about the wrong thing. Many people think they have a non-material thing, which they call a soul and which makes them who they are. It's what gives them a mind and makes them conscious. It doesn't disintegrate when the body dies, and it can end up in Heaven. According to this view, your immaterial soul's surviving amounts to you surviving.

Why immaterial? One reason is that the material part of us doesn't last. Of course, this hardly guarantees that non-material things are permanent. However, set all that aside. Does such a thing as a non-material soul exist?

The idea that there are both non-material souls and material bodies is a form of **substance dualism**. According to substance dualism, two fundamentally different kinds of things exist: physical and mental. This idea has a long history and various philosophers have made arguments for the existence of an immaterial self or mind or soul. Because the world "dualism" often goes hand-in-hand with the word "Cartesian," we'll describe Descartes' argument here. René Descartes (1596–1650) saw that he could doubt the existence of his body—for example, he could imagine that everything he seems to see is an idea implanted in his mind by an evil demon. However, he couldn't doubt his own existence because to doubt requires someone who exists to do the doubting. Since it's possible to doubt the existence of the body but not to doubt the existence of the self, Descartes concluded that they can't be the same thing.

This isn't a very good argument. What we can and can't doubt isn't a reliable guide to the nature of things themselves. The planet Venus is sometimes called the Morning Star because it's visible just before dawn. The ancient Greeks also called it Phosphorus. Venus is also called the Evening Star because we can see it just after sunset. The Greeks also called it Hesperus. But it took a while before anyone figured out that Phosphorus and Hesperus are one and the same thing, and in fact some people still don't know it. Jared presumably can't doubt that Hesperus is Hesperus, but he can doubt that Hesperus is Phosphorus. If we followed Descartes' reasoning, we'd have to conclude that Phosphorus ≠ Hesperus because there's something we can doubt about Phosphorus (that it's Hesperus) that we can't doubt about Hesperus. Obviously, that's wrong. Both of them are just the planet Venus.

Descartes may have given a bad argument, but there are other reasons for thinking that the self or soul isn't physical. It's hard to see how what goes on in our bodies and brains can create consciousness. No matter how much we learn about the workings of our brains, it might seem that we would still be left with a mystery about how we could get from the scientific story about neuron firings, brain chemicals, and physiology to an explanation of conscious experience. This leads some people to think that no purely physical story could ever do the trick.

The question of whether consciousness can be explained physically is a controversial one, and many good philosophers are ready to defend the view that science really can do the job (for example, see Carruthers

2000). All we need to admit is that things aren't obvious here. There's an interesting issue about how our mental life could be accounted for in purely physical terms. This provides a reason for considering some sort of dualism, but that doesn't get us as far as you might think.

2.2.1 Non-Physical Things vs. Non-Physical Non-Things

Suppose we were to decide that there's something more to us than our physical bodies and their physical properties. Even if that were true, the "something more" wouldn't necessarily help explain how life after death could be possible. Suppose that what we need to be conscious isn't a non-physical *thing* at all. What we need could be non-physical mental "properties" or "qualities" that can't exist apart from the physical things that possess them. In that case, we would have **property dualism** rather then substance dualism, and property dualism doesn't give us anything that survives the death of the body. Or suppose that bodies only become conscious when a flow of non-physical "energy" runs through them (whatever that might mean). The "energy" wouldn't be the consciousness; it would merely make consciousness possible. Compare: your computer only operates when a current runs through it, but the physical computer does the calculating. If the current in the computer doesn't amount to computation, why should the flow of "psychic energy" amount to sensation or thought?

The point is that even if some sort of dualism is true, it might not provide for life after death in the way people sometimes think it would. But suppose we grant that each of has some sort of non-physical thing, which we'll call a soul, and that it's capable of existing apart from our bodies. Suppose we grant that we wouldn't have a mind unless we had a soul. The problem is that whatever our minds have to do with souls, they pretty clearly have an enormous amount to do with our brains. Damage to the brain can take away our memories or mobility or speech. At least some mental illnesses seem to depend on the balance of chemicals in the brain. The idea that we need a soul to think and feel is speculation. The idea that our minds depend on our brains is difficult to deny. This makes it doubtful that your soul by itself could be you.

So far, we haven't made a lot of headway. Unless van Inwagen's body-snatching story is true, our bodies disintegrate after we die. It's not obvious how putting the compost back together would amount to bringing us back. But talk of a non-physical soul doesn't clearly get us any further. Are we doomed to die and never rise?

3 THE GOSPEL ACCORDING TO GENE RODDENBERRY

The problem we've been dealing with so far is the problem of **personal identity**. Roughly, it's the problem of explaining when a person at one time and a person at another time are one and the same person. The problem comes up because even if we grant that there could be a heavenly being who is like you, it doesn't immediately follow that it really is you. Philosophers writing about personal identity in the last few decades found a useful tool for conducting **thought experiments** in the science-fiction series *Star Trek*, created by Gene Roddenberry (1921–1991). A thought experiment is a hypothetical scenario that helps us explore the limits of our concepts, and what makes *Star Trek* relevant to our problem is the fact that characters on board the *Enterprise* and other Starfleet ships have a handy mode of personal travel. They can step into the **transporter** and be beamed where they need to go. The transporter works by dematerializing you, beaming the appropriate data, and then rematerializing you at your destination. Philosophers took an interest in this imaginary gadget because it raises intriguing puzzles about personal identity.

No one expects anyone to build a functioning transporter any time soon, but that's not the point. Asking what we think about the possibility is a way of exploring our concept of personal identity. Three things are worth noting about the transporter. The first is that whoever steps into it doesn't have literally the same body as whoever steps out the other end, so if the transporter idea makes sense, we don't need to keep the same body to keep existing. The second point is that souls have nothing to do with how the thing is supposed to work. There's no suggestion that the transporter is a way of moving immaterial souls from place to place. The third point has to do with our reactions. Most people watching an episode of *Star Trek* don't hesitate to think of the transporter as a way of getting one and the same person from one place to another. Most people don't have any problem with the idea that the transporter preserves personal identity.

By itself, this doesn't tell us a lot. There are science-fiction stories in which characters travel back in time and change the past. Most viewers don't worry about whether this makes any sense; they simply accept it. In fact, whether the idea of changing the past actually makes any sense is open to a good deal of doubt (see David Lewis, 1976). The same thing holds for the transporter beam; perhaps it's a mistake to think that it could preserve personal identity.

Interestingly enough, many philosophers who specialize in the problem of personal identity disagree. The most notable is Derek Parfit, whose *Reasons and Persons* (1984) is the most important book in the field of the last several decades and the one that introduced the transporter example into the personal identity debate. What Parfit has in common with many other philosophers is that he doesn't think of problems of personal identity in terms of whether some thing survives from one time to another. Rather, the question is how various "stages"—persons-at-a-moment, if you will—are related to one another. Views like this are called *relational views* of personal identity because they claim that what make you-earlier the same person as you-later lies in the details of how the two are related rather than the existence of some "thing" that makes you who you are.

3.1 Relational Views of Personal Identity

A full discussion of relational views of personal identity is beyond our scope. Also, in this section we are ignoring a complication: a case in which there is more than one "duplicate" of you (more on that later). Still, the main points we want to make will stand in spite of the simplifications. Let's start with the idea of "stages."

At this moment, you are reading this chapter. We might say that a certain "person-stage" is reading this chapter. Not all philosophers who favor relational views talk about person-stages, but the terminology provides a good way to get a feel for the ideas. At some time in the past, a person-stage got hold of a copy of this chapter. The relational approach to personal identity doesn't ask if some one thing is present at both times (soul or body). It asks whether these two stages are related in the right sort of way to count as parts of one continuing person. John Perry offers an analogy in his *Dialogue on Personal Identity and Immortality* (1978). You're out driving and you come to a river. Later, after a lot of meandering, you come to a river once again. You ask your companion if it's the same river you saw before. What you want to know is whether the stretch of water you see now is connected in the right sort of way to the one you saw an hour ago. For relational theorists, questions of personal identity are similar—they're questions about whether the right sort of relationship exists among person-stages to make them "time-slices" of a single person.

What would the right sort of relationship be? The most minimal answer would be that any later stage that's enough like an earlier stage of a person would do, no matter how it got to be that way. (We'll ignore ties for now.) For example, suppose that at the moment of your bodily death, a 1 in a googolplex (10 to the power of one **googol**, where a googol is 1 followed by 100 zeros) cosmic fluke takes place. By sheer chance, a person pops into existence who looks, acts, thinks, and "remembers" just like you. Would that be you? If bare similarity is the basis of personal identity, then the answer is yes. However, most people think the answer is no. Accidental resemblance doesn't seem to be enough. There must be some stronger connection, or so many people think.

A stronger but still minimalist story is the one favored by the Buddha (Siddhartha Gautama, roughly 623 BCE–543 BCE), David Hume, (1711–1776) and the contemporary philosopher Derek Parfit. Hume puts it vividly:

> For my part, when I enter most intimately into what I call myself, I always stumble on some particular perception or other, or heat or cold, light or shade, love or hatred, pain or pleasure. I never catch myself at any time without a perception, and never can observe any thing but the perception. When my perceptions are removed for any time, as by sound sleep; so long am I insensible of myself, and may truly be said not to exist (Hume 1784, p. 252; the odd punctuation is his).

Hume claims that no self really exists. Instead, if he's correct there are perceptions, sensations, thoughts, and so on. They shift from moment to moment and intermittently disappear. The bundle doesn't have a soul at its core; it's a matter of resemblance and succession, later bundles caused by earlier ones. Hume's version of the idea gives us a particularly thin notion of personal identity. Hume saw the relation of cause and effect itself as a matter of what he called "constant conjunction"—of one sort of event always being associated with another without some underlying "impetus" or "force" or "connexion" (Hume's spelling) between the two. The difference between the absolute minimal view described in the previous paragraph and Hume's view is not all that large.

Notice that the body has no special role to play in Hume's account of personal identity. It's also not central for Parfit, nor was it for the Buddha. Most philosophers who hold a relational view of personal identity would say that *psychological continuity* is what matters. Although details would differ from philosopher to philosopher, connections of memory would be important for most: later stages should have memories whose contents link up in the correct way with earlier stages. Other kinds of psychological continuity could be added to fill out the story and might include beliefs, mental habits, and other psychological features. In any case, if a view like Hume's is correct, there's no reason why the transporter beam couldn't preserve personal identity.

Hume sees the connections among stages as very weak because he has such a weak idea of what cause and effect is. Someone might be sympathetic to the general outline of Hume's account but think that we need a stronger notion of casual connection. Still, such a philosopher might say that any causal process that provides a reliable way to move information from the old body to the new one would be good enough. Others would insist on more yet. For instance, Mark Johnston thinks that even if the transporter preserved enough information to make a perfect copy of you, that copy would merely be a deluded duplicate who thinks they're you even though you have been destroyed (Johnston 1997). If that's correct, preserving information isn't enough. Perhaps only certain kinds of causal connections can link earlier conscious states to later ones.

Just which view is correct is difficult to say, and the question is complicated because questions about personal identity and survival are bound up with questions about what matters to us—what we value. (Raymond Martin discusses this issue extensively. See Martin 1992 and 1997.) But if an acceptable version of the relational view allows the transporter beam to be a way of surviving, then clearly life after death is at least conceivable. After all, the transporter story would be a form of surviving bodily death because the process destroys your original body. And we might note that in one episode of the sequel series *Star Trek: The Next Generation*, Scotty, a crew member from the original series, has survived for 70 years in the buffer of a transporter. If the relational view of personal identity is correct, there's no reason why an omniscient and omnipotent God couldn't "beam" you to heaven, as it were. God would ensure that all of the appropriate information about you arrives, just as the transporter does. And because many theists claim that God is the source of all causal powers, it would be no problem for God to guarantee that your earthly self and your heavenly successor were connected in the right sort of way. We conclude that there's no deep philosophical problem about the possibility of an afterlife, whether or not anyone actually survives their bodily death.

*3.2 A Side Issue: Fission

Though this section isn't essential to the discussion, it deals with a problem that can't be avoided if you read the literature on personal identity. Suppose you step into the transporter and two copies of you emerge at the other end of the process—call them x and y. Now x and y might be exactly alike—might be **qualitatively identical**—but they aren't one and the same thing—aren't **numerically identical**; for short, $x \neq y$. Now if you = x, then you $\neq y$. After all, things that are identical to the same thing must be identical to one another. But likewise, if you = y, then you $\neq x$. And worse still, it's hard to see what could make you identical with one without also making you identical to the other. This leads most philosophers to conclude that *you* wouldn't survive this process, called **fission**. (Think of nuclear fission—the splitting of an atom—or the way that one amoeba divides into two.)

Another example: suppose that either half of your brain could support your full psychology. You are in an accident that has wrecked your body but left your brain intact. Doctors decide to save you by putting each half of your brain into a copy of your body. (They do it twice in case one operation fails.) Both operations succeed. You can't be both of the resulting people, but because nothing favors one over the other, it seems that you can't be either. That means you haven't survived this form of fission, but this conclusion seems perverse. If either operation had failed while the other succeeded, you would have survived. How can getting it right twice be not getting it right at all?

The answer that many philosophers give is that identity isn't what matters in survival. What matters is the kind of connection between you and a future being. Your consciousness could divide and if it did, this would still give you many if not all of the benefits of ordinary survival. Though we agree that the disadvantages of fission are sometimes underestimated (see Johnston 1997), we agree that fission wouldn't have to be fatal to meaningful survival.

4 WOULD IMMORTALITY BE A GOOD THING?

Life after bodily death might be finite, but most people who hope for an afterlife hope it will go on forever. Most people also assume that everlasting life would be a good thing if we had it, but not everyone agrees. Some people argue that the fact that life is finite is what allows it to have meaning. These people say that if life went on forever, it would eventually degenerate into boredom and despair. Bernard Williams is one such skeptic. Williams takes his inspiration from the fictional account of Elena Makropulos, the protagonist of a play by Karel Capek. When she was 42, her father discovered an elixir that would keep her alive indefinitely so long as she continued to take it, at the physical age of 42. Three hundred years later, her life has become frozen and unbearably boring. As Williams sees it, this is no accident. He argues that

> an endless life would be a meaningless one; . . . we could have no reason for living eternally a human life. There is no desirable or significant property which life could have more of, or have more unqualifiedly, if we lasted for ever (Williams 1973, p. 89).

There are two issues for Williams. The first is that for unending life to be meaningful, it must be you who lives everlastingly. John Martin Fischer calls this the identity condition. The second issue is that assuming if it is you who lasts, we must be able to make human sense of the idea that this unending life would be worth living. Fischer calls this the attractiveness condition (Fischer 1994, p. 257). We'll start with the second worry.

4.1 The Attractiveness Condition and Williams' Dilemma

One way we might continue to survive is with essentially the same character and personality that we have now. On the other hand, our character might well change as the eons pass. Williams offers a dilemma: if our character stays the same, eventually everything we might reasonably care about will have happened to us, and we will become detached and bored. However, if our characters change it's unclear that the attractiveness condition is satisfied because it's unclear how to evaluate in light of our character now whatever new interests, goals, and so on, we will develop as we change.

Take the first issue: we keep our character. Fischer doesn't see why boredom would have to be inevitable. It's true that some pleasures are what Fischer calls "self exhausting" (p. 262) worth having once or a few times but not worth repeating indefinitely. You might be eager to visit Antarctica once to experience what such a harsh and foreign landscape is like. Having done it once, you might be glad you did, but you might not have any desire to do it again. If all pleasures were self-exhausting, it might be that a person with a given character couldn't find enough of them to last through endless time. But Fischer maintains that there are repeatable pleasures that need never become tiresome so long as they aren't repeated single-mindedly or too closely together in time. They are pleasures that a person could always return to. Sex is perhaps the most obvious example, but it's by no means the only one. Good athletes might never get tired of playing their favorite sport, and in the sort of infinite life we're imagining, they would never have to lose that ability. For some people, hearing a favorite piece of music might be a repeatable pleasure (again, so long as it's not a case of listening to it obsessively). For others, it might be visiting a particular wilderness spot. And as Fischer points out, certain spiritual and religious experiences seem to qualify—a reminder that seems especially important in this context. For some people, the experiences they have in prayer and meditation are a seemingly endless source of deep satisfaction. As Fischer sees it, Williams makes the mistake of assuming that all pleasures are self-exhausting.

Fischer may be right. Certainly within the span of a finite life, there are repeatable pleasures. But is that enough? What Fischer and Williams are imagining is an embodied, very human life. Repeatable pleasures are important in such a life, but there's an extra element that matters to some people. If we were never challenged, if we never took any risks, if we never faced the possibility of being disappointed, many of us would find life a little dull. But if we imagine an unending life like the life of Elena Makropulos, it's hard to see how there could be any challenge or risk. You decide to free climb the heavenly equivalent of the Northwest Face of Half Dome in Yosemite Valley. Where's the risk? You're immortal. If you fall, it doesn't matter; you know you'll survive. In fact, if we add the backdrop of assumptions that people often make about paradise to the embodied human existence that Williams and Fischer have in mind, things might start to sound a little silly. You have some version of your human body, but you're in paradise. Everything is perfect; you can't come to any harm. We're being asked to imagine being human in a world very unlike the human world we know. Williams might say that there's a hollowness in this picture that talk of repeatable versus self-exhausting pleasures simply misses.

This is a difficult objection to meet directly. Few serious believers think of the afterlife as just a jazzed-up version of earthly life. Most would agree that they have only a dim idea of what it might be like. We'll return to this point below. For the moment, let's consider the second horn of Williams' dilemma. He worries that if our characters change over the course of infinite time, we won't have a way to decide in advance what to make of our new values and goals. Fischer correctly points out that mere change of character needn't be an issue. After all, in this life we not only find that what matters to us changes over time but if we have any self-awareness, this is what we expect. If our new aims and interests evolve in a natural way from our old ones, and if they reflect decisions we've made as opposed to things forced on us, it's difficult to see why what we might call the development of our characters is a problem at all for the prospect of a meaningful life.

4.2 The Identity Condition

There's another way of trying to dissolve Williams' concern but to explain it, we'll need to talk about the identity condition. Some repeatable pleasures have a distinctive character—we can, as we say, lose ourselves in them. Most of us know what it's like to become so absorbed in something that we lose track of time and of what's going on around us and even of our own usual stock of worries and cares. Williams sees a problem here:

> [I]f one is totally and perpetually absorbed in such an activity, and loses oneself in it, then as those words suggest, we come back to the problem of satisfying the condition that it is me who lives forever (Williams 1973, p. 96).

Williams thinks that the disconnect with one's self is especially strong if what we have in mind is pure intellectual activity, detached from any of our unconscious motives. Given our human nature, it's difficult to deny that unconscious motives and desires are part of who we are. For example, pursuing a purely mathematical argument with complete absorption takes us out of touch with a deep part of ourselves.

Fischer has a reply that's plausible, as far as it goes:

> An engrossing activity causes one to 'lose oneself' in the sense that one is not self-absorbed. But it is quite another matter to claim that the experiences involved in such activities are themselves not one's own ... the crucial distinction is between the content of the relevant experiences and their ownership. (Fischer 1994, pp. 259–260)

This is a perfectly reasonable point: if you're lost in a mathematical thought or completely absorbed by the music you're hearing, you aren't focused on yourself but the experiences are still your experiences. Still, this might not be enough. Williams writes of some activity in which we are "totally and perpetually absorbed." To be totally and perpetually absorbed is a different matter than spending a few minutes or an hour or two "out of ourselves." We might still exist if we were eternally absorbed, but the sense in which it would be us would be minimal, or so the objection would go.

Someone might protest that there's no need to imagine an afterlife of perpetual absorption in any one activity. Perhaps we could be absorbed some of the time by one thing and some of the time by another. It's also not clear that when we are absorbed, our unconscious is not at work. After all, what makes certain things absorbing might have to do with the deepest parts of ourselves; our absorbed activity might be a pure expression of the depths of our beings.

Clearly, not all kinds of absorption would count. For example, imagine someone who spends the afterlife endlessly absorbed in playing computer solitaire. A minimal sense of "self" might well be left here but the word "zombie" comes to mind. However, we need to be careful that we're not misled by the example. Eternal solitaire seems trivial, quite apart from any questions about whether it amounts to losing ourselves. Other possibilities seem a lot less silly. The believer might think that contemplating the divine is a clear example—that this sort of unending activity would be valuable beyond measure.

Even if complete absorption threatens the self, we should keep in mind that in many of the great religious traditions, overcoming the self is part of the goal. Christians may recall the words of Jesus on the Mount of Olives: "Not my will, but thine be done" (Luke, ch. 22, v. 42). In Buddhism, the self is seen as an illusion and, as such, is associated with the craving that causes suffering in the first place. Nirvana, although not a condition in which we have simply ceased to be, is described in terms of the extinction of the self. Meditators from various traditions describe (or try to describe) a state in which the boundaries between the self and the universe dissolve. And religious ecstasy, whatever else it may be, is called "ecstasy" because people who experience it have a sense of being outside the self.

The larger point is that trying to think of the afterlife as a mere extension of ordinary mortal life is religiously suspect. As we pointed out above, thoughtful believers tend to shy away from telling us what it would be like to live on after the death of the body. A state that has no meaningful connection with our self as we tend to think of it might be of no interest, but trying to decide if an afterlife is worth caring about by thinking of it on the model of life as it's usually lived is probably not very helpful. If someone believes in an afterlife and is asked what it will be like, the best answer is probably "I don't know."

4.2.1 A New Problem?

What we've said might suggest a new difficulty. If life after death is so unlike ordinary life, aren't believers forced to admit that they have no way of deciding whether it's worth having?

If making that evaluation called for detailed knowledge of what's in store, the answer would be yes. But analogies from ordinary life suggest another way to think about it. Suppose you're facing an experience unlike any that you've ever had. You might be nervous; you might not be sure that you'll like what's in store. But you can imagine being calmed by someone who knows you, knows the experience, and tells you that all will be well. Believers might see themselves as being in something like this position. They might take themselves to have assurances of various sorts. If they're theists, they might believe that they have had the experience of divine comfort and reassurance that this life isn't the end. They might believe that they can put their trust in what the mystics of their faith have hinted at, even if they haven't had the experiences they have had. And if the experiences of religious prayer and meditation are taken into account, even an ordinary believer might well insist that she has had a foretaste of something worth caring about in the deepest possible way.

5 CAN WE KNOW?

We've put off what might seem to be the most urgent question. Can we know or have good reason to believe that there's an afterlife? We can consider three broad sorts of evidence. One is philosophical argument. Another is *empirical* evidence—information gleaned from experience, either informally or through science. The third is what we might call religious inference.

5.1 Philosophical Arguments

In this section, we'll sketch the arguments of two philosophers, Plato and Immanuel Kant. A detailed treatment of their views would require a good deal more space, but we're not convinced that it would lead to more convincing arguments.

Plato (427 BCE–347 BCE) thought that we innately know at least some things. (Geometry was one of them. See his dialogue *Meno*.) As he saw it, the only way to explain this was to assume that we have immortal souls that existed in the pure real of Eternal Forms before we were born. This argument seems weak. Even if we come wired for certain types of knowledge, this could be a matter of the genetically determined structure of our brains. Plato also thought that only compound things could decay and dissolve. He argued that the soul is not compound, and so it can't break down; it's immortal. (You can read this argument in his *Phaedo*.) Once again, this isn't very convincing. First, if the soul is what gives us a mind, it's not obvious that a soul could be non-compound. Second, even if non-compound things can't disintegrate, they could just stop existing or, like elementary particles, change their form.

Immanuel Kant (1724–1804) starts from the fact that we realize that we have moral duties—that we're bound by the moral law, as he puts it. However, Kant thought that if we really understand what the moral law calls for from us, we'll see that it calls for a level of perfection that we could never reach in a finite human life. According to Kant, the only way that we can make sense of our conviction that we're still bound by the moral law is by presupposing that we are actually immortal—that we won't be kept from living up to the full demands of morality just because we run out of time. (You can read this argument in Chapter II of his *Critique of Practical Reason*.) Kant doesn't see this as a proof of immortality but as a reason for seeing it as a "presupposition of practical reason"—of reasoning about what we ought to do. Once again, this isn't an argument that has stood the test of time. Most of us see things like stealing and cruelty as wrong whether or not we think there's any hope of an everlasting afterlife. We might never expect to be perfect, but we don't think that excuses bad behavior.

5.2 Empirical Evidence

Empirical arguments tend to rely on things like experiences that seem to be communications from the dead, out-of-body experiences, and near-death experiences. Suppose there's some family dispute and you feel that you've received a message from your long-dead grandfather telling you to look in a moldy corner of the family attic, where you find a box rusted shut and covered with dust. You manage to get it open and find a letter in it, dated many decades ago, that settles the dispute. This would be impressive. It might well lead you to think that Grandpa is still somehow alive, even though his body is long since gone.

One problem is that it's hard to find clear cases where anything this remarkable has happened. There are anecdotes aplenty, but as someone once put it, "the plural of anecdote is not data." And even if we found a case like this, the question of how it might best be explained would still come up. Did Grandpa really communicate? Or was it a case of "remote viewing"—of psychically perceiving distant information? Or did you unconsciously remember some remark Grandpa made in the distant past? Settling those questions might be very difficult.

People whose hearts have stopped and who have been resuscitated sometimes recall "near death experiences." These often include a sense of passing through a tunnel toward a light and encountering a loving being. Some people interpret these as cases in which someone has actually died and returned to life—offering, as it were, a first-hand report. Obviously, we have the problem of getting data that's not corrupted by wishful thinking and faulty memory and for obvious ethical reasons, controlled experiments are out of the question. However, even if we had a clean case, what's reported might possibly be: (i) an experience that the patient had before the EEG went flat and remembered later; (ii) an experience the patient had while emerging from the coma; (iii) an experience that amounts to a sincere but false memory constructed after the patient has regained consciousness. No doubt other possible explanations exist. The "near-death experience" could be a fusion of unusual but perfectly natural experiences with information gleaned from various sources, including hearing things while in a semi-conscious state, confusion in the memories of witnesses about what happened, "memories" of things that never happened, and so on. (For a brief discussion of near-death experiences, see Blackmore 2003, pp. 361–365.)

5.3 Religious Reasons

Perhaps good empirical evidence is possible and might even exist, though it's very likely to be plagued by problems about how to interpret it. However, most people who believe in life after death don't rest their belief on paranormal stories. Most of them believe at least partly because it's part of the religious faith that they accept. If accepting Islam or the Baha'i faith is reasonable, then accepting the claims that these traditions make about the afterlife could be reasonable as well. In the case of Christianity, believers claim that they have a special reason for believing in life after death: Jesus died, was buried, rose again, and ascended into Heaven. Various Christian thinkers argue that the reality of the Resurrection is the best explanation for various pieces of evidence, including the rapid development of Christianity in the years after the crucifixion.

(For a lively debate on this topic, see *Did Jesus Rise From the Dead?* by Habermas and Flew, 1987.) One could also offer more general theological reasons. Assuming that a basis exists for the belief in something like the God of classical theism, the idea that this God would not let our lives end at death seems like a reasonable further piece of theology.

If there's a case to be made for life after death, we suspect that an appeal to more general religious beliefs is the best way to make it. Just how good the case will be however, depends on how reasonable you think it is to believe in the existence of God. Since we've devoted a good deal of this book to presenting various arguments pro and con, we'll have nothing more to say about that. You'll have to decide for yourself.

6 ETERNAL LIFE?

Some sharp-eyed readers may have noticed that up until this point, we have never once used the phrase "eternal life." We quoted Williams as asking whether there would be any point to "living eternally a human life," but we didn't follow his usage. That's because we're keeping to the distinction we made back in Chapter 1 between eternal and everlasting. Something everlasting goes on in time without any end. The eternal is outside time. Therefore, it's interesting to note therefore, that at least one major religious thinker rejects the idea of everlasting life in favor of eternal life. The Protestant theologian Paul Tillich, whom we met in Chapter 1, writes

> Many people . . . hope for a continuation of this life after death . . . This is a prevalent attitude about the future, and also a very simple one . . . It refuses to accept that we are creatures, that we come from the eternal ground of time and return to the eternal ground of time . . . It replaces eternity by an endless future.
>
> But endless future is without a final aim; it repeats itself and could well be described as an image of hell (Tillich 1963, p. 125).

According to Tillich, the Bible itself doesn't speak of "the hereafter" or "life after death." This is controversial, at least as a claim about the Christian New Testament. Even if the Greek equivalents of the words "hereafter" or "life after death" don't appear, it would be very difficult for most people to read the fifteenth chapter of First Corinthians without seeing it as a promise that we will be raised from the dead with new, incorruptible bodies. However, rather than trying to sort out the questions of biblical exegesis, let's ask what Tillich might have in mind.

That's not exactly easy to say. He writes:

> If we want to speak in truth without foolish, wishful thinking, we should speak about the eternal that is neither timelessness nor endless time (Tillich 1963, p. 125).

Neither timelessness nor endless time; what Tillich is trying to express has a long philosophical history. Eleonore Stump and Norman Kretzmann (1981) trace it back to Plato, Plotinus (c.204–270) and Boethius (480–c.525). Stump and Kretzmann sum up Boethius's definition of eternity this way:

> Eternity is the complete possession all at once of illimitable life (Stump and Kretzmann 1981, p. 431).

Whatever this means, it doesn't mean some sort of frozen abstraction like the way numbers exist outside time—assuming it really makes sense to think that numbers exist in the first place. On the contrary, Stump and Kretzmann stress that eternity isn't in the least defective compared to existence in time. They write:

> Atemporal duration is duration none of which is not—none of which is absent (and hence future) or flowed away (and hence past). Eternity, not time, is the mode of existence that admits of fully realized duration (Stump and Kretzmann 1981, p. 445).

This seems to be what Tillich has in mind. If we think of the present from our limited, time-bound perspective, it's a mere nothing—a width-less border between what was and what is to come. But Tillich thinks the wonder is that in spite of this, we can sometimes have a vibrant sense of the present and of "presence."

Explaining this is a struggle. Tillich writes:

> It is the eternal "now" which provides for us a temporal "now." Not everybody, and nobody all the time, is aware of this "eternal now" in the temporal "now." But sometimes it breaks powerfully into our consciousness and gives us the certainty of the eternal, of a dimension of time which cuts into our time and gives us our time (Tillich 1963, p. 131).

We are still wrestling with metaphor. What Tillich believes is that even though we are enmeshed in time, we also have a dimension that reaches out of time. That is why we are sometimes able, from our place in the flow of time, to have a sense of the eternal and thus of our eternal life. And recalling Stump and Kretzmann, if the "complete" possession of illimitable life" is good enough for God, then it should be good enough for us.

It's hard to know what to make of such metaphysics, though not so hard to understand what gives it its allure. If you have ever made a serious attempt at centering prayer or meditation or any similar discipline, you have probably had at least moments that combine a profound sense of being present in the moment with a lack of awareness of time—whether you are a Christian, or a Muslim, or a Buddhist, or someone with no religious perspective at all. And as Tillich points out, sometimes such moments come to us in the midst of life. Perhaps they don't mean what Tillich takes them to mean. Perhaps the reality is the conventional conception of everlasting life. Or perhaps the skeptic is correct and there's nothing more to our lives than a finite string of moments. But if Tillich and others with his view are correct, there is something more and it's not somewhere else and it's not at some other time. If so, then though we don't always know it, we are eternally where we're meant to be.

AT A GLANCE: LIFE AFTER DEATH

1. A Puzzling Possibility?
   - Question: what is the difference between your own survival in heaven and the existence of a heavenly duplicate who wasn't you?
2. Substance Views
   2.1. Bodily Resurrection
      - Problem: our bodies decay and even if the matter was put back together, it wouldn't obviously be us.
      - Possible solution: God takes our bodies away at the moment of death. This is not a solution that most people find plausible.
   2.2. Souls
      - Another version: our immaterial souls survive after our bodies die.
      - This is a form of substance dualism.
      - Question: why believe souls exist?
      - Possible answer: it's not obvious how to account for consciousness purely physically.
      2.2.1. Problems
         - Property dualism rather than substance dualism might be true. If so, no *thing* exists to survive.
         - Consciousness might depend on a non-physical "energy" flowing through the body rather than on a non-physical thing. If so, the energy itself isn't us.
         - Even if a thing exists that is the soul and that our minds depend on, it's even clearer that our minds depend on our brains.

3. The Transporter

- The *Star Trek* transporter suggests a view of personal identity that doesn't depend on things surviving.

    3.1. Relational Views of Personal Identity

    - Two "person-stages" are parts of one person if the relationship between the stages is the correct kind of relationship.
    - Different views of the "right kind of relationship" are possible, ranging from mere strong resemblance to requiring certain particular kinds of causal connections.
    - If a relational view is correct, then it could account for the possibility of an afterlife.

    3.2. Fission

    - If you undergo fission, then you couldn't be both successors because if $x = y$ and $x = z$, then we must have $y = z$.
    - Some philosophers think that the possibility of fission simply shows that meaningful survival doesn't require identity.

4. Would Immortality Be a Good Thing?

- Bernard Williams questions whether unending life would be a good thing.
- Two conditions must be considered: the identity condition and the attractiveness condition.

    4.1. The Attractiveness Condition

    - This condition leads to a dilemma:
        i. If your character stays the same, then you will eventually become bored.
        ii. If your character changes, we don't know how to evaluate from your present position whether what is to come will be attractive.
    - On (i): Fischer argues that Williams ignores repeatable pleasures.
    - Problem: if unending life means a human life with no risk, then life could still seem meaningless, even with repeatable pleasures.
    - On (ii): Our characters change even in this life without creating a problem for the meaningfulness of life. But if unending life is risk-free, we still have the problem noted under (i).

    4.2. The Identity Condition

    - An activity that completely absorbed us might seem to solve the problem.
    - Objection: if we "lose ourselves" in the activity, then in a sense, we don't survive.
    - Fischer points out that "losing ourselves" in an experience means we aren't focused on ourselves, not that the experiences aren't ours.
    - Problem: given the difficulties so far, it might be that only a permanently absorbing activity would do. But in that case, the "self" that's left seems very minimal.
    - Possible reply: first, some completely absorbing activities (e.g., contemplating the divine) might be extremely valuable. Second, many

religions hold that losing one's self in the right way is a good thing. Finally, most believers in an afterlife will agree that they don't know what it will be like.

    4.2.1. Problem: if we don't know what the afterlife will be like, we don't know how to decide if it's a good thing.

- Possible solution: we can sometimes have reason to think something will be valuable even if we don't know what it will be like.

5. Arguments for Establishing Life after Death
   5.1. Three Sample Philosophical Arguments

- We need to assume an immortal soul to account for some kinds of knowledge.
- Reply: there are other ways to do this, e.g., genetically determined brain structure.
- The soul is non-compound and therefore can't dissolve or break down.
- Reply: (a) it's not obvious That a soul would be non-compound, and (b) even if it is, it could still cease to exist or change forms like an elementary particle.
- We need the idea of life after death to make sense of the moral law.
- Reply: most of us believe we have moral obligations whether or not we will have time to meet them all.

   5.2. Empirical Arguments

- Reports of communications from the dead, out-of-body experiences, and near-death experiences are hampered by lack of solid evidence and by problems of interpretation.

   5.3. Religious Reasons

- If belief in the existence of the God of theism is reasonable, belief in life after death might be reasonable as well.

6. Other Views

- Some thinkers (e.g., Tillich) reject unending life in favor of eternal life— a mode of life outside time.

FURTHER READINGS AND WEB RESOURCES

A great deal of discussion of near-death experiences is found at http://www.near-death.com.

Psychologist Susan Blackmore has written extensively on this topic. You can find a short essay and other resources at http://www.susanblackmore. co.uk/si91nde.html.

John Perry's *A Dialogue on Personal Identity and Immorality* (Hackett Publishing Company, 1978) covers many of the philosophical issues in a lively and engaging way.

Plato's dialogue *Meno*, in which he argues that mathematical knowledge is innate, can be found at http://classics.mit.edu/Plato/meno.html.

Plato's *Phaedo* is online at http://classics.mit.edu/Plato/phaedo.html.

Kant's discussion of immortality is in his *Critique of Practical Reason*, online at http://www.gutenberg.org/etext/5683.

To read more about the *Star Trek* transporter and how it works, go to http://en.wikipedia.org/wiki/Transporter_(Star_Trek).

Scotty's sojourn in the buffer of the transporter is discussed at http://en.wikipedia.org/wiki/Relics_%28TNG_episode%29.

Glossary

abduction, abductive argument. An inference to the best explanation. Abductive arguments try to show that a claim is true by arguing that it is the best explanation for a set of facts. A detective might reason that a suspect committed the crime because that assumption gives the best overall explanation for the evidence (his fingerprints were at the crime scene, he had a motive, he can't account for his whereabouts at the time the crime was committed). The term "abduction" was introduced by the American philosopher Charles Sanders Peirce.

ad hoc explanation. From the Latin *ad hoc*, meaning "for this." An explanation developed after the fact to make evidence fit a theory. It usually involves changing one's theory for the sole purpose of avoiding counterevidence.

agnostic, agnosticism. Agnostics neither believe nor disbelieve that God exists. Instead, they suspend judgment. Philosophical agnosticism holds that in principle, we can't know whether a God exists, but many agnostics simply claim not to be able to settle the question for themselves.

analytic. A sentence is analytic if the subject contains the concept in the predicate. The statement, "All bachelors are unmarried," is an analytic sentence because the subject "bachelor" already contains the concept of the predicate "unmarried." What it *means* to be a bachelor includes being unmarried (for a contrast, see **synthetic**).

anthropic principle. Anthropic principles deal with the relationship between what we observe about the universe and our nature as observers. The *strong anthropic principle (SAP)* holds that the physical laws and constants of the universe are restricted to those ranges that allow the emergence of life. The *weak anthropic principle (WAP)* says only that the physical laws and constants scientists can expect to observe are restricted by the conditions necessary for their presence as observers.

a posteriori. A Latin phrase that literally means "from after," but in philosophy, it means "after experience." *A posteriori* knowledge is knowledge justified on the basis of experience.

a priori. A Latin phrase that literally means "from before," but in philosophy, it means "prior to experience." *A priori* knowledge is knowledge that doesn't rely on experience for its justification.

argument. A series of sentences consisting of one or more premises and a conclusion such that the premises are meant to support the conclusion.

argument from evil. The argument that the existence of suffering is evidence against the existence of God. The argument from evil comes in two forms: logical and evidential. According the logical argument from evil, the existence of suffering makes the existence of God logically impossible. The evidential form of the argument makes the more modest claim that the existence of suffering makes the existence of God unlikely or at least less likely.

argument from queerness. This is an argument due to the philosopher J. L. Mackie that is meant to support the conclusion that no objective moral values or moral facts exist. Mackie sees two types of problems. One is **metaphysical**: if moral facts existed, they would be utterly different in kind from other sorts of facts. The other problem is **epistemological**: given that moral facts would have to be so different, the way we knew them or recognized them would have to be completely different from the way we know or recognize other sorts of facts. In Mackie's view, these two premises provide a powerful reason for accepting the conclusion that there are no objective moral values or facts. The problem of trying to respond to this argument is sometimes called the **queerness problem**.

atheism. Atheism is the view that God does not exist. Some philosophers distinguish between positive or strong atheism, which is the affirmative view that God does not exist, and negative, or weak, atheism, which is simply a lack of belief that God exists. Other philosophers question whether negative atheism is really different than **agnosticism**.

basic belief. Any belief not held on the basis of other beliefs.

behaviorism. This is a philosophical view about the nature of the mind, according to which the mind is to be understood in terms of behavior or disposition to behave in certain ways. Philosophical behaviorism is different from but related to psychological behaviorism. Psychological behaviorism is a strictly *empirical* approach to psychology that emphasizes the importance of behavior as the only phenomena that psychologists can directly observe.

begging the question. A fallacy in reasoning that comes in two varieties. In one variety, the reasoner argues in a circle. In the other form, the argument contains a premise that's so controversial that someone who doubts the conclusion couldn't be expected to accept it.

Big Bang. According to modern cosmology, the universe as we know it began about 15 billion years ago with a cataclysmic explosion called the Big Bang. Before the explosion, matter/energy was condensed into a tiny region that gave rise to subatomic particles, atoms, molecules, and eventually stars and galaxies as the universe expanded outward. Cosmologists have also offered theories about what might have happened before the Big Bang. According to one major theory, the Big Bang itself arose when fluctuations in something called a "Higgs Field" gave rise to a "false vacuum," where the field variables all took the value zero (hence the "vacuum") but where the energy density was very high. According to the inflationary model of the universe, this "false vacuum" was the beginning of the process that led to our physical universe.

blik. A term introduced by the philosopher R. M. Hare in response to Antony Flew's assertion that religious claims are not **falsifiable**. Bliks are comprehensive viewpoints that supposedly lie behind out ordinary beliefs, even if they can't be falsified.

Buffy the Vampire Slayer. An American television series that ran from 1997 to 2003, based on the original script of the 1992 movie *Buffy the Vampire Slayer* (see http://en.wikipedia.org/wiki/Buffy_the_Vampire_Slayer for more details). The main character, Buffy Summers, was a young woman who possessed "super-natural" powers that enabled her to battle vampires—once-human creatures who had lost their souls but who would live forever unless they were killed by burning or by a wooden stake through the heart.

The series developed an academic following and resulted in conferences, journal articles, books, and Ph.D. dissertations. Philosophy students will find the series a source of witty writing and sometimes unintentional philosophical puzzles.

central perfections. The central perfections are the attributes that **classical theism** ascribes to God: **omnipotence, omniscience** and **omnibenevolence.**

circular argument. Any argument where the truth of one or more of the premises depends on the truth of the conclusion.

classical theism (see **theism**)

cognitive meaning. This term is used by **logical positivists** to refer to the kind of meaning that factual statements are supposed to have. Statements like, "George Washington was the first president of the United States," have cognitive meaning. Questions, commands, expressions of taste, and some poetry for example, may be meaningful but they are not cognitively meaningful.

coherentism. A view about the structure of beliefs according to which one's beliefs are related in a web-like manner, so that a belief is justified by how well it "coheres" with the total family or web of beliefs.

compatibilism (see **determinism**)

complexity (see **irreducible complexity**)

conditional probability (see **probability**)

conjunction. In logic, a conjunction is the resulting of joining two or more statements or **propositions** by "and." This sense of the term is different from the sense often used by grammarians.

contingent, contingency (see **modality, modal logic**)

contradiction. A statement that must be false for reasons of logic. For example, "Martin is bald and not bald."

cosmological. From the Greek word "kosmos" which in turn comes from the Greek word "kosmeo," which means, roughly an orderly or pleasing arrangement. When we talk about the cosmos, we mean the whole of the ordered physical universe. Cosmological questions in philosophy are questions about the nature and ultimate origins of the universe.

cosmological argument. The argument for God based upon the need to explain the existence of the universe.

creationism. The view that God created the universe. Creationism in this very broad sense is compatible with both **scientific creationism** and **theistic evolution.**

deduction. A form of reasoning in which one attempts to see what follows strictly from a set of claims rather than what the claims make probable. Mathematical reasoning is deductive reasoning.

de facto. Pertaining to facts as opposed to justification.

defense. As used in connection with the **argument from evil,** any response that tries to undermine the argument without telling us why God permits evil.

de jure. Pertaining to justification as opposed to facts.

dependent being. A being that depends on something else for its existence.

determinism. The doctrine that everything that happens is strictly determined by earlier states of the world and the laws of nature. The major philosophical issue about determinism has been whether it is compatible with free will. The thesis that free will and determinism are not compatible is called *incompatibilism.* If we add the claim that the world really is deterministic, we get the doctrine called *hard determinism.* Other philosophers argue that free will is compatible with determinism. The view that free will and determinism are compatible is called *compatibilism.* If we add determinism to compatibilism, we get *soft determinism.*

A further position that should be mentioned is *libertarianism.* This is the view that free will requires indeterminism, and that indeterminism is true. (This use of the word "libertarianism" is not to be confused with the meaning found in political theory.)

divine command theory. The view that things are right or wrong because God commands or forbids them.

disjunction, disjunctive. In logic, a disjunction is the result of joining two or more statements or **propositions** by "or," and the result is a disjunctive statement or proposition. Although the components ("disjuncts") of a disjunction are sometimes understood to exclude one another, this is not always the case. In particular, someone who proposes a disjunctive theodicy need not claim that exactly *one* of the disjuncts provides the unique explanation for evil. A non-exclusive (or "inclusive") disjunction is true so long as at least one of its disjuncts is.

doctrinal exclusivism (see **exclusivism**)

dualism. This is the view that there is a fundamental division in reality, typically between the physical and the mental. Dualism can be contrasted with monism, which holds that there is no such divide. A monist could be a physicalist, holding that everything is physical; or an idealist (the word has a technical meaning here), holding that everything is mental; or could be a neutral monist, holding that though there is no fundamental divide in reality, and that what exists has physical and material aspects.

There are two kinds of dualism: substance dualism and property dualism. Without offering a definition of the word "property," we can simply say that properties in the sense relevant here are the qualities or characteristics of things. Some properties are properties of other properties (for example, a certain color property—a certain shade of blue might have a property of saturation or intensity). In contrast, things like stones or molecules or animals, on the other hand, have properties but are not themselves properties of anything; they are substances.

Substance dualists claim that two fundamentally different sorts of substances exist—physical and mental. Property dualists believe that only one kind of substance exists, namely physical substance, but that physical things have properties that are different from any of the sorts of properties for which physical science can account. The usual examples are properties associated with consciousness.

efficient cause. In the philosophical system of the Greek philosopher Aristotle (384 BCE–322 BCE), the efficient cause of something is what creates it or brings it into being. According to many commentators, when Aquinas discussed efficient causes in his Second Way, he meant a *sustaining cause*, which is a cause that acts not before something exists but simultaneously with it, to keep it in existence.

empirical knowledge. Knowledge based upon experience.

empty set (see **set**)

epistemological. Pertaining to the theory of knowledge.

epistemic. Pertaining to knowledge.

eschatology. From the Greek word meaning "end" or "last." This is the branch of theology that pertains to the End Times. Personal eschatology has to do with life after death (e.g., survival of bodily death, resurrection, Heaven, Hell, and so on). Historical eschatology is about the end of history (e.g., the second coming of Christ, the battle of Armageddon, the Beast of Revelation, the judgment of mankind, the fullness of the kingdom of God, and so on).

eternal. As used in this text, something is eternal if it exists outside time. Abstract entities such as numbers are eternal if they exist. Some theologians claim that God is **eternal**. (See also **everlasting**.)

Eucharist, eucharistic. The Eucharist is the ritual re-enactment of the Last Supper between Jesus and his disciples, depicted in the Gospels—the four narratives of the life and death of Jesus that are found in the Christian Bible. Roman Catholics, Orthodox Christians, Lutherans, and Anglicans use the term Eucharist. Members of other Christian denominations are more likely to use terms such as Last Supper or Communion. This difference in terminology tends to be accompanied by deep theological differences about the nature and meaning of the ceremony. Catholics believe that the bread that the priest consecrates becomes the body of Christ. Many Protestants regard the Last Supper or Communion simply as a memorial.

everlasting. Something is everlasting if it exists in time, but has no beginning and no end. (See also **eternal.**)

evidentialism. The view that beliefs must be based on arguments and evidence.

evidentialist objection. The view that belief in the existence of God is unjustified because there is no evidence for God's existence.

evolution. The view that life developed in gradual steps by a process of random genetic mutations and natural selection.

exclusivism. Exclusivism in religion is the belief that some one particular religion—one's own—is privileged compared to others. Two sorts of privilege might be at issue. One is privilege with respect to truth. The *doctrinal exclusivist* holds that his or her religion is true and that where other religions disagree with it, they are false. A *salvific exclusivist* is someone who thinks not only that his or her religion is true but that only those who explicitly believe the religion's doctrines can hope to attain the ultimate good. See also **inclusivism** and **pluralism.**

expected utility. The expected utility of a choice is roughly the average benefit or loss you would expect if you repeated the choice many times. For example, you might enter a contest with four possible outcomes: you win nothing, you win a television, you win a trip to Hawaii, or you win a new car. You might assign the values or *utilities* 0 to winning nothing, 20 to winning the television, 40 to winning the trip, and 100 to winning the car. Suppose the probabilities of these outcomes were, respectively, .8, .1, .09, and .01. Then the expected utility would be

$$.8 \times 0 + .1 \times 20 + .09 \times 40 + .01 \times 100 = 6.6$$

This means that if you entered this contest many times, the average of the values of the outcomes you'd realize is 6.6.

According to many theorists, when we're faced with a number of options, we should always prefer the option with the greatest expected utility. Others disagree, especially in cases where the opportunity won't repeat itself and therefore the "average" has no practical meaning.

A note on money and utility: utility isn't a dollar-for-dollar function of money. Getting an extra $1000 will matter a lot to you if you are a starving student working your way through school. If you're a multimillionaire, getting an extra $1000 might not matter much at all. This is the "diminishing marginal utility" of money. The mathematical theory of utility has straight-forward ways of dealing with this.

externalism, externalistic. This is the view of knowledge according to which the factors that confer justification or warrant are external to the introspective awareness of the knower.

faculty. An ability or capacity of the mind (e.g., reason, memory, sense perception).

falsifiable. This term is used in two different ways in philosophy. In the context of linguistic meaning, a statement is said to be falsifiable if it is possible—in principle—to show that the statement is false. In the context of the philosophy of science, it is used especially in connection with Karl Popper's view of science. According to Popper, a legitimate scientific theory must be falsifiable. That is, there must be some circumstances that would be in conflict with what the theory requires and would lead us to reject the theory. On this view, science doesn't show us what statements are true about the world; rather, it shows us which statements are false. Science expands our knowledge of the world by showing us which factual claims are false.

fission. Splitting or dividing; in philosophical discussions of *personal identity*, "fission" refers to a process in which a thing divides into two successors. (For example, suppose that God makes two copies of you in Heaven.) Because you can't be both copies (things identical to the same thing must be identical to one another), it's difficult to see how you could be either. Many philosophers argue that even though neither fission product is identical to you, the results of fission might be almost as valuable to you as ordinary survival.

foundationalism. A view about the structure of knowledge according to which one's beliefs resemble a building with a superstructure and foundation. According to classical foundationalism, only three types of beliefs are in the foundation: **incorrigible beliefs, self-evident beliefs,** and **perceptual beliefs.** According to modern foundationalism, two types of beliefs are in the foundation: incorrigible beliefs and self-evident beliefs.

functionalism. This is a view about the nature of mind, according to which it is the way a system is organized—not the material that something is made of—that makes it a mind. What is important in determining whether something is a mind is not what it is made of but how it functions as a system.

According to functionalism, mental states are defined in terms of their cause and effect relations. More specifically, mental states (e.g., beliefs and desires) are constituted by their causal relations to other mental states, sensory inputs, and behavioral outputs. Because many state types could play the relevant causal role, mental states can be multiply realized.

This brings up an interesting aside. As Hilary Putnam points out, one consequence of defining mental states in terms of their causal roles alone is that functionalism is compatible with substance dualism:

> The brain-state theorist usually mentions (with a certain pride, slightly reminiscent of the Village Atheist) the incompatibility of his hypothesis with all forms of dualism. This is natural if physical-chemical states of the brain are what is at issue. However, functional states of whole systems are something quite different. In particular, the functional-state hypothesis is not incompatible with dualism (Putnam 1991, p. 200)!

However, functionalism is equally consistent with the view that the functional states in question are physical. Indeed, this is the view most functionalists hold. Functionalism allows for a particular mental state token (i.e., a particular instance of pain) to be identified with a particular brain state, but the mental state type (i.e., pain itself) is to be identified only with its functional role.

goal-directed complexity. The property of having parts arranged in a complex way that work together towards a goal.

googol, googolplex. A googol is a very large number—1 followed by 100 zeros, or 10 to the power of 100. The mathematician Edward Kasner, it seems, asked his 9-year old nephew Milton Sirotta what a number that big should be called. His nephew came up with the word "googol," which Kasner introduced to the world of mathematics. A googolplex is vastly larger: it is 10 to the power of one googol, which is 1 followed by one googol zeros. There is, indeed, a connection between "googol" and the search engine Google.com. Go to http://www.google.com/corporate/history.html.

Holy Trinity. In Christianity, God is conceived of as three persons in one being. The three persons of the Christian Trinity are the Father, the Son, and the Holy Spirit.

hypothesis. A proposed explanation or a proposition offered for consideration.

identity, identical. There are two main senses in which we say that things are identical. One is *numerical identity*. The Morning Star is numerically identical to the Evening Star. That is, only one thing exists rather than two. The other sense is *qualitative identity*, or exact similarity. When objects are only qualitatively identical, each one gets counted separately.

Numerical identity satisfies Euclid's Axiom 1: things that are identical to a third thing are identical to one another. Because the Evening Star is identical to Venus, and because the Morning Star is also identical to Venus, it follows that the Evening Star is identical to the Morning Star. This means that identity is a transitive relation. Qualitative identity is transitive so long as we mean exact similarity.

An important principle arises in connection with identity. It was formulated by the German philosopher Gottfried Leibniz (1646–1751) and is often called Leibniz's Law. It says that if X and Y are numerically identical, then they share all their properties. If X has a property P and X = Y, then Y must also have the property P. (For example, if the Morning Star turns on its axis, then the Evening Star must also.) This principle is uncontroversial, although it must be qualified. Leibniz's Law does not hold for "properties" that things have because of someone's beliefs, attitudes, and so on—for what are sometimes called "intentional properties." For example, Ruth might believe that the mayor is paid a low salary. She might also doubt that Cohen is paid a low salary. So the mayor seemingly has a property (being believed by Ruth to be paid a low salary) that Cohen lacks. But Cohen could still be the mayor. This is why Descartes' argument for the distinctness of mind and body isn't a good one. The fact that someone can doubt the existence of their body without doubting their own existence doesn't allow us to use Leibniz's Law to conclude that the self and the body are distinct. The properties in question are intentional properties.

idolatry. Idol-worship. An idolater is someone who worships an idol instead of worshiping God. The term is sometimes used in a broad sense that includes any sort of devotion to a false ideal. It's important to keep in mind that what might seem like idolatry might in fact not be. People who bow to images or statues may perfectly well understand that the image or statue itself is not divine. Rather, it is a symbol or representation of the divine and if it's used as an aid to devotion rather than as a direct object of worship, it would be wrong to talk of idolatry.

immanence, immanent. When used in connection with God, immanence refers to God's presence in or interaction with the world. This is contrasted with the **transcendence** of God. Conceived of as transcendent, God is apart from and more elevated than the physical world. Many religious outlooks see God as having both an immanent and a transcendent aspect.

Incarnation. The Christian doctrine of the Incarnation holds that God became human in the person of Jesus of Nazareth, so that Jesus, although fully human, was also fully God.

inclusivism. Religious inclusivists believe that the claims of their own religion are true, but that people with other beliefs may still attain salvation, or paradise, or blessedness, or Nirvana, or whatever term the religion uses to describe the Ultimate Good. See also **exclusivism** and **pluralism**.

incorrigible belief. A belief about which one cannot be wrong—for example, the belief that one is in pain.

inductive reasoning. A form of inference that involves extending a description beyond a limited sample set to a larger set. For example, based on the fact that all the copper we have encountered so far conducts electricity, we might conclude that all copper conducts electricity.

infinite regress. a process of reasoning or justification that can be traced back into infinity.

intelligent design theory. A theory according to which science can legitimately make the inference that there is intelligent design in nature. The intelligent design need not be by God but most proponents of intelligent design believe that God is, in fact, the designer.

internalism, internalistic. The view that the individual knower has introspective access to the factors that convey justification.

instrumentalism, instrumentalist (see **realism, realist**)

irreducible complexity. A system is irreducibly complex if it is composed of several interacting parts such that the removal of any one part causes the whole system to cease functioning.

justification. The basis for a knowledge claim. The exact nature of justification is controversial. The usual view is that a belief is justified if it is held for good reason.

Koran. The sacred text of Islam. Muslims believe that it was delivered to the prophet Mohammed by the angel Gabriel. Also spelled "Qur'an" in English, the word literally means "recitation."

libertarian freedom (see **determinism**)

logical positivism. A school of thought about the nature of linguistic meaning that originated in the 1920s and 1930s from a group of philosophers known as the Vienna Circle. The positivists urged a theory of cognitive meaning according to which a putative factual statement is cognitively meaningful if and only if (i) it is *analytic* or (ii) it is *synthetic* and can, in principle, be verified by experience. This view of meaning is referred to as **verificationism**.

logician, A scholar of logic, usually a philosopher or mathematician.

macroevolution. Large-scale evolutionary change, including the evolution of a new species. Scientific creationists deny macroevolution is possible.

metaphysical, metaphysics. Metaphysics is the branch of philosophy that studies questions about the structure and nature of reality at the most abstract level. Questions about the existence and nature of God are metaphysical, as are, for instance, questions about whether there is such a thing as free will.

microevolution. Small-scale evolutionary change, falling short of the appearance of a new species. Most Scientific creationists affirm microevolution while denying macroevolution.

modality, modal logic. Modal logic deals with the so-called "alethic modalities" of possibility, impossibility, contingency, and necessity. For example, some things are true:

> *The United States has 50 states.*
> *Beethoven was born on December 16.*
> $2 + 3 = 5.$
> *Dogs are mammals.*

Each of the following, on the other hand, is false:

> *The United States has 60 states.*
> *Beethoven was born on July 4.*
> *2 + 3 = 7.*
> *Dogs are reptiles.*

In reading these lists, however, there seem to be important differences among the entries. While it's true that the United States has 50 states we can perfectly well imagine that it might have been more or fewer. The fact that the United States has 50 states is a contingent truth: in some important sense, it could have been false. In particular, there could have been 60. On the other hand, "2 + 3 = 5" seems not just to be true but we can't make sense of the idea that it might have been false. It is a necessary truth.

There is more than one sort of possibility. **Epistemic** possibility has to do with what's possible "for all we know." In that sense, it's not possible that the United States has 60 states. The sense of possibility under discussion here is a matter of whether the thing itself, so to speak, is possible. In thinking about these matters, philosophers and logicians have found talking about possible worlds helpful. When we say that it's possible that the United States has 60 states, we mean that there could have been 60, and one way to think of this is to say that a possible world exists in which the United States has 60 states.

A minority of philosophers think that possible worlds are every bit as real and concrete as the actual world. However, most philosophers think of possible worlds as abstract entities, not in competition with the physical, concrete world. On this way of thinking, a possible world is more like a **proposition** or a collection of propositions that specify a complete, detailed way the world could be.

No matter which of these views is correct, once we have the concept of a possible world we can explain the relationships among modal concepts straightforwardly and clearly. A statement represents a possibility (for short, "is possible") if a possible world exists where the statement is true. If P is a statement, it's common to write "possibly P" as "◇P." P is *necessary* if P is true in every possible world. As we've seen, "5 + 2 = 7" is an example. Necessity is standardly written as "□P." A contingent proposition is one that's true in at least one world and false in at least one. That is, P is contingent if "◇P" and "◇~P" are both true, where "~" is the symbol for "not." An impossible proposition is one that's false in every possible world—"2 + 5 = 8" would be an example.

So far, we've been discussing possibility and necessity in the broadest sense. Talk of possible worlds allows us to consider more specific kinds of possibility. For example, we can say that something is physically possible if it's true in at least one world that has the same laws of nature as our world. And we can say that something is physically necessary if it's true in every possible world that shares our laws.

modus ponens. Any logical inference of the following form: "If P then Q; P, therefore Q."

monotheism. The belief that only one god exists.

naturalism. This is the view that nothing supernatural exists. It is difficult to give a clear meaning to the word "supernatural." For example, ghosts and magic are often thought of as supernatural, but it's not exactly clear why. If ghost exist and can interact with ordinary matter, or if saying magic words can make things happen, that would be very surprising but it would be a fact about the world we live in, and might even be amenable to scientific explanation. However, an uncreated creator of the physical world would be supernatural by any reasonable definition, and so if such a being exists, naturalism is false.

natural theology. The project of learning about God from reason and nature. This usually involves constructing proofs of the existence of God based on observations about the world.

necessary, necessity. Something is necessary if it couldn't be otherwise. However, when we say that something couldn't be otherwise, we sometimes mean relative to certain principles or assumptions. It's physically necessary that nothing travels faster than light, but not necessary in the strongest sense. See also **modality, modal logic.**

necessary existence. A being or thing has necessary existence if it is impossible for it not to exist. Whether any things possess necessary existence is controversial. Most philosophers would agree that no space-time object could exist necessarily. Some philosophers might think that space and time themselves exist necessarily, but many would disagree. Most philosophers would agree that if mathematical objects such as sets and numbers exist, then they exist necessarily, but there would be considerable disagreement about whether there really are such things really exist at all. The **ontological argument** attempts to show that God exists necessarily. See also **modality, modal logic.**

necessary truth. In the strongest sense, a necessary truth is one that would hold no matter how the world differed from the way things actually are. Truths of mathematics are examples: that $2 + 3 = 5$ is a necessary truth. Certain statements about the nature of things might also be necessary truths—for example, that water is made of H_2O. See also **modality, modal logic.**

necessary condition. To say that a statement P is a necessary condition for Q is to say that unless P is true, Q is not true. For example, the statement "John is in Maryland" is a necessary condition for "John is in College Park." Similarly, to say that a state of affairs or fact P is a necessary condition for a state of affairs or fact Q is to say that unless P obtains, Q doesn't or won't obtain. The presence of oxygen is a necessary condition for a match to light.

necessary truth (see **modality, modal logic**)

necessary being. A being whose nonexistence is impossible.

negative atheism (see **atheism**)

neoplatonism. A form of Platonism developed by Plotinus in the second century AD. Neoplatonism was a mystical descendent of Platonism. As it relates to the argument from evil, the basic idea is that everything ultimately derives from the Platonic form of the good. Evil and suffering are not forms of the good so, strictly speaking, they are not things. They are privations of things.

New Testament. Christians and Jews recognize certain books of the Bible in common. These biblical books are referred to as the Tanakh by Jews and as the Old Testament by Christians. Christians also recognize another set of books, referred to as the New Testament and written after the death of Jesus. These include the four Gospels, which tell about the life, death, and resurrection of Jesus, and a number of other books, including letters written by St. Paul to various congregations.

non-basic beliefs. Beliefs that are held on the basis of other beliefs.

numerical identity, numerically identical (see **identity, identical**)

observational selection effect. An observational selection effect involves the distortion of evidence caused by the observer of the evidence. Usually the distortion is caused by the method used to collect the data. For example, a poll of American political views would be distorted if it only polled rich people. The method of polling only the rich acts as a filter of political views as well. An observational selection effect need not be the result of the method of data collection. Data may be filtered by the condition that someone exists to make observations.

omnibenevolent. Perfectly good. According to classical theism, God possess the perfection of being perfectly good. This claim leads to the logical version of the **problem of evil**.

omnipotent. All-powerful. Omnipotence is one of the perfections of the God of classical theism. Some philosophers and theologians have claimed that the concept of omnipotence leads to paradoxes.

omnipresent. Present everywhere. God is often held to be omnipresent.

omniscient. All-knowing. Classical theism holds that God's knowledge is perfect, and hence that God is omniscient. The question of whether God's omniscience is compatible with human freedom is a perennial theological and philosophical issue.

ontology. The area of philosophy concerned with what exists.

ontological. Pertaining to what things exist.

ontological argument. An argument for the existence of God initially developed in the eleventh century by St. Anselm of Canterbury. The argument is that the concept of God has necessary existence built into it and so when someone denies the existence of God, they contradict themselves. In effect, they are saying that a being who must exist doesn't exist. Therefore, the argument concludes, God must exist.

panentheism. The doctrine that the universe is in God, though not identical with God. Panentheism stresses God's **immanence** as opposed to God's **transcendence**.

pantheism, pantheist. Pantheism claims that God is identical with the universe.

perceptual beliefs. Beliefs formed directly on the basis of sensory experience.

personal identity, problem of. The philosophical problem of explaining the conditions under which a person at one time is the same person as a person at another time. Relevant questions include: is psychological continuity enough to establish personal identity? Is physical continuity required? Is there a deep unity to a person? Or is identity a relatively shallow matter of appropriate resemblances among "stages" of a person?

philosophy of science. The branch of philosophy that concerns itself with the nature of science and scientific concepts. Philosophers of science ask such questions as: do scientists explain the world or merely describe it? What constitutes confirmation of a scientific hypothesis? What is a law of nature?

physical constants. Unvarying numbers that enter into physical laws—for example, the speed of light in a vacuum is a constant. The strength of the force of gravity is a constant; its value doesn't change.

pluralism. A religious pluralist is someone who thinks that many religions are on a par with respect to truth and goodness. Pluralists often believe that there is one goal that most religions seek, and they seek it in different but equally valid ways. Pluralists such as John Hick claim that fully grasping the nature of the divine is beyond our human abilities, but that many religions perceive aspects of ultimate reality in partial and fragmentary ways. See also *inclusivism* and *exclusivism*.

polytheism. The belief that many gods exist.

possible, possibility (see modality, modal logic)

positive atheism (see atheism)

posterior probability. The probability of a hypothesis in light of the evidence (see also **probability**)

pragmatic reason. A pragmatic reason for a belief is a reason that doesn't bear on the likelihood that the belief is true but instead appeals to some sort of benefit (psychological, for example) that comes from holding the belief.

predicate. The term "predicate" has several senses. In the most familiar sense, a predicate is a descriptive term or phrase, such as "is red" or "is taller than the

Empire State Building." As Kant uses the term in his discussion of the onto-logical argument, a predicate is a property or quality that a thing might have.

prima facie. On the face of it; at first appearance. For example, we might say that if witnesses say that a suspect was seen running from the crime scene, that is *prima facie* evidence that he's guilty.

Principle of Credulity. A principle proposed by Richard Swinburne that deals with the circumstances in which simply taking what one seems to experience at face value is acceptable. The Principle says that unless there are special reasons to think otherwise, if it seems to you that something a tree, say, is present, then it probably is present.

Swinburne believes that this Principle can be applied to religious experiences. Thus if it seems to you that God is present or is telling you some-thing, then you are entitled to think that this is probably so, according to Swinburne.

principle of satisfying reason. A principle considered in this text according to which the existence of **contingent** things can be accounted for in a way that is intellectually satisfying, even if the explanation doesn't strictly imply what it explains.

principle of sufficient reason. Any of several principles according to which everything is either self-explaining or has an explanation in terms of something else. To count as an explanation in the sense relevant to principles of sufficient reason, the explanation must *imply* what it explains in the strict sense of logic. (See the entry on **valid** for further discussion of implication.)

prior probability. The probability of a hypothesis "before" or apart from the evidence. See also **probability**.

privation. A lack of some power or ability. Blindness is a privation of sight.

probability. The mathematical theory of probability allows us to reason about uncertainty. There are various concepts of probability, but we can divide them into *objective* and *subjective*. Objective probabilities most commonly tell us about frequencies or ratios. For example, if we toss a fair coin many times, we expect to get heads about half the time. That means the probability of heads is 1/2. A physicist might tell us that the probability that an atom will decay in the next hour is 3/4. That means that if we had many atoms like this one, three-quarters of them could be expected to decay in the next hour. Those are objective probabilities.

Alternatively, if you ask someone for the probability that life exists on other planets, they might say 70%. But that figure doesn't tell us anything about how often we could expect something to happen. It represents degree or strength of belief. Probabilities like this are called subjective probabilities, although the word "subjective" does not mean "arbitrary" or "idiosyncratic." Subjective probabilities can be more-or-less reasonable.

Objective and subjective probabilities obey the same rules. Probabilities are numbers that range from 0 to 1—from 0% to 100%. They follow these rules:

(1) If two possibilities exclude one another (for example, Jones is over 6 feet tall vs. Jones is under 6 feet tall), then the probability that one or the other is true is the sum of the individual probabilities. Formally,

If X and Y are mutually exclusive, then $p(X \text{ or } Y) = p(X) + p(Y)$

(2) The probability that something doesn't happen is 1 minus the probability that it does happen. For example, the probability that the die doesn't come up 6 is 5/6, which is $1 - 1/6$. Formally:

$$p(not\text{-}X) = 1 - p(X)$$

By applying logic to these rules, we could show that if two possibilities exclude one another, the probability that they both happen is 0. We could also show that the probability of "X or not-X" is 1.

We can define the *conditional probability* of X given Y, which we write as $p(X|Y)$:

$$p(X|Y) = \frac{p(X \text{ and } Y)}{p(Y)}$$

For example, suppose you roll a single die. What's the probability that it comes up even given that it came up greater than 2? Intuitively, the answer is 1/2 because of the four numbers greater than 2, two are even. But notice that the probability that the die came up even and greater than 2 is 2/6. The probability that the die came up greater than 2 is 4/6. And

$$\frac{^{2}/_{6}}{^{4}/_{6}} = \frac{1}{2}$$

In the chapter on miracles, we talk about the probability of a hypothesis—call it H—given some piece of evidence E. This is the *posterior probability* of the hypothesis. If we simply use the definition of conditional probability, we get

$$p(H|E) = \frac{p(H \text{ and } E)}{p(E)}$$

However, often not directly clear is to what $p(H \text{ and } E)$ and $p(E)$ amount. Some formal tinkering leads to a very important result called Bayes' Theorem, which directs us to think about three things: (i) How likely is the hypothesis apart from the evidence? This is the *prior probability* of the hypothesis. (ii) Supposing the hypothesis is true, how likely is that we would find this evidence? In other words, what is $p(E|H)$? (iii) Supposing the hypothesis is false, how likely is that we would see the evidence? In other words, what is $p(E|not\text{-}H)$? The formula—which we display only for illustration—is

$$p(H|E) = \frac{p(E|H) \times p(H)}{p(E|H) \times p(H) + p(E|\bar{H}) \times p(\bar{H})}$$

("Here "*H̄*" represents *not-H*.") The lessons of the formula are more important. First, the more improbable a hypothesis is, the harder it is to establish by evidence—the lower the *posterior probability*, other things being equal. Second, if the evidence is more-or-less equally likely whether the hypothesis is true or false, the evidence doesn't count for much. Put another way, if $p(E|H)$ and $p(E|not\text{-}H)$ are roughly equal, then the evidence is not very relevant to the hypothesis. As an illustration, suppose someone said that eating hot peppers helps cure a cold. Their evidence is that people who eat a hot pepper every day while they have a cold generally get better in about a week. Because this is what we'd expect in any case, the evidence counts for little if anything. However, if the evidence was that people with a cold who ate a hot pepper every day got better in two days, this would be surprising and this evidence would be highly relevant to the hypothesis.

problem of evil. The problem of explaining why an all-powerful, perfectly good God permits suffering.

problem of induction. The problem of justifying inductive inferences. We infer that the Sun will rise tomorrow because it has risen every day for a long time. Our inference about the Sun is inductive because it extends past observations into the future. How do we know inductive inferences are good? We might try to justify making inductive inferences based on our past observations of the success of inductive inferences. The problem is that this is circular. It amounts to using inductive inference to show that inductive inference is reliable. But that amounts to assuming from the outset that inductive inference is reliable.

problem of other minds. The problem of justifying our belief that others have minds given that no one has direct access to other minds.

process theology. A non-classical view of God that is rooted in the philosophy of Alfred North Whitehead (1861–1947) and was developed especially by Charles Hartshorne (1897–2000). In process theology, the world does not consist of "things" but of momentary processes that sometimes cluster together into configurations that we normally view as objects. According to process theology, God interacts with these processes in a way that doesn't coerce or fix the outcome. For this reason, process theologians reject the classical understanding of **omniscience** because what God knows depends on what entities in the world determine to do or become. Process theologians also deny that God is **omnipotent** in the sense of having all power or controlling everything. Process theologians also stress the idea that God is affected by the world—God is responsive to the world, and this includes suffering with us. Various useful links on this topic are found at http://www.ctr4process.org/process/CPSWhatIs.htm.

property dualism (see **dualism**)

Protestants, Protestant reformers. Theologians and ministers who protested corruption in the Catholic church and wanted reform but ended up breaking off and starting Protestant denominations. Prominent reformers include Martin Luther and John Calvin.

proposition. The content of a statement or sentence. Two very different sentences could express the same proposition. For example, the English statement "Snow is white" and the German statement "Schnee is weiss" both express the same proposition.

proper subset (see **set**)

pseudo-task. A "task" that nothing would count as carrying out. Asking someone to make a square circle is asking them to perform a pseudo-task. According to some theologians, asking God to make a stone so heavy that he cannot lift it is asking God to perform a pseudo-task.

psychological continuity. A term used in discussions of **personal identity**. It refers to such things as continuity of memory, beliefs, and personality among stages of a person.

qualitative identity, qualitatively identical (see **identity, identical**)

queerness problem (see **argument from queerness**)

realism, realist. To be a realist about a theory is to believe that the world is the way the theory says it is. We can contrast realism with instrumentalism. Ancient astronomers were very interested in predicting the exact positions of the planets, and they developed a complex system for doing this. The picture they offered put the earth at the center of the universe and depicted the planets and stars as revolving around the earth. The scientific problem was that the motion of planets through the sky is very complicated. They speed up, slow down, and in some cases even appear to go backwards. The ancient astronomers assigned each planet a primary orbit—a circular path around the earth. However, to account for the complicated behavior of the planets, they added orbits within orbits. A planet might revolve in one direction around a smaller circle that is carried along in the opposite direction on a larger circle. These extra circles were called epicycles.

The main goal of the astronomers in positing these epicycles was to "save the appearances"—to come up with a mathematical scheme that predicted what we would actually observe in the night sky. However, the goal was not necessarily to describe the real structure of the planetary system. The system of epicycles was an "instrument" for making predictions. The corresponding attitude is instrumentalism—the view that a theory should be treated simply as a predictive tool, setting aside the question of whether it really describes the true structure of things.

reductio ad absurdum. An argument that establishes its conclusion by showing that the denial of the conclusion leads to absurdities or contradiction.

relevance, relevant. Technical terms introduced for purposes of this book that deal with the relationship between a hypothesis and evidence for the hypothesis. If our hypothesis is H (for example, that Joe robbed the bank) and the evidence is E (for example, that Joe's fingerprints are on the safe), then the relevance of the evidence to the hypothesis depends on two things: (i) the **probability** of finding the evidence assuming that the hypothesis is true, that is, the **conditional probability** $p(E|H)$; and (ii) the probability of finding the evidence even if the hypothesis is false—the conditional probability $p(E|not\text{-}H)$. The higher the ratio of $p(E|H)$ to $p(E|not\text{-}H)$, the more relevant the evidence.

In nontechnical terms, relevance is a matter of the surprise value of the evidence. If it would be surprising to find this bit of evidence supposing that the hypothesis is wrong but unsurprising to find it if the hypothesis is correct, then the evidence is relevant.

reliable, reliabilism. The view of justification according to which a belief is justified if it was formed by reliable process. A reliable process is a process that tends to produce true beliefs.

salvific exclusivism (see **exclusivism**)

scientific creationism. A scientific creationist is someone who thinks that science supports the direct creation of the universe by God, a literal reading of Genesis, a relatively young Earth (6,000 to 10,000 years old), and a prominent place for Noah's flood in explaining the geology of Earth.

self-evident beliefs. A belief is self-evident if its truth is immediately apparent, without the need for making observations. Examples might include beliefs such as "$1 + 1 = 2$" or "If it is raining then it is raining."

sense of presence. A felt sensation of someone being present apart from perceiving the person by means of the usual five senses.

sensus divinitatis. A Latin phrase meaning "divine sense." Alvin Plantinga uses the term to refer to a cognitive mechanism that outputs belief in God, given the appropriate input. So, the input of seeing a majestic mountain might trigger one to believe in God.

set, set theory. A set is a collection of elements entirely defined by its members or elements. If two apparently different sets have the same members, they are the same set.

One set P is a subset of another set Q when every member of P is also a member of Q. Thus, if P = {1, 2, 3} and Q = {1, 2, 3, 4, 5}, then P is a subset of Q, which we write:

$$P \subseteq Q$$

Every set S is a subset of itself. That is, for any set S, $S \subseteq S$. We say that a set P is a proper subset of a set Q when P is a subset of Q, but Q is not a subset of P—that is, when every member of P is a member of Q, but some members of Q are not members of P. The sets P and Q noted above illustrate this concept.

Set theory is the branch of mathematics that studies the properties of sets. Some of what set theory tells us is quite surprising. For example, different sizes of infinity exist. (We consider this in Chapter 3 in connection with the Kalam Cosmological Argument.) In standard set theory, we can show that there can be no set of all sets. The assumption that one exists leads to paradox.

skeptic, skepticism. In philosophy, skepticism is a view about knowledge—either knowledge in general or some particular sort of knowledge. For example, a skeptic about the external world would say that we are never in a position to know that a world exists beyond our senses. A skeptic about morality would say that we are never in a position to know that anything is right or wrong. Skeptical views go back at least to such ancient Greek philosophers as Sextus Empiricus, and there are contemporary defenders of skeptical views. One example is Peter Unger, whose book *Ignorance* offers a defense of skepticism.

Skepticism typically relies on arguing that knowledge is subject to very stringent requirements—for example, as Descartes believed, that if it's possible to doubt something then it can't amount to knowledge. Most contemporary philosophers don't so much argue against skepticism as assume that it's a bad place to start thinking about knowledge. These philosophers take for granted that we have knowledge and see the task of **epistemology**—the philosophical theory of knowledge—as setting forth an account that makes sense of this fact.

sound, soundness (see **valid, validity**)

specified complexity. As popularized by intelligent design advocate William Dembski, this phrase refers to that property that reliably indicates intelligent design. To make a reliable design inference, Dembski argues that the organization of the parts of an object must be complex, not simple. More specifically, the organization and arrangement of an object must be so complex that the chance that the odds of it occurring randomly is less than 1 chance in 10^{150} (Dembski's original value for the **Universal Probability Bound**).

This complexity must also be specified in the sense that the particular improbable pattern of organization must be specified independently of the result and not in a purely *ad hoc* manner. Dembski illustrates the concept of specificity with an analogy: suppose a person shot an arrow into a wall and then, after the fact, drew a target around the arrow in a way that results in a bull's-eye. That the arrow hit the exact spot it did is relatively unlikely given the hundreds or thousands of other spots on the wall it could also have hit. But the results are not impressive because the arrow had to hit some point in the wall. Now assume that the archer pre-specified the result by drawing the target on the wall before he shot the arrow. If the arrow now makes a bull's-eye, it is more impressive because it is an improbable event that is also specified.

The term "specified complexity" was originally coined by Leslie Orgel in his book, *The Origins of Life*. Orgel used the word differently than Dembski does. He used it merely to refer to that property which distinguished living organisms from nonliving matter. Physicist Paul Davies has also used the term, but he follows Orgel's usage.

Star Trek. A popular science fiction television series that ran from 1966 through 1969 and spawned several movies and spin-offs. Many of the episodes raised philosophical questions, and the **transporter** device, which apparently allowed people to be "beamed" from one place to another, gave rise to its own set of philosophical **thought experiments**.

strong anthropic principle (SAP). (see **anthropic principle**)

substance. A technical term that means a particular thing, as opposed to an event or a process or a property of a thing. A person is a substance in this sense. Water is not; neither is a flash or lightning. The term entered philosophy as the Latin translation (*substantia*) of the Greek term *ousia*, or "being." The Latin word refers to something that "stands under." What a substance "stands under" are the properties or qualities that it has. Thus, a person may be tall but his tallness is not a substance. On this view, properties inhere in substances, but the substances are fundamental.

substance dualism (see **dualism**)

sufficient condition. To say that a statement P is a sufficient condition for a statement Q is to say that if P is true, Q is also true. For example, the statement "John is in College Park" is a sufficient condition for "John is in Maryland." Similarly, to say that a state of affairs or fact P is a sufficient condition for a state of affairs or fact Q is to say that if P obtains, Q does or will also obtain. Putting a piece of sodium into water is a sufficient condition for a violent chemical reaction.

superstring theory. The physical theory according to which the most fundamental physical entities are like multidimensional, fantastically small vibrating strings. Elementary physical particles can be thought of as excitation modes of elementary physical strings.

synthetic. Sentences are synthetic when the subject does not include the concepts of the predicate phrase. So the sentence, "This raven is black," is synthetic because the concept of a raven does not necessarily include the concept of blackness. Ravens are black, but we know this based on observation. You can at least imagine finding an albino raven. (For a contrast see **analytic**.)

teleological argument. The argument for the existence of God based on apparent design in nature.

teleology. The study of purpose or design in the natural world.

teletransportation (see **transporter**)

theism. The belief that God exists. **Classical theism** holds that one God exists who is the creator of the world, who is separate from the world, and who is **omnipotent, omniscient** and **omnibenevolent.**

theistic evolution. The view that God creates indirectly through the ordinary operations of both the laws of nature and evolution.

theodicy. A response to the argument from evil that attempts to explain why God permits suffering.

thought experiment. An imaginary scenario used both in science and in philosophy to probe the limits of our concepts. Einstein and Newton used thought experiments to explore concepts such as absolute motion (Newton's bucket thought experiment) and the relationship between gravitation and acceleration (Einstein's elevator thought experiment). Philosophers exploring the concept of **personal identity** indulged in thought experiments based on the **transporter** in the television series **Star Trek.** For more on thought experiments, go to http://plato.stanford.edu/entries/thought-experiment.

transcendent, transcendence. Something that is transcendent is beyond, above, or surpasses some common standard. Transcendence is the quality or property of being transcendent. However, when we describe God as transcendent, we mean more specifically that God surpasses, is above, or goes beyond the limits of the physical world. A transcendent being is not an ordinary physical being, and in God's case, calling God transcendent also implies that God possesses various perfections that no worldly thing could possess.

transfer of necessity. This is our term for a principle of **modal logic** according to which if a truth is necessary, and another truth follows strictly from the first truth, then the second truth is necessary as well:

> *If P is necessary, and P strictly implies Q, then Q is also necessary.*

An alternative version:

> *Suppose that P is necessary; if P then Q is necessary, then Q is necessary.*

transporter. A fictional device from the television series *Star Trek* used for accomplishing what philosophers came to call teletransportation. One entered the device, was dematerialized and then—apparently—reappeared elsewhere, wherever the beam was aimed. Philosophers in the late twentieth-century found the transporter beam to be a rich source of philosophical **thought experiments.** For more on the theory of the transporter beam, go to http://en.wikipedia.org/wiki/Transporter_(Star_Trek).

Trinity. The Christian doctrine of the Trinity holds that though God is only one being, he is three persons: Father, Son, and Holy Spirit. The classic phrase is "three persons in one being." Christians insist that this view is consistent with **monotheism,** but monotheists from other faiths are not so sure.

truth-preserving. Certain **arguments** or forms of inference have the property that if their premises are true, then their conclusions must be true as well. Such arguments and inferences are called **truth-preserving** and consequently, they are **valid**.

Universal Probability Bound. A degree of improbability that is so unlikely, given the physical resources of the universe, that it cannot realistically be thought to have occurred by chance. William Dembski, who popularized the concept, originally calculated the Universal Probability Bound to be 1 in 10^{150}. He calculated this value by multiplying the following three values:

1. 10^{80} (the number of elementary particles in the observable universe)
2. 10^{45} (the maximum rate per second at which transitions in physical states can occur, or the inverse of the Plank Time)
3. 10^{25} (a billion times longer than the estimated age of universe in seconds)

unfalsifiable (see **falsifiable**)

unjustified (see **justification**)

unwarranted (see **warrant**)

utility (see **expected utility**)

valid, validity. The term "valid" applies to arguments or reasoning. Intuitively, an **argument** – a set of premises together with a conclusion – is valid if there is no way for the premises to be true unless the conclusion is also true. Put slightly differently, when an argument is valid, all the information that the conclusion contains is implicitly or explicitly contained in the premises. Here is an example of a valid argument:

> *If John is in Hartford, then Sally is in Milwaukee.*
> *John is in Hartford.*
> *Therefore, Sally is in Milwaukee.*

There is no way for the premises of this argument to be true unless the conclusion is also true. By contrast, the following argument is not valid, that is, it is invalid:

> *If John is in Bloomington, then Sally is in Milwaukee.*
> *Sally is in Milwaukee.*
> *Therefore, John is in Bloomington.*

Here it's possible for the premises to be true and the conclusion false. Suppose the reason the first statement is true is that John and Sally are in sales. Whenever John's boss sends him to Bloomington, he sends Sally to Milwaukee. However, also true is that whenever John's boss sends him to Indianapolis, he also sends Sally to Milwaukee. In that case, both premises could be true but the conclusion could still be false. The argument is invalid.

When an argument is valid, we say that the conclusion "follows from" the premises, or that the premises "logically imply" or "entail" the conclusion. We sometimes shorten "logically imply" to "imply" when no chance of confusion exists.

For those interested in more detail, here is some further discussion.

Our original, intuitive definition was framed in terms of whether it's possible for the premises to be true and the conclusion simultaneously false, but this way of doing things has drawbacks. Some philosophers would say that the following is an absolute impossibility:

Water is not H_2O.

If we agree with them, and if we use our original definition, we end up saying that the following is a valid argument:

The glass contains water.
The glass does not contain H_2O.
Therefore, the Moon is made of green cheese.

This isn't like our previous example. In that example, the fact that the premises couldn't both be true was itself a matter of logic. This case isn't like that. It also isn't logic plus definitions. "Water" doesn't mean "H_2O" (people in the sixteenth century understood the word "water"). Logicians treat these two cases differently, and to do so, they call on a more sophisticated definition of validity:

An argument is valid exactly when it has a valid form.

An argument has a valid form if there is no counterexample to the form. A counterexample would be an argument with the same form but with true premises and a false conclusion. The argument above has this form:

All X are Y.
All Y are Z.
Therefore, all X are Z.

No argument with this form has true premises and a false conclusion. No matter what we use in the variables, we will never come up with an example in which the premises are true and the conclusion false. On the other hand, this argument is invalid:

All dogs are animals.
All mammals are animals.
Therefore, all dogs are mammals.

The form is

All X are Y.
All Z are Y.
Therefore, all X are Z.

As a counterexample, we could take

All roses are plants.
All cabbages are plants.
Therefore, all roses are cabbages.

Validity is important because valid reasoning is *truth-preserving*. That is, when we reason validly from true premises, we end up with a true conclusion. Valid arguments with true premises are called sound arguments. Their conclusions are true because they follow from true premises.

Vatican II. The Second Vatican Council, called in 1962 by Pope John XXIII. (The dates of the First Vatican Council were 1869–1870.) Vatican II was the beginning of a period of liberalization in the Roman Catholic Church and some of its decisions (e.g., the decision to allow the Mass to be spoken in modern languages rather than in Latin) were controversial.

veridical. An experience or perception is veridical if things really are as they seem to be. If it seems to you that you see an elephant on your lawn, then your perception is veridical if an elephant really is there, and if that fact explains why you see what you see. If your experience is a hallucination, then it isn't veridical.

The term works the same way when applied to religious experience. For example, if someone believes that God is telling them to change their life, then the experience is veridical if God really is communicating this message to them. The central philosophical question about religious experiences is whether they are ever veridical.

verificationism. A theory of meaning urged by the logical positivists of the Vienna Circle. According to verificationism, a supposedly factual statement is cognitively meaningful if and only if (i) it is **analytic** or (ii) it is **synthetic** and can, in principle, be verified by experience.

warrant. Warrant is whatever must be added to true belief to turn it into knowledge. According to Alvin Plantinga, a belief has warrant if and only if the belief is produced by properly functioning cognitive faculties in circumstances in which those faculties are designed to operate. Warrant is an *externalist* epistemological concept because a belief could be produced by properly functioning cognitive faculties without the knower being aware of it.

weak anthropic principle *(WAP)*. (see **anthropic principle**)

Zeno's paradoxes. A series of paradoxes developed by the Greek philosopher Zeno of Elea (490 BCE–430 BCE). The point of these paradoxes was to defend the claim that motion and change are illusions. For example, if you move from point A to point B in a straight line, you must cross the midpoint of line AB. But to get to the midpoint of the line you must cross the midpoint between the starting point and the original midpoint. In fact, you must cross an infinite number of points. No finite person can perform an infinite number of tasks, so no one can walk from point A to point B. You seem to move but reason tells us it is impossible. Thus, motion is an illusion.

Bibliography

Adams, J. R. (1989). *So You Think You're Not Religious?: A Thinking Person's Guide to the Church*. Cambridge, MA: Cowley Publications.

Adams, M. M. (1999). *Horrendous Evils and the Goodness of God*. Ithaca, NY: Cornell University Press.

Adams, R. (1973). "A Modified Divine Command Theory of Ethics." In *Religion and Morality: A Collection of Essays*. Outka, G. and Reeded, J. (Eds). New York: Oxford University Press.

Adams, R. M. (1979). "Divine Command Meta-Ethics Modified Again." *The Journal of Religious Ethics*, 7(1): 66–79.

Adams, R. M. (1987). *The Virtue of Faith and Other Essays in Philosophical Theology*. New York: Oxford University Press.

Alston, W. (1981). "Can We Speak Literally of God?" In *Is God GOD?* Steur, A. D. and Mclendon, J. W. Nashville, TN: Abington Press.

Alston, W. (1991). *Perceiving God: The Epistemology of Religious Experience*. Ithaca, NY: Cornell University Press.

Alston, W. (1996). "Some (Temporarily) Final Thoughts on Evidential Arguments from Evil." In *The Evidential Argument from Evil*. Howard-Snyder. D. Bloomington, IN: Indiana University Press.

Ayer, A. J. (1946). *Language, Truth, and Logic*. New York: Dover Publications.

Barker, D. (1992). *Losing Faith In Faith*. Madison, WI: Freedom from Religion Foundation, Inc.

Batchelor, S. (1998). *Buddhism Without Beliefs: A Contemporary Guide to Awakening*. New York: Riverhead Books.

Behe, M. (1996). "Evidence for Intelligent Design from Biochemistry." From an unpublished speech delivered at Discovery Institute's God & Culture Conference. Seattle, WA: Discovery Institute.

Behe, M. J. (1998). "Intelligent Design Theory as a Tool for Analyzing Biochemical Systems." In *Mere Creation*. Dembski, W. A. Downers Grove, IL: InterVarsity Press.

Behe, M. J. (2001). "The Modern Intelligent Design Hypothesis." *Philosophia Christi*, 3(1): 165.

Behe, M. J. (1996). *Darwin's Black Box : The Biochemical Challenge to Evolution*. New York: Free Press.

Behe, M. J., Miller, K. R. et al. (2002). "Intelligent Design?" Milner, R. and Maestro, V. (Eds). New York: Natural History Magazine. (This is a special report on Intelligent Design by Natural History Magazine, 2005.)

Blackmore, S. (2003) *Consciousness: an Introduction*. New York: Oxford University Press.

Carter, B. (1974). "Large Number Coincidences and the Anthropic Principle in Cosmology." In *Confrontation of Cosmological Theory with Observational Data*. Longair, M. S. (Ed.). Dordtecht: Reidel.

Charlesworth, M. (1965). *St. Anselm's Proslogion*. Oxford: Oxford University Press.

Clark, K. J. (2000). "Reformed Epistemology Apologetics." In *Five Views on Apologetics*. Cowan, S. B. (Ed.). Grand Rapids, MI: Zondervan.

Clifford, W. K. (1901). "The Ethics of Belief." *Essay and Lectures*. London: Macmillan & Co Reprinted in *Philosophy of Religion: an Anthology*. Pojman, L. P. (Ed.). New York: Wadsworth Publishing Co.

Cobb, J. B. and Griffin, D. R. (1976). *Process Theology: An Introductory Exposition*. Louisville, KY: Westminster/John Knox Press.

Collins, R. (2003). "Evidence for Fine-Tuning." In *God and Design: The Teleological Argument and Modern Science*. Manson, N. (Ed.). New York: Routledge.

Cooper, W. (Trans.) (1902). *Boethius: The Consolation of Philosophy*. London: J. M. Dent.

Craig, W. L. (1992). "Philosophical and Scientific Pointers to *Creatio Ex Nihilo*." In *Contemporary Perspectives on Religious Epistemology*. Geivett, R. D. and Sweetman, B. (Eds). New York: Oxford University Press.

Craig, W. L. (2003). "Design and the Anthropic Fine-Tuning of the Universe." In *God and Design: The Teleological Argument and Modern Science*. Manson, N. (Ed.). New York: Routledge.

Darwin, C. (1859, 1964). *On the Origin of Species*. Cambridge, MA: Harvard University Press.

Davies, P. (1992). *Mind of God*. New York: Simon & Schuster.

Dawkins, R. (1996). *The Blind Watchmaker: Why the Evidence of Evolution Reveals a Universe without Design*. New York: W. W. Norton & Co.

Dawkins, R. (1996). *Climbing Mount Improbable*. New York: W. W. Norton.

Dembski, W. A. (Ed.) (1998). *Mere Creation: Science, Faith and Intelligent Design*. Downers Grove, IL: InterVarsity Press.

Dembski, W. A. (1999). *Intelligent Design: The Bridge between Science and Theology*. Downers Grove, IL: InterVarsity Press.

Dembski, W. A. (2001). *Signs of Intelligence*. Grand Rapids, MI: Brazos Press.

Dembski, W. A. (2002). *No Free Lunch: Why Specified Complexity Cannot Be Purchased without Intelligence*. New York: Rowman & Littlefield Publishers.

Dennett, D. C. (1995). *Darwin's Dangerous Idea*. New York: Simon & Schuster.

Denton, M. (1986). *Evolution: A Theory in Crisis*. Bethesda, MD: Adler & Adler.

Descartes, R. (1971). *Philosophical Writings*. New York: Macmillan Publishing Co.

Dorit, R. (1997). "A Review of Darwin's Black Box: The Biochemical Challenge to Evolution." *American Scientist*, http://www.americanscientist.org/template/AssetDetail/assetid/22794.

Draper, P. (1996). "Pain and Pleasure: An Evidential Problem for Theists." In *The Evidential Argument from Evil*. Howard-Snyder, D. (Ed.). Bloomington, IN: Indiana University Press.

Earman, J. (2000). *Hume's Abject Failure: The Argument Against Miracles.* New York: Oxford University Press.

Fischer, John Martin (1994) "Why Immortality is Not So Bad." *International Journal of Philosophical Studies,* Vol. 2, No. 2: 257–270.

Flew, A., Hare, R. M. et al. (1955). "Theology and Falsification." In *Philosophy of Religion: Selected Readings.* Rowe, W. and Wainwright, W. (Eds). Chicago: Harcourt Brace Jovanovich Publishers.

Flint, T. (1998). "Omniscience." In *The Routledge Encyclopedia of Philosophy.* Craig, E. (Ed.). New York: Routledge. 7: 107–112.

Gettier, E. (1963) "Is Justified True Belief Knowledge?" *Analysis,* 23(6): 121–123.

Gish, D. T. (1979). *Evolution: The Fossils Say No!* San Diego, CA: Creation-Life Publishers.

Goodenough, U. (2000). *The Sacred Depths of Nature.* Oxford: Oxford University Press.

Gutting, G. (1982). *Religious Belief and Religious Skepticism.* Notre Dame, IN: University of Notre Dame Press.

Gutting, G. (1996, 1982). "A Modified Version of the Argument from Religious Experience." In *Philosophy of Religion: An Anthology of Contemporary Views.* Stewart, M. Y. (Ed.). Sudbury, MA: Jones and Bartlett Publishers.

Harman, G. (1995). "Rationality." In *Thinking.* Smith, E. E. and Osherson, D. N. (Eds). Cambridge, MA: MIT Press.

Hasker, W. (1986). "On Justifying the Christian Practice." *The New Scholasticism,* 60: 129–144.

Heim, S. M. (1995). *Salvations: Truth and Difference in Religion.* Maryknoll: Orbis Books.

Hick, J. (1977). *Evil and the God of Love.* New York: Harper & Row.

Hick, J. (1989). *An Interpretation of Religion.* New Haven, CT: Yale University Press.

Hick, J. (1994). "Interfaith and the Future." *Baha'i Studies Review,* 4(1): 1–8.

Hick, J. (1964). "Skeptics and Believers." In *Faith and the Philosophers,* Hick, J. (Ed.). New York: St. Martin's Press.

Hitt, J. (1999). "This Is Your Brain on God." *Wired,* 7, http://www.wired.com/wired/archive/7.11/persinger.html.

Hoffman, J. and Rosenkrantz, G. (2002). "Omnipotence." In *Stanford Encyclopedia of Philosophy.* Zalta, E. N. (Ed.).

Howard-Snyder, D. (Ed.) (1996). *The Evidential Argument from Evil.* The Indiana Series in the Philosophy of Religion. Bloomington, IN: Indiana University Press.

Hume, D. (1975, 1784). *An Enquiry Concerning Human Understanding, in Enquiries Concerning Human Understanding and Concerning the Principles of Morals.* Oxford: Clarendon Press.

Hume, D. (1989). *Dialogues Concerning Natural Religion.* Amherst, MA: Prometheus Books.

Jackson, F. (1982). "Epiphenomenal Qualia." *Philosophical Quarterly,* 32: 127–136.

James, W. (1985, 1902). *The Varieties of Religious Experience.* New York: Penguin Classics.

James, W. (2003, 1896). "The Will to Believe." In *God Matters: Readings in the Philosophy of Religion*. Martin, R. and Bernard, C. (Eds). New York: Longman Press.

Johnson, J. L. (1994). "Procedure, Substance, and the Divine Command Theory." *International Journal for Philosophy of Religion*, 35: 39–55.

Johnson, P. E. (1991). *Darwin on Trial*. Downers Grove, IL: InterVarsity Press.

Kenny, A. (1983). *Faith and Reason*. New York: Columbia University Press.

Keown, D. (1996). *Buddhism: A Very Short Introduction*. Oxford: Oxford University Press.

Kitcher, P. (1982). *Abusing Science: The Case against Creationism*: Cambridge, MA: MIT Press.

Leslie, J. (1989). *Universes*. London: Routledge.

Lewis, C. S. (1943). *Mere Christianity*. New York: Macmillian Publishing Co.

Lewis, C. S. (1947). *Miracles: A Preliminary Study*. New York: The McMillan Co.

Lewis, D. (1976). "The Paradoxes of Time Travel." *American Philosophical Quarterly*, 13: 145–152.

Lycan, W. and Schlesinger, G. (1989). "You Bet Your Life." In *Reason and Responsibility*. Feinberg, J. (Ed.). Belmont, CA: Wadsworth Publishing Co.

Mackie, J. L. (1977). *Ethics: Inventing Right and Wrong*. Harmondsworth, UK: Penguin Books.

Mackie, J. L. (1982). *The Miracle of Theism*. Oxford: Clarendon Press.

Mackie, J. L. (1992). "Evil and Omnipotence." In *The Problem of Evil: Selected Readings*. Peterson, M. (Ed.). Notre Dame, IN: University of Notre Dame Press.

Malcolm, N. (1960). "Anselm's Ontological Arguments." *Philosophical Review*, 69(1): 41–62.

Martin, R. and Bernard, C. (2003). *God Matters: Readings in the Philosophy of Religion*. New York: Longman.

Manson, N. A. (Ed.) (2003). *God and Design*. New York: Routledge.

Matthews, D., McCollough, M., Larson, D., Koenig, H., Swyers, J., and Milano, M. (1998). "Religious Commitment and Health Status." *Archives of Family Medicine*, 7(2): 118–124.

Martin, M. (1990). *Atheism: A Philosophical Justification*. Philadelphia: Temple University Press.

Mavrodes, G. (1963). "Some Puzzles Concerning Omnipotence." *Philosophical Review*, 72: 221–223.

McCloskey, H. J. (1997). "God and Evil." In *Critiques of God: Making the Case Against Belief in God*. Angeles, P. (Ed.). Amherst, MA: Prometheus Books.

McFague, S. (1987). *Models of God: Theology for an Ecological, Nuclear Age*. Minneapolis, MN: Augsburg Fortress Publishers.

McMurrin, S. (2000, 1959). *The Theological Foundations of the Mormon Religion*. Salt Lake City, UT: Signature Books.

Meeker, K. (2002). "Exclusivism, Pluralism, and Anarchy." In *God Matters: Readings in the Philosophy of Religion*. Martin, R. and Bernard, C. (Eds). New York: Longman Press. 524–534.

Miller, K. R. (1999). *Finding Darwin's God*. New York: HarperCollins Publishers.

Miller, K. R. (2003). "Answering the Biochemical Argument from Design." In *God and Design*. Manson, N. A. (Eds). New York: Routledge.

Morris, H. M. (1974). *Scientific Creationism*. San Diego, CA: Creation-Life Publishers.

Musgrave, I. (2005). "The Evolution of the Bacterial Flagellum." In *Why Intelligent Design Fails*. Young, M. and Edis, T. New Brunswick, NJ: Rutgers University Press.

Murphy, M. (2002). "The Natural Law Tradition in Ethics." In *Stanford Encyclopedia of Philosophy*, http://plato.stanford.edu/entries/natural-law-ethics.

Nachman, M. W. and Crowell, S. L. (2000). "Estimate of the mutation rate per nucleotide in humans." *Genetics*, 156(1): 297–304.

National Academy of Sciences. (1999). *Science and Creationism: A View from the National Academy of Sciences*. Washington, DC: National Academy Press.

Olding, A. (1971). "The Argument From Design—A Reply to R.G. Swinburne." *Religious Studies*, VII: 361–373.

O'Leary-Hawthorne, J. and Andrew, C. (1993). "The Principle of Necessary Reason." *Faith and Philosophy*, 10(1): 60–67.

Otte, R. (1996). "Mackie's Treatment of Miracles." *International Journal for Philosophy of Religion*, 39: 151–158.

Otto, R. (1923) *The Idea of the Holy*. Harvey, J. (Trans.). Originally *Die Heilige* (1917). Oxford: Oxford University Press.

Paley, W. (1963). *Natural Theology*. New York: The Bobbs-Merril Co.

Parsons, K. M. (1989). *God and the Burden of Proof*. Buffalo, NY: Prometheus Books.

Pascal, B. (1995, 1670). *Pensees*. London: Penguin Books.

Pegis, A. C. (1945). *The Basic Writings of Saint Thomas Aquinas*. New York: Random House.

Pennock, R. T. (1999). *Tower of Babel: The Evidence against the New Creationism*. Cambridge, MA: MIT Press.

Pennock, R. T. (Ed.) (2001). *Intelligent Design Creationism and Its Critics: Philosophical, Theological, and Scientific Perspectives*. Cambridge, MA: MIT Press.

Perakh, M. (2004). *Unintelligent Design*. Buffalo, NY: Prometheus Books.

Perloff, J. (1999). *Tornado in a Junkyard: The Relentless Myth of Darwinism*. Arlington, MA: Refuge Books.

Perry, J. (1978). *A Dialogue on Personal Identity and Immortality*. Indianapolis, IN: Hackett Publishing Company.

Petersen, M., Hasker, W., Reichenbach, B., and Basinger, D. (2003). *Reason and Religious Belief* (3rd ed.). New York: Oxford University Press.

Pinnock, C., Rice, R. et al. (1994). *The Openness of God: A Biblical Challenge to the Traditional Understanding of God*. Downer's Grove, IL: InterVarsity Press.

Plantinga, A. (1977). *God, Freedom, and Evil*. Grand Rapids, MI: William B. Eerdmans Publishing Co.

Plantinga, A. (1983). "Reason and Belief in God." In *Faith and Rationality: Reason and Belief in God*. Plantinga, A. and Wolterstorff, N. (Eds). Notre Dame, IN: Notre Dame University Press.

Plantinga, A. (1984). "Advice to Christian Philosophers." *Faith and Philosophy*, 1(3): 253–271.

Plantinga, A. (1993). *Warrant and Proper Function*. New York: Oxford University Press.

Plantinga, A. (1995). "Pluralism: A Defense of Religious Exclusivism." In *The Rationality of Belief & the Plurality of Faith*. Senor, T. D. (Ed.). Ithaca, NY: Cornell University Press.

Plantinga, A. (1996). "On Being Evidentially Challenged." In *The Evidential Argument from Evil*. Howard-Snyder, D. (Ed.). Bloomington, IN: Indiana University Press.

Plantinga, A. (2000). *Warranted Christian Belief*. New York: Oxford University Press.

Plantinga, A. (1992). "Is Belief in God Properly Basic." In *Contemporary Perspectives on Religious Epistemology*. Geivett, R. D. and Sweetman, B. (Eds). New York: Oxford University Press.

Putnam, H. (1991). "The Nature of Mental States." In *The Nature of Mind*. Rosenthal, D. (Ed.). New York: Oxford University Press.

Quinn, P. (1990). "The Recent Revival of Divine Command Ethics." *Philosophy and Phenomenological Research*, L: 345–365.

Quinn, P. (1992). "The Primacy of God's Will in Christian Ethics." *Philosophical Perspectives*, 6: 493–513.

Reid, T. (1997). *An Inquiry into the Human Mind on the Principles of Common Sense*. Edinburgh, UK: Edinburgh University Press.

Rowe, W. (1978). "An Examination of the Cosmological Argument." In *Philosophy of Religion: An Anthology*. Pojman, L. P. (Ed.). New York: Wadsworth Publishing Co.

Rowe, W. (1988). "Evil and Theodicy." *Philosophical Topics*, XVI(2): 119–132.

Rowe, W. (1996a) "Modal Versions of the Ontological Argument." Reprinted in *Philosophy of Religion: An Anthology of Contemporary View*. Melville Y. Stewart (Ed.) Sudbury, MA; Jones and Bartlett.

Rowe, W. (1996b). "The Problem of Evil and Some Varieties of Atheism." In *The Evidential Argument from Evil*. Howard-Snyder, D. (Ed.). Bloomington, IN: Indiana University Press.

Ruse, M. (Ed.) (1988). *But Is It Science?* Buffalo, NY: Prometheus Books.

Ruse, M. (2003). *Darwin and Design: Does Evolution Have Purpose?* Cambridge, MA: Harvard University Press.

Ryle, G. (1949). *The Concept of Mind*. London: Hutchinson & Co.

Shackleton, E. (1998). *South*. New York: Carroll & Graf Publishers.

Shanks, N. (2004). *God, the Devil and Darwin: A Critique of Intelligent Design Theory*. New York: Oxford University Press.

Smith, G. (1989). *Atheism: The Case Against God*. Buffalo, NY: Prometheus Books.

Smith, G. H. (1980). "Atheism: The Case Against God." In *An Anthology of Atheism and Rationalism*. Stein, G. (Ed.). Buffalo, NY: Prometheus.

Smith, Q. (1995). "A Defense of a Principle of Sufficient Reason." *Metaphilosophy*, 26(1 & 2): 97–106.

Sobel, J. H. (1987). "On the Evidence of Testimony for Miracles: A Bayesian Interpretation of David Hume's Analysis." *Philosophical Quarterly*, 37: 166–186.

Sober, E. (2001). *Core Questions in Philosophy: A Text with Readings.* Upper Saddle River, NJ: Prentice Hall.

Sober, E. (2003). "The Design Argument." In *God and Design: The Teleological Argument and Modern Science.* Manson, N. A. (Ed.). New York: Routledge.

Strassman, R. (2001). *DMT: The Spirit Molecule.* Rochester, NY: Park Street Press.

Stump, E. and Kretzmann, N. (1981). "Eternity." *Journal of Philosophy*, 78(1981): 429–458.

Swinburne, R. (1968). "The Argument from Design." *Philosophy*, 43: 202–215.

Swinburne, R. (1979). *The Existence of God.* Oxford: Clarendon Press.

Taylor, R. (1983). *Metaphysics* (3rd ed.). Englewood Cliffs, NJ: Prentice Hall.

Tillich, P. (1957). *Dynamics of Faith.* New York: Harper & Row.

Unger, P. (1975). *Ignorance: A Case for Skepticism.* Oxford: Oxford University Press.

Van Inwagen, P. (1995). "Non Est Hick." In *The Rationality of Belief & the Plurality of Faith.* Senor, T. D. (Ed.). Ithaca, NY: Cornell University Press.

Van Inwagen, P. (1996). "The Problem of Evil, the Problem of Air, and the Problem of Silence." In *The Evidential Argument from Evil.* Howard-Snyder, D. (Ed.). Bloomington, IN: Indiana University Press.

Wells, J. (2000). *Icons of Evolution: Science or Myth.* Washington DC: Regnery Publishing.

Whitcomb, J. C. and Morris, H. M. (1961). *The Genesis Flood: The Biblical Record and Its Scientific Implications.* Philadelphia: Presbyterian & Reformed Publishing Co.

White, R. (2003). "Fine-Tuning and the Multiple Universes." In *God and Design: The Teleological Argument and Modern Science.* Manson, N. (Ed.). New York: Routledge.

Wiesel, E. (1992). "Night." In *The Problem of Evil: Selected Readings.* Peterson, M. (Ed.). Notre Dame, IN: University of Notre Dame Press.

Wykstra, S. J. (1990). "The Human Obstacle to Evidential Arguments from Suffering: On Avoiding the Evils of 'Appearance.'" In *The Problem of Evil.* Adams, M. M. and Adams, R. M. (Eds). New York: Oxford University Press.

Wykstra, S. J. (1996). "Rowe's Noseeum Argument from Evil." In *The Evidential Argument from Evil.* Howard-Snyder, D. (Ed.). Bloomington, IN: Indiana University Press.

Yancey, P. (1990). *Where is God When It Hurts?* Grand Rapids, MI: Zondervan.

Yandell, D. and Yandell, K. (2003). "The Cosmological Argument." In *God Matters: Readings in the Philosophy of Religion.* Martin, R. and Bernard, C. (Eds). New York: Longman Press. 64–76.

Young, M. and Edis, T. (Eds) (2005). *Why Intelligent Design Fails.* New Brunswick, CT: Rutgers University Press.

Index